The Mediated Construction of Reality

The Mediated Construction of Reality

NICK COULDRY AND ANDREAS HEPP

polity

The right of Nick Couldry and Andreas Hepp to be identified as Authors of this Work has been asserted in accordance with the UK Copyright, Designs and Patents Act 1988.

© Cover picture by Beate Koehler, http://beate-koehler.name

First published in 2017 by Polity Press
Reprinted 2017 (twice), 2018

Polity Press
65 Bridge Street
Cambridge CB2 1UR, UK

Polity Press
350 Main Street
Malden, MA 02148, USA

ISBN-13: 978-0-7456-8130-6 (hardback)
ISBN-13: 978-0-7456-8131-3 (paperback)

A catalogue record for this book is available from the British Library.
Library of Congress Cataloging-in-Publication Data
Names: Couldry, Nick, author. I Hepp, Andreas, author.
Title: The mediated construction of reality: society, culture, mediatization
    / Nick Couldry, Andreas Hepp.
Description: Cambridge, UK; Malden, MA: Polity Press, 2016. I Includes bibliographical references
    and index.
Identifiers: LCCN 2016011836 (print) I LCCN 2016019395 (ebook) I ISBN 9780745681306 (hardback) I
    ISBN 9780745681313 (pbk.) I ISBN 9780745686523
    (Mobi) I ISBN 9780745686530 (Epub)
Subjects: LCSH: Mass media--Social aspects. Mass media and culture.
Classification: LCC HM1206 .C683 2016 (print) I LCC HM1206 (ebook) I DDC 302.23--dc23
LC record available at https://lccn.loc.gov/2016011836

Typeset in 11.25/13 Dante by
Servis Filmsetting Limited, Stockport, Cheshire
Printed and bound in Great Britain by CPI Group (UK) Ltd, Croydon

For further information on Polity, visit our website:
politybooks.com

Contents

Preface and Acknowledgements

This book brings to a temporary resting point more than ten years of shared discussion and enquiry.

When we met and discovered each other's work in 2003, we also quickly realized that we had a shared interest in social theory, and a dissatisfaction with the limited dialogue existing between social theory and media theory in the UK, Germany and elsewhere. For a decade we have been organizing and writing together, with various interruptions; but only in mid 2012, during a Visiting Fellowship by Andreas in the Department at Goldsmiths, University of London, did we conceive the idea of something more ambitious: a jointly written book, where we would try to answer that dissatisfaction by setting out the social theory we saw as necessary for an age of digital media. We were inspired in part by the tradition of social phenomenology, but by many other sources besides, and provoked by the clear inadequacy of the treatment of media and communications in a famous offshoot of that tradition, Berger and Luckmann's *The Social Construction of Reality*, which marks the half-century of its publication this year. A particular inspiration for us both had been listening to a keynote talk by Hubert Knoblauch at the Mediatized World Conference at the University of Bremen in April 2011, which suggested a more satisfying way of reconnecting the UK and German traditions of social theory than had been found before. After Nick moved back to the London School of Economics in September 2013, it was fortunately possible for Andreas to return to London during 2015 and 2016 as a Visiting Senior Fellow in LSE's Department of Media and Communications, in order to help focus on an intense phase of the book's writing. We thank both the LSE and Goldsmiths departments for their support for these two fellowships, the University of Bremen and, especially, Andreas' colleagues at the ZeMKI for making possible two longer stays abroad in such a short time.

A word on how the book was written: while a first rough draft of a chapter was written by one of us, we discussed and reworked such drafts intensively, contributing on such a basis further parts to the chapters, which were discussed and reworked again. By that method we hope to have developed a consistent analytical approach across the whole book. As writers, we have been shaped by different intellectual traditions that have distinctive writing styles: we have debated each turn of the argument along the way, and hope to have integrated the best of each tradition. We are happy for our distinctive voices to be discernible in each chapter, and hope as a reader you will be too.

During this book's researching and writing, we each had to contend with many other responsibilities. We must single out for thanks a number of people without whom this book could not have been written on this time-scale. Most notable is Anthony Kelly, Nick's research assistant from November 2013 to October 2015, who did vital work on the literature searches underlying Chapters 5, 6 and 8, and who provided much support on other related topics and projects during this time. We are also very grateful to Miriam Rahali, who took over as Nick's research assistant during November 2015, providing invaluable help in pulling together the book's references, and also reading the manuscript just before final submission. Nick also wants to thank for her support Natalie Fenton, who was joint Head of Department with Nick at Goldsmiths during the first year of preparing the book's ideas. Our work for Chapters 2, 3 and 4 was very much supported by literature searches conducted by Ulrike Gerhard, student research assistant at the University of Bremen. Later in this role, Anna Heinemann and Linda Siegel undertook many final checks of references. Organizationally, all our work was supported by Heide Pawlik and Leif Kramp at the ZeMKI, University of Bremen.

We are grateful to various institutions for giving us the opportunity to present ideas from the book: the Time, Memory and Representation Group, Södertörn University, Stockholm, March 2014 (thanks to Hans Ruin and Staffan Ericsson); the Institute for Advanced Studies, Helsinki (thanks to Johanna Sumiala); the Perspectives of Communicative Constructivism Conference, Berlin, November 2014 (thanks to Hubert Knoblauch and Jo Reichertz); the Media and Social Theory Research Network, LSE, which we launched with a joint talk in May 2015; the Reflexive Mediatization Workshop, the Technical University Dortmund, April 2015 (thanks to Ronald Hitzler and Michaela Pfadenhauer); the Meaning Across Media Conference, Copenhagen University, May 2015 (thanks to Kjetil Sandvik); the Social Ontology of Digital Data and Digital Technology Symposium, by the Warwick University Centre for Social Ontology, London, July 2015 (thanks to Mark Carrigan); the ECREA Doctoral Summer School, Bremen University, August 2015; the New Directions in Mediatization

Research Workshop, Copenhagen, October 2015 (thanks to Stig Hjarvard); and the Media Communications between Complexity and Simplification Conference at the Alexander von Humboldt Institute for Internet and Society, Berlin, November 2015.

We are grateful to a number of people for helpful discussions and inspiration along the way: Mark Andrejevic, Veronica Barassi, Andreas Breiter, Kenzie Burchell, Craig Calhoun, Tarleton Gillespie, Anthony Giddens, Uwe Hasebrink, Daniel Knapp, Hubert Knoblauch, Friedrich Krotz, Risto Kunelius, Jannis Kallinikos, Knut Lundby, Peter Lunt, Sonia Livingstone, Gina Neff, Thomas Poell, Alison Powell, Jo Reichertz, Michaela Pfadenhauer, Uwe Schimank, Kim Schrøder, Justus Uitermark, Jose van Dijck. In addition, Andreas' work on the book benefited greatly from the discussions in the research network 'Communicative Figurations', funded by the German Initiative of Excellence as one of the University of Bremen's Creative Units, and he would like to thank all its members for the stimulating collaboration. Thanks also to the anonymous readers of our manuscript for encouraging us to clarify various aspects of the book's argument, to Susan Beer, our copy-editor, and to Miriam Rahali, whose proof-reading skills saved us from many errors.

Nick would like to dedicate this book to the memory of John Edwards, much loved father-in-law (1926–2015). Andreas would like to dedicate this book to Beate Köhler.

We are deeply grateful to our partners, Louise Edwards and Beate Köhler, for their love, patience and support during our many absences. A special thank you to Beate for supporting us with the cover picture of the book – and her willingness to stay at various times in London.

Nick Couldry and Andreas Hepp
London and Bremen, February 2016

1

Introduction

Suppose the social to be mediated – what? This question (with apologies to Nietzsche)[1] has hovered over social theory, and everyday accounts of the social and public world, since the late nineteenth century. When not ignored, the question has received myths or slogans for answers: the few serious answers have tended to be based on a reading of social infrastructures at least a quarter of a century old. This is a book of social theory that tries to do better than that.

So, how do we rethink the character of the social world (including 'sociality', 'socialization', 'social order', 'society'), starting out from the principle that the social is constructed from, and through, technologically mediated processes and infrastructures of communication, that is, through what we have come to call 'media'? Since our 'reality' as human beings who must live together is constructed through social processes, what are the consequences for that reality if the social itself is *already* 'mediated'; that is, shaped and formed through media? These questions generate our book's title: the *mediated* construction of reality.

The basic terms of these questions need some discussion. 'The social'? This term has been attacked in recent decades from many directions. Quite apart from neoliberal attacks on the 'social' – Margaret Thatcher's notorious slogan 'there is no such thing as society' – the importance of the social as an object of *theoretical enquiry* has increasingly been displaced by other priorities in the social sciences. So, for example, the philosopher and sociologist of science, Bruno Latour, has sought to deconstruct, or at least reassemble, 'the social' as a sociologist's fiction, that generally obscures from us the actual material arrangements by which various entities, human and non-human, are connected for various purposes and on various scales.[2] Latour's key target was the sociology of Emile Durkheim. Durkheim[3] argued in the late nineteenth and early twentieth centuries that society is a fact constructed out of the acts and imaginings of human beings; a 'fact' just as much as the 'facts' of natural science. Durkheim's reference point for this notion of society was primarily the emotional and cognitive reality of the face-to-face gathering. Durkheim did not live to consider how the notion of society must change when it is presented to us, in part, through technological processes of mediation that, in turn, are necessarily outcomes of economic and political forces: clearly this is an omission that needs correction. In addition, other writers have seen a problem in Durkheim's emphasis on the work that *representations* of the social do in reproducing its reality, looking elsewhere for forms of connection, friction and resonance that bypass 'meaning' altogether (Thrift, 2008). Still others want to shift our focus away from human interactions to the 'posthuman' from which perspective 'the social' can seem quaintly parochial (Hayles, 1999). At the very least, the term 'social' needs some repair work – if, that is, the project of social theory is to be renewed.

What of *'media'*? Serious reflection on how media institutions represent – perhaps distort – the social already requires us to put certain versions of 'the social' or 'society' within scare quotes. The problem multiplies in the digital era when the most promising source of new economic value appears to be what are called *'social media'* platforms. The very term 'media' masks huge changes. In the mid to late twentieth century, debate about media's implications for the values and realities on which social life was based focused on television and film,[4] that is, the consequences of *particular* news frames or *exemplary* images. Only radio in the age of mass media plausibly involved a *continuous* form of social shaping, although Tarde's (1901) suggestive work on the continuous influence of how news circulates through newspapers already pointed in this direction.[5] But the expansion of internet access via the World Wide Web from the 1990s and its move to smart mobile devices from the 2000s profoundly changed the questions that social theory needed to answer about media and media theory about the social. Particularly with the introduction of social media networks from the mid 2000s, 'media' now are much more than specific channels of centralized content: they comprise platforms which, for many humans, literally *are* the spaces where, through communication, they *enact* the social. If the basic building-blocks of social life are potentially themselves now shaped by 'media' – that is, the contents and infrastructure derived from institutionally sustained technologies of communication – then social theory must *rethink* the implications of 'media' for its basic term, 'the social'. 'The digital revolution' as it is often called – but it involves much more than digitalization and the internet – must, as Anthony Giddens (2015) has argued, be answered by a major transformation in sociological thinking too. That transformation in sociological thought and its reorientation towards these key changes in media *and* social infrastructures is the principal focus of this book.

For that reason – that is, our double focus on the mutual transformations of media *and* the social world together – we will give less emphasis to specific media texts, representations and imaginative forms than we might do in a book focused exclusively on media themselves. For the same reason, when we discuss 'reality' in this book, we refer not to specific media representations or enactments of reality (for example 'reality TV'), but to the achieved sense of a social world to which media practices, on the largest scale, contribute. In this, starting out from the detailed scholarship of media and communications studies, we hope to make a substantive contribution both to media *and* social theory. Indeed our point is that social theory is no longer viable, unless it has been, in part, transformed by media theory.

Yet, once we have acknowledged the complexity of the institutional 'figurations' we now call 'media' (we will come back to the term 'figurations') and deconstructed the various representations of the social that different power blocs make, some might be tempted to abandon the term 'social' entirely. But that would be a huge mistake. For the term 'social' is one we cannot do without if we are to grasp the complexities that interest us. The term 'social' points to a basic feature of human life: what historian and social theorist William Sewell calls 'the various mediations that place people into "social" relations with one another'.[6] Indeed the word 'social' signifies something fundamental that even recent detractors of the social would not deny: the basis of our human life-in-common in relations of interdependence. These always include relations of *communication*: as Axel Honneth says, 'the process of social construction can [. . .] only be analysed as a communicative process' (Honneth, 1995, p. 58). The fundamentally *mediated* nature of the social – our necessarily mediated interdependence as human beings – is therefore based not in some internal mental reality, but rather on the *material* processes (objects, linkages, infrastructures, platforms) through which communication, and the construction of meaning, take place. Those material processes of mediation constitute much of the *stuff* of the social. As a result, Sewell argues, the social is always double in character: both form of meaning *and* built environment.[7] Yet this inherent complexity of the social is lost if we abandon the term 'social' and go off to analyse either meanings or technologies of connection in isolation. Meanwhile, the infrastructures of the 'media' that help constitute the social get ever more complex.

Our argument involves new conceptual and historical work. For example, in Part I of this book, we introduce the reading of communications history on which our conceptual framework is based, and adapt the term 'mediatization' as shorthand for *all* the transformations of

communicative and social processes, and the social and practical forms
built from them, which follow from our increasing reliance on technologically and institutionally based processes of mediation. Quite clearly such
transformations are complex, meaning that 'mediatization' is not just one
type of thing, one 'logic' of doing things; indeed it is best understood as not
a 'thing' or 'logic' at all, but as the variety of ways in which *possible* orderings of the social by media are further transformed and stabilized through
continuous feedback loops.

Particularly important as a mid-range concept for grasping those more
complex transformations is the term 'figuration', which we borrow from
the late work of Norbert Elias in the 1970s and 1980s. We find it encouraging for the long-term project of social theory that concepts developed
decades ago have their full analytical power only today. Now we can
appreciate their openness to processes that, on a larger scale, are gaining
in importance today, when the 'stuff' of the social is being transformed by
data-based processes, largely automated and on vast scales, something that
could not possibly have been anticipated when those concepts were developed. Much about today's infrastructures of social interaction seems alien
to most earlier versions of social theory, as discussed further later in our
argument. Yet this growing interdependence of sociality *on system* – the
growing 'institutionalization' of both self and collectivity (as reflected in
the book's third part) – is at root hardly contrary to the vision of social life
that Georg Simmel had, already, at the dawn of the modern media age. In
a chapter on 'sociability' Simmel offered an insight into the paradoxical –
certainly complex and recursive – nature of mediated social life:

> the world of sociability [. . .] is an artificial world [. . .]. If now we have
> the conception that we enter into sociability purely as "human beings",
> as that which we really are [. . .] it is because modern life is *overburdened*
> with objective content and material demands. (1971, p. 133)

This captures well the tension between our ever-changing sense of who
'we' are (and what our lives together mean) and the material demands
of our technologically supported lives in view of, and in touch with,
each other. The more intense our social life feels, the greater its recursive
dependence on technological media of communication. We must sharpen
our grasp of this paradox, and that is the purpose of this book.

Towards a Materialist Phenomenology of the Social World

We want in this book to understand better the construction of everyday reality as part of the social world. We agree with philosopher of science Ian Hacking when he writes (1999, p. 49) that the concept of 'construction has become stale. It needs to be freshened up'. A theory of the construction of *social* reality must at the very least pay attention to a key element in the construction of social life today, which is mediated communications. This simple recognition turns out to have profound consequences for social theory.

Our goal is to develop *a materialist phenomenology* of the types of social world in which media play an obvious and unavoidable part. Let us unpack this a little more. The word *materialist* refers back to an approach called 'cultural materialism', linked closely with the writing of Raymond Williams (1980). Williams' main point was to include the *material* as well as the *symbolic* aspects of everyday practices when analysing culture as a 'whole way of life'. Williams (1990) himself demonstrated the importance of this point of departure when he discussed television as both (material) technology and (symbolic) cultural form. It is not a matter of positioning the material against the symbolic, but of grasping both in their interrelatedness, as part of a proper analysis of how media and communications contribute to the construction of the social world. We need, in other words, to consider media both as technologies including infrastructures *and* as processes of sense-making, if we want to understand how today's social worlds come into being. By using the term 'materiality' we want to emphasize this full complexity.

We offer a *phenomenology* of the social world, because we believe that, whatever its appearance of complexity, even of opacity, the social world remains something accessible to interpretation and understanding by human actors, indeed a structure built up, in part, *through* those interpretations and understandings. Weber's definition of sociology as 'the *interpretative* understanding of social action' (1947, p. 88) has much more than definitional force, since social life, as Paul Ricoeur (1980, p. 219) wrote, has its 'very foundation' in 'substituting signs for things': that is, signs that embody interpretations. Phenomenology, however, goes further in taking seriously the world as it appears for interpretation to particular *situated* social actors, from *their* point of view within wider relations of interdependence. There is an implicitly humanist dimension to phenomenology by which we fully stand.[8] We do not claim however to have done detailed phenomenological empirical work behind every claim in our book: not only would that have been impossible, given the range it tries to cover, but it would ignore the excellent literature on how a mediated social world appears to social actors that already exists. Our account throughout however, even where based on secondary literature, is developed from the standpoint of a *possible* phenomenology that is oriented to empirical research.

A fully *materialist* phenomenology is able to bypass some standard and important objections to what has been associated with the 'classic' tradition of social phenomenology. Take, for example, Michel Foucault's firm rejection of phenomenology for giving 'absolute priority to the observing subject' (Foucault, 1970, p. xiv), or Pierre Bourdieu's related objection to symbolic interactionism for 'reducing relations of power to relations of communication' (Bourdieu, 1991, p. 167). With our materialist phenomenology we hope to commit neither of these sins. If the social world is built up, in part, of interpretations and communications, as phenomenology insists, our account of that world must look closely at the material infrastructures *through which, and on the basis of which*, communications today take place. Phenomenology cannot then *only* focus on how the world appears for interpretation by particular social actors.[9] What is needed instead is a full-blown rethinking of the social construction of everyday reality, in all its interconnectedness, for the digital age. That means reoccupying the space associated with Berger and Luckmann's well-known book, *The Social Construction of Reality*, published exactly half a century ago and one of the most read sociology texts of the 1960s and 1970s. But our aim is emphatically *not* to rework Berger and Luckmann's book, or even to reinterpret it. Our aim instead, starting out from something like their basic ambition, is to build a different but comparable account of how social reality is constructed, an account that is adequate to the communicative forms of the digital age.

There is incidentally still much to admire about Berger and Luckmann's book, developing as it did the mid twentieth-century's tradition of phenomenological sociology into a satisfying version of the sociology of knowledge. Yet this book seems very distant from us now. A basic reason is that Berger and Luckmann say almost nothing about technologically based media of communication. Take for example this rare passage where media are mentioned obliquely in a discussion of the lifeworld's dialectic of near and far:

> The reality of everyday life is organized around the 'here' of my body and the 'now' of my present [. . .] Typically my interest in the far zones is less

intense and certainly less urgent. I am intensely interested in the cluster of objects involved in my daily occupation [. . .] I may also be interested in what goes on at Cape Kennedy or in outer space, but this interest is a matter of private, 'leisure-time' choice rather than an urgent matter of my everyday life. (1966, p. 36)

Media feature in passing here, but only as the window onto a distant world of fascination that helps us while away our leisure hours. Berger and Luckmann do not even consider the importance of media-based narratives for shaping our sense of everyday reality. Was this plausible even in the 1960s? Probably not, and it had long since ceased to be plausible by the 1990s when we both became researchers, after which the embedding of media in the fabric of daily life has intensified considerably. Not surprisingly, therefore, Berger and Luckmann's work has not had much influence on the international cross-disciplinary field of media and communications research.[10]

Our challenge is in any case quite different from Berger and Luckmann's: it is to build a fully materialist phenomenology that starts out from the fact not just of digital media but also of the new data-driven infrastructures and communications on which today's social interfaces increasingly rely. It means understanding how the social is constructed in an age of *deep* mediatization when the very *elements and building-blocks* from which a sense of the social is constructed become *themselves* based in technologically based processes of mediation. As a result, the ways in which we make sense of the world phenomenologically become necessarily entangled with the constraints, affordances and power-relations that are features of media as infrastructures for communication. We explore the concept of 'deep' mediatization further in Chapter 3, but we signal now that it involves a fundamental transformation in how the social world is constructed, and so can be described. Offering such an account will involve returning as much to Berger and Luckmann's predecessor, Alfred Schutz, who had insights already into the consequences of media technologies for social reality that Berger and Luckmann failed to develop.

Our reworking of Berger and Luckmann's legacy has consequences for this book's position in the history of sociology. Step by step we extend the scope of Berger and Luckmann's original project – 'The social construction of reality' – to acknowledge the fully mediated character of today's everyday reality. And while Berger and Luckmann originally sketched a 'sociology of knowledge' itself (as they subtitled their book), we develop instead a sociological account of how media and communications are embedded in everyday life, as the basis for a new account of how the social world and social reality are constructed in an age whose communications infrastructure is radically different from what Berger and Luckmann knew[11] This is the reason why we called this book 'The *mediated* construction of reality'. In that sense, this book can also be read as a contribution to the sociology of knowledge, although our argument at no point depends on making that claim.

Our Inspirations

Before we get started on our analysis, we would like to explain some wider sources that have inspired this project, and note some others that we have tended to avoid.

A surprising source of inspiration for our reinterpretation of Berger and Luckmann comes from the great Jesuit priest and radical educator, Ivan Illich. The last book he wrote before he died offered a reinterpretation of the shift in the communicative lifeworld during Europe's twelfth century that *preceded* the more celebrated transformations that flowed from printing technology. Illich describes the shift from a world where written manuscripts served as the inert repository where revered texts in sacred languages were stored for eternity – while being kept alive through oral recitation, often from memory (compare also Ong, 2002) – to a world where writing itself became the site where *new meanings* were made. Writing became used for storage, but also for contemporary expression, and in *any* language, including meanings intended by the 'ordinary' literate person (for example, a note-taker or diary-writer). Illich describes a complete reorientation of how humans make meaning through technologies of storage: this shift took place over half a century, and introduced a new type of reading, writing, speaking and thinking self. Illich characterized the change involved as a change in 'the relations between *the axioms of conceptual space and social reality* insofar as this interrelationship is mediated and shaped by techniques that employ *letters*'.[12]

We only need to extend Illich's term 'axioms' to today's techniques that employ codes and hyperlinks, and we have an elegant phrase for capturing the superficially simple, yet radical, nature of the digital age's transformations. Illich's word 'axioms' has its root in a Greek word, 'axioma', meaning 'what is *valued*'; in mathematics, Aristotle used this word to refer to what is valued so much, as knowledge, that it can be taken for granted in building an argument or proof. If we have a suspicion that, in the digital age, the things we take for granted in our imaginative and practical relations to the world – our 'axioms' – are *changing*, what better time to revisit the sociology of knowledge with Illich's historical work in mind?[13]

Social theory has offered various routes for making sense of the trans-formation in the axioms of everyday life through media, but each has its limitations. Niklas Luhmann's 'systems theory' appears to offer insights into the digital world, insofar as the latter can be reduced to the opera-tion of an interlocking set of systems. But the theoretical price paid for adopting Luhmann's system theory is very high: not only assuming that the *lived* world of everyday experience and social meaning *is* generally systematic and functionally differentiated, when in reality it may be much more complex and pluri-centred than that, but also masking from view the highly motivated and institutionally directed attempts to *impose* (or pow-erfully propose) systematicity that are increasingly an important feature of the digital communications infrastructure.[14] Another route to making sense of these transformations must be found.

It is more promising to trace the stretched-out patterns of technological formation and linkage that *underlie* how our external actions are organized in the world. Here Bruno Latour has had enormous influence in reorient-ing our sense of what is sociologically interesting. Deeply sceptical about wider notions of 'society' and the 'social', Latour has rightly insisted we pay attention to the huge variety of ways in which people and objects become associated with each other. This is a promising way of registering innovations of practice at a time when the basics of what we value (the 'axioms' of daily life) are being stretched and transformed by our uses of a new digital infrastructure. But here too there is a cost, since Latour, in his scepticism towards sociology's claims of explanatory order, seems to lose touch with what remains at stake for everyday actors in *interpreting* the spaces of interaction ('the social') in which we are entangled. 'The social' is not a space, necessarily, of order; but it is a space *where order is at stake*, and where the absence of order brings severe costs. This is one key contri-bution of phenomenology: to insist that there is something fundamentally (and, we might say, *naturally*) at stake for us, as human beings, in the order that we manage to make in and of the world, an order whose normative force goes far beyond the particular arrangements that, as individuals and collectivities, we assemble. We must therefore hold onto that sense of what is at stake in 'the social' if we are to register the human dilemmas of the digital age, dilemmas which stem from our continuing attempts to *preserve* agency and some satisfactory degree of order under ever more complex, perhaps contradictory, conditions.[15]

We do, however, follow Latour in abandoning the modern idea of 'society', if by that we mean a *sui generis* 'human' construction somehow built up 'against' nature. Latour is not the only writer to see problems in this modern view of nature, science and society.[16] Indeed two major philosophical traditions – the Aristotelian tradition, recently revised in neo-Aristotelian form, and the Hegelian tradition – have insisted on the need to understand the social not as something opposed to 'nature', but as a 'second nature' into which, as human beings, we grow:[17] a contingently evolved but, as such, natural tendency to develop institutional arrangements within which a common life can be lived. Media and communications infrastructures have become part of this second nature and, as such, may, or may not, be evolving in ways that are congenial to other human needs and goals. It is not easy to find a word for this evolving second nature, but it remains important to hold onto a sense of how the shaping of meaning, over time, takes on cumulative and inherited forms without which human life is impossible (McDowell, 1994, p. 95). For this we propose the term 'figurational order', building on the word 'figuration' which we introduce shortly.[18] This figurational order has always been socially shaped, but potentially now is being dislocated by the impact of new contradictions, with radical implications for the sustainability of existing ways of life and forms of social order.

At the root of our concern as social theorists, therefore, is the question of how we come to be embedded *in* a world: that embedding carries for us a moral and ethical charge. Technologically based media of communication are now fundamental to the construction of everyday reality, that is, to building and replicating the world in which we are embedded, but in ways that are producing new costs, tensions and pain. As Anthony Giddens put it more than two decades ago, 'in conditions of late modernity we live "in the world" in a different sense from previous eras in history' (1994a, p. 187). The phenomenological task of following how the world 'hangs together'[19] for us as human actors – as beings who have no choice but to be dependent on others – is, we propose, the best route to grasp the sense of contradiction that we feel in relation to many of the deep transformations within what Jose van Dijck (2013) has called 'the age of connectivity'.

The sociologist who offers most towards understanding the phenomenological contradictions of our digital age is Norbert Elias. His analysis of modern society's increasing 'civilizing' of the body and mind does not separate the individual from society. Elias was interested in how a certain form of civilized 'subject' is linked with a certain form of society. This way of thinking becomes much clearer in his later books such as *The Society of Individuals* and especially *What is Sociology?*. Here Elias understands the social not as static and given, but as articulated in an ongoing process. To analyse the process of building and sustaining the social, Elias introduces the term *'figuration'* as a conceptual tool to grasp the complex problems of interdependence that living together in large numbers generates, how those problems find solutions. Social change is always in part, Elias argues, a change at the level of figurations. It is here too – in the detail of specific figurations, and more complex figurations of figurations, and in the overall web of the 'figurational order' that such figurations constitute – that the consequences of technological processes of mediation for our *possible* social worlds are best traced.

Are the figurations of social life today becoming less positive, *more disordered*, than those of the past? If so, what *social* resources can we find to address this? And what if, as yet, there are none? These are the unsettling questions that our book tries ultimately to pose and at least begin to answer.

When we pose such questions, we become aware how far social theory has ignored until now this emergent media-derived complexity in what it was meant to theorize: 'the social'. That standoff is no longer defensible. For the social *is* mediated, and that mediation is increasingly *sustained* by manifold technologies of communication: by 'manifold', we refer not just to the plurality of today's media channels and interfaces, but also to their interlinked nature, and to the many-dimensional order that results and that encompasses our whole media environment.[20]

The Shape of the Argument to Come

The chapters of Part I of this book are devoted to unfolding the various layers of this relationship between 'the social', 'media' and 'communication' on a broad, historical scale. We start in Chapter 2 by reflecting on the social world as a communicative construction. On the basis of this we move into a historical analysis of the different waves of mediatization that cumulate in the current stage of deep mediatization (Chapter 3). In Chapter 4 we move to the level of everyday living and analyse how we live with the complex figurations of a mediatized social world. In this way, Part I of the book offers an overall understanding of the construction of the social world under conditions of deep mediatization.

We are then ready in Part II to explore the implications of the social's mediation for the dimensions of the social world as building-blocks of everyday experience: for the *spaces* in and over which the social is enacted (Chapter 5) and the *times* in and through which the social occurs (Chapter 6); for our grasp of the types of complexity which the social now displays, because of the increasing importance of *data-based* processes that operate, as it were, behind the scenes of everyday interaction (Chapter 7).

This, in turn, provides the basis in Part III for considering agency in the social world and the larger organizational forms that are built 'on top of' this mediated social, as worked through in our practices as 'selves' (Chapter 8), as 'collectivities' (Chapter 9), and as institutions that attempt to order, even govern, the social world (Chapter 10). Only through these various levels of analysis can we get into view the wider question with which the book ends: is our ever more technologically mediated life together sustainable, or at least compatible with maintaining good relations of interdependence? If not, how can we begin to remedy this?

Across this set of arguments will be a normative trajectory that underlies our book's analysis as a whole: while we want to avoid any naive criticism that claims deep mediatization is *per se* 'good' or 'bad', we reflect throughout on the question of how far certain forms of mediatization offer agency to certain figurations of people and institutions, giving them particular opportunities in the construction of the social world, while limiting the agency of others. In this sense, we are concerned with how far, at the highest level of complexity, today's 'figurational order' has negative or positive implications overall for human lives-in-common. The first part of this book provides the foundation for such a kind of analysis. In the second and third parts of the book we reflect from many angles on these questions of agency in times of deep mediatization. We bring together our sense of how the figurational order of the digital age fits with the normative demands that humans are entitled to make of *any* way of life in Chapter 11, the Conclusion.

Part I

Constructing the Social World

2

The Social World as Communicative Construction

In this chapter we introduce our approach to understanding how communication, and specifically mediated communication, contribute to the construction of the social world. This is the essential starting-point, if we are to explain how the social world *changes* when it becomes fundamentally interwoven with media. What does it mean when the social world, as we know it, is constructed in and through mediated communication? A way of capturing this deep, consistent and self-reinforcing role of media in the construction of the social world is to say that the social world is not just mediated but media*tized*: that is, *changed* in its dynamics and structure by the role that media continuously (indeed recursively)[1] play in its construction.

We do not mean by this to say that the social world is totally 'colonized' – to use a Habermasian term (Habermas, 1984 [1981], p. 117) – by the media, or subjected throughout to something as simple or direct as a 'media logic' (Altheide and Snow, 1979). Nor do we intend to imply that the salience of media in the construction of the social world operates in the same way everywhere: of course, the *degree* of media's interweaving in the social varies in different regions of the world, as does even what we mean by 'media' (Slater, 2013, pp. 29f.). We *do* mean by this that the social world has significantly more complexity when its forms and patterns are, in part, sustained in and through media and their infrastructures. Even if we do things without directly using media, the horizon of our practices is a social world for which media are fundamental reference-points and resources. This is the sense in which we speak about the social world as 'mediatized'.

The term 'mediatization' can be further explained by a more basic reflection on the concept of communication. Communication is a process necessary to the construction of a social world: as Hubert Knoblauch puts it, 'communicative action [is] the basic process in the social construction of reality' (Knoblauch, 2013b, p. 297). This does not mean that all practices within the social world are communicative (they are not), but it means *more* than saying that communication is just one of many acts we do in the world (of course it is). Because communication is the set of practices through which we 'make sense' of our world, and build arrangements (simple or complex) for coordinating our behaviour, the communicative dimension of our practices is critical to how the social world *becomes* constructed. Some social constructivism, as formulated by Berger and Luckmann (1966) for example, rather underplayed *communication* in general, in the course of overplaying '*language* as the empirical medium of action' (Knoblauch, 2013b, p. 298). As a result, that approach was poorly placed to grasp the sheer variety of communicative practices through media. But the inadequacy of that position becomes all the clearer with deep mediatization (see Chapter 1) when more and more aspects of our daily practice are saturated by new forms of mediated communication.

Our first step therefore is to build an approach that understands the social world as *fundamentally interwoven with media*. Already, we turn away here from the original thinking of Berger and Luckmann. We also establish another key difference. While Berger and Luckmann understood their book as a 'treatise in the sociology of knowledge' (its subtitle), defined in a rather universal manner, our starting-point in understanding the construction of the social world in an age of digital media is fundamentally different. *Because* media have changed the reference-points of human practice so dramatically, it is now obvious not only that the social world is something *constructed* by us as humans, but that those processes of construction can only be understood if seen as *historically located*, with one of the main recent historical changes being the increasing social relevance of technologies of mediated communication. In this chapter we sketch the consequences of this for understanding the social world. The terminology we introduce – everyday reality and the domains of the social world, institutional facts, and communicative practices by which we construct the social world as meaningful – will be the basis for our critical reflection on social agency that we develop over the course of this book.

We cannot analyse the social world via a simple division between 'pure' face-to-face communication and a separate presentation of the world to us 'through' media. Many of the communicative practices by which we construct our social world are media-related ones. Our daily communication comprises much more than direct face-to-face communication: mediated communication – by television, phones, platforms, apps, etc. – is interwoven with our face-to-face communication in manifold ways. Our face-to-face interaction is continuously *inter*woven with media-related practices: while we talk to someone, we might check something on our mobile phones, get text messages, refer to various media contents.

Sonia Livingstone (2009) sums this up as 'the mediation of everything'. However, because the social world is not just a series of discrete things laid alongside each other (a first-order complexity) but a web of *interconnections* operating on a huge number of levels and scales, 'the mediation of everything' automatically generates new complexities, since each part of 'everything' is itself already mediated. This huge *second-order* complexity is what we try to capture by the term 'media*tization*', and it derives from the mediation of the communicative practices that at every level contributes to the construction of the social world. If we are to grasp how processes of communicative construction take place across a variety of different media, our analysis must go to a higher dimension of complexity than is possible by concentrating on the 'face to face' and 'here and now'.

To ground an approach like this we make a three-step argument. First, we clarify what we understand by 'social world': what does this term imply? Second, we outline how the construction of the social world and its everyday reality takes place. And third, we develop an understanding of the complexity of media and communication's role in this process of construction.

2.1 Theorizing the Social World

In everyday language, as well as in social sciences, the term 'social world' is a more or less widely used concept. It sometimes requires no further explanation, indicating the 'common dimension' of the world – the 'empirical world' in which we as human beings live. In this sense, for example, Herbert Blumer wrote about the 'empirical social world' (Blumer, 1954, p. 4) in his famous article entitled 'What is wrong with social theory?' This is also the very general sense in which Tim Dant (1999) described 'material culture' as part of the 'social world'. In contrast to such general understandings, a very specific concept of the social world can be found in symbolic interactionism with its so-called 'social world perspective' (Clarke, 2011; Shibutani, 1955; Strauss, 1978). From this perspective, society consists of various bounded 'social worlds'; for example, the social world of football playing, the social world of schools, or the social world of the family. Each of these social worlds – so the argument goes – is defined by a 'primary activity', by certain 'sites' where these activities occur, and by 'technologies' and 'organizations' that are involved (Strauss, 1978, p. 122).

In our view, these understandings of the social world are either too generalized (more or less a metaphor for human togetherness) or too narrow (understanding certain social domains as social worlds).[2] Our definition of the social world is both inclusive and focused at the same time. The social world, put most simply, is the overall outcome of our joint processes of social – specifically, communicative – construction. Through the variety of our sense-making practices, we construct our social world, as something 'common' to us from the beginning. It is in this sense that the philosopher John Searle (2011) discusses the construction of social reality as 'making the social world'.

Such a definition of the social world echoes the reflections of social phenomenology but in a more historically sensitive way. We can trace this understanding back to the book *The Phenomenology of the Social World* by Alfred Schutz (1967 [1932]). If we follow his arguments, the social world is an intersubjective world, that is, a world we share with other human beings (Schutz, 1967, p. 9). This creates the possibility that the social world is 'meaningful, not only for those living in that world, but for its scientific interpreters as well' (Schutz, 1967, p. 9). Schutz attempted to reconstruct the fundamental phenomenology of the social world, using in his later work the concept of the 'lifeworld' to emphasize its rootedness in our 'unproblematic' and 'natural' experiences of everyday reality (Schutz and Luckmann, 1973). Berger and Luckmann picked this up in their approach to the social construction of reality, which for them, too, is based in 'everyday life' (Berger and Luckmann, 1966, pp. 31–62). While we will have some critical things to say about the limits of some work in this classic tradition of social phenomenology, there are three fundamental points we can learn from it.

1. *The social world is intersubjective.* Describing the social world requires an analysis that considers the various subjective perspectives of the different actors within the social world, but, at the same time, taking into account that the social world has an existence beyond (that is, independent of) the individual. The social world existed before we as individuals were born, and it will last when as individuals we are gone. Various media are important means towards securing the intersubjective character of our social world. Media offer the possibility to communicate across time and space, developing a shared understanding of the social world and representing the social world for further reflection and action. Media here include not only so-called mass media, which, in the form of broadcasting and print, for a long time constituted the dominant definitions of the social world. Media here also include the various digital platforms we use to communicate with our friends and colleagues and to represent these social relations. The intersubjectivity of today's social world is something we articulate to a distinct degree through our many media in structures of connection or, as we will call them later, figurations.

2. *Everyday reality is the foundation of the social world.* According to Schutz, everyday reality is *constitutive* for our living in the social world. What does this mean? As Alfred Schutz and Thomas Luckmann formulated it, everyday life 'is the province of reality in which man [sic!] continuously participates in ways which are at once inevitable and patterned' (Schutz and Luckmann, 1973, p. 3). It is the 'region of reality' in which we can engage as individual human beings and which we can change through our bodily operations. Berger and Luckmann went further, describing this everyday reality as deserving the title of the 'paramount reality' (Berger and Luckmann, 1966, p. 35), which grounds the possibility of a social world. It is important here, as elsewhere, to be clear on what we are, and are not, saying if we follow this classical phenomenological position. Because we have bodies and it is *only* through the capacities of our bodies that we act in the world, there is no other possible grounding of our social world than our embodied actions: by 'everyday life' we mean then, quite simply, what each of us *does* in the world, individually and in relation to each other. But what we do in the world is not somehow separate, or cut off, from the technological means by which we act in the world. Berger and Luckmann, as was common in sociology for a long time, wrote as if there is *first* face-to-face 'everyday life' *and then there is a supplement*: what we do, technologically, to mediate that everyday life. This was hardly true through most of human history, at least since the discovery of writing, but today it would simply be bizarre to ignore how the reality of everyday life is inseparably linked with media, when supermarket checkouts read our credit cards with our personal data, when our everyday communication happens to a high degree via mobile devices, platforms and interactive systems, and when children learn to play through the means of internet-connected tablets. Under these circumstances it makes no sense at all to think of everyday reality as a 'pure experience' that can be contrasted with a (somehow secondary) 'mediated experience'. Everyday reality, from the beginning, is in many respects mediated, which means that the complex social world of *interconnections* constructed from everyday life's foundations is mediatized.

3. *The social world is internally differentiated in domains.* The social world is not one homogeneous thing; 'it is internally diverse, exhibit[ing] a multi-form structure' (Schutz, 1967, p. 139). The structuring force of the social world is quite consistent with much of our everyday life being de facto lived within 'sub-universes of human existence' (Luckmann, 1970, p. 580), 'a variety of small "worlds"' (Luckmann, 1970, p. 587) like, for example, single-purpose communities, or work and leisure groups. This perhaps sounds like symbolic interactionism's 'social worlds perspective'

(Clarke, 2011; Shibutani, 1955; Strauss, 1978), but a risk with that latter approach was to neglect the common links and constraining forces that sustain those sub-worlds *as structurally related*. We would rather say that the social world is differentiated into various domains. Each of these social domains is defined by a shared practical orientation of the humans acting within this domain. That said, we cannot understand these domains as closed systems, in the way traditional systems theory does. The boundaries of each domain are rather blurred and in various ways they intersect with each other. Yet they are also, in principle, linked to each other as part of a larger social world. Media play a double role in relation to these social domains: first they stimulate the *differentiation* of these domains by offering a high variety of symbolic resources; second, they support the *intersection* of these domains by sustaining communication across them.

In summary, the social world is the intersubjective sphere of the social relations that we as human beings experience. Those relations are rooted in everyday reality, a reality nowadays always interwoven with media to some degree. The social world is, in turn, differentiated into many domains of meaning, even though it is also bound together by multiple relations of interdependence and constraint.

Notice that we have talked so far of a social world, not 'society'. For sure, we cannot avoid considering how our various overlapping experiences of the social world contribute to, and are embedded within, 'social orders' (Wrong, 1994) of various sorts, including at the level of 'national societies'. Those wider orders impact on our possible sense of membership of a social world often in violent ways; increasingly, through globalization, we live in a social world that is shaped by multiple, overlapping and (in their effects) contradictory social orders. But – and this is the key move of social phenomenology – those orders are not primary. A social world *can* be built, and experienced, without them, and so *their* complexities and contradictions do not contradict the possibility of a social world itself. This enables us, for example, to hold onto the fundamental notion of the social world, while avoiding any assumption of 'methodological nationalism' (Beck, 2006; Couldry and Hepp, 2012; Wimmer and Glick Schiller, 2002): we do not take the borders of 'national societies', whatever their practical importance for various purposes, as 'natural' limits of the social world. We also avoid assuming that any single 'society' (whether local, regional, national or global) is the only and exclusive 'order' in which the social world is embedded for particular sets of actors. Media today play a key role in the proliferating complexity of social *ordering*, that is, in shaping the *possibilities* for social order. We will come back later in Chapter 10 to the question of social order, but on various scales, not just those of the nation. With deep mediatization, it is often, as we will find, *ambiguities* at the level of social ordering that characterize our experience. All the more important then that we take the social world in general (not any particular social order) as the departure of our analysis.

2.2 Reality and the Construction of the Social World

The social world is not just a given. We *make it*, as human beings; it is, in this sense, socially constructed. This is the fundamental position of social constructivism, and it has nothing to do with the philosophical traps of anti-materialism or idealism (see Hacking, 1999, pp. 24–25; Ferreux, 2006, p. 50). Indeed it involves insisting that the social *is* material, a materiality that is not a 'pre-given' stratum into which human beings are inserted, but a product of human interaction itself, with all its power-relations and inequalities. This basic idea of what we call materialist phenomenology is perhaps self-explanatory, but things get more complicated if we ask what 'construction' means in detail. As for the trap of idealism, our fundamental point is that the social world is grounded not in ideas, but in *everyday action*, that is, in *practice*: the reality in which we as human beings act and that we articulate by our interaction. The approach to social *construction* that is involved in materialist phenomenology should not therefore be confused with the idealist notion that the world does not exist except through our imagination of it. On the contrary, we insist that there is one material world, with determinate features, in which we act: as John Searle puts it, 'we live in exactly one world, not two or three or seventeen' (Searle, 1995, p. xi).

Social construction, the material world and institutions

Factual claims about the material world can be made within any number of frameworks of understanding, all of which at some level refer to values and orientations that may not be universally held. So it was possible for large groups of people to believe, at the same time, that the earth moved around the sun, or that the sun moved round the earth, even if only one of those factual claims could be true; and the degree of consensus over such frameworks of understanding is historically contingent. However, to the extent that there is consensus, those sharing the consensus can use shared procedures to agree on specific facts, and other frameworks of understanding can be built by reference to those facts, including frameworks for constructing everyday reality in a specific way. There is, in other words, one physical world, but many possible, and even conflicting, constructions of it.

In thinking about the facts of the world, we need to consider the special status of social facts. Émile Durkheim in his early outline of the discipline of sociology used the term 'social facts' to describe 'any way of acting [. . .] which is general over the whole of a given society whilst having an existence of its own, independent of its individual manifestations' (Durkheim, 1982 [1895], p. 59). What Durkheim calls 'social facts' are very close to what philosopher John Searle calls 'institutional facts' (Searle, 1995, p. 2)[3] and have some crucial features (pointed out by Searle) which distinguish them from, say, facts about the natural physical world. Institutional facts are constituted by people recognizing and accepting certain common rules and functions, and so they *only exist* to the extent that people *go on* accepting those things: that is, they exist *when* people continue to act according to those common rules and functions and without that, they cease to exist (see Berger and Luckmann, 1966, p. 72).

This brings us to the necessity of defining institutions. The process of social construction spreads far beyond the domains of what, in everyday terms, we would recognize as institutions (corporations, courts, schools, governments). Berger and Luckmann point out the importance of a wider process of 'institutionalization' which involves not only habit at the level of individual actors, but, more subtly, the way actors mutually adjust their expectations of each other: what Berger and Luckmann, following Schutz, call the reciprocal typification of habitualized actions (Berger and Luckmann, 1966, p. 72). From this perspective, even the family, which typifies particular forms of action in terms of types of actors ('father', 'mother', 'current partner', 'child', 'aunt', and so forth), is part of the process of institutionalization. So too are our habits of mobile communication, which sustain for us our everyday space of interaction with family, friends and work colleagues. In this last respect, media's involvement in processes of institutionalization has expanded with deep mediatization, and is no longer limited to the role of large-scale media organizations and their authority over the changing construction of the social world. This also includes institutions on a much higher level of complexity, so-called 'institutional fields' (Friedland and Alford, 1991) such as education, economy and politics where distinctive kinds of social domains come together on the basis of distinctive relations of meaning. Building on Bourdieu's (1993) theory of fields, this approach emphasizes the *institutionalized* character of each social field and its different sorts of capital.

Many institutional facts have a basic feature that derives from their basis in constitutive rules of the form 'X counts as Y in context Z' (Searle, 1995, p. 28): that is, they are context-relative. In addition, they are often ordered in hierarchies. So, for example, the fact that, in chess, a move that captures the king is called 'checkmate' and ends the game is subordinate to the fact that there is a game with certain properties and rules which is called 'chess'; if that game stops being recognized as a game, then the institutional facts constituted by its specific rules automatically fall away, too. Because a special feature of institutional facts is that they are constituted by people continuing to accept them – that is, they exist *only and insofar as* they are reproduced continuously – there has been a strong temptation to claim that all of everyday reality is like that: that is, it exists only through its regular *reproduction* in the form of performed acceptance. This approach is known as 'structuration theory', one of the core principles of which is, according to its proponent Anthony Giddens (1984, p. 19, added emphasis), that 'the rules and resources *drawn upon* in the production and reproduction of social action are at the same time the means of system reproduction': this is what he calls 'the duality of structure'. But there are certain problems with this view, which we discuss next.

While it clearly follows from the basic features of institutional facts that *some* elements of everyday reality exist by virtue of 'structuration' over time and across space (rather than being abstract facts that apply to all time and space), it is not plausible to say that *all* elements of everyday reality are the result, and *only* the result, of ongoing reproduction through action.

'Resources' certainly are constituted, in part, by institutional facts. So, if the authority of a king is considered a resource, it depends on people recognizing that authority and acting upon it, whatever their grounds for doing so (they may have none: the emperor's new clothes scenario). Yet the resource of, say, the global financial system surely involves many elements that are not institutional facts, but rather the arrangement of material objects in highly ordered ways (see Searle, 1995, p.121). However, 'structuration theory' tends to blur this by claiming that society is made up of rules (that is, social facts) and resources, and depends on *both* rules and resources being reproduced through our ongoing actions in the world.

The existence of resources, unlike rules or institutional facts, is generally not subject to the control or influence of social actors, not least because of the distributed materiality of many of these resources. What counts is the *interplay* between institutional facts and resources, as William Sewell notes

(2005, p. 137). A general problem for all accounts that think of social reality as 'structure' is how far they can recognize *the degrees of agency* that actors have even within a highly patterned resource distribution. This varies depending on which aspect of structure we are talking about. So, as Sewell says, the structure of language is very durable, but the degree to which it constrains specific linguistic actions is weak, whereas political structures may be much less durable, while constraining action in highly specific ways (Sewell, 2005, pp. 147f.). Indeed, the 'strength' of structure – the force of its constraining power – is of great importance in relation to today's growing information infrastructure: it is part of what binds the social world together notwithstanding its diversity, but perhaps in ways that are not durable, but fast-changing.

There may even be times and places when different structures – different institutional facts, and different systems of rules and interpretations that underlie them – potentially apply *to the same situation*. This is exactly what happens when actions in everyday life are performed on online platforms within certain affordances and constraints, yet similar acts are performed elsewhere according to different constraints. Such conflicts are deeply disruptive and may trigger situations where important classes of institutional facts *disappear*, because they no longer are accepted by sufficient numbers of those who are potentially affected by them (Searle, 1995, p. 45, 57). With deep mediatization, major new infrastructures for human interaction and socialization have been built in a matter of two decades, which means (whether we acknowledge it or not) that the construction of everyday reality has *itself* become subject to major new disturbance and conflict.

The Radical Uncertainty of Social Construction

It is important, however, before we get to those larger disruptions, to say more about the process of construction *as such*. We have talked so far at a general level about the social world and its construction, and have been explicit about the degrees of contingency (if you like, the *constitutive* uncertainty) inherent to this term. These uncertainties seem rather different from the degrees of uncertainty about basic physical facts; for example, that the earth revolves around the sun (although every 'fact' only appears as such within a certain framework of reference and such frameworks have not remained static throughout history). In spite however of the contingencies inherent to institutional facts, their consistent place within everyday life generally encourages us to equate them with *reality* itself. It is important, however, not to make this logical slide.

Here a recent discussion by the French sociologist Luc Boltanski is helpful.[4] For Boltanski, 'reality tends to coincide with what appears to hang together [. . .] [that is,] with order' (2011, p. 57). Two points are crucial to Boltanski. First, that the 'everyday reality' of the social world is not all there is, since what is *constructed as* reality stands out against a larger set of possibilities which forms the background to whatever *can* be constructed as the 'everyday reality' of the social world.[5] Second, based on the first point, we must 'abandon [. . .] the idea of an implicit [and fixed] agreement which would somehow be imminent in the functioning of social life'. Instead, we should 'put *dispute* and, with it, the *divergence* of points of view, interpretation and usages at the heart of social bonds' (Boltanski, 2011, p. 61, added emphasis). If we follow Boltanski, this means *diverging sharply* from 'social constructionism' as generally interpreted. *Like* 'standard' social constructionism, it foregrounds agency, and specifically recognizes the ongoing agency of human beings and their institutions, in the construction of reality, that is, the sociological reality *of* 'reality' construction.[6] *Unlike* 'standard' social constructionism, this approach in addition emphasizes the irreducible and conflicted *uncertainty* at the heart of the process of social construction: the unending conflicts about the ontology of the social or, as Luc Boltanski puts it more poetically, 'the whatness of what is [. . .], what matters, what has value, what it is right to respect and look at twice' (Boltanski, 2011, p. 56).

Let us say something more specific about the construction of institutions. The basic idea of materialist phenomenology – that the social world depends on the material processes whereby human beings construct it – does not rely on an account of institutions. But it is beyond dispute that, over time, social life has come to require, as it has grown more complex, various stabilizations of resource within institutions. Those institutions have become associated with particular types of practice, including practices of interpreting the social world in a particular way. Institutions play an important role, down to the level of everyday language, in constructing reality and making possible a particular reality's appearance of hanging together against a background of much greater flux (see Berger and Luckmann, 1966, pp. 53–67). More than that, particular institutions (such as the law) are distinctive in that to them is 'delegated the task of stating the whatness of what is' (Boltanski, 2011, p. 75), that is, the general *representation* of social reality. This repeats, from a different perspective (that of the institutions which try to stabilize it), Searle's fundamental point about the underlying contingency of social facts, but rejects any functionalist idea that 'social construction' is equivalent to a continuous and integrated social order without conflict, tension or institutional effort. The institutions with specific responsibility for representing reality in its general and specific forms have gone on developing throughout history, and in the current age of internet-based connectivity include institutions as seemingly remote from everyday intervention as the algorithms at work within search engines (Halavais, 2009). But, as Adrian MacKenzie notes, even the software that implements such processes 'is very intimately linked with how code is read and by whom or by what [whether] by person or machine' (MacKenzie, 2006, p. 6): in other words, algorithms, software, and databases too are not 'reality', but *constructed* reality.

The social world and its everyday reality – at every level – is not a metaphysical notion but a concept inextricably linked to *action*. As Ian Hacking, following in the tradition of Wittgenstein, put it, 'we [. . .] count as real what we can use to intervene in the world to affect something else, or what the world can use to affect us' (Hacking, 1983, p. 146). Put another way, everyday reality is the context in which actors are 'immersed in the *flux of life*' (Boltanski, 2011, p. 98) and so they must act. The complexity, however, is that different social forces have varying degrees of *power over* what comes to count as everyday reality, and the role of social sciences is to get at such power, abstracting it from the seemingly unproblematic everyday order that we need to endure as acting beings. For Boltanski, it is law that is particularly important as an institutional force constructing reality, and we do not deny law's importance. But we would suggest that *communication, media and their infrastructures* matter increasingly today in 'stating the whatness of what is'.

Let us sum up our argument to this point. The social world has a reality of its own – everyday reality. This social world and its everyday reality are constructed. This means they are not naturally given but 'made' by human practices and the side-consequences of those practices. However, this does *not* mean that the social world is 'random' or 'idiosyncratic'. On the contrary, this process of construction is based on many patterns of practice whose validity is generally accepted (institutional facts). Institutional facts involve the work of institutions (in the everyday sense – major concentrations of material resource, like governments and courts) but also broader patterns of institutionalization: all contribute to the construction of the social world in a process Berger and Luckmann call 'objectivation'. Indeed, we depend on it seeming that way to us: social conditions where the interpretation of reality becomes itself the site of intense contestation (for example, societies on the path towards dictatorship) are times of the greatest anxiety and distress. The paradox of the social world is that it is both grounded in complex and historically contingent interrelations of individual and collective action, yet tends to be grasped by us as a *single* interconnected reality. We *know* that we live in just *one* material world: we cannot individually or collectively choose *another* world in which we prefer to act. But the specific and (relatively) stable *features* of the social world in which we live are themselves part of *the construction* that institutions strive to sustain, against the background of a more complex and uncertain flux of possible states of the social world.

2.3 Media and the Communicative Construction of the Social World

So far we have outlined a materialist phenomenological approach to understanding how the social world is constructed. This immediately provokes another question: what is the role of communication in this process? Communication as a meaning-making practice is the core of how the social world gets constructed as *meaningful*, while media and their infrastructures have become increasingly crucial for everyday communicative practices. This has implications for how we think about social constructivism. Already in the 1930s Alfred Schutz had a certain feeling for the importance of media – something he shared with some other great exponents of social science (see Manheim, 1933; Tarde, 1901; Weber, 1911). If we follow Schutz (1967, pp. 163–207), the social world in which we live can be divided into two spheres. This is, first, the 'world of consociates' (*Umwelt*), our 'directly experienced social reality'. Second, there is the sphere of the 'world of contemporaries' (*Mitwelt*). For each of us, 'directly experienced social reality' – the reality of the face-to-face situation – is the core of our experience of the social world. It is where we are present with all our senses, and where we experience the other and our social relationship to him or her in a direct way. The 'world of contemporaries' is somewhat distant from this: we know that they exist and that they build with us the social world, but we are not in direct contact with them.

Interestingly Schutz himself in his early writings indicated some caution about the distinction between consociates and contemporaries, or more crudely, between interactors near and far (Knoblauch, 2013a). Schutz argued that, *because of media*, the distinction between face-to-face experiences and other experiences of the social world as already less absolute and more of a *continuous gradation*. As early as the 1930s, Schutz used the example of the telephone to explain this: 'imagine a face-to-face conversation, followed by a telephone call, followed by an exchange of letters, and finally messages exchanged through a third party. Here too we have a gradual progression from the world of immediately experienced social reality to the world of contemporaries' (Schutz, 1967, p. 177). Other examples he discusses include the role of media for constructing 'collective entities' (Schutz, 1967, pp. 180f.) like the nation.[7] Therefore, media play a role in the increasing 'mediatedness' (*Mittelbarkeit*) of our experience of the social world, which affects *how* our social world is constructed as a reality.[8]

The 'Mediatedness' of the Social World

Back in the 1930s, Schutz could only have had a first impression of this complex connection between technological media of communication and the changing 'mediatedness' of the social world. He called for a more detailed analysis of the 'contact situations' (Schutz, 1967, p. 177) between direct and indirect experience, but could not develop it. In the context of processes of deep mediatization, we must elaborate Schutz's early insights much further.

Today's forms of 'mediatedness' have potentially deepened in at least four ways unforeseen by Schutz. First, as Schutz already saw, we have an increasing mediation of our communicative stream, that is, a shift in the overall balance from direct communication to mediated communication as the regular means of sustaining social relations. But, unimaginably for Schutz or anyone writing up to the 1980s, even our mediated communication can have enhancements which make them closer in specific responses to the face-to-face communication; for instance, video calls with simultaneous text messaging and email stream, enabling two parties to share simultaneous focused attention on the same external communicative stream, that is, an email attachment or website (contrast the simple phone call). A second deepening is the embedding not just of particular communicative streams into everyday life, but of the inputs from *past* communications (continuous streams of information from both *Mitwelt* and *Umwelt*): think of the feedback loop that operates when, while communicating with somebody else face to face, we are also checking information on earlier interactions on our smartphone, involving other communication partners. We are involved in a 'multi-level' construction of the social world, acting on various 'levels' of communication at the same time. Third, and also unimaginable to Schutz, is the already discussed continuous availability of media as a *current resource* in face-to-face communication, from showing pictures on one's digital device to the use of video even in the most intimate of settings. And fourth, we are living through an integration of all these three shifts into the *habits and norms* of all communicative behaviour, both face to face and mediated. Increasingly we expect that our comments and gestures can be mediated for future commentary, circulation, etc., *unless*, that is, we insist they should not be re-circulated (Tomlinson, 2007, pp. 94–123).

Our communication today in the here and now is thoroughly interwoven with various media. The point is not that the face to face becomes less important, but that *in order to sustain its primacy* (for example, the importance of family meal times) we now *require* continuous *mediated coordination*, within processes of 'connected presence' that enable us to coordinate the possibility of that face-to-face situation (Licoppe, 2004).[9] We regularly rely on having access to communication inputs comprised of past processes of mediated communication: much of that information is comprised of data automatically collected via platforms, which then feeds back into our perception of ourselves and our perception of 'others'. As a result, the social world can no longer be understood in terms of classic social constructionism, which claimed that the 'most important experience of others takes place in the face-to-face situation' (Berger and Luckmann, 1966, p. 43). It is not just that media extend direct experience via a gradual process towards more indirect experiences: *from the outset* our social world is suffused with technological media of communication, and the 'directness' and 'mediatedness' of experience are inextricably interwoven with each other. In this respect, media are changing not only our *Mitwelt* but, more basically, our *Umwelt*: 'our directly experienced social reality', as Schutz put it. This goes beyond mere definition[10] into questions of action, what we can do in the world: technologically based media of communication are bringing about the refiguring of the world in and on which we act.

Communication and Practice

We cannot grasp this transformation unless we understand *communication as action and practice*. While these terms – action and practice – have different origins and nuances of meaning, the core idea linked with both terms is the same: to communicate is a form of 'doing' comparable to other forms of 'human doing', like, for example, constructing a table. As language is so important for social construction, our 'communicative doing' is as far-reaching as our 'physical doing'. The case of performative rituals – for example, rites of passage like 'educational qualifications' or 'marriages' – is just a more elaborate version of the same basic point: typically they are acts of communication. In many cases it is just one word or phrase – a 'yes' or

'I do' when getting married – that has considerable consequences for the life of a person. As pragmatism in linguistics emphasized (see Austin, 1962; Levinson, 1983; Searle, 1969), we should take communicative action as being just as real in its effects as other forms of human action.

Communicative action is inherently 'social': it is a practice of interaction. This means that communication doesn't just 'happen', but that we communicate on the basis of the objectivizations of language that we have learned in the process of our socialization. We learn not only the basic communicative signs, but also patterns of *how* to communicate: the way to 'question', to 'answer', to 'discuss', etc., is based on certain social patterns – 'rules' based in institutional facts – which we learn during our socialization. Such patterns can have a high level of complexity, including 'schemes' showing how to articulate a 'speech' in a correct way or how a multi-layered 'dispute' should take place. But regardless of how complex these patterns are, they are built on the basis of forms of communication that remain in place independently of the concrete *contents* of communication.[11]

Communication is a complex process, with many levels, some more consciously formulated than others; communication is a complex skill that, to be performed, draws on many types of socialized competence, and we cannot always say why we communicate as we do. Communication is based on what Giddens (1984, p. 375) calls 'practical conscious[ness]': people have the capacity to act in a communicatively appropriate manner. But they are not necessarily in a position to express discursively this practical knowledge of 'how to do communication'.

Allowing for this complexity, we define communication to mean any form of symbolic interaction either conscious and planned or habitualized and situated. We also use the term 'communicative' to refer to any thing or action that is related to, or has the property of being, 'communication' in this broad sense. Communication depends upon the use of signs, which humans learn during socialization and which, as symbols, are for the most part arbitrary so that they are founded upon social rules. Interaction here means mutually oriented action, which usually does, although it need not, depend on a wider set of interrelations (that is, a 'social' context). Communication is required for there to be a social world at all, because it is the key means *by which* the interactions and interrelations that make the world social are performed. But the social world of everyday reality also involves many non-communicative processes too.

The role of communication as a process in the construction of the social world can be understood, in more detail, as working through a number of levels. First, there are *communicative actions*, that is, single acts of communication, such as an 'order', a 'question', or a 'statement', that share a distinct and bounded form linked to the specific action which that act performs. Second, there are *communicative practices*, that is, groups of communicative actions that together constitute a larger unit; for example, the practice of discussion. Various actions – 'questioning', 'replying', 'contradicting', etc. – may come together, sometimes in a single flow and sometimes as part of wider practices. Of course, our practices of communication are interwoven with other forms of action and our use of objects,[12] and we must consider these complex interrelations if we want to arrive at an understanding of the character of a communicative practice. And even practices that we do not consider to be primarily communicative may have a *communicative dimension*: we can therefore imagine human practice as a continuum between 'pure occupation' (no communication: for example, a physical task performed without commentary or accompanying symbols) and 'pure communication' (a conversation without any other simultaneous actions).

The third and fourth levels concern how the social world is built up *out of* practices of communication. So, on the third level, for example, the social domain of an office environment is incomprehensible unless one grasps the interrelations between the many sets of practices (with their underlying acts) in which people are involved. But those interrelations are themselves not accidental, but structured: they involve *'forms'* of action in which the performers recognize themselves to be involved (for example, 'preparing for a sales conference', or 'doing an audit' or 'designing a new web platform'), each form involving the convergence of a number of practices. Or, on a fourth level and still larger scale, there are *'patterns'* made up from the articulation together of communicative forms towards certain aggregate effects at the level of institutional fields: for example, reinforcing the power of one set of actors over another set of actors. The whole field of education (comprised as it is of patterns of complex communicative forms, involving many coordinated actors and their acts and practices) can be understood in this way. Institutions play a key role in reinforcing such patterned inequalities of power through the organization of communicative action.

Media and Communicative Construction

All these forms of communication – on various levels of complexity – are processes of construction: a *meaningful* social world is therefore built up by acts of communication. And these happen *through* media, relying on an infrastructure of mediated communication that of course is not a neutral tool but brings with it certain consequences. But what *are* media? Up to now, when discussing media, we have implicitly referred to what we might call technologically based media of communication, that is, we have excluded 'generalized symbolic media' like 'money' just as we excluded 'primary media' like 'language'. Therefore, our focus has been on these technologically based means of communication that *extend or modify* our basic human possibilities of communication (McLuhan and Lapham, 1994). These include the modern mass media like television, radio or printed newspaper, but also the mobile devices and platforms we use to communicate with each other, including the companies that are 'behind' these platforms and infrastructures. Therefore, we need an understanding of media that is specific enough to focus our reflections on technological media of communication, but at the same time open enough to capture their contemporary variety.

By *media* therefore we mean technologically based media of communication which institutionalize communication. Media *institutionalize* our communicative practices on various levels. We are moving here from practices not just to forms (watching television) but also to complex patterns of practices: the level of how we arrange ourselves in the moment of media use, the level of forms and patterns of our communication through a medium, and the level of a medium as a certain organization – to name just the most important levels. Linked with such processes of institutionalization is the *materialization* of a medium, as a way of interfacing with the world. We use the term 'materialization' in a comprehensive sense, referring here both to the material presence of each medium and at the same time the norms and beliefs about 'how things are' in relation to this medium, including the habits we develop with regard to and around this medium. Each medium has a characteristic materiality: not only the materiality of the device as such (the TV set, the mobile phone, the computer, etc.), but also the materiality of the underlying communication infrastructure: the cable network, the satellites, the broadcasting stations, and so on. 'Naturalization' is often an aspect of this materiality: certain forms and material aspects of media use, over time, have come to be so basic to everyday action that they seem 'natural'. For example, it seems to be 'natural' to use the radio as a broadcasting medium centred on a particular communicative 'centre' because its existing infrastructure suggests this. In the same sense it seems to be 'natural' to use internet platforms for networking because they are coded like that. As soon as a medium acquires a certain materiality, it comes to seem to social actors reified; as Bruno Latour (1991) put it, technology is 'society made durable'. And in a certain sense we can find this idea already within the concept of 'affordances' (Gibson, 1967): using this concept, each medium has a characteristic, or 'affordance', that offers the possibility for specific actions as part of its 'usability'.

Focusing on media not only as objects but also as means of communication, we can link these ideas with the 'double articulation' (Silverstone, 2006, pp. 239f.) of each medium: the 'content dimension' and 'object dimension'. Both refer to a medium's fundamental character as a means of communication that involves at the same time institutionalization and materialization. Because of this, media are never neutral in the act of communication. They are a stage in how our communication is 'moulded' (Hepp, 2013a, pp. 54–60). And this is the reason why our communicative construction of the social world and its everyday reality *changes* when media are involved in this process. All forms of media communication have in common that they extend communication from a mere 'here' and 'now' into a 'there and now' (Zhao, 2006) and enable us to communicate across space and time. Therefore, most situations of media communication are, in some sense, 'translocal': through processes of communication, they link up activity and meaning-making across various localities (even the act of updating one's contacts on one's phone can rely on the background activity of a distributed memory function).

What can we conclude from our reflections in this chapter? Referring back to the question we posed at its beginning – how does the social world change when it fundamentally becomes interwoven with media? – our main argument has been the need to develop a theory of the social world that does not any more take face-to-face interaction as its unquestioned centre. Even when we communicate directly, we do so by reference to everyday reality that is deeply interwoven with media. To capture the complex consequences of this, we need to develop the term 'mediatization', a concept we will unpack further in Chapter 3 when we read the history of the social world in terms of successive overlapping 'waves' of mediatization. Thinking about the social world and its different domains as 'mediatized' means grasping that its construction involves practices of communication that are, in turn, moulded by the long-term processes of institutionalization and materialization that we refer to as 'media'. The more intricately the construction of the social world becomes implicated in our uses of media, the more intricate are the interdependences between media themselves. That is the double shift we characterize by the term '*deep* mediatization', which we also take further in the next chapter. In times of deep mediatization, to grasp the communicative construction of our social world, it is not enough to consider single media in isolation: our analysis must go to a higher level of complexity.

3

History as Waves of Mediatization

This chapter offers a rereading of the history of media and communications, as an entry-point to a *theoretical* argument about how the construction of the social world through communications has changed over time. Some versions of media history[1] have a tendency to offer a narrative of the influence of *single* media, the emergence of which supposedly transformed society. A recent book offers a 'push theory of media effects' (Poe, 2011, p. 23), that is, a theory of how the emergence of each 'new' medium had an identifiable 'effect' on culture and society. While we do not deny that each medium has a specificity that 'shapes' or 'moulds' communication in particular ways, such a medium-based perspective ignores the many overlapping layers of communication (acts, practices, forms, patterns) whereby the social world is constructed. We need a more far-reaching understanding of the mediatization of culture and society to grasp the current transformations of the social world and our 'media environment' (Hasebrink and Hölig, 2013). Communications' role in history does not move, like a relay-race, from one 'influencing' medium to another. It is rather a continuous and cumulative *enfolding* of communications *within* the social world that has resulted today in ever more complex relations between the media environment, social actors, and therefore the social world.

Specifically, we argue in this chapter that the history of mediatization over the past five to six centuries can be understood in terms of three successive and overlapping waves in which modes of communications have developed and their interrelations have become significantly more complex: the wave of *mechanization*, the wave of *electrification* and the wave of *digitalization*. Arguably, we are now living at the start of a fourth wave, the wave of *datafication*, a point we discuss towards the end of the chapter. The latest wave(s) of digitalization and datafication correspond to phases of *deep* mediatization, because they are associated with a much more intense embedding of media in social processes than ever before. Towards the end of the chapter, we introduce the term 'media manifold' – that is, a large 'universe' of variously connected digital media through which (in various figurations) we actualize *social* relations – as a way of capturing the multiple relations to the overall media environment that characterize everyday life in times of deep mediatization.

3.1 Mediatization in a Transcultural Perspective

Over recent years mediatization has become an important concept in media and communications research for grasping media-related transformations in society (Lundby, 2009, 2014). The relevance of this concept derives from the increasing salience of technologically based media of communication in contemporary cultures and societies. As we argued elsewhere (Couldry and Hepp, 2013, p. 197), mediatization is a concept that helps us to analyse critically the *interrelation* between changes in media and communications on the one hand, and changes in culture and society on the other. It is not a concept of 'media effects', but rather a *dialectical –* two-way – concept for understanding how the transformations of culture and society are interwoven with specific changes in media and communications. We cannot theorize media and communications as 'external' influences on culture and society, for the simple reason that they are an integral part of it. At this general level, mediatization has quantitative as well as qualitative dimensions. In its quantitative dimensions, mediatization refers to the increasing temporal, spatial and social spread of mediated communications; over time we have become more and more used to communicating across distance via media in an increasing range of contexts. But mediatization also refers to qualitative dimensions, that is, to the social and cultural differences that mediated communications make at higher levels of organizational complexity.

For clarity, it is worth drawing a sharp distinction between the related terms 'mediation' and 'mediatization' (see Hepp, 2013a, pp. 31–38; Hjarvard, 2013, pp. 2–3; Lundby, 2014, pp. 6–8). While mediation refers to the process of communication in general – that is, the way that technology-based communication involves the ongoing mediation of meaning-production (Couldry, 2008; Martín-Barbero, 1993; Silverstone, 2005) – mediatization describes the higher-order processes of transformation and change *across society* that result from mediation going on at every level of interaction. More than that, mediatization as a term enables us to grasp how, over time, the consequences that multiple processes of mediated communication have for the construction of the social world have *themselves* changed with the emergence of different kinds of media and different types of relation between media. Mediatization is, in short, a meta-process (Krotz, 2009), a process of change in how social processes *go on through media* and are articulated together in ever more complex organizational patterns.

It is important also to see the various stages of mediatization in a *transcultural* perspective, which means grasping the multiple forms that mediatization has taken over its long duration in various sites across the world: these variations cannot be neatly mapped onto the boundaries of specific nations or national cultures (Hepp, 2015, pp. 28–34), because media as resources of symbolic power are entangled inevitably with the development of elites, particularly urban elites. We reject also any simple linking of mediatization with (European) modernity (see Esser and Strömbäck, 2014b, pp. 6–11; Hjarvard, 2013, pp. 5–7, 16–23; Lundby, 2013, p. 197; Thompson, 1995, pp. 44–80). Certainly 'the development of media *organizations*' – that is, independent organizations for the production and circulation of communications, that 'first appeared in the second half of the fifteenth century and have expanded their activities ever since' (Thompson, 1995, p. 46) – was a precondition for European modernity, even though the theoretical *term* mediatization did not emerge until the early twentieth century (Manheim, 1933, pp. 23f.; Averbeck-Lietz, 2014, pp. 199–123). There is a danger here, however, of framing mediatization in a too Eurocentric way (see Madianou and Miller, 2012, pp. 141–143; Slater, 2013, pp. 27–57): the idea that mediatization involves independent media organizations – that is, organizations independent of political or religious institutions – does not apply to every region of the world, like Latin America, where media organizations are much more interwoven with religious, political or other social institutions (Martín-Barbero, 2006; Waisbord, 2013b). It is especially problematic to link mediatization too closely with European specificities and then assume that it unfolds identically wherever we go in the world. Indeed, the term 'medium' itself involves a certain form of classification, and may be bundled together in one set of means of communication in one cultural context and in another set in another context (Slater, 2013, p. 40). Therefore, we should not accept a one-dimensional understanding of modernization based on specific media (Slater, 2013, p. 28). However, none of that means we should abandon the term 'media' entirely (and as a consequence devalue any attention to higher-order processes of 'mediatization'), as Slater (2013, p. 20) sometimes appears to suggest. We need these terms to grasp the wider processes of social change that result from the increasing quantitative spread and qualitative relevance of particular combinations of media in many particular places. But we will attempt to do so in what follows without reproducing a 'provincial' (Chakrabarty, 2001) European perspective.

A parallel from longer-term debates about globalization may help here (Waisbord, 2013b, p. 7). For sure, today's everyday *experiences* of 'the global' are at least partly based on the massive spread of media (Hepp, 2015, pp. 13–18). But at the outset, globalization as a process was analysed from a Western perspective, and understood as a kind of time–space compression that had its origins in European social institutions of modernity (Giddens, 1990, p. 63; Harvey, 1990, pp. 260–283). This definition of globalization as a consequence of (European) modernity was criticized for its Western-centric bias and a provincial time-narrative.[2] Postcolonial criticism of such Western-centric approaches had been important (Gunaratne, 2010, pp. 477f.), substantiated by empirical analysis of globalization from non-Western regions of the world, especially Latin America.[3] In response, globalization research moved to an understanding of multiple 'global modernities' (Featherstone, 1995) within 'many globalizations' (Berger, 2002), and plural 'modernizations' and 'modernities' (see Calhoun, 2010; García Canclini, 1995). Far from 'global modernity' being a unique 'historical period' (Tomlinson, 1999, p. 33), there were forms of globalization long before modernity. Yet it is still plausible to argue that globalization has *deepened* over the past few decades, in that globalization is nowadays rooted in the everyday practices of *most* regions of the world (García Canclini, 2014, p. 21; Tomlinson, 1999, p. 13), even if the details still vary widely from context to context.

We can make the same points about mediatization. If we understand by mediatization the increasing spread of communications media (quantitative) and the social and experiential consequences of this (qualitative), both differ significantly from one context to another and we must find a dialectical way of analysing this. For example, the appropriation of television in Brazilian favelas (Leal, 1995) was highly different from that in rural India (Johnson, 2000); the same can be said for the use of the internet by the Chinese working class (Qiu, 2009) and the middle class in suburban Malaysia (Postill, 2014). However, one main point remains across all the variations: that the embedding of technologically based means of communication in the practices of everyday life is a long-term process that deepened dramatically over the past 150 years. This is what we mean by mediatization, and, because it is a matter of the accumulating inter-relations that derive from such embedding, it is appropriate to talk of it as becoming 'deeper' over time. The deepening of mediatization is a matter of the increased reliance of *all social processes* on infrastructures of communication on scales up to the global; put more broadly, it is a shift in the *modalities* whereby the social world is constructed in and across various locations. Mediatization, then, involves a progressive increase in the complexity of social change that derives from the increasing prevalence, among the factors that drive social change, of factors related to underlying infrastructures of communication.

It goes without saying that the ways in which mediatization plays out in particular places will depend on the particular histories of infrastructure, resources and inequality in that place, and also on the particular human needs that media use in that location predominantly fulfils, and this, in turn, will depend on deeper variations in social, economic and political organization (Couldry, 2012, pp. 156–179). Which is not to say, for example, that *no* significance can be attached to the increasing spread of particular platforms such as Facebook across many countries: the common affordances of such platforms provide starting-points for asking about how, for example, social needs get actualized through those platforms, and how those local actualizations are available to be connected up, practically, with actualizations elsewhere. Nor does it mean that there are no general trends, linked for example to the coordinated development of media markets and state actions, under way in large parts of the globe at the same time, if in uneven ways. The growing trend towards datafication is one such overall trend that we will discuss across many chapters.

After these introductory remarks, it is time to turn to the three – or perhaps four – waves of mediatization that we mentioned earlier.

3.2 Waves of mediatization

Referring back to scholars of medium theory like Harold Innis (1950, 1951) and Marshall McLuhan (1962), it became common to narrate the history of communications as phases of the domination of a certain kind of medium that must then be understood as having had a deep and global cultural influence. The history of humankind then gets read as a sequence of media-*dominated* cultures: 'traditional oral cultures' are superseded by 'scribal cultures', followed by 'print cultures' and 'global electronic cultures' (Meyrowitz, 1995, pp. 54–57). This version of communications history is also widespread in sociology (Baecker, 2007, pp. 7–13; Tenbruck, 1972, pp. 56–71), where the differentiation of societies is related to the 'dissemination media' (Luhmann, 2012, p. 120) of writing, printing and electronic communication.[4] As already noted, this history – especially when presented as a global history – is inadequate, because of its focus on one dominant medium and the tendency to think in 'communications revolutions' (Behringer, 2006) driven by certain media-technological innovations.

If we look more carefully at what changes over time, it is not a matter of the revolutionary emergence of any one kind of medium at particular points in history. Rather, what changes over time is the *aggregate* of accessible communications media, and the role that (in their *inter*relations) they play in moulding the social world. In short, what we have to focus on is the changing media *environment*: the totality of communications media available at one point in space–time. This emphasis on the media environment of interrelating media rather than a single medium has its basis in a fundamental point about technology in general, which is that technologies do not tend to work in isolation, but in clusters that Brian Arthur calls 'domains', that is 'mutually supporting set[s] of technologies' (Arthur, 2009, pp. 70–71). Media are no different. From this perspective, it is not hard to recognize some decisive changes in media environments across the last 600 years, and these changes are the starting-point for a transcultural account of mediatization.

Such changes in the media environment can be related to certain 'surges' or 'waves' of technological innovation (Briggs and Burke, 2009, p. 234; Rosa, 2013, p. 41; Verón, 2014, p. 165). The metaphor of the 'wave' emphasizes, on the one hand, certain fundamental innovations (the 'peak of the wave'), which, on the other hand, have long-term consequences and side-consequences (the 'propagation' of the 'wave'). This idea has a parallel in William H. Sewell's (2005) approach to social transformation in which both prominent events and long-term structural changes are of importance, and this analogy makes clear that there are multiple ways of interpreting these waves, depending on one's analytical perspective.

We define a *wave of mediatization* as a fundamental qualitative change in media environments sufficiently decisive to constitute a *distinct phase* in the ongoing process of mediatization, even when one allows for the very different forms that such media environments may take in particular local, regional and national contexts. Underlying such waves are fundamental technological changes in the character of media (and media relations) that make up media environments. Our argument is *not* (as in medium theory) that each new media wave results globally in a certain kind of culture and society. At most, we claim that the *starting-points* for grasping social transformation, insofar as they involve media, can change decisively from stage to stage. Differences remain, of course, in relation to the specific context. However, even allowing for these differences, we can trace distinct waves of mediatization that relate to fundamental qualitative changes in the media environment.

Looking back over the last 600 years, we can distinguish at least three waves of mediatization (see figure 1).[5] First, we have the *mechanization* of communications media that can be traced back to the invention of the printing press, which was based on even earlier forms of handling written documents (compare our analysis in Chapter 10) and was continued by the increasing industrialization of the communication process, resulting in what is called print mass media. Second, we have the *electrification* of communications media. This started mainly with the electronic telegraph, and ended with the various broadcast media, but also the telephone and other forms of telecommunication. The third wave is *digitalization* that can be related to the computer and the various digital media but also to the internet, the mobile phone, and the increasing integration of computer-based 'intelligence' in everyday life, through all of which digital contents are freely exchangeable.

The reason why we can understand mechanization, electrification and digitalization as waves of mediatization is that each of these captures a distinctive way in which the constellation of media generally available at a particular time and place operate as an environment – not only through upcoming 'new' media but also through continuing 'old' media. So 'mechanization' does not only refer to the book, but also to smaller kinds of media (for example, the broadsheet), and encompasses the consequences of the typewriter for (private) letter-writing and for the role of the hand-written manuscript. 'Electrification' includes various once 'new' media, beginning with the telegraph and ending with radio and television, but also transformations in the newspaper and other pre-existing 'mechanical' media. The same can be said for 'digitalization': this wave of mediatization also concerns 'new' and 'old' media at the same time, for example, digital television: it is even possible, as we will see, that a new wave of datafication is under way within the wave of digitalization.

To get a deeper understanding of the related changes we first have to consider each of these waves in more detail, contextualizing the rather crude dates in the figure opposite.

Mechanization

By *mechanization* we mean the wave of mediatization through which the media environment became a mechanical one. In Europe and Northern America, the printing press – invented in its mechanical form around 1450 by Johannes Gutenberg – can be understood as the main origin of this process. However, we have to bear in mind that this invention is not just a European fact: already between 700 and 750 block printing arose in China

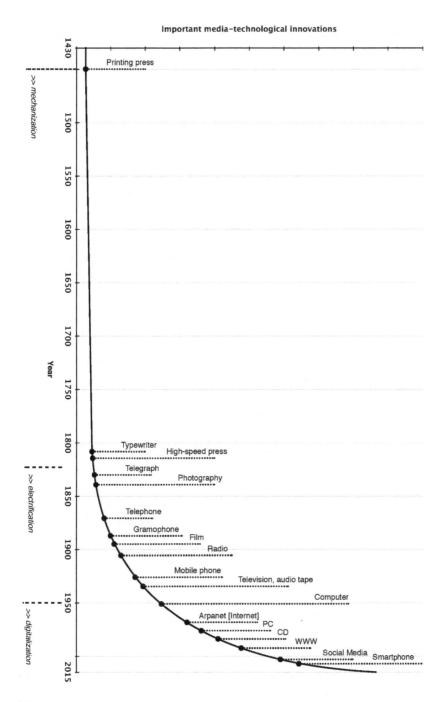

Figure 1

and Korea, and the first experiments with ceramic letters were undertaken around 1040 in China. Later these techniques were developed further in Korea using bronze letters (Chow, 2003; McDermott, 2006, pp. 9–13; Moon-Year, 2004).

The printing press did not change the appearance and structure of the book, but rather 'mechanized', indeed materialized through technology, a previous shift in how text was organized into a new form of production (Illich, 1996, pp. 3–4; Neddermeyer, 1998, pp. 389–536). In this sense, the invention of the printing press was less an event of a single 'communication revolution' (Albion, 1932, p. 718; Behringer, 2006, p. 333; Kovarik, 2011) and more a 'long revolution' (Eisenstein, 2005, p. 335), or, maybe better, an important step in a long-term process of mechanization. This mechanization involved an increase in the co-existence and co-influence of mechanically printed media with handwritten manuscripts and other media (Bösch, 2015, p. 20), but it also made a number of 'new' media possible: besides the printed book these were pamphlets and broadsheets, later the newspaper (Oggolder, 2014). Interestingly, these media – mechanical or not – influenced each other in various ways. For example, printed treatises on the art of letter-writing stimulated the handwritten letters in early modern Europe. And for a long time manuscripts remained in use as they offered the chance to communicate controversial issues to a wider audience, which was embedded in practices of rewriting and 'publish-it-yourself' (Briggs and Burke, 2009, p. 38).

It would be too crude therefore to equate the invention of the printing press with a leap into a media environment consisting only of books and newspapers. The media environment remained diverse and was characterized by interactions between various media (Bösch, 2015, p. 65; Briggs and Burke, 2009, p. 37; 56). However, print became fundamental for the media environment because it changed the interrelation of other media, a change that has to be understood in a wider context. This mechanization of the media was a specific variant of other forms of mechanization like, for example, the invention of the mechanical clock, the railway, and machines in factories – just to mention some important further innovations that resulted in the 'machine speed' of the nineteenth century (Tomlinson, 2007, pp. 14–43). Therefore, we have to understand mechanization within the overall contradictory process of industrialization (Williams, 1965, pp. 10–11, 88, 141).

To understand what such a fundamental qualitative change of the media environment meant for the everyday, we have to look at audiences: that is, people and their media use. If we consult historical studies, in Europe already within the seventeenth century the readership of newspapers (and books) was quite diverse, including the aristocracy, scholars and state officials, but also merchants, craftsmen, soldiers and women (Bösch, 2015, pp. 47f.). While the absolute number of copies of a newspaper in these times was a lot lower than today (between 300 and 400 copies), each copy had between ten and thirty readers (Bellingradt, 2011, p. 243). Media appropriation was much more a *collective* venture than an individual one. An expression of this is the foundation of various reading clubs to share the costs of subscriptions and to have access to a wider variety of newspapers, journals and books. Starting around the seventeenth century, women became more and more part of the readership, and various journals and books were dedicated especially to them, building up their own communities of readers (Briggs and Burke, 2009, pp. 50–55).

While it is obvious that mechanization changed media environments substantially, we must be very cautious in attempting to deduce from this that the communicative construction of the social world was transformed in a homogeneous way. Rather, we can say that, with mechanization, media environments became more diverse and complex. They involved an increasing number of different media based on the mechanical reproduction of print: mainly broadsheets, pamphlets, books, posters, newspapers and journals. These print media were interrelated with non-print media. Mechanical reproduction offered through its standardized reproduction the possibility of reaching a wider group of people via one kind of media outlet. As a result, communication on a larger scale could 'disembed' (Giddens, 1990, p. 21) from the here and now. Hand in hand with this, new practices of communicative construction emerged, and it is a matter of contextual analysis to decipher these practices and to investigate under which historical circumstances and in which contexts they are located.

Within this plurality of possible transformations, mechanization helped to 'thicken' more extensive communicative spaces by intensifying translocal communications. In Europe, these spaces were related historically to the rise of (national) states, something that is reflected by the concept of the (mediated) 'public sphere' (Habermas, 1989; Meyer and Moors, 2006). The thickening of these national communicative spaces supported the emergence of 'modern societies' (Thompson, 1995, pp. 44–80) with their national 'imagined community' (Anderson, 1983). But it is important to remember that the late Benedict Anderson's model of the imagined community is just as much an account of the rise of new nations under or against colonialism (Thailand, the Philippines), and that the nation is only *one* type of imagined community made possible by print communication

(Anderson, 1983, p. 6). The thickening of translocal communications can also refer to completely different social entities: dispersed scholarly groups of experts, religious and ethnical diasporas, or other groups with distinctive world-views, can just as much be associated with the articulation of social conflict as the stabilization of nation-states. In Africa for example the emergence of the printed press was closely related to colonialism, that is, the attempt to *impose* a new colonial state on pre-existing societies (Larkin, 2008). This was a long-term process and involved, on the one hand, the construction of a 'united "imagined community" of white settlers' as a citizen public and, on the other hand, the encouragement of a 'black readership aimed at entertainment' (Willems, 2014, p. 83) – with all its related problematic constructions. It is here that we start to see the consequences of a transformed media environment for *larger* possibilities of social change, that is, for media's role in the construction of social reality itself (mediatization).

Electrification

A second wave of mediatization is electrification, which again changed the whole media environment, and also transformed mechanical print to a higher level of reproduction. In contrast to mechanization, electrification cannot be related to any single important media technological innovation like print, but to multiple ones (see figure 1), most importantly the telegraph, telephone, gramophone, turntable and audiotape, film, radio and television. By the term 'electrification', we mean the transformation of communications media into technologies and infrastructures based on electronic transmission. In electrification, media of various sorts became increasingly embedded in wider technological networks: in electricity grids, cable networks, networks of directional radio, and so on. This move is also a further step of *interrelating* media closer with each other, and so increasing the interdependences within the media environment.

The electric telegraph was invented in the 1830s. After the 1850s an intense wiring of the world began, starting from London and Paris, and having a first peak with the successful transatlantic submarine cable in 1866 (Hugill, 1999, pp. 27–32). However, this infrastructure of electric communication was far from egalitarian, centred first in the UK and later the USA, and in the hands of a limited number of companies funded by capital from particular investor countries (Winseck and Pike, 2007). The basic technologies of the telephone go back to the nineteenth century, and already in the 1920s long-distance calls became possible. The development of wireless telephone technology – radio telephony – began at the end of the nineteenth century (Hugill, 1999, pp. 83–107), with the first mobile train phones in Europe in 1926 and first mobile car phones in North America in 1946.

If we consider electric telegraphy and telephony, the striking fact is that electrification was in the beginning predominantly related to what is called 'personal communication' and not to 'mass communication' (Balbi, 2013). Initially, the benefits went to selected elite groups, especially in the fields of the military, economy and government (Mattelart, 1994, pp. 3–31). In addition, the electric telegraph transformed print journalism as it made possible quicker access to transnational and transcultural information, which became first important for war coverage (Mortensen, 2013, pp. 332–334; Wobring, 2005, pp. 39–92).

Electrification involved incremental moves from mechanization, through partly electrified media, to fully electronic media. This becomes apparent if we refer to audio communication, where we have a sequence of innovations like the gramophone, turntable and audiotape. While the phonograph and gramophone were mechanical, the turntable was an electronic audio device for producing sound from the combination of phonograph and record. Audiotapes followed in the second half of the 1920s, as commercial products in the mid 1930s, again with many mechanical parts. In visual communication, we once again notice electrification on the basis of a sophisticated *mechanization*. Photography in the 1830s was a mechanical-chemical procedure; its electrification started in the 1950s through the use of electric parts in cameras. In a much faster way, film production also moved into electrification. Being in the beginning a mechanical-chemical medium like photography, the projection of films in cinemas made strong lights necessary as well as electric motors to drive the film reels. A further step into electrification was sound films. Over time, we have come to consider film as an electronic medium.

Typically, however, electrification is thought of in terms of broadcast media, that is, radio and television. Developed as technologies at the end of the nineteenth century, the first radio broadcast took place in 1906. However, not before the end of the First World War and the beginning of the 1920s did radio become a more widespread medium. In the beginning the medium was technically open for a mutual transmission of private messages; this fascinated Bertolt Brecht, for instance, who was interested in its capacity as a horizontal 'communication system' (Brecht, 1979, p. 25). Driven, however, by commercial and political interests it quickly became sender-centred, being legally regulated and technically materialized as broadcasting (Scannell, 1989, pp. 137–139; Barnouw, 1990, pp. 25–96). Already by the 1920s and 1930s, radio was established in Europe, North and South America, and also in Asian and later African countries (see Bösch, 2015, pp. 113–116). Television goes back to a late nineteenth-century vision of making the transmission of (moving) pictures by telegraph possible (Fickers, 2013, pp. 241–243), but regular television broadcasting did not start until the mid 1930s in Germany, the UK and the USA (Hickethier, 1998, pp. 33–39). The main breakthrough of television happened in the late 1940s in the USA, and in the 1950s and 1960s in Europe and many other parts of the world. Television changed its character continuously, becoming in the 1970s a coloured medium with increasingly new and original formats, additional related devices (remote control, VCR), and the spread of satellite television across borders in the 1970s and 1980s (Barker, 1997; Hepp, 2015, pp. 39–51; Parks and Schwoch, 2012).

These historical moments demonstrate again how by electrification the whole media environment became transformed. 'New' media emerged, but also 'older' media like the press underwent change, too. Electrification was the trigger for a deep qualitative change of the whole media environment within a rapid sequence of media technological innovations, perhaps having its first peak at the beginning of the twentieth century – a time in which contemporaries already imagined a 'wireless age' (Sloss, 1910, p. 27). Across the world, electrification was an enormous endeavour, with high public and private investments being necessary to build up the appropriate technical infrastructure, first by landline and cross-Atlantic telegraphy cables, later by broadcasting stations and cable networks.

Electrification can nonetheless be seen – at least in its beginning – as an extension of mechanization, but with the key difference that it involved a deeper *inter*linking of media through a new technological infrastructure: the electricity grid, cable and broadcasting networks etc. Single media came to appear less 'independent'; increasingly, technical capacity was not only on the producers' side of the media, but also on the users' side. Therefore, at a fundamental level electrification can be understood as a move into a deeper, and technically more intertwined, media environment.

How should we understand the social and cultural consequences of electrification? We must again be very careful not to oversimplify the related social and cultural transformations around the globe. It is too crude to run together all forms of technical connectivity by assuming they had a single global consequence (the idea of the 'global village': McLuhan and Powers, 1992). It would be too reductionist also to assume that electrification of media caused something like a 'global neighbourhood' (Commission on

Global Governance, 1995). However, proceeding in a more open way, we can notice at least three interdependencies involved in electrification, as it came to shape the media environment.

First, with reference to all kinds of produced media communication, electrification made possible *simultaneous transmission* of media content across space. Crucial here was the emergence of powerful media organizations in the film, but especially broadcasting, industries. The connectivity they enabled through their production cycles generated shared *rhythms* of simultaneous experience and new narratives of commonality, whose clearest form was the 'media event' in which there emerged the 'rare realization of the full potential of electronic media technology' (Dayan and Katz, 1992, p. 15).

Second, electrical transmission made new forms of near-instantaneous, reciprocal communication feasible across long distances: the new possibility of *simultaneity in personal communication* across space. Various media like telegraph, telephone etc., some of which were widespread before the electronic mass media, support this. As a consequence, this wave of mediatization is not only related to the emergence of new types *of media organizations,* but in addition and much more far reaching it made possible completely new kinds of *social institutions.* For example, already with telegraphy in the 1860s, a globalized economy began to emerge, when 'the first tickers clicked out stock prices' (Bösch, 2015, p. 94).

Third, these forms of communication offered possibilities for constructing cultures in new ways across space and time. Electrification brought media that supported a further thickening of translocal spaces of communication. It was a wider support for stabilizing national communicative spaces and at the same time for a possible social and cultural differentiation within and across those spaces then, for example among diasporas: that is, transnationally dispersed cultural groups which maintain their relations in real time through electronic media (Dayan, 1999). But this is only one example of a broader possibility: the establishment, through structures of simultaneity and shared rhythms of media flow, of translocally configured cultures of many sorts, including at the most general level the emergence of large-scale popular culture since the 1950s.

We are not, of course, saying that electrified media environments were, or are, the same across the world and would have resulted in one kind of global change at the social and cultural level. Other dynamics took place in Nigeria, for example, where videocassettes and the infrastructure of privacy had an important role for building up counter-spaces and alternative collectivities (Larkin, 2008, pp. 217–242). In general, 'indigenous media' (Spitulnik, 1993, p. 303) supported a range of possible dynamics and consequences: coming together through media as a collectivity, constructing shared memories through media, and gaining a 'voice' in public discourse. In Latin America, there has been a 'hybrid history' (García Canclini, 1995, p. 44) of appropriating technologically based media of communication: beyond a linear 'Western' modernization this has supported processes of transculturation, especially in urban areas. These media environments made possible not just nationalized but also highly de-centred and globalized processes of communicative construction, each of which must be analysed contextually.

Digitalization

Digitalization is the third wave of mediatization within the last few centuries, and is typically related to the computer, internet and mobile phone.[6] All three are key inventions for this wave of mediatization, but again we should be reserved about describing them as 'revolutions' (Rainie and Wellman, 2012, pp. 1–108): like all other inventions, they are the result of complex distributed social processes of making. One perspective on this history sees algorithms and software as the fundamental level of digital media;[7] another emphasizes the perspective of politics in the history of digitalization;[8] while a third brings out the cultural contexts and 'pioneering' groups behind these developments.[9] However, we want to start our analysis by moving the development of 'the internet' itself into the foreground. As we emphasized earlier, a main characteristic of waves of mediatization is the intensified *interrelatedness* between media that they involve: the internet *is* the infrastructure that makes possible the linkages between contemporary media devices with mainframe computers, large data centres, and – in the near future – social robots and autonomous systems like self-driving cars, as well as links all our activities on countless digital platforms.

The history of 'the internet' has been told many times. Everyone knows that it emerged from the research arm of the USA's military establishment through its connections with university research labs. In this sense, it is a strong example of how developments for which 'the market' claims ultimate credit usually derive from deep underlying subsidies by the state and other forms of public institution (Mazzucatto, 2013). Particularly important is the combination of steps – some state-led, some driven by markets – as a result of which in 2015 a small number of corporations that loosely can still be called 'media' – Google, Facebook, Apple, Instagram, perhaps also Twitter and, in China, Alibaba – can through their 'platforms' act *directly* on the world of consumption and the world of everyday social interaction. The stages involved in that development are worth setting out more fully.[10]

First, there was the building of 'distributed' networks of communications between (initially very few) computers through the innovative process of 'packet switching', as a means, initially, to ensure more secure forms of communication when facing military attack (the formation of ARPANET in October 1969 and NSFNET in 1985, with various parallel commercial networks also forming in the mid 1980s). The next stage was the development (originally anticipated by Vannevar Bush in 1945) of the TCP/IP protocol[11] for connecting up groups of already linked computers into a wider network, originally implemented in the early 1980s, and leading by 1989 to an 'internet' of around 160,000 computers in the public sector. The defining stage was the emergence of the World Wide Web, which occurred through two key inventions: the idea that texts could be linked together if they were associated with ordered sets of 'metadata' called 'hypertext', and CERN's Tim Berners-Lee's formalization of the means to ensure the reliable transmission of hypertext between linked computers (HTML, or Hypertext Markup Language; HTTP, or the Hypertext Transfer Protocol; and URL, or Universal Resource Locator, which provided an address code for each hypertext file). Taken together, they enabled the proposal in 1990 for a 'web' of files on networked computers and the first system for 'browsing' the domain of those texts (the World Wide Web), and the first 'web' site in November 1991 (info.cern.ch). This publicly subsidized development had produced by the early 1990s the skeleton of a connective infrastructure, but this was not yet linked to everyday commercial activity, or even non-specialist everyday use.

A rather different and accelerated sequence generated the deeply commercialized internet and WWW that we know in the second decade of the twenty-first century. In 1991, NSFNET was closed and the internet's operations handed over by the US government to commercial providers. From this new starting-point, the first commercial web browser (MOSAIC) was developed by a researcher, Marc Andreesen, who had left the public research sector (the NCSA, or US National Centre for Supercomputing Applications) to found his own commercial company called Netscape Communications, which went on to produce and mass-market Netscape. In the late 1990s and early 2000s, the means to access the exponentially growing domain of internet-linked files shifted from the model of managed directories (Yahoo) to Google's algorithmically based model of indexing pages based on a hierarchy developed from, at its most basic, counting the number of *links in* to each internet page. The distinctiveness of Google was that, rather than process a bounded and finite directory, its operations were, in a technical sense, recursive, with each new link increasing the data over which its calculations ranged, and increasing the mechanism's power, without end. This key innovation facilitated internet use considerably, and emerged alongside the diffusion of small desktop computers and then laptops as means for accessing the internet easily.

Building on the huge success of its Google search engine, Google bolted onto it the foundations of a much more robust commercial infrastructure: a new model for advertising tied to terms searched through the Google search engine ('Google Adwords') and a system of live-auction advertising (Adsense), which together opened up a new basis for the marketization of online 'space'.

The crucial next step was the independent development of 'smart' mobile phones with the capacity not just to provide access to the traditional modalities of phone use (talking/listening, plus the key discovery of the mobile phone device: the sending and receiving of text, or SMS), but also to the domain of the World Wide Web. The emergence of 'smart' phones was followed relatively quickly by the design (led by Apple, but quickly followed by most other smartphone providers) of applications, or 'apps', installable on each phone, to provide accelerated and simplified access to particular domains of web data. A further crucial step involved the emergence (tentatively in 2002 and on a larger scale from 2006) of a new type of website which provided platforms for hundreds of millions of users to network with each other, but within the parameters of form and content management designed by that platform's owners: so-called 'social media networks'. This is the twenty-first-century replaying of the emergence of possibilities for lateral communications which Craig Calhoun (1992a, p. 214) noticed in the history of nineteenth-century communications, but this time harnessed to the capacity for every message, in principle, to be directed at, or subsequently re-circulated to, the whole domain of the WWW through acts of 'mass self-communication' (Castells, 2009, pp. 65–72).

The result of these cumulative and interlocking steps is a strikingly complete transformation of 'the internet' from a closed, publicly funded and publicly oriented network for specialist communication into a deeply commercialized, increasingly banal *space for the conduct of social life itself.* The sheer size of the data transmissions now occurring via the internet has generated entirely unprecedented infrastructural demands (especially for storage, but also to support data processing) that are being satisfied, once more, not by public interests, but by a small number of private corporations that dominate the so-called 'cloud' (Mosco, 2014).

Again, the wave of digitalization was not only a matter of so-called 'new' media. 'Old' print and electronic media also became more and more digital. This is very well documented for print, especially the book and newspaper industry (Brock, 2013; Thompson, 2005a, pp. 309–329; 2010, pp. 312–368). Indeed, television and film also became digital, from the perspectives of both production and use, most recently with internet television, second screens and digital film projectors. As digital products they could be pirated and reached further audiences and users across the globe who build 'underground networks driving globalization from below' (Mattelart, 2009, p. 322). Related to digitalization is also a fundamental shift in the business models of media derived, in part, from shifts in how advertisers can reach their target audiences, that is, increasingly through personalized tracking of individuals and related data collection (Turow, 2011). Another emerging trend is the increasing embedding of digital media capacities in objects that accompany everyday practices: 'virtualized media communication', such as computer and mobile phone 'assistants' simulating a living communication partner, or 'social robots' as 'artificial companions' in our lives (Pfadenhauer, 2014, p. 136), something that more and more becomes realized through software (Sandry, 2015).

How should we understand the cultural and social consequences of these changes? It is certainly not enough to talk, as we often do, of media saturation, of even supersaturation (Gitlin, 2001, p. 67; Couldry, 2012, pp. 4–5). The saturated nature of the media environment was already being noted back in 2003, that is, towards the beginning of the wave of digitalization, and long before its peak (Bird, 2003, pp. 2–3). Some writers have sought to accentuate the abruptness of the digital transition, arguing that the new capacities of receivers of communication to send communications from the same device, and often as part of the same communication cycle, have led to the disappearance of the 'person formerly known as the audience' (Rosen, 2006), or the emergence of the hybrid 'produser' (Bruns, 2005). Undoubtedly, the starting possibilities for our relations to media have changed, but it is unhelpful to read the resulting forms and patterns of use in too polarized a way. Audiences are able to do an extended range of things with media (Livingstone, 2004): for example, their commentary on media is now available to be folded back into production cycles in ways that were previously impossible. But media produced by media organizations have not disappeared, and today's forms of media saturation are only an intensification (driven by the capacities of mobile phones and social media networks) of – not a fundamental break from – cultural forms that emerged late in the wave of electrification with the late 1990s growth of reality media and celebrity culture in many parts of the world (from Brazil to Korea, from Lebanon to South Africa).

We would do better to look for change at the level of the increasingly individualized patterns through which people can *access, follow and comment upon* (in other words, 'actualize') what we propose to call the media manifold (defined shortly). As yet, we do not know much about those figurations, except that they are much more varied than were possible in the electronic wave of mediatization, when most media content came from a limited number of synchronized central sources, when opportunities for media production were very limited and tied to the operations and gatekeeping power of those central resources, and when commentary on media was almost always lost to the air.

Put more generally, digitalization involves a further deepening, both in the *connectedness* of the infrastructures on which media-related practice depends – so, for example, the digital is now dependent on the development of Wi-Fi and other mobile services – and in the *layering* of connected media practices in which individuals or groups are now routinely engaged. Media environments have become characterized increasingly by 'convergence' (Jenkins, 2006b; Jensen, 2010),[12] meaning less a merger of all media devices into one kind of super-device, and more convergence at the level of the 'data' or content which, being *digital*, becomes *communicable* across multiple devices, some new, some older.

Living in the midst of this third wave of mediatization, it is obvious that it has far-reaching consequences for the communicative construction of the social world. But it must be understood merely as the *provisional* climax of this latest wave of deep mediatization. We now see signs of a *further* wave of mediatization, a wave that is related to data. If we consider how far datafication changes the way we produce knowledge (see Chapter 7), how deeply it is related to the constitution of the self, of collectivities and organizations (see Chapters 8, 9, 10), these media-related changes may well be more far-reaching than those we currently associate with digitalization. Certainly, we can expect a further deepening of the relations of interdependence between media and between people, when an increasing proportion of communication relies on infrastructures of communication based on the collection and processing of data. The degree to which this is the harbinger of a further qualitative shift of the whole media environment must remain, in part, an open question, but one to which we will return at various points in the chapters that follow.

3.3 Deep Mediatization and the Media Manifold

Mediatization came in waves – mechanization, electrification, digitalization – which each changed the whole media environment fundamentally. But since it is the whole media environment we are talking about, such mediatization waves cannot be understood as the 'diffusion' (Rogers, 2003) of *one* dominant medium, and it is much too crude to say that we have always lived in a newspaper, television or internet/mobile phone era. To understand mediatization, we must understand it as a process of the increasing deepening of *technology-based interdependence*. This deepening has two senses; first, that over the past 600 years an acceleration of technological innovations in media has taken place; and second that, over the same period, media have become increasingly relevant to articulating the *kind* of cultures and societies we live in, *because of* media's changing role in the conditions of human interdependence.

Acceleration of change means in a basic sense that the sequence of more or less fundamental technological innovations in the field of communications becomes shorter. While for example the interval between the invention of the printing press and the printed newspaper was around 150 years, telephone, film, radio and television were invented within fifty years, and the innovation of various digital media took place within thirty years. In a more complex way, comparing the three waves of mediatization – mechanization, electrification and digitalization – the change of the whole media environment in which they resulted took place in increasingly short time-periods, linked to the increasing causal weight of *pre-existing* media in shaping the new interconnected media environment that emerged. Both can be related to a more general phenomenon: what Hartmut Rosa has called the 'progressive acceleration of social change' (Rosa, 2013, p. 110). If we recall innovations in media technologies presented in the earlier figure, we can follow Rosa's proposal of a transformation 'from an *intergenerational* speed of change in early modernity through a phase of approximate synchronization with the sequence of generations in "classical modernity" to a tendency toward an *intragenerational* tempo in late modernity' (Rosa, 2013, p. 110). But once again, we should avoid tying this acceleration automatically to 'European' modernization: with that caveat, Rosa's metaphor may help us to grasp the acceleration of media's role in processes of globalization themselves.

Such cumulated waves of mediatization have resulted in a media environment that is unique in its present form: many communications media – even the stone tablet and manuscript – have not disappeared but kept a special functional role, partly within the arts. Some early electronic media, like vinyl records for example, even have a revival (Malvern, 2015). Beside that, a further landscape of digital media has been established – the mobile phone, online platforms and computer games are just some examples – while older electronic media such as the television, radio or cinema themselves became digital; all of this in a sustained and ever more distributed infrastructure. There remains, however, a significant challenge in grasping the complexity of the contemporary media environment adequately.

Underlying these changes has been a deeper change, that media's degree of *technical interrelatedness* has considerably increased from mechanization to electrification, and then again from electrification to digitalization. The technical interrelatedness of mechanization was limited insofar as technology was mainly used on the side of media production and far less on the side of media use. Think of the printing press: the distribution of printed books, magazines and broadsheets took place through physical mobility, and the *use* of these print media did not involve any use technology at all. This changed with electronic media: media became technologically intertwined, with the wider power grid of electricity distribution being a precondition for electronic media's subsequent distribution, and media themselves becoming dependent on their own technological infrastructure, including broadcasting networks, cable networks, radio networks etc. This technological relatedness partly became manifested in new kinds of devices that integrated various 'different' media into one terminal, like for example 'compact systems' combining radio, audio cassette, records and sometimes even television into one end-device at the user's side. In the broadest sense, digitalization has been a further move in the direction of technological interrelatedness:[13] through digitalization, it became possible to move various kinds of 'content' across a connective infrastructure, the internet. In turn, our devices for accessing the internet may no longer be specialist computers, but can be multi-purpose devices such as smartphones and tablets. Even so, while in such a media environment most devices are based on aspects of computer technology, we do not yet have a convergence into one 'meta-device'.[14] What we have instead is a deep technical interrelatedness of the *increasing variety* of different devices; this is what makes connectivity so omnipresent as a requirement of our present times. In addition to this, the character of each medium is more and more defined by the particular software and calculative functions on which its underlying functions are based, and not just by the technological device as such. What we call a 'mobile phone' is a device that can 'represent' to us *multiple* media, and can even be extended by adding further apps that give filtered access to other media streams.

The resulting *increased interrelatedness* of contemporary digital media cannot just be considered as a question of choice: which medium an individual selects for what purpose. The deepened interrelatedness associated with the wave of digitalization defines a new *kind of* media environment different from earlier media environments. We need therefore to develop the right analytic tools to grasp what is distinctive about this environment, and our relations to it.

As the wave of digitalization has proceeded, various kinds of description have been proposed to capture the new types of interrelation that have been emerging. Some terms put emphasis on the interchanges of content between various media; for example, 'remediation' (the 'representation of one medium in another' (Bolter and Grusin, 2000, p. 45), 'transmediality' (narrations that work across various kinds of media: Evans, 2011), and 'spreadable media' of 'viral' communications across various platforms (Jenkins et al., 2013, p. 295). Other concepts foreground the appropriations of multiple media by users: the terms 'cross-media' (Schrøder and Kobbernagel, 2010; Westlund, 2011), 'media repertoires' (Hasebrink and Domeyer, 2012) and 'polymedia' (Madianou and Miller, 2013; Madianou, 2014) are examples of this. Such a terminology understands the contemporary media landscape as a 'composite environment within which each medium [and its use] is defined relationally to all other media' (Madianou, 2014, p. 330): 'media repertoires' are not just a sum of the media a person uses but the meaningful relation between them in everyday practice. Deep mediatization on this view is marked by user practices that move across a variety of media.

Such concepts hint at the fundamental transformation of the social world that flows from deep mediatization and they are correct in trying to grasp the relations of interdependence that characterize the digital media environment. However, they do not capture the interrelated *complexity* that is characteristic of the digitalized media environment as a whole. To capture this, we offer the concept of the *media manifold*.[15]

The term 'manifold' comes from mathematics, specifically topology, where it refers to a topological space in many dimensions that can be adequately described by a shape in a lesser-dimensional (for example, Euclidian) space. So the earth is a three-dimensional shape that can, with reasonable fidelity, be reduced to a set of two-dimensional 'maps' of parts of its surface. Deleuze used this notion to emphasize the open-ended complexity of the world, but his emphasis was rather on how that order *escapes* any simple reduction to a model (DeLanda, 2006, pp. 12–15). The Deleuzian usage however seems to lose touch with the *two-level* aspect of the manifold concept that, we would argue, is most useful in grasping how we stand now with media: that is, the *relation between* a many-dimensional object and the approximation to that object in another object with fewer dimensions.

Our suggestion is that this double concept (the 'manifold') well captures the doubleness of our embedding in today's extremely complex media environment. The set of media and information possibilities on which a typical social actor, at least in rich countries, can now draw is almost infinite, and organized on very many dimensions. But it is in fact a reduced set of possibilities from which we choose every day: that reduced set is how, in practice, we actualize, for daily usage, that many-dimensional media universe.[16] What we then do with media on particular occasions actualizes, in turn, that reduced selection, and comprises itself a distinct and important level of variation. There are therefore three levels in operation; but here, as we try to understand our relations as social actors to the wider universe of media, it is only the first two levels (and their interrelations) that most concern us. The *relation* between this reduced set of daily options and the infinity of options in principle available is what we mean when we talk of our *relations with a 'media manifold'*, holding onto the idea of 'manifold' as a many-dimensional object that can be captured adequately in a lesser number of dimensions.

The term 'media manifold' enables us to keep in view both the social actor's position within a much larger institutionalized environment of interdependent media *and* the situated complexity of that actor's everyday choices of media. We need to understand both, and their interrelations, since the dynamics of that wider environment, particularly its overriding pressures towards datafication, are of major consequences for all actors and for the organization of social life as a whole.[17]

In the next chapter we turn to how we can think sociologically about the consequences of our relations with today's very complex media environment for the construction of the social world.

4

How We Live with Media

We have in the previous chapter argued that our complex media environment is best described as a media manifold. Such complexity can, perhaps,
be seen as characteristic of social practice in general: Theodor Schatzki,
the leading exponent of practice theory, writes of 'the manifolds of linked
doings and sayings that compose practices' (1996, p. 131). But the term
'*media* manifold' refers to a degree of *institutionalized interdependence* in
everyday practices with media that creates a distinctive *type* of social complexity. How do we live with this complexity? What does this complexity
mean for us? Posing this question brings us to recent social science debates
about the relationship between technology, systems and complexity, and
requires us to develop and extend a further concept from social theory,
that of 'figurations'. The result is an approach to 'society' itself that is
not functionalist, yet it registers the ordering *force* of the *interdependent*
institutional arrangements that we call 'media' and in which our lives are
implicated.

This chapter will take further the conceptual innovations on which our
overall argument relies. Our task will be twofold: first, within the broader
context of recent social science thought about complexity, to insist that the
two most popular options for thinking about interdependence ('networks'
and 'assemblage') are, in spite of some virtues, inadequate for understanding the distinctive processes of institutionalization characteristic of social
life under conditions of deep mediatization. We then take on the challenge of developing Elias' concept of figuration, which remains relatively
underdeveloped, into an analytic tool that can help us grasp many levels
of complexity in a social life whose every element and layer depends
on linked processes of mediated communication: that, in turn, requires
further conceptual innovation, involving the extended concept of '*figurations of* figurations'. This will be hard work, but it is necessary to complete
the foundations of our larger argument.

However, before we come to this overall argument, we have to reflect
on the deeply interconnected nature of infrastructures and organizational

processes today, which inevitably encourages *some* idea that the social world is a complex technologically driven 'system' dispersed across space, or rather many interlinked technological systems. Indeed, without some notion of systematicity (Walby, 2007), how could we understand the *claims to* a system made, for example, by powerful actors such as governments, platform operators, or infrastructure owners? But acknowledging the force of pressures towards a system is very different from saying that we have a clear grasp already of what the phrase 'technological system' might mean in a social context, or that 'system' concepts from mathematics and the physical sciences are necessarily a helpful starting-point.

Some have seen the rise of time–space measurement and signalling systems based on GPS as an example of complexity in social life. Should we rethink how we are 'in the world' in terms of a 'converged locatedness' which relies entirely on distributed technological systems that gather, process and transmit information (Dennis, 2007, p. 152)? The surveillance mechanisms routinely embedded in particular types of work – such as online trading – have been another source of 'complexity' theorizing (de Angelis, 2002). Complexity theory has been readily adapted in management theory as a way of grasping the operations and flow of large organizations (Lissack, 1999). Meanwhile, in sociology, one highly developed theory of the social has been built on the notion of hierarchical relations between multiple self-sustaining systems: Niklas Luhmann's (2012) systems theory, which drew heavily on the early work on biological systems by Varela.[1]

But two basic problems arise with such theorizing. First, they depend on metaphor, as even enthusiasts of complexity theory acknowledge (Lissack, 1999, p. 117). The social world is *not* composed of elements whose interactions can be measured and analysed numerically, and this flows directly from the nature of the social world: each of its actors not only acts but *interprets*, and those processes of interpretation are themselves often complex, creating 'complexities of complexities' (Mesjasz, 2010, p. 709). For that reason, all applications to the social world of complexity theory from the physical sciences or mathematics depend on a decision to apply such theory *metaphorically* in a social context for which it was not designed (Mesjasz, 2010, p. 713). Second, the choice of interpreting the complex social world *as system* is already arbitrary. Consider the assumption in Luhmann's work that the social system, whatever its complex interlinked nature, is self-adjusting and generally in equilibrium; or (even stranger) the assumption by Luhmann-follower Qvortrup that the (primary) role of the institutions we have known as 'media' is not to make profit, or tell stories, or provide employment, but instead to 'manage social complexity'

(Qvortrup, 2006, p. 355). What would count as evidence for such claims? Why believe that the social world is comprised of large-scale 'components' that have come to interrelate seamlessly together in terms of certain 'basic functions'? This approach to the understanding of the social world reads order *backwards* into emergent processes, and so misreads historically produced differentiation as functionally derived differentiation; it also assumes the boundedness of systems that may in fact be overlapping (Walby, 2007, pp. 457–459).

A different problem arises with attempts to talk about the social world in terms of 'topology'. Topology is the field of mathematics that concerns the properties of geometrical shapes that remain *invariant* under various transformations (stretching, twisting, and so on). Topology is interested in how different shapes, however unrecognizably we transform them, can remain the same (and so distinct from other topological shapes) in certain fundamental respects. Confusingly, however, the notion of topology has been adopted in social science as a stand-in for fluidity, not invariance. For sure, a sense of the overwhelming complexity of rapid transformation generates something like a topological *question* about whether, for example, globalization has really changed 'the very ontology of place and territoriality' (Amin, 2002, p. 387). But so-called 'topological thinking' in the social sciences, instead of explaining what might be gained by thinking of enduring *invariances* as topological forms, uses 'topology' as a byword for fluidity (Allen, 2011; Harvey, 2012; Lury et al., 2012; Tucker and Goodings, 2014), exactly missing the point of 'topology' itself (Martin and Secor, 2014, p. 12). 'Topology' can only help us understand a world outside mathematics if there is a 'technical translation' or 'functional mapping' between a domain of 'mathematical activity' and 'social or cultural activity' (Phillips, 2013, p. 13): that requires further work, which goes beyond the scope of this book.

We need alternative understandings of the complexity of our contemporary life with media that do not work through metaphor, but focus on the core concerns of social theory. As early as the 1970s the sociologist Norbert Elias built a social theory for describing an increasingly complex social world that did not reduce it to functional description or pure metaphor. He understood the social world through its increasingly complex ways of interweaving human beings in *relations of interdependence* that he called 'figurations'. Or as Elias puts it: 'the indices of complexity set out here may perhaps help to make everyday matters appear rather strange. This is necessary if one is to understand why sociology's field of investigation – the processes and structures of interweaving, the figurations formed by the actions of interdependent people, in short, societies – is a problem at all' (Elias, 1978, p. 103).

For sure, Elias' theory requires some development if it is to be adequate to describe the complexity of our contemporary life with media. However, Elias was already sensitive to how the complexity of figurations might increase with media's expansion (Elias, 1991, p. 163). We want to develop in this chapter a *figurational approach* to describe our life with media. But first we need briefly to survey two rival concepts for understanding complexity – network and assemblage – that, in spite of their usefulness, fall short of grasping how the social world is built, in part, out of accumulated relations *of meaning*.

4.1 Beyond Networks and Assemblages

Network and assemblage are both concepts for capturing complex structural relations. Both assume *some* notion of how the social world holds together in a regular and ordered way. The idea of analysing networks goes back many decades and has generated an important branch of social science methodology. Assemblage derives from philosophy and has become an important approach in wider cultural analysis. Each approach has crucial limits.

Network is a structural metaphor to describe the relations of human actors within a certain social entity (group, family, etc.) and in between such entities. Network research developed long before the internet and contemporary processes of deep mediatization.[2] But, during the wave of digitalization, network analysis became increasingly a *dominant* analytical perspective. Already in the 1990s Barry Wellman (1997) sought to apply the concept of network to understand how 'electronic groups' operate: as the intensity of the internet's connective infrastructure developed, so too did the notions of 'networked individualism' (Wellman et al., 2003, p. 3) and the possibility of conceiving the social itself as based on a new 'operating system' (Rainie and Wellman, 2012). On this view, society appears as nothing more than a large, complex network: 'societies – like computer systems – have networked structures that provide opportunities and constraints, rules and procedures' (Rainie and Wellman, 2012, p. 7).

Manuel Castells' (1996; 2000) idea of the network society is more far-reaching, as he is concerned with power-relations that operate on all scales up to the global. Networks for Castells are 'complex structures of communication' (Castells, 2009, p. 21) that are transformed, as media technologies themselves change, making possible what he calls 'mass self-communication' (Castells, 2009, p. 55), as individuals increasingly, if very unevenly, have access to the 'broadcasting' capacity that previously was reserved to institutions. More recent work has developed the concept of network further (Wasserman and Faust, 1994, pp. 729–731; Castells et al., 2011, pp. 788–790), distinguishing between networks where many modalities operate across the same node ('multi-modal, uniplex networks') and networks in which multiple relations (of the same sort) reach out from a single object ('unimodal, multiplex networks').

All such approaches to network analysis contribute something valuable to our overall understanding of how the social world is constructed, because they map the changing dynamics of 'actor constellations' (Schimank, 2010, p. 202) as social structures – what Simmel (1992 [1908], p. 19) called *Wechselwirkungen* of individuals – as a fundamental unit of social structure. Media uses are clearly crucial for such networking dynamics (Baym, 2015, pp. 101–102, 112–141).

The problem of 'network' as a concept is that it reduces the social world to *nothing more than* the actor-constellations of networks. In so doing, many further features of the social world and our life within it are ignored. Try as they might to acknowledge the importance also of the 'production of meaning' in communication networks (Castells, 2009, pp. 21f.) or the 'stories' that 'mark ties within networks' (White, 2008, p. 20), leading network theorists are unable to integrate these processes of meaning into their overall picture of how the social world is constructed. In addition, notions of 'network society' are still *reifying* networks as entities that can simply be positioned *against* other social groups,[3] without considering the full complexity of the contextualized relations of interdependence in which both networks and groups are embedded. The concept of 'network' always falls short therefore of understanding the *overall* constructions of meaning that *orientate* human action.

By contrast, the term 'assemblage' was developed first in the arts to describe collages, and more recently has acquired a rich philosophical trajectory that captures 'wholes' characterized by relations of exteriority (Deleuze and Guattari, 2004 [1980]). In French the word is not 'assemblage' but 'agencement', meaning 'arrangement' or 'fitting' like the arrangement of the parts of a body (or machine) or the fitting of two or more parts together (see Phillips, 2006; Bucher, 2012b, p. 481). In the social sciences, 'social assemblage' has come to refer to a 'set of human bodies properly oriented (physically or psychologically) towards each other' (DeLanda, 2006, p. 12), but without any assumption that they form a natural or functional unity. From here, some argue the social world *consists of* various, differently scaled assemblages (DeLanda 2006), and we sympathize with this anti-functionalist line of thinking. Particularly popular has been the use of the term 'assemblages' to attribute to 'non-human' objects an agency of their own that unfolds in an assemblage with acting humans (Latour, 2007, p. 67), which connects with other scholarly work in the tradition of 'socio-technical co-production' and 'socio-materiality'.[4] Indeed, the anti-functionalist emphasis of work on 'assemblages' is well suited to help us to grasp the contribution of many heterogeneous elements in the contingent historical arrangements that we have come to call 'media' (Slater, 2013, pp. 27–67). The term 'assemblage' is valuable, because it helps us grasp the variety of ways in which communicative practices (of every sort) are today *deeply interwoven* with media technologies (of every sort), and we will draw on it in later chapters.

Yet again there are some weaknesses of this term. First, it is often used in a rather metaphorical way to describe just the fact that different things and practices 'come together' in a field of interest: but, in itself, that tells us little about the type of 'coming together' involved, and the varying forms of order at work. Second, and even less helpful, much writing about assemblages involves the claim that the 'ontology' of assemblages is flat: that is, 'it contains nothing but differently scaled individual singularities' (DeLanda, 2006, p. 28). In other words, there is nothing 'behind' social aggregates, only endless 'reassembling' (Latour, 2007, pp. 8–9). However, such an analysis closes off many important questions. Can we grasp the (mediated) construction of the social world just by considering the 'assembling' of practices and things in a 'flat landscape'? Are there not forms of structural relatedness that have consequences beyond the particular assemblage itself? And when material objects are arranged in ways that help stabilize social processes, are the arrangements all the same?

Missing from both concepts (network and assemblage) is an attention to the complexity of our changing interrelations and interactions through communications, and specifically mediated communications. The strength of 'network' is the attention to the structural features of actor constellations, whereas the strength of 'assemblage' is its attention to the fine detail of practice and its entanglement with material technologies. But neither concept discusses comprehensively how complexity is built up *in and through* processes of meaning-construction and resource-distribution.

Throughout this book, we understand the social world as the *space of interrelatedness* that involves and encompasses a particular set of actors (however large): as such, it must be more than the sum of its networks and assemblages. Nor can it be flat, in the sense of without structure or hierarchy.[5] Let us then move beyond network *and* assemblage to explore a different concept for grasping our life within the complexity of the media manifold: the concept of figurations.

4.2 Figurations for Living with Media

The idea behind the term 'figurations' for Elias was to critique 'reifying ways of speaking' (Elias, 1978, p. 13) about the social world: by the 1970s, it had become usual to describe social phenomena, such as families, groups or organizations, as if they were objects 'beyond' the individual, positioning the social 'against' the individual, and understanding social phenomena as static, not dynamic and processual. Yet there is no social world 'over and above' the interrelations of individuals, and no individual is understandable outside her/his embedding in the social world (Elias, 1978, pp. 14f., 128f.). This is why we must think about social entities as *figurations* that are formed, and reformed, in an open-ended process.

Understanding Figurations

At its most basic, figuration is 'a simple conceptual tool' (Elias, 1978, p. 130) to allow a thinking in which 'the individual' and 'society' are not treated as antagonistic. A figuration is a kind of 'mode[l] of processes of interweaving' (Elias, 1978, p. 130), a more or less stable interaction of individuals which produce in this interrelation a certain kind of social meaning. One can take a football match or card game as examples to explain what a figuration is: the people involved form a figuration as their interactions are oriented to each other in an interdependent way. The game is the 'outcome' of the interrelated practices of the involved individuals and their ongoing process of playing. It is 'more' than just the gatherings of individuals but at the same time not something 'beyond' them. Or put differently: figuration means the 'changing pattern created by the players as a whole – not only by their intellects but by their whole selves, the totality of their dealings in their relationships with each other' (Elias, 1978, p. 130). If we follow Elias, the fundamental idea is to understand more or less durable social formations of humans as figurations: they are constituted by the interdependencies and interactions of the involved individuals and can be characterized by a certain 'balance of power' (Elias, 1978, p. 131), that is, power relations. The boundaries of each figuration are defined by the shared meaning that the individuals involved produce through their interrelated social practices, which is also the basis of their mutual orientation to each other.

The idea of figuration has parallels to the concepts of network. Elias himself emphasized repeatedly the relation of his idea to the structural category of the network, for example when he describes the interrelation of individuals in figurations as 'networks of individuals' (Elias, 1978, p. 15). Elsewhere he argues that 'social figurations' are a kind of 'human network' (Elias, 1978, p. 20) or 'ordered network' (Elias, 1978, p. 84). His distinctive take on networks becomes clearer when we consider his detailed analysis of different figurations. In these analyses 'network' is an important term to describe the *relations of the intertwined actors*, especially when it comes to what he calls 'game models' of figurations (see Elias, 1978, p. 87, 91). But Elias goes far beyond network as a metaphor. The latter is helpful to analyse the interrelations of actors in a figuration and to describe some fundamental characteristics of them as 'models of interweaving' (Elias, 1978, p. 80). But the network does not yet describe the co-oriented practices of sense-making in a figuration. Therefore, a figurational approach means much more than describing the network of actors: it means considering also the power relations, the characteristic roles in a figuration's actor constellation and the overall meanings that are thereby produced.

Figuration has also certain parallels to assemblage, as both describe the social world in terms of processes of individuals' mutual interweaving. Indeed Latour explicitly refers to the idea of figuration (Latour, 2007, pp. 52–58), although without discussing Elias. However, figuration for Latour is not only a figuration of human actors as 'there exist many more figures than anthropomorphic ones' (Latour, 2007, p. 53) and we must, he argues, analyse figurations of humans and non-humans (Latour, 2007, p. 71). On this view, methodologically grounded research into assemblages might itself appear to be nothing more than the investigation of certain figurations, but with the crucial difference that Elias, when reflecting on the role of objects and technologies in figurations (see Elias, 1991, pp. 162–164), always makes a clear analytical distinction between objects and human actors. This is an important point to which we will return.[6]

A figurational approach allows us to integrate the strengths of network and assemblage analyses – their focus respectively on constellations of actors and socio-materiality – while going further in explaining how the embedded complexity of communicative practices works. A figurational approach indeed has all the strengths of complexity theory, especially its sensitivity to nonlinear causal processes, respect for the contingency of process and the possibility of multiple outcomes, and insistence on the importance of emerging relations rather than fixed objects. But it manages to achieve this directly within the language of sociology and social theory.

Indeed Elias' notion of figuration was introduced as a way of *changing* the social sciences' 'means of speaking and thinking'. Sociology's inherited vocabulary, Elias argued, freezes processes into things, specifically things such as 'norms and values', 'structure and function', 'society' and 'individual' (Elias, 1978, p. 113). Instead, we need to grasp 'the *special kind* of order associated with processes of *social interweaving*', which means 'start[ing] [. . .] from the connections, the relationships, and work[ing] [. . .] out from there to the elements involved in them' (1978, p. 116, added emphasis). A 'figuration' is 'a flexible lattice-work of tensions' (1978, p. 130) which, while its development is open-ended, remains regular and interconnected enough to form something relatively stable, and so worth analysing as a pattern.

The force of the figuration lies in its basis in an understanding of relationships of *meaning*. Elias wrote that 'the behaviour of many separate people *intermeshes* to form interwoven structures' (1978, p. 132, added emphasis). The term 'intermeshing' sounds like mere metaphor, but the metaphor precisely captures a number of things: first, a *feedback* loop (so much is common with complexity theory, systems theory and assemblage theory); second, a feedback loop whose paths are comprised of interlocking *practices*, acting back on themselves; third, practices that interlock because, *as meanings*, they are in a mutual relationship, answering, inviting, challenging, questioning and so on. The elements of a figuration only have a common form (a con-figuration), because there is something at stake in them, something that matters (is meaningful) to the actors involved.

We can see plenty of examples of figurations in times of a deep mediatization. Many are new, involving us in new types of action in which new things are at stake. Figurations may involve, at one end of the spectrum, chains of photo-exchange on Flickr and information or debate threads on Twitter and (at the more elaborate end of the spectrum) the whole interlinked ecology of platform-based message circulation in which, for example, celebrity promotions, or friendship building, or project promotion now evolve. We cannot grasp the dynamics of these new processes unless we understand them as *more than* associations of heterogeneous elements (assemblages) and *more than* structures of linkages (networks). The figurations of online practice comprise an open (expanding) set of spaces for interaction and dependency, in which we are enmeshed, as we try to go on doing what we ordinarily do. Their dynamics also cannot be understood except within a larger strategy to build an infrastructure for sociality online that is a feature of the wave of digitalization.

The Basic Features of Figurations

The basic idea of figuration already offers many of the conceptual tools we need for analysing the complexity of our life with media (see Hepp, 2013b; 2015, pp. 29–33; Hepp and Hasebrink, 2014). As a figuration coalesces, it begins to stabilize relations between what until then were disparate sites of practice. However, Elias could not foresee the deepening of mediatization – with its waves of mechanization, electrification, digitalization and now also (possibly) datafication. As a result, for this context of deep media-based interdependency, we need to specify three distinct dimensions of how figurations stabilize: their relevance-frames, actor-constellations and communicative practices, each of which is founded, in part, on relations of meaning. Let us explain. First, each figuration has certain *relevance-frames*. By this we mean that the people involved in a figuration have a common orientation to a shared 'purpose', whether it be as a family, a group of friends, a collectivity or as users of a particular digital platform. The relevance-frames of a figuration express its social meaning as a distinct way of acting together. Sharing this set of relevance does not of course rule out conflicts or disagreements. There can be, for example, many conflicts in families as in any other kind of figuration, but the point is that these are understood as *family* conflicts. When it comes to our living with the media manifold, new questions arise: do older relevance-frames get transformed by our relations with the contemporary media manifold? How far are certain relevance-frames related to the new media environment? And does this enable new *types* of figuration to arise?

Second, each figuration involves a distinctive *constellation of actors*. This phrase has a double meaning. First, the individuals in a figuration are not just a random accumulation of individuals. They are related to each other in typical ways, for example, because they have specific roles in the figuration (parents and children in a family). There are certain social definitions of that relatedness (close or less close relationships between friends etc.). Second, a figuration is a constellation of 'human beings' (Elias, 2003, p. 89). This does not mean that we should not consider objects and technologies – including media – as elements in figurations, but simply insists that objects and technologies are not part of the constellation of actors who understand themselves to be acting together in this way. Figurations *can* exist without objects and technologies, but they *cannot* exist at all without individuals. Therefore, its actor-constellation is more fundamental to a figuration than the objects and technologies involved in it. It is an arrangement of individual actions that is characteristic for that figuration, but the constellation is also open to change.[7]

Third, each figuration is based on certain *practices* that in turn depend on an *ensemble of objects and technologies*. Put another way, each figuration is based on certain distinctive practices *of communication* and a related *media ensemble* (Bausinger, 1984, p. 349). It is through the interrelated actions of such practices that individuals construct figurations: that is, figurations involve ways of doing certain things together, or in coordination, very often with and through media. The communications that arise around those practices contribute to the overall 'meaning' of the figuration. But we cannot understand the practices of such figurations without the objects and technologies we use in relation to them. While not being necessarily a *constitutive* feature of figurations – as relevance-frames, actor-constellation and practices (of communication) are – figurations typically *come together with* certain objects and technologies. Families, whether located at a single place or mobile (like migrant families), have certain possessions: household goods, maybe even apartments or houses. But they also have a variety of media to communicate with each other. Nowadays, this is even the case for homeless people for whom media can offer a certain 'ontological security' while being forced to live on the streets.[8] The character of these properties has a lot to do with the specificity of these figurations and in addition supports a certain stability. A family with a great amount of property and a rich media ensemble can develop a much greater durability than families that primarily rely on personal relations. So it is not just technology that makes figurations more 'durable' (Latour, 1991, p. 103); it is physical objects of all sorts.

To sum up, the formation of figurations as patterns of communication in which something distinctive is at stake emerges through the interrelations between three dimensions: relevance-frames, constellations of actors, and communicative practices, that have, as their basis, a particular ensemble of objects and media technologies. These dimensions are relatively autonomous, but because each is involved in the situation in which action occurs, processes of acting together generally tend to reinforce them, and stabilize patterns of association between them. *All these dimensions are based in relations of meaning.* It is this attention to the distinctive consequences that flow from social worlds *as communicative orders between human beings*, built in part through regularities of communication and meaning that is missing from the notions of network and assemblage.

Power and Belonging

What of the larger social arrangements that emerge through figurations? We can approach this from two angles: power and belonging. In
both cases, a double perspective is needed, asking on the one hand how
figurations *internally* can be characterized by their power-relations and
belongings, and on the other how figurations build power and belonging
externally in the wider social world.

Each figuration has a distinctive actor-constellation, with certain characteristic *power-relations*. Elias wrote about 'balance of power' (Elias,
1978, p. 64), but that term can be misleading if we read it as evenness.
Particular figurations are characterized by certain 'conflict-ridden figurational dynamics' (Dunning and Hughes, 2013, p. 63). But power-relations
in figurations are not just a matter of *positioning* in the actor-constellation.
They have a lot to do with practices of communication that *make sense
of* these power-relations. Analysing power in figurations involves at least
three levels: the positioning in the actor-constellation, the practices that
support power-relations, and the inscription of power in the media ensemble. For example, as the analysis of gender relations in families has demonstrated, power within them correlates with the disposition of certain
media technologies: the remote control, VCR etc. (Morley, 1986, pp. 158f.).
If we think about contemporary media technologies, the inscription of
power with reference to gender even goes further: for example, the pre-
selection of a certain gender ('male', 'female', ...) when joining a specific
platform predefines how as an individual one is represented and so can act
through communication.[9] And if we not only reflect on the internal power-
relations of this figuration but also its external relation to other figurations,
we have to consider how far the overall orientation of a figuration – its
relevance-frames – is related to the power of this figuration more broadly.
For example, being part of a certain collectivity – a group of male refugees
or the community of a shared office – is related to the power that the
members of this figuration have in the wider social world, to which media
discourses about this collectivity.

Figurations are also closely involved in the construction of *belonging* (see
the detailed analysis of collectivities in Chapter 9). Belonging can have a
purely situational meaning. Think here about the figurations of games or
the dance (Elias' regular example): sharing orientation to common interactions creates a certain situational belonging of being part of, for example,
the game or the dance. Think of the figuration of spectators in a stadium.
In such a figuration we experience a deep feeling of communitization

(*Vergemeinschaftung*: Weber (1972 [1921], p. 21)), a situational feeling of being part of a crowd within an event (Hitzler, 2010, pp. 13f.). However, this does not necessarily result in being part of a longer-lasting community (*Gemeinschaft*). In cases like these the deeply felt belonging is built up through the intensity of the figurations' practices. Today, occasions for figurations with such an intense contextual meaning are more and more interwoven *with media*. The figuration of stadium spectatorship cannot be understood outside of its media ensemble: loudspeakers, scoreboard, display panels, and spectators' parallel communications via their mobile phones and tablets. But even more media-related are figurations of music concerts or collective viewing of television and cinema in public places. And with digital media we have the new figurations of online gatherings – in chats, on platforms, through apps – through which we construct an intense situational belonging to each other.

Figurations and Media Infrastructure

At this point, we reach and need to go beyond the limits of the *original* concept of figurations as Elias developed it. Starting from the late 1960s to the 1980s – all before the emergence of the internet as an infrastructure for everyday social interaction – Elias offers basically a hydraulic metaphor for capturing the process whereby particular human beings become increasingly interdependent through the flow of meanings, promises, obligations and performances. The term captures well the *length* of these potential chains of interdependence, but tells us less about *the sorts of entities* that are bound into figurations. As a result, it tells us little – without at least the additional work we do later in this chapter – about the forms of dependence on *system-infrastructure* that are crucial to the very complex figurations characteristic of our relations to the media manifold. Elias only seems to conceptualize the figuration as an order that emerges from the moves of the individual themselves: 'by figuration we mean the changing pattern created by the players as a whole [. . .] a flexible lattice-work of tensions [. . .] a fluctuating tensile equilibrium, a balance of power moving to and fro' (Elias, 1978, pp. 130–131). Yet, his own later reflections already by the 1980s acknowledged that media and communications technologies, and the large-scale systems they generate, were themselves already intensifying the complexity of the social, and its degrees of interdependence, generating 'fluctuations in what might be called "social pressure", in particular the "internal pressure" in a society' (Elias, 1991, p. 145).

Certain types of figuration – associated with distinctive ensembles of media technologies – generate obligations and dependencies not just between individuals, but also between individuals and communication systems, obligations that are distinctive features of how we live within the media manifold, but which also characterize *new types* of figuration.

Let us start with the most basic examples. Take the figuration of a family: this figuration is now increasingly characterized by a distinctive media ensemble, whether it is particular patterns of watching television together or in sequence, particular uses of smartphones to organize family practices and interactions, the photographs we share in printed photo albums or (more usually) via online platforms. All these media contribute to the ongoing construction of a group of people *as* a family, with all its contradictions, conflicts etc. So too with the figurations of organizations where, with 'ubiquitous computing', both inside and outside its formal structure, it has become, some argue, 'increasingly difficult to separate people's interactions with other people from people's interactions with technologies' (Contractor et al., 2011, p. 684).

But we have to go a step further: the media ensemble of a certain figuration is significant in the way it moulds its various practices of communication. Mobile phones and digital platforms mean a lot for families, when it becomes possible to locate family members wherever they are, when family members can be reached at all times, and when family members have reference to mediated representations of themselves as a family on a continuous basis. These material possibilities of contemporary media and related infrastructures not only offer better chances of sustaining the family figuration in a particular way; they also mould our practices of communication.

However, this is not a 'one-way-street' of media effects. Figurations produce certain needs of communication and therefore are an ongoing source for developing new media technologies and adapting present. The digital platforms we live with, for example, did *not* come out of nowhere. On the contrary, they responded to families' needs to be reachable across space and time. 'New' technologies get appropriated within a figuration's media ensemble (Silverstone and Hirsch, 1992; Mansell and Silverstone, 1998; Berker et al., 2006), quite possibly changing the figuration, and generating *new* demands for media, and so on in an endless feedback loop. This offers again chances for further media adaptations by 'producers' and 'designers'.

Many of the most recent media developments refer to fundamental human needs of *connection*. This is reproduced, further institutionalized and materialized in the *connectivity* of digital platforms (van Dijck, 2013, pp. 46–50). Understanding our lives with media means therefore grasping an ever more complex range of media-related figurations. But to do this fully, we need to conceptualize the transformed scale on which many contemporary figurations work.

4.3 The Scaling and Transformation of Figurations

Up to this point we discussed figurations on the level of partnerships, groups and organizations: that is, on the level of figurations that might be accessed through an analysis of individuals who interact in an observable way. However, there are figurations of much greater complexity, for example the figuration of the global financial market. How can we grasp figurations like these without becoming purely metaphorical? Asking this question means starting to think about what we can call the 'scaling' of figurations.

Scaling is widely discussed in complexity theory as a term to 'describe how one property of a system will change if a related property changes' (Mitchell, 2009, p. 258): complexity theory notes that there is no linear correlation between an increase in scale and the changes in internal characteristics associated with this increase. In assemblage theory, problems of scaling are also discussed, but dismissed, with the insistence that it is not helpful to understand 'macro' phenomena as a container in which 'meso' and 'micro' are embedded: on this view, the 'macro' is 'another equally local, equally 'micro' place, which is *connected* to many others through some medium transporting specific types of traces' (Latour, 2007, p. 176). However, the 'macro' remains even on this account a place where decision-making power is centred: governmental offices, corporate headquarters and the like. But what is a government HQ if not a site where *very many* (rather than few) connections are directly or indirectly coordinated? So the question of 'scale' or at least, as Saskia Sassen (2006) puts it, of 'scaling', cannot be avoided.[10] Remember that we have already insisted that the media environment we access is a manifold, that is, a many-dimensional object: why would we believe that the social world in which we put that manifold to use in varying ways has any *fewer* dimensions? The social world is a higher-dimensional manifold within which we can distinguish two distinct principles of scaling or complexification: scaling through relations between *figurations* and scaling through the *meaningful arrangements* of figurations.

Relations Between Figurations

There are two ways of *relating* figurations to each other: first, by linking their actor constellations directly together, and, second, by building figurations *of figurations*. Linking actor constellations takes place when one actor of a figuration becomes part of the actor constellation of another figuration. There are many researched examples of this, especially in network analysis. Some actors have power because they are 'switchers' (Castells, 2009, p. 45) that link different networks. When powerful actors make such links between figurations, they build hierarchical relations between them. Take companies as an example: the heads of certain working groups – themselves figurations – build a cross-cutting figuration (of department management) which is headed by one of its members who is again part of the figuration of heads of department etc. So by following the links between the actor-constellations we get an understanding of how a certain company is internally structured and how its power relations work. We can integrate more informal figurations into such a description; for example, the figuration of an interest group that meets regularly in this company to discuss certain interests, linking up diverse groups of people across the company. Similar ways of relating figurations through linked actor-constellations can be found in other parts of the social world: in relation to the various associations of public and private life, educational institutions, political parties etc. Such relations between actor-constellations depend however on there being figurations which share something in terms of frames of relevance.

A more complex way of joining up figurations (and so enabling figurations to operate on much larger scales) is what we can call *figurations of figurations*. In this case the actor-constellation of a figuration consists not only of individual actors but of 'supra-individual actors' (Schimank, 2010, p. 327), that is, actors that themselves can each be considered as figurations in their own right. Saskia Sassen (2006) uses the term 'configuration' similarly to describe European or even global relations of states, companies and other complex kinds of actors. But how far does it make sense to conceptualize supra-individual actors in this way? In our everyday language we have no problem naming certain organizations, social movements or even states as actors when we say that they 'do' this or that. Analytically speaking, supra-individual actors are always 'composite actors' (Scharpf, 1997, pp. 42–50), that is, actors made out of individual actors, or composed of figurations of individual actors. As a consequence, the agency of these supra-individual actors is nothing other than the agency produced by this figuration. But when does a figuration gain this kind of agency?

Some figurations are either too situational or too conflictual to be incorporated into wider figurations of figurations. The supra-individual agency of event spectatorship has no sustainability beyond the event; the 'established and outsider figuration' in the suburb investigated by Norbert Elias and John Scotson (1994 [1965]) is also too conflictual to have a shared agency. Conversely, a figuration of otherwise unconnected individuals can become a supra-individual actor when the practices of the involved individuals 'result in a orderly whole, thus not only occasionally but systematically build on one another in a way that an *overall objective* is pursued' (Schimank, 2010, p. 329; our translation). In the contemporary social world, there are two kinds of figurations in which this is the case: 'collective actors' (or 'collectivities', discussed further in Chapter 9) with intense shared patterns of interpretation as in social movements; and 'corporate actors' (or 'organizations', discussed in Chapter 10) such as companies and public authorities, associations and clubs in which binding agreements on their agency are constructed in more or less formal negotiation procedures (Schimank, 2010, pp. 329–341). Both kinds of 'supra-individual actors' can themselves contribute to a figuration of figurations: companies can build groups of companies, associations can build umbrella associations. A figurational perspective therefore is not just about recognizing that groups, organizations, cities and nations are different kinds of 'assembled' individuals (DeLanda, 2006, pp. 47–119): of course they are, but this doesn't tell us very much! More important is analysing the *interrelation* of the figurations involved, their actor-constellations, their practices and the *new* relations of meaning (including pressures to sustain *new* relevance-frames, actor-constellations, practices in common and underlying media ensembles) that result from building pre-existing figurations into a larger arrangement, or figuration of figurations.

Media ensembles may be crucial to this process. Collective actors like social movements and other corporate actors use media to construct their common agency in various ways. It can be by shared communication via digital platforms as in many contemporary social movements (Mattoni and Treré, 2014), or it can be through organized communication processes like in many companies (Orlikowski, 2010). The negotiated shared 'will' of these supra-individual actors is typically materialized in a media form and by this made durable.[11] Indeed, more boldly, we might look back on the history of the internet discussed in Chapter 3, and see this as the emergence over time of a many-dimensional 'figuration of figurations', achieved through the ever-expanding meaning-based linkages, that is, through hyperlinks.

Also crucial are the infrastructures that can be built through the links between communications under particular controlled conditions, such as social media platforms. Social media platforms provide a space for specific figurations to be sustained or created: the overall structure of interdependency that results includes also our relations to the underlying platform. That is what we mean by saying that we are now involved not just in single figurations, but also in *figurations of* figurations. When, for example, Facebook breaks down or imposes unacceptable privacy conditions, the multiple levels of the interdependencies in which we are involved become suddenly and brutally clear to us.

Meaningful Arrangements of Figurations

There is however a second principle for scaling figurations: *meaningful arrangements*. Several times already we have emphasized that any attempt to understand the construction of the social world through communication is necessarily a theory about shared meaning production. We understand meaning at this point in the original sense of Max Weber (1988 [1904], p. 200) as *Kulturbedeutung*, that is, cultural meaning as actors in the social world produce it. In such a perspective the figurations of the social world also have – beyond any concrete links between actor-constellations – meaningful arrangements with each other. So, for example, national government agencies are figurations that are *understood as* 'centres of power' in relation to many other figurations. Such constructions of some figurations as 'powerful', 'public', and so on, and others as 'weak', 'private', and so on are only *partly* explicable through the interrelatedness of their actors or through the composition of 'figurations of figurations'. For, in addition to such structural links, figurations in which we live also 'hang together' (Boltanski, 2011) with each other through relations of meaning, and this 'hanging together'[12] derives from two distinct sources: certain *discourses* that connect these figurations and their meanings in the social world, and certain *larger-scale relations of interdependency between domains of action* (for example, the transport infrastructure and the economic infrastructure) that come to be associated with *assumed* relations of meaning. Both types of arrangement go beyond the simple inclusion of actors or figurations in a larger or more complex figuration (or figurations of figurations).

Peter Berger and Thomas Luckmann tried to explain something like such arrangements of meaning through the notion of 'symbolic universes' (see for this Berger and Luckmann, 1966, pp. 110–122). Symbolic universes were for them 'meaningful totalities' that share an overall understanding of the social world. They offer an 'all-embracing frame of reference, which now constitutes a universe in the literal sense of the word, because *all* human experience can now be conceived of as taking place within in' (Berger and Luckmann, 1966, p. 114). But this functionalist reading of how meaning contributes to order was never fully plausible even when they wrote, and it is absolutely implausible today in an age of proliferating meaning-making across countless national and transnational digital media.

Berger and Luckmann's language of 'symbolic universes', if applied here, would suggest that all figurations fit neatly within functioning meaningful wholes. But this underestimates the *variety of different discourses* that relate figurations to each other by 'telling' or 'explaining' the 'overall sense' of certain figurations, and so, over time, construct larger-scale patterns of related figurations sustained by interrelations of meaning (rather than by the structural linkages that make up, for example, figurations of figurations). Such discourses are not just rational constructions.[13] First and foremost, they establish 'affective bonds' (Elias, 1978, p. 134) or, as we would prefer to put it, relations of meaningful interdependency, *across* different figurations, and in a variety of ways. Let us think about the web of figurations in which the figuration of a contemporary family is involved: that family has the responsibility of organizing the leisure and upbringing of its children; it interacts over many years with organizations (schools, adult education centres, universities) that are regarded as having certain responsibilities for education. But over time, those children develop independent relations with external institutions (cultural institutions for leisure purposes; companies and organizations that are responsible for providing employment), and so the family over time develops meaningful relationships with an ever-expanding, indeed changing, set of other external figurations (and figurations of figurations), right up until the parents become old and in need of care. Those external figurations are themselves further understood to stand in relation to various levels of government in a public domain, which media institutions themselves help to define and shape.

Our argument is *not* that such webs of figurations connect up in such a way as to create an overall functional whole of societies. Our approach is precisely not functionalist, since relations of meaning within such webs are always potentially contestable and interruptible. We want instead to insist on the importance of such connecting discourses whereby the 'macro' becomes embedded in the specificities of 'micro' actions through relationships of meaning. Put another way, individual actors come to learn to act in a social world characterized by discourses about what 'society is' and how 'society works' (in this sense, the 'macro' is always present in the 'micro': Morley, 2000, pp. 9–12).

Such relations of meaning can emerge in another way too, not directly through discourses of meaning but through deep practical relations of interdependency that 'hang together' as what seems to be a 'way of life' that, as such, gets taken to be meaningful 'as a whole'. So for example actors in an economic market depend on the workings of the transport system, and actors in the financial markets depend on the workings of communications systems. If one breaks down, the other cannot continue. Such relations of interdependency continue up to higher dimensions without limit. Such is the complexity of the practical interdependencies on which contemporary life depends that actors struggle to make sense of *all of it* as a meaningful whole: this is where new types of discourse or myth emerge to make sense of it all, *as* a whole, *as* a reality (Laclau, 1990; Boltanski, 2011).

What we call 'society' is much more than a container for different figurations (Beck, 2000b, pp. 23–26); rather it is the overall 'hanging together' of figurations (and figurations of figurations) across the many domains of action associated with a large spatial territory. Insofar as these forms of hanging together are based on meaning, they have a mythical rather than material character. Those myths do not describe an 'objective reality' of the social world, but are particular constructions of it, which help hold in place *assumptions* about how its domains of action 'fit together' in a wider 'order' (see Chapter 10 for more details). There is a long history of such myths, which have been associated with media institutions and their ongoing claims to social legitimacy, and this is not the place to unpack this history in detail. But it is enough to mention that today's myths of this sort go far beyond the legitimacy claims of old media institutions (for example, major public media), and encompass the mythical claims about collectivities brought together on social media platforms and the access to the 'social' supposedly achieved through 'big data'.[14]

Figurations and Social Transformation

In the process perspective we are taking here, no social phenomenon is just given. Even figurations that remain over a long time 'the same' – figurations of religious organizations, for example – have to be *constructed as* 'the same' through action and interpretation. Alongside change, there is also 'inertia', yet attempts to preserve figurations and to avoid change can have the unintended side-effects of 'strengthen[ing]' a figuration's 'tendency to change' (Elias, 1978, p. 147). Good examples are religious organizations or political parties in which the efforts of the organizational elite to keep them stable stimulate tendencies of critique, long-term instability, and so change. And equally it is possible that practices which are intended to change a figuration might strengthen its tendency to remain unchanged. For example, some actors' ideas of change might be oriented in different directions, and by this make specific changes difficult. Any description of figurational transformation on a large scale is necessarily complex.

What weight finally should we give to media technologies of communication in such transformations? It is a question of the 'moulding' *potential* that derives from a figuration's media ensemble. A changing media ensemble in a family, in a peer group or in a shared office community does not necessarily transform the figuration itself: the family, peer group or office community might stay the same. A changing media ensemble only results in transformation if a figuration's practices of communication are also transformed and with them the ways in which meaning is produced within that figuration.

Nor is internal change of the media ensemble simply driven by external changes in the media environment. In many cases where figurations transform – maybe in most of them – it rather will be as a result of an interaction between internal and external forces. Think of a company: very often the reason to change its media ensemble does not take place accidentally but by management decisions. New internal data systems or new social media platforms are introduced to fulfil certain aims better: to process information more efficiently, or to reach customers more effectively. The media ensemble *is made* to change because at least some of the actors hope to better achieve their aims. But the side-consequences may be very different from how these actors intended it. Employees might, for example, appropriate data systems in subversive ways to build up their work procedures in a more convenient way. And *whether* changes in a media ensemble change the *dynamics* of a figuration remains a complex matter for local investigation. So, as already noted, some figurations (religious organizations) may remain quite stable in spite of their increased uses of digital media: the fact that the office of the pope is active on digital platforms does not change its power-balance as an institution. In each case, it is a matter of understanding the dynamics of *particular interrelations*. There is no 'logic' of media that drives changes in figurations: there is at most media-related change of various sorts in the field where the relations that make up a figuration, or figurations of figurations, unfold in a non-linear way.

Both internal and external aspects of a figuration can transform fundamentally in a changing media environment. This has first to do with new possibilities of how figurations can become related to each other. As we have argued in Chapter 2, the fundamental characteristic of each medium is that it offers possibilities to act beyond the here and now, and by this to extend the reach of human agency. It is, as Elias already noted, especially through *media* that 'chains of interdependence become more differentiated and grow longer', and so 'become more opaque and, for any single group or individual, more uncontrollable' (Elias, 1978, p. 68). This means that figurations can more easily spread across space and time (something we will discuss in the next section of this book). A company, for example, can much better integrate dispersed parts of its organization; administrations can reach different places; a family can hold together while being at the same time located transnationally. This does not mean that location ceases to matter in an age of deep mediatization. On the contrary, our relations with the media manifold *privilege* locations of high media connectivity (Zook, 2005): across such locations figurations can spread much more easily, and come into contact with each other, for example the transcultural environments of cities that offer opportunities for linking actor-constellations in multiple ways (Georgiou, 2013, pp. 92–116; Hepp, 2015, pp. 113–123). It is a key characteristic of huge cities and metropolises, that these are places where very different figurations cross and intertwine.

Life with media in the age of the media manifold is inseparable, we have argued, from involvement in a variety of different figurations that exist in complex and sometimes contradictory constellations. Such figurations exist in arrangements of varying levels of complexity, involving, on the one hand, links between actors or the incorporation of pre-existing figurations within 'figurations of figurations', or, on the other hand, relationships of meaning that in practice bind particular figurations (and figurations of figurations) into large-scale interdependent relationships. So far, we have just described the 'how' of figurations, and we have not yet reached the question of 'so what?', that is, the consequences of figurational patterns for wider social order, or what we might call the 'figurational order' of contemporary societies. We reach this finally in Chapter 10, but before that, in the preceding chapters of Parts II and III, we need to pass through various intermediate stages of analysis: in Part II, space, time and data; and in Part III, the implications of deep mediatization for the self, for collectivities, and for our possibilities of governing social space.

Part II

Dimensions of the Social World

5

Space

Space is an important means by which communication contributes to the construction of the social world. There are three aspects to this. First, technologies of transmission may enable communication between two entities that are spatially distant from each other, creating new first-order interactions. Second, communication-at-a-distance also enables new links between those such first-order interactions, establishing through this new second-order communicative relations. Examples of this are the development of royal sovereignty across a territory and the emergence of power through information systems or platforms. Third, second-order communicative relations change, more broadly, the basic *possibilities* for interaction of all sorts in a particular social domain (for example, where protocols govern information processes in a way that underlies the space of communication that we call the internet). Each of these spatial aspects of how communication contributes to the construction of the social world involves figurations of various sorts. In this chapter, we unpack these processes, which are of varying degrees of complexity.

In a sense, there is nothing new here: the entanglement between space and communication is a *banal* feature of modernity. Modernity has been based on increasingly *many* forms of communication-at-a-distance, from communication by horse, pigeon or letter – the older forms of mail – to more recent forms of communication by television, radio signal or computer-to-computer linkage. Through those forms, new types of social space have been built: broadcasting territories constituted by the space where a signal reaches; online communities of people who have never physically met; password-guarded domains of online interaction. There are few, if any, parts of the world which are untouched by these changes, even if, as we signalled in Chapter 3, the spread of media remains in some respects highly uneven and the idea that modernity or mediatization takes just one form, framed by the West, is deeply misleading. A decade ago, one of us (Couldry and McCarthy, 2004) tried to capture this interaction between media and space through the concept of 'MediaSpace': a dialectical concept that captures the many levels on which the spatiality of media's operations may contribute to the wider ordering of space and society. Much of this contribution occurs implicitly. Mass media contents do not usually *refer* to the spatial aspects of their own production, distribution and reception – they represent the world instead from a generalized, de-spatialized standpoint – yet the spatiality of media always operates in the background, *dis*placing social reality in various ways (Couldry and McCarthy, 2004, pp. 4–5). We explore such processes of displacement further in this chapter, before at the end considering briefly the new displacements that derive from the role of software and data-processing.

Transformations of space through media have generally been combined with transformations in time. Take the telegraph and the telephone: they enabled the *speeding-up* of translocal communication (Hepp, 2004, pp. 182–184) and led to distant actors being able to sustain communication between each other regularly in time, at least if they travelled to key network nodes (the telegraph station, the landline phone). The media manifold, and particularly the embedding of 'social' online platforms in everyday interaction, have involved a huge deepening of this first shift. They have enabled in many parts of the world not just discrete many-to-one (broadcasting) or one-to-one (interpersonal) communications sustained regularly at a distance, but, through the infinite communicative reserve of the internet, *reciprocal and continuous* communication-at-a-distance from (almost) any and all points to (almost) any and all other points, and within a range of temporalities.

These more recent extensions of communication across space, however uneven they may be geographically, generate fundamental new issues for the social organization of communication. For example, there is the problem of communicative excess. This occurs when the volume of communications received, and requiring response, at one point in space becomes *arbitrarily large* by reference to the processing capacity available at that point, as has happened through the massive expansion of the means for non-synchronous communication: as a result, what we call the 'figurational order' of the social world (see Chapter 1) risks becoming unstable. Put paradoxically, the increasing mutual entanglement or *practical* 'hanging together' of actors and processes in space (and time) facilitated by today's online communications may undermine the wider order of our habits and practices (its *normative* 'hanging-together' as an arrangement for living in common).[1] 'Keeping up with things' is no longer a matter of improving one's efficiency of response in only one communications interface like email, but rather managing a communicative excess *across* multiple independent platforms. But how, if at all, do we *sort between* the various communicative infinities with which we each must deal? We will come back to the consequences for our experience of time in the next chapter. There is however a contradictory movement which points, in some domains, to a massive intensification of coordination across space achieved through communication: we refer to what Karin Knorr-Cetina calls the 'synthetic situation' of 'scopic media' (2014, p. 45; see also Knorr-Cetina and Bruegger, 2002) which in, say, the global financial markets provides a shared focus for thousands of dispersed actors, based on the commonly available visual displays taken-for-granted. These movements need to be understood together.

We separate time and space in these two chapters purely to make the presentation of our argument more manageable. Both are affected by the same progressing deep mediatization of the social world, and the analysis of spatial relations cannot be neatly separated from the analysis of temporal relations: what matters are the interconnected relations of *space–time* (Massey, 1992, pp. 79–84). By the end of the next chapter, we will be able to put all this together in an account of the changing figurational order of contemporary societies.

This chapter is organized as follows. First, we review some general principles for thinking about the space of the social world, and how communications contribute to its transformation; then, we discuss particular types of social space and their communicative features; finally, we turn to the disruptive implications for social space of software and the information and data infrastructure more generally.

5.1 Media and the Changing Spatiality of the Social World

We are now 'in space' in a different way from those who lived in the pre-internet era. Translated into the language of our argument in preceding chapters, media – and specifically the media manifold of digitalization – have changed something fundamental about the spatiality of the social world.

Sociologist Sanyang Zhao (2006) expressed the point most clearly when he noted that online communications have transformed the starting-point for a phenomenology of the social world: Schutz's key distinction between consociates (*Umwelt*) and contemporaries (*Mitwelt*). If consociates are those with whom a human being comes into direct contact, the internet has expanded this set of people beyond those one meets face to face. As Zhao puts it: 'instead of using corporeal copresence as the standard for judging all forms of human contact, we must now treat face-to-face interaction as one of the many ways in which individuals come to connect [as consociates] with each other in the [. . .] internet era' (Zhao, 2006, p. 459). Online communication is not therefore a supplement to face-to-face interactions, but one of the *basic* ways in which we encounter and get to know people. It is a 'there and now' (Zhao, 2006, pp. 459–460) which supplements the 'here and now' of face-to-face interaction described by classic phenomenology. We gather online to meet others whom we do not ordinarily meet face to face. This has two basic consequences: first, 'the internet has [. . .] expanded the lifeworld' to include the online domain (Zhao, 2007, p. 156), and, second, no longer is the face-to-face situation 'the prototypical case of social interaction' (Zhao, 2006, p. 417, commenting on Berger and Luckmann, 1966, p. 28).

This changes the dynamics of how we learn as social actors. Online consociates, in principle, become 'legitimate source[s] of mutual knowledge' (Zhao, 2007, p. 149; contrast Berger and Luckmann, 1966, p. 32). Yet Schutz had already anticipated something like this in his reflections on the telephone (Schutz and Luckmann, 1973, p. 44). As Schutz, solo, wrote in 1964, 'we are less and less determined in our social situation by relationships with individual partners within our immediate or mediate reach, and more and more by highly anonymous types which have no fixed place in the social cosmos' (Schutz, 1964, p. 129; see also Knoblauch, 2013a, p. 330). Through a later form of telephone – the almost universally adopted mobile phone – we have in the past two decades become accustomed to operating in more than one space 'at once', with surprising consequences on occasion for the contexts in which some interaction streams get received (Moores, 2004). Such shifts in how social resources and processes are configured cannot be understood if we think about the consumption and production of media in a narrow media-centric way that focuses only on media contents and not on mediaspace. When the (more or less) continuous availability of an online *Mitwelt* changes people's conception of the 'space where [they] meet people' (interviewee quoted by Jansson, 2013, p. 283), then broader aspects of social coordination also change, as new 'sociospatial regimes of dependence' (Jansson, 2013, p. 281) emerge.[2] Meanwhile, in a very different way, the installing of information technologies embedded via radio transmission devices in ever smaller and more widely distributed units across everyday life (Hayles, 1999; Klauser and Alberchtslund, 2014, p. 277) is changing the ways in which space and society become ordered. The increasing saturation of everyday space by processes of tracking and monitoring, involving the continuous capture and combination of data, is changing the way space 'feels' in many parts of the world, and particularly, but not exclusively, cities.

Before getting lost in the details of these transformations, we need to take a step back and think in general about the nature of spatial relations within the social world. 'The relation between space and social life is [. . .] very poorly understood': so wrote two remarkable architects whose book on the power-relations that flow from the design and organization of living space has been unjustly neglected (Hillier and Hanson, 1984, p. ix). There is a reason for the blind spot of which Hillier and Hanson complain (and indeed for the neglect of their work): the reason is that we live *embedded* in places, moving from one to another through the day, and building our path through life out of more or less successful *appropriations* of space in the form of the places that we occupy. Those who are fortunate to have security of spatial relations – and the recent 'migrant' and 'refugee crisis' in Europe, Africa and Asia reminds us that this is very far from everyone – move from the security of their living-space to that of their workplace, easily forgetting the importance of the spatial resources needed for everything they do, and every movement they make. Yet space is a scarce resource (Pred, 1990, p. 13), and our achievements of 'place' – the ability to impose a 'schema' of interpretation and organization *onto* particular regions of space (Tuan, 1977, p. 34) – rarely get grasped as appropriations of that scarce resource. A materialist phenomenology however requires an appreciation of space and, more specifically of the role that technologies of communication play in the construction of place, locality and scale.[3]

Place, Locality and Scale

A geographical perspective is essential here, because it looks unwaveringly at the inequalities in the distribution of spatial resources that may not be visible from particular locations. Attention to space is not just a matter of noticing the differences of resource within and across space, but also of grasping the spatiality of the larger spaces of circulation that *connect up* all the points of economic, social and cultural life and their highly uneven consequences (Smith, 1990, pp. 105–106). Attending to 'space' means thinking about the materiality of relations.

According to the great French spatial theorist, Henri Lefebvre, 'social space' is 'not a thing among things', but 'a relation between things', something that 'encompasses their interrelationships in their coexistence and simultaneity' (Lefebvre, 1991, pp. 73, 83). This approach fits well within a figurational approach to social life. The production of social space, Lefebvre argued, is crucial to our possibility of social experience in and between particular places. More than that, space's basis in material relations means that space cannot be understood without some reference also to time, that is, relations across space and within time. The very notion of space – that is, the frame through which we conceive of things happening or being situated in the 'same' space – depends on 'the simultaneous coexistence of social interrelations and interactions at all spatial scales, from the most local level to the most global' (Massey, 1992, p. 80).

For that reason, space cannot be exclusively understood in terms of place or locality. Space, insofar as it is relational, is, as Bruno Latour pointed out, in large part an achievement of actors themselves, as they build new material connections *between* localities that can be embedded into action-contexts (Latour, 2005, p. 184). The increasing complexity and variety of how, in our contemporary modernities, social and economic relations are sustained across space through globalized communication and exchange means that many spatial relations are today not strongly anchored in particular 'places' or 'localities' – that is, in fixed and bounded space-containers. One of the first to grasp this connection was Wolfgang Schivelbusch in his reflections on the impacts of the railway in the nineteenth century in Europe. Schivelbusch wrote that 'henceforth, the localities are no longer spatially individual or autonomous: they are moments in the traffic that makes them possible' (Schivelbusch, 1986, p. 40). The point has been developed in relation to late twentieth-century technological acceleration, leading some geographers to suggest that globalization (and specifically 'transnational connectivity') changes 'the very ontology of place and territoriality itself' (Amin, 2002, p. 387). The argument is not that place, locality, and scalar relations disappear completely, but that they are not the only type of spatial relation in a world of 'multiple geographies of belonging' and 'multiple spatialities of organization' (Amin, 2002, pp. 395–396). We must acknowledge therefore the distinctive contributions that the concepts of place, locality and scale make to our understanding of space (Jessop et al., 2008): *all* are transformed potentially by deep mediatization. It is particularly important not to abandon the notion of scale.[4] As the Brazilian cultural theorist Roberto Da Matta put it, 'it is basic to study the "&" that ties the mansion to the slum dwelling, and the enormous, terrible, fearsome space that relates the dominant to the dominated' (Da Matta, 1985; quoted in Martín-Barbero, 1993, p. 186). Relations of scale, and breakdowns in relations across scale, are crucial to understanding inequality, and the power-relations that flow from inequality.

That is quite consistent however with arguing that the relations between localities are intensified with mediatization and globalization. What more and more matters is a 'translocality' (Hepp, 2015, p. 12; Nederveen Pieterse, 1995, p. 45): that is, the mediated *interrelations* between various localities. Localities do not dissolve: as embodied human beings, we have no choice but to act *from* a certain locality, even if the resources on which action from that place relies are themselves distributed. But these localities change their meaning in a social world made up of ever more complex translocal connections. As a result, a certain degree of spatial complexity becomes intrinsic to the social world: this complexity is enacted through the operations of figurations.

Media and the Organization of Social Space

Sites of social experience vary hugely in their spatial organization: indeed their different feel may depend directly on the difference in how key resources – from housing to food to culture – are distributed across them. As Lefebvre (1991, p. 31) puts it, 'every society [. . .] produces a space, its own space', and that space may be profoundly differentiated, even while particular institutions represent it as 'unified'. From a historical perspective, a key aspect of our modernities was shifts in spatial relations caused by a new ability to sustain economic (and other) relations across large distances and in increasingly rapid time-rhythms. Ever since the early inventions of news relays (Rantanen, 2009), media have played a role in the shaping of space and territory. The modern nation in 'the West' and outside 'the West' (Anderson, 1983; Thompson, 1995; Giddens, 1990; Larkin, 2008; Spitulnik, 2010) was always a translocal space sustained in part by the production and circulation of media and by the linked improvement of other material things and bodies (transportation). Media's key role in sustaining 'nationhood' does not stop today, even if media do not always work to sustain particular nations: nationhood, through media and other forces, remains part of the 'deep structures' of modern life (Skey, 2014; Calhoun, 2007).

What specific challenges for our understanding of social space do digital media throw up? New forms of translocal communication – above all, via the internet – have intensified the complexity of spatial relations, and created new types of spatial inequality. Imagine two living spaces, one connected to the internet and the other not: they are very differently embedded in the distribution of both communications and wider resources, with major implications for their inhabitants' ability to act on various scales. Once common claims that new technologies of communication abolish space are profoundly misleading: what matters instead for the contemporary social world is the 'adjusted distribution of co-presence' (Boden and Molotch, 1994, p. 278). Put another way, the history of spatial relations has always been a history of exclusion, sometimes morally disguised as 'purification' (Sibley, 1988), and there is no reason to think that an age of deep mediatization is any different. Indeed some geographers argue that the intensified infrastructures of late modern life splinter cities into segregated networked spaces that variably benefit from 'bundles' of networked infrastructure, including digital communications (Graham and Marvin, 2001). Meanwhile, behind the apparently free global flow of media representations and information signals lie hidden inequalities of news production which shape the sources and therefore contents of those representations (Brooker-Gross, 1983). To get at this, we need to think not about individual actions or the space where individual actions are performed, but about the relation between wider patterns of action, and the hidden constraints that shape their distribution: what Swedish geographer Torsten Hagerstrand called 'coupling constraints' (Schwanen and Kwan, 2008, discussing Hagerstrand, 1975).

Think for a moment about specific actor-constellations and their problems of space- (and time-) *coordination*. As everyday action assumes increasingly the ability to adjust continuously 'in real time' to the demands of distant others through mediated communications, plans for managing, say, a family's movements across space become more complex. Prima facie this reduces 'coupling constraints' by solving some problems of how this movement can be coordinated with that movement; but, through the levels of coordination now relied upon, it may create new problems. Contemporary families, as figurations characterized by coordinated media use, are able to cope with much greater spatial complexity than families previously did, but, by the same token, they become ever more *reliant on* the consistent availability of the resources that make such coping possible: that is, continuous access to the same flows of communications across the family. When this breaks down – a phone battery loses charge, someone enters a zone without signal, or some more serious obstacle to communication intervenes – then a breakdown at all levels of communication can ensue. The figuration of the family is increasingly dependent today, even for its basic functioning, on the wider figuration of figurations of which internet infrastructure forms just one part, and this applies (even if in very different forms) to rich elites who own large numbers of media devices *and* to poor families for whom 'media' is a single shared mobile phone through which signals can be sent (by dropped call) or money remitted across borders.

From another perspective, the *folded* nature of digital communications – with every webpage containing many additional links and possible pathways or resources – only intensifies the complexity of how people's relations to space are differentiated through their variable uses of media. Whereas a great majority of communications today assume some access to the internet, it does not follow that all people have the same level of access: quite the opposite is true. As a result, the way that social space is ordered has also changed. The process of locative media, for example, provides space-related information, but also signals actors' positions in space to systems that track this: in this way locative media create, as the Brazilian writer André Lemos notes, 'augmented realities [. . .] integrated, mixed processes that merge electronic and physical territories, creating new forms and new senses of place' (Lemos, 2009, p. 96). These augmented spaces are intensely differentiated, and important new power-relations are constituted by control over space-related information.

More generally, the diversity of how actors interact with the infinities of spatially relevant information may require a notion of 'metaspace' to get at the changing possibilities for how we move through space and socialize with others (close or distant), and the role that media interfaces and formats play in shaping these changes (Humphreys, 2012). For some actors, as Humphreys puts it (2012, p. 508), 'mobility, sociality and mediality' converge. Media in various configurations now involve us in multiple and changing relations to space and place. As a result, one person's 'metaspace' – her or his way of operating on space and so configuring their life spatially – may be incompatible with another's.

It goes without saying that networks are important, and that effective network access (for example, through social media) positions us differently in relation to resources, as they are distributed in space, compared with the lack of such access. When, for example, sitting with our laptop or phone, we ask a network, or consult YouTube, for advice on how to cook a certain dish, or fix a computer problem, we access a networked resource. Rather, however, than rely on broad claims about the relations between 'networks' and 'society' – for example, Manuel Castells' (2009, p. 53) claim that networks and their interrelations structure the very possibility of society – we need a more differentiated account of 'how the connections are implemented' (Knorr-Cetina and Bruegger, 2002, p. 392).

The next section will explore some entry-points to a richer account of how media's embedding in the social world affects spatial relations.

5.2 Communicative Practices and Spatial Relations

One way of getting clear on *'where people are' through media* is to think about where they gravitate (where they tend to be, and to be oriented), when relatively free to choose what they do. We will come shortly to how people act socially in work environments, where they use media but may lack control over the particular media platforms they use.

'Where We Are' Through Media

It is a measure of how much has changed in the relations between media and space that we even feel the need to ask a question about 'where people are' with and through media. In the era of modern media before the past eight to ten years with its wave of digitalization – when hundreds of millions of people across the planet became used to continuous fast internet connection within the media manifold – *we were where our bodies were*, plain and simple, situated within the social context where our bodies were set: at work or in our bedroom, at school, in a factory or office. Maybe we would have had media on in the background, or would have been using media as an occasional tool to find something out that we could put to use in our immediate context; maybe we would have been consuming (or, if we were a media professional, producing) media content in a focused way. True, we already knew by the early 2000s that mobile phone use could cause a layering of places and localities that was sometimes problematic (Moores, 2004, drawing on Schlegloff, 2002), but when the mobile phone call ended, so did the problem. Immersive games through computer-based interfaces (Turkle, 1996) were already a first indication of a broader transformation: the possibility of seeming to be 'somewhere else' although situated, through our bodies, in a particular place. But games have always been a special domain of social life and, except in pathological cases, their liminal status is not generally assumed to affect the normal flow of everyday interaction.

Within, however, a context of deep mediatization and the media manifold it *is* meaningful to ask 'where people are' with and through media, whether they are sitting in a classroom, an auditorium, a café or a park. Even if they are not immersed in games, they may be involved through media in a significant number of non-playful interactions with distant others. People may be visible to *many* distant others – or watching *many* distant others while remaining invisible themselves – through their relation to interactive spaces where a large number of things are going on, some involving them and some not. People may be commenting on things going on (on Twitter, Facebook, a chat stream, email) in 'live' interaction spaces involving a stream of others, but with traditional media content (say, a downloaded TV programme) watched in the background. They may have various feeds coming in from a range of sources, hooking them temporarily into new interactions. It is still possible of course for someone to be watching a live broadcast TV programme or reading an online newspaper intensely, but many of those will simultaneously be following one or more streams of commentary *around* that media content on other media.[5]

As a result, the primary 'where' of the social world may, for many people, be shifting *over* to the sites sustained by media platforms and people's interactions with and across them, as well as to a general orientation towards an expanded set of online information and personal encounters. As a result (as Sanyang Zhao notes), the boundary between the private embodied 'here' of the computer, tablet or phone user and the public 'out there' of the audience for a particular communication may be blurred, weakening our sense of an offline world which is *not part* of the online world, and irreducible to it. Spaces of work and spaces of family interaction are two good places to look for detailed examples.

Mediated Workplaces and Intimate Life

In working environments, extensions of everyday social interaction may change some of the mutualities built into face-to-face interaction. This may lead to problems of reciprocity, responsibility and mutual visibility: so Heath and Hindmarsh (2000) argue in a study of working environments that depended on the heavy use of screens linking to remote spaces. The resulting 'disconnection between action, object and environment' (2000, p. 102) may, they argue, undermine the assumption of *reciprocal substitutability of perspectives* that for Schutz was essential to the face to face, yet these working environments have to be managed and lived through somehow, so workarounds and repairs develop.

The consequences of such extensions are likely to be complex. Take the case of telemedicine, where the spatial reorganization of the people, resources and information flows in the complex process of caring for patients at a physical distance leads, according to one writer (Nicolini, p. 2007), not just to a spatial extension, but to a change *in the meaning* of the process. There are shifts in authority and legitimacy, which have to be managed by the actors, and 'an expansion [. . .] of what it means to care for distant patients' (2007, p. 915). The medical practice in question has been 'stretched out': 'when extended in space and time, medical practices are put under pressure in that some of the existing taken for granted assumptions and practical arrangements become unsuitable for the new conditions of work' (Nicolini, 2007, p. 891). So for example the informal and partly improvised exchanges of expertise normal on the hospital ward-round need to be newly configured, with a new distribution of roles in the figurations' actor-constellations, when human and non-human members of the therapeutic team (doctors, nurses, administrators, measuring devices, etc.) are placed in multiple locations. The outcomes may well be positive for some actors; for example, carving out a space of autonomy for the nurse which did not exist on the ward round.

The everyday reliance in many types of work on distributed information systems (for example, the so-called ERP or 'Enterprise Resource Planning' system) is one example whose consequences cannot be understood phenomenologically if we think about one situated context (Campagnolo et al., 2015). It is necessary also to consider how various actors, coordinating across multiple sites, are enabled to co-orient themselves to a reality that is distant *from all of them*, through a process that Schutz and Luckmann called 'appresentation', that is, the perception of something 'as present when we have no original experience of it' (see Campagnolo et al., 2015, discussing Schutz and Luckmann, 1973).

In the sphere of political 'work', there are also examples of the positive extension of the political process, as when situations online generate new possibilities of action. An interesting example was the political campaign that emerged around a YouTube video portraying a protest against corruption in Mexico in 2012; it showed 131 protesters challenging a Mexican minister after the government had dismissed the corruption and protest as of no consequence. When new people started adding the comment on YouTube 'I am number 132' ('Yo soy #132'), this led to a campaign with that name (Gómez García and Treré, 2014). Here the extension of political process, drawing in actors across a large nation in a chain of communication and affirmation, depended on the flexible (because indexical) reference point of the Twitter hashtag: a new figuration of action emerged, based on the simple grammar of repetitive textual practice across a distributed platform. No distortions or stretching out of space seemed to be involved. Rather, this was a new type of action, although the grammar was limited to an additive one: it was not possible to do more than add one's name, for example by commenting on the complexity of the case or related injustices. Sadly, the surveillance structure of digital space made participants in this network subsequently vulnerable to government spying and the capture of their data (Treré, 2015), a point to which we return later.

The transformation of work practices by media technologies has parallels in family practice. First of all, the distribution of media use and degrees of online connectivity becomes a key factor in the structuring of family living-space, giving new meaning to the organization of the space of the home (Bengtsson, 2006). On the face of it, extended communication and money transfer networks allow family relations to be maintained at new distances to the benefit of all concerned. Media anthropologists (Madianou and Miller, 2012) and the media sociologist Jack Qiu (2009) argue this for extended families of migrant workers in the Philippines and China respectively.[6] Even for families who are not always stretched out across space, ICT and mobile media enable them to coordinate their activities, and their thoughts and intimacies, while their spatial trajectories are temporarily dispersed (Wajcman et al., 2008; Green, 2002). The contemporary figurations of families can maintain a 'connected presence' (Licoppe, 2004) even across complex spatial schedules: in that sense the family becomes a 'distributed family' (Christensen, 2009). In a corollary of the point about the extension in space of social actors' *Mitwelt*, our closest and most familiar consociates (family) can now *perform that role* continuously in time in spite of physical separation (Christensen, 2009, p. 445). This tendency of apparently de-spatializing technologies to *reinforce* close ties, not diffuse them, was already noted for the landline phone in the early twentieth century (Fischer, 1992). The role that continuous online chat forums play in linking generations within a family is also significant. It is not trivial when a sick elderly relative can be 'present' at a wedding through interaction on Facetime: the boundaries of the ritual space have been extended, allowing 'family' to be performed in a new way. But whether these various forms of intensified ties are overall positive for families is a much more complex question: Christensen already noted the 'dual role' of media technologies in 'both integrating and dispersing families' (2009, p. 439). Insightful work on Cameroonian migrants also suggests a different outcome: 'experiences and expressions of pressure, compulsions and expectations', because they cannot be fulfilled (perhaps when those at a distance lack the time and money to maintain support), may lead to the 'disintegration of relationships' (Tazanu, 2012, p. 259).

For young people who either still live with their families or have left home but are looking for relationships, media have transformed friendship and peer relations just as profoundly as in families if not more so. Here too it is a mistake to think that the *potential* extension of friendship relationships to larger scales has been the dominant change, when more important is the intensified *maintenance* of friendships across space. For young people of school age in richer countries, still under full parental and school control, the ability to maintain continuous exchange and conversation with their friends and peers while remaining in the confines of their bedrooms or while travelling to and from school, is a major extension of not just their sociality but also their sense of the *space* where their lives play out. The closed bedroom door is no longer a protective wall around solitude or isolated absorption in an imaginative world through media; it is a wall that guards the entry-point *back out* into the world of peer interchange that had stopped at the front door.

danah boyd's (2014) authoritative study of US youth's use of online media is clear about the importance of the extended spaces of agency and sociality that social media platforms provide, but also about how they bring additional pressures, strains and responsibilities: subtle new distinctions may emerge within the 'space' of social media platforms, for example between the 'publicly private' and the 'privately public' (Lange, 2007). Extending the space (and time) when peer pressure can be communicated and modulated increases the scope of mutual surveillance or co-veillance (Andrejevic, 2008). In a number of countries a rise in bullying is a concern of policymakers and educationalists: it may not be accidental that in a recent international survey the two countries where young people were most unhappy (the UK and South Korea) were also the countries in that sample with most intense connectivity.[7] Such problems, and the accompanying benefits, matter because they transform relations of meaning, as Mexican researcher Rosalia Winocur makes clear: 'it is not digital convergence in itself that provokes the transformations in the realms of society and communication, but the way in which its possibilities are *imaginatively transposed* into the diverse socio-cultural conditions of young people's everyday lives [. . .] [by] the *confluence of meaning* that it organizes' (Winocur, 2009, p. 184, added emphasis).

For young people who are seeking new friends, whether to find company with peer-types not available in their normal milieu, or, if a little older, to find romantic partners, media act as a clear extension of the space where connections can be made, public presence achieved or experimented with, and identity performed. This extended space may be of particular importance for those whose sexual identity and its performance is discouraged or punished in public space, such as young gay or lesbian people living in conservative rural America (Gray, 2012). And even later in life, long-interrupted friendship or acquaintances can be revived more reliably and effectively than was possible before the age of social media platforms through the use of social networks.

So is the following recent story from a Spanish newspaper typical, or precisely exceptional and so in need of advertorial puff?

> She is from a village where he used to spend all his summers ([name of village], 2360 inhabitants), one of those places where people greet each other in the street and hang out together in the same bars, shops and plazas as each other. But they didn't meet there, but in the world's most populated country: Facebook.[8]

It is not easy to separate out the actual degree of change here from the hype. But the fact that major extensions in the modalities of possible sociality are under way is beyond doubt.

More Complex Transformations

So far we have discussed the increasingly complex spatiality of figurations such as the family and groups of co-workers. But media transform interdependencies also on higher levels of organizational complexity, for example, within figurations of figurations.

On this scale, technologically based communication media enable entirely new *types* of work-space and work-relation, and so help sustain new practices of work. Karin Knorr-Cetina's pioneering studies of the global financial market start out from Schutz's reflections on shared worlds of work, with their intense sense of special time and common focus. While for Schutz such shared focus required physical co-presence, this is no longer the case, as the case of global financial markets shows. Screens that present a filtering of multiple streams of events, data and actions marshalled into a continuous ordered flow of 'information' can provide the shared focus of attention for micro-interactions among actors in multiple locations, bringing 'the territorially distant and invisible "near" to participants, rendering it interactionally or response-present' (Knorr-Cetina and Bruegger, 2002, p. 392). Knorr-Cetina calls these distinctive types of media, which depend not just on networked screens but on a huge *background* computing power to process and sort data from many sources, 'scopic media': through their concentrated action, they enable new, shared acts of seeing (from the Greek word *skopein*). As she writes, 'scopic media visually present and project events, phenomena, and actors that would otherwise be separated by distance and would not be visible from a single standpoint' (Knorr-Cetina, 2014, p. 43). The result is a transformation of what counts *as reality* for the thousands of actors involved: 'the screen is not simply a "medium" for the transmission of messages and information. It is *a building site on which a whole economic and epistemological world is erected*' (Knorr-Cetina and Bruegger, 2002, p. 395). The force which scopic media have depends not just however on the infrastructure of transmission but also on the *claim* of comprehensiveness made on behalf of what is brought together through that transmission: they '[stitch] together an analytically constituted *world* made up of "everything" potentially relevant to the interaction' (Knorr-Cetina, 2014, p. 48, added emphasis). The result is the creation of a new space not just of vision, but of *action*.

While the scopic media of the global financial markets seem a special case, because of their extremely high levels of technological infrastructure, geographical span and intensity of time-interactions, it is not hard to find other, less extreme, examples of how, through the reliable concentration of technological media to focus a particular type of *attention*, the centre of gravity of social interaction shifts. Locative media may become embedded in collective behaviour, but always against the background of distinctive cultural norms and histories. So Hjorth and Gu (2012) write about the use of the locative platform Jiepang in Shanghai (a platform similar to the US Foursquare) and argue that, given the very different cultural attitudes to privacy in China from in the USA or Europe, the platform enables a form of social coordination across space: 'the key motivation is to both see where their friends are and report on new "cool" places' (Hjorth and Gu, 2012, p. 704). 'It's like a diary with location', one 25-year-old woman they interviewed said, but of course a diary that is continuously available to a distributed group (2012, p. 755). A great deal of complex variation lies behind the term 'infrastructure': the affordances of particular technologies such as mobile phones may be experienced very differently on the ground in different places, depending on economic, regulatory and cultural circumstances, since 'infrastructure' is a 'dynamic process that is simultaneously made and unmade' (Horst, 2013, p. 151).

Yet such enhancements of local information can induce an intensified 'parochialization', as people are encouraged to link up with those who are physically very close to them, but based on a proximity encountered not through ordinary social interaction, but through an institutional push ('X is near you right now'), leading even to a 'social molecularization', rather than an enriched appreciation of social space.[9] There are counter-examples of course: for example, artistic projects that draw on the enhanced place- and information-coordination possible through digital platforms to generate new forms of awareness of the spatial regularities of city life that are largely hidden, because they are not 'seen together'. A fine example is the Barcelona art project called Canal Accessible, which asked disabled people to identify via their phones physical obstacles they encountered as they tried to move across the city.[10] Media are then involved in multiple types of 'scopic regime', more or less intense and integrated, and with many varied consequences for how their users are embedded 'in' space.

Perhaps there is a general paradox here. As Hartmut Rosa suggests (2013, p. 101), by being more connected through digital media, we may become more self-sufficient in any one place, and so less *in need* of mobility. But since face-to-face communication time still counts for a lot, this paradox is probably more apparent than real. It is also misleading to see all these transformations as only involving space: the trajectory of all these transformations is, after all, not to enhance mobility for its own sake, but to increase people's capacity *to act*. We start to see here the importance of the myths, discussed in general terms at the end of the last chapter, which hold beliefs in such possibilities of coordinated action 'in place'. Those myths may however be very much at odds with a deeper *differentiation* in people's powers to act that continues in spite of, indeed reinforced by, technologies' role in extending communications in space. Most obvious are differences between women and men. Whereas marketing for smartphones always emphasizes their power to coordinate lives for anyone (man or woman), it is generally women for whom technologies of communication lead their family pressures to spill over into the work space (Chesley, 2005), while it is particularly men's work pressures that spill over into the family space, reproducing a very old division of domestic labour (Wajcman, 2015) in which women have, by default, the primary responsibility for domestic labour and caring, including any unexpected demands.

Meanwhile, other communications infrastructures – figurations of figurations – sustain new everyday spaces of interaction. By contrast with the augmented reality of locative media, which tend to benefit individual actors in particular ways, social media platforms can, in general terms, work as a space to act together and in concert, a collectively identified space of encounter and action (boyd, 2014, p. 39). As boyd argues, the key contribution of social network sites, at least for young people in the USA, is not to extend the range of *people* with whom they interact (an extension of existing interactions), but rather to provide an otherwise unavailable space *of action*, a new centre of gravity, as it were, that was not there before and which escapes the control of parents and so potentially reshapes the symbolic organization of everyday life (boyd, 2014, pp. 55–57).

It is tempting to read these transformations as involving solely the extension, via transmission, of communicative relations in space (and time). Facebook indeed makes sense this way, because it allows extended exchanges between those who have previously been in contact, or who can readily imagine being in contact with each other. Other platforms such as Twitter are however very different. One does not have to be a celebrity used to communicating to a mass audience to end up interacting with people one does not know at all: people who have retweeted or commented on something one has posted. Indeed, Twitter, although experienced as a space of exchange, is not a space at all but a *presentation* of linked data in a continuous flow that creates the illusion of a space for direct exchange. Yet, unlike in a physical space, ordinary users of Twitter cannot know or imagine the set of texts potentially relevant to them that are *not* presented in that flow. The 'space' in which they act is therefore shaped by the selective productions of software and data processing: it is, as Zizi Papacharissi puts it, 'an algorithmically rendered materiality' for the social (2015, p. 119). It is time then to turn to software's implications for social space more generally.

5.3 Software and Social Space

A materialist phenomenology cannot avoid the challenge of thinking about how the experience of social space is now being transformed by the embedding of ICTs and data processes of deep mediatization. This is happening in fundamental ways never envisaged by classical phenomenology. Social space is being transformed by the ability of unseen others (or unseen systems) to *see us* from a variable distance, whether we are stationary or moving around. This is not, as in science fiction, because we literally carry cameras on our bodies, but because software allows the textual and image traces we leave online, and the data derived from them, to be captured remotely and made available for further exchange and processing.

We need to consider cases where new types of trans-spatial encounter change our possibilities for *performing* self within an enlarged horizon of visibility, that is, both in front of others we do not and cannot know (Brighenti, 2007; Voirol, 2005) and for continued mobile contact with those we know and care about. It is impossible to live on a permanent and boundless stage: in the film *The Truman Show*, Truman only survived as long as he didn't *know* his world was a stage. So there may in all this be an intensified need to *maintain* boundaries around the interactions with loved ones we want to protect. Our continuous, if unwitting, 'transmission' via the GPS function of our mobile communication devices, creates new issues about social order and the legitimacy of surveillance. As Mark Andrejevic puts it, the new 'revelatory role of location' (2014), based on data transmission, takes the risks of 'public' space to a quite different level.

Meanwhile, as a number of geographers have shown, the spaces of ordinary locations – or at least the spaces many take for 'ordinary' such as airport lounges and supermarkets – are deepened through the operation of software, which enables new types of movement by some agents while restricting that of others. As Kirchin and Dodge note, there are now many spaces (so-called 'code/spaces') that are constituted only and entirely through the operation of software: 'space is not simply a container in which things happen; rather, spaces are subtly evolving layers of context and practices that fold together people and things and *actively shape* social relations', such as the airport security zone (Kitchin and Dodge, 2011, p. 13, added emphasis). The embedding of software in the organization of everyday life (Thrift and French, 2002, pp. 232, 309) is of even wider importance, but it is less clear whether it shows that space is *changing as such*, or rather that actions in, and mobility across, the social world are increasingly subject to *differentiating control* through ever more discriminating software systems. Such discriminatory control affects physical movement – the system that decides whether a particular passport holder is able to leave her or his country, or arrive in another (Amoore, 2013) – but it can segregate and order non-physical spaces: the system that rejects one's credit card as one sits in a restaurant waiting to pay. Either way, the action-space of everyday reality (and the institutional decision-space built around everyday life) is now increasingly 'software-sorted' (Graham, 2005). This has implications, directly, for how urban and other spaces *feel*: we may become aware of a 'splintering' (Graham and Marvin, 2001) of the urban which operates by principles that are not visible, and indeed not directly accessible, to individual actors.

We can go further. The spatial conditions of self-formation in everyday reality are changing significantly. Everyday space in the digital era is not just mediated but 'networked', that is, its action-possibilities are structured by the hierarchical and differentiating work of informational networks. A space where your Wi-Fi password works is a different action-space from one where it does not; a system which only allows you limited access and action-options is very different from one which allows you full access and freedom to act. As a result, just beneath the spatial surface of everyday reality are developing new topologies: networks that link one set of persons into certain possibilities for action, but *cut off* another set of persons from those same possibilities.[11] Such implications are relevant to the consideration of the self to which we come in Chapter 8 and are themselves in need of a more extended treatment of the implications of 'data' for materialist phenomenology (Chapter 7). First, however, we must move to some concomitant transformations of social time in the era of deep mediatization.

6

Time

It is through time that we grasp the process of everyday life. Time, whatever particular forms it takes, is a fundamental dimension of life. We understand this directly when we consider that to have one's life spatially confined may still be consistent with a possible 'good life', whereas to have one's life cut short is, except in cases of extreme suffering, an absolute loss.[1] Life *is* the process of living forward *in time.*[2] This chapter will however be concerned less with the sense of inner time that each of us has, and more with the social aspects of time, that is, time as a dimension of the social world.

When we consider time in the social world, we cannot ignore space. We have already emphasized this at the beginning of the last chapter, where we quoted Henri Lefebvre's definition of social space as 'a relation between things [. . .] [that] encompasses their interrelationships in their existence *and their simultaneity*' (1991, p. 73, added emphasis). The possibility of distant things being in a relationship to each other continuously, at each *moment in time*, is the reason why we must think relationally about social space, as we did in the last chapter. Time is not just extended duration but involves relations of *simultaneity* across *space*. That is why, as one of the leading UK analysts of people's experience of time-pressure notes, 'coordination is as much about space as it is about time' (Southerton, 2003, p. 23). Time – the experience of time moment-by-moment – is therefore, in this sense, the vehicle through which individuals experience the *relatedness* of life, the costs and benefits of such relatedness, and the connection between such relatedness and the underlying organization of space. Figurations will, as we shall see, be a particularly important entry-point for grasping how such relatedness is sustained and managed through media.

Time has always, in part, been imagined in terms of relations. Religious concepts of time, as ways of thinking about the relatedness of all things and beings, continue to be important today. So, when Evangelical Christians in the UK seek to challenge the fragmentation of a secular modern urban life, they ask 'what time is it?' (Engelke, 2013, pp. 20–21). Particularly important for our discussions of media and information infrastructures is the modern concept of clock time (Benjamin, 1968; Thompson, 1967). Clock time matters for our understanding of *media's* relations to time for three reasons. First, this is because media institutions (like other institutions) operate in accordance with clock time. Second, because media are one of the most important institutions for reinforcing our awareness of the passing of clock time: for example, radio stations announce the time throughout the day and news websites generally have an embedded clock. Third, because media, as the primary modern means for focusing the attention of large dispersed populations around shared reference-points, are part of the infrastructure of time, with interpersonal media such as the mobile phone extending the domestication of timekeeping in new ways (Ling, 2012, chs. 3 and 7). In this respect, media are concrete means by which the inherently *social* basis of time-differentiation (Durkheim, 1995 [1912], pp. 9–10, 353–354) is worked through in practice. For all these reasons, major changes in the way that media bind space together are likely also to have major consequences for the objective and subjective aspects of time. This was the lesson of important research into nineteenth-century transformations in communications technologies (Beniger, 1986), and it is equally relevant today.

Time – in the sense of simultaneity-across-space – is part of what media institutions *sustain*. Media and information infrastructures have long been involved in marking the passing of life's socially recognized stages and events. Indeed that may be one of their more important roles, as Paddy Scannell (1989) was one of the first to point out. It is generally accepted that 'modern technologies of communication' are 'changing the human perception of time' (Nowotny, 1994, p. 8). However, to understand fully the role of changing media and information infrastructures for the social world we have to go further in times of deep mediatization. Time may be one key way in which media can *disrupt* the embedding of the individual in our increasingly complex social world. Time, felt as a sense of necessary interrelation and obligated connectedness, may not always be compatible with the sense of time as duration that we might want to sustain for ourselves and our loved ones. Time is therefore intimately connected with the *compatibility* between lived experience and social relations, that is, with the *sustainability* of what in Chapter 1 we called 'figurational order'. That is the importance of phenomenology's insistence on understanding the social world from the starting-point of reciprocal obligations: the importance of time for sociological analysis is missed entirely if we start from the premise that relations with others are merely options for an isolated consciousness.

In his book *Social Acceleration*, Hartmut Rosa (2013, p. 28) proposes that time plays an even more decisive role than space in the shaping of modernity, because the spatial aspects of everyday life are more fixed and inflexible, whereas the temporal dimensions are more fluid. As already argued, time and space cannot be analysed in separation from each other, at least when we think of time as simultaneity-across-space. Nor is it necessarily helpful to characterize temporal relations as more fluid than spatial relations. But Rosa points us towards something important. Time, because of its intrinsic relation to consciousness, is an *inherent* dimension of action, and of communicative action in particular. While a conversation's basic nature and meaning is unchanged by being sent across distance, for example by telephone, it *is* changed by being elongated in time: silence is eloquent. Communication, in other words, always depends on a continuous unfolding of time for its enactment, whereas communication does not depend, in general, for its enactment on a continuous movement across space.

As a result, the relations of space and time to power are not the same. We can sometimes feel immune from spatial power (that is, power over space): we often only discover spatial power when we try to move from one place to another and find ourselves blocked. But wherever we are, we can never feel immune from temporal power (power over time), since it is implied within communication itself ('you will do this *now, later etc.*'): perhaps drugs are the only release from our sense of onward time (time-pressure being a common theme of anxious dreams), but it is temporary at best.

Put more formally, time is the principal dimension along which social order itself is worked out through communication, the only limits being its acceptance by people across space as an exercise of power from somewhere else. The normative force of figurations – and figurations of figurations – is therefore worked out *in time* and cannot be understood without consideration of how meaning unfolds in time. For this reason, time is a key dimension of how communications are involved in the construction of the social world. Time is the dimension where we see a social life's 'figurational order' put to the test.

In this chapter, we will give emphasis to certain tendencies of time-pressure that are based in the potentially global connective infrastructure of the internet (and the data processes associated with the internet), but have their prominence, for sure, not everywhere, but in particular rich countries and among other countries' elites. We are not claiming that these tendencies are, or are destined to be, universal, or that the internet is the only factor today shaping the figurational orders of the social world (once again, we take seriously the critique of media-centrism).[3]

6.1 Media and the Temporality of the Social World

It is worth at this point going back to Schutz. Schutz's understanding of the social world begins from the experience of intersubjectivity: the necessity of being 'oriented' towards others. Schutz (in his solo writings at least) insists that 'communicative action also implies some kind of anticipation of the other's understanding of one's action' (Knoblauch, 2013a, p. 331, 332); this in turn implies a shared time in which understanding can be achieved and worked through in time (Knoblauch, 2013a, pp. 333–334). Elsewhere, Schutz acknowledges the variable role of communications technologies in maintaining such simultaneity in spite of (perhaps increasing) physical distance:

> Depending on the state of communications technology, the symptoms whereby the other is apprehended can decrease while the synchronization of the streams of consciousness can still, to a certain extent, be maintained. (Schutz and Luckmann, 1973, p. 90)

Schutz here provides the beginning of an insight into time-relations as a key focus for understanding our obligations of reciprocity, and their potential vulnerability to technological change.

Luckmann later acknowledged that 'abstract social categories of time' which operationalize individuals' sense of time can organize social interactions 'in total disregard of the rhythms of inner time' that get synchronized when two individuals are in direct face-to-face interaction (Luckmann, 1991, p. 158). But in Luckmann's discussion it is hard to see beyond this clash between these two types of time-organization, 'abstract' and 'inner': there is no sense of how time works to *organize* the social world in a broader way, including by the deep embedding of external coordination *into* the fabric of individual lives. Indeed there is a bias in Luckmann's approach towards the dynamics of inner time and the synchronization of the inner times of face-to-face interlocutors and interactors rather than the broader dynamics of *social* coordination and control through a socially sustained sense of time.[4] Was this view ever plausible, for example, in the early stages of Western modernity? We doubt it, but certainly it has absolutely no plausibility in an age when the rhythms and categories of media's operations play a major role in social coordination. It is important to be clear about the difference that media and communications infrastructures make here.

Media make time concrete: individual time, social time, and the reference-points (for example, time-measurement) on which both individual and social time are based. Therefore, media are 'social metronomes of the everyday' (Neverla, 2010, p. 183). As a result, media provide a focus for new ways of systematizing and regulating the social world: with mobile phones enabling new practices of micro-coordination.[5] Media therefore play a key role in establishing and instantiating the 'system of tensions' in society (Elias, 1994 [1939], p. 32), with social media platforms intensifying this process massively.[6] For Elias, the sustaining across ever larger spaces of a *shared* sense of time was the entry-point for grasping how modernity itself evolved as an ever larger system of interdependence and obligation. Elias' discussion of 'tempo' is vivid:

> This 'tempo' is in fact nothing other than a manifestation of the multitude of intertwining chains of interdependence which run through every single social function people have to perform [. . .] the tempo is an expression of the multitude of interdependent actions, of the length and density of the chains composed by the individual actions, and of the intensity of the struggles that keep this whole interdependent network in motion. [. . .] a function situated at a junction of so many chains of action demands an *exact allocation of time*; it makes people accustomed to subordinating momentary inclinations to the *overriding necessities* of interdependence; it trains them to eliminate all irregularities from behaviour and to achieve permanent self-control. (Elias, 1994 [1939], p. 457, added emphasis)

A dense network of connection exacts its 'price' in individuals' felt obligation to manage themselves *in time*. From Elias' great insight, the contemporary social theorist Hartmut Rosa has developed a theory of late modernity as an age of intensified 'social acceleration'. We will come to details of Rosa's thesis later, but its core is that, with deep mediatization through the acceleration of technologically based communications and many other processes, an increasing gulf emerges between our *space of experience* and our *horizon of expectation* (2013, p. xxxvi, drawing on Kosseleck, 2004 [1979], ch. 14).[7] For Rosa, the 'temporal structures' of any society have huge consequences for its members' possible ways of life. The reason for this is that 'temporal structures and horizons represent one, if not the, systematic link between actor and system perspectives' (2013, p. 4). Rosa's extension of Elias' work is both plausible and important. A similar sense of the importance of time in constructing social order is found in Niklas Luhmann's work. Luhmann pointed out the special role that time plays in the weighting of activities against each other, and even, potentially, in 'confound[ing] the order of values' (Luhmann, 1994 [1968],

p. 143). Temporal structures then, as Elias discovered, have a 'normaliz*ing* character' because they create a frame in which local coordination is not optional but necessary, if wider coordination is not to break down: they provide in this way a privileged point for grasping *overall* patterns of order and disorder.

From here, we can directly see the importance of media's relations to time within the mediated construction of reality.[8] Yet the media manifold and the particular figurations embedded within it arguably lead to distinctive types of time-pressure, more intense than any Elias envisaged.

The Distinctiveness of Simultaneity in an Age of Deep Mediatization

We noted, in the last chapter, media institutions' historic role in sustaining ever larger collectivities' sense of togetherness and practical coordination across space. Because of the interlocking of space and time, we could just as readily insist that media institutions have for a long time played a key role in sustaining spatially bounded collectivities in time (Scannell, 1989; Carey, 1989). There are some distinctive features of how today, with deep mediatization, media and information infrastructures sustain relations of co-consciousness (as Schutz would put it) across space *and* time. First, they do so between *any one point and any other*, since the building of internet access into many mobile phones and devices means that simultaneity need not be orchestrated only from an institutional centre of production: I can draw you and others into continuously tracking me simply by uploading to a digital platform a picture of what I have just done in a different continent, although in doing so I am of course relying on an infrastructure that depends on many networked concentrations of resource. Second, *transmission* speeds are close to instantaneous, whatever the size of content transmitted. This does not lead to the erasure of time *as experienced*, but, quite the contrary, to a growing sensitivity to the 'little temporal differences' (Nowotny, 1994, p. 10): we notice (and often judge negatively) when an SMS or chat message goes unanswered for some hours, or when an email goes unanswered for a day. Third, there seems in principle no limit to how much the size of transmitted *content* can go on growing, even if, at a certain point, speed of transmission becomes for most purposes instantaneous, which implies that the burden of interpreting and processing content *received* from co-conscious interactors can also grow without limit.

Two decades ago Paul Virilio prophetically expressed the resulting superfluity of information as 'the generalized arrival of data' (1997, p. 56). The relative acceleration of digital information transmission means that, rather than actors relying on moving themselves or their objects across space, they may stay in the same place and access information about most things where they are: the importance of the space in-between seems erased (Tomlinson, 2007, pp. 90–91). But the outcome is certainly not a *universal* sense of acceleration. Not only do people react against acceleration (as they perceive it), but intensified flows of communication lead to breakdowns of figurations and new forms of inertia or slowed-down reaction (Rosa, 2013, p. 80; Wajcman, 2015). Meanwhile, our access to the past is changed by the expansion of information available in and across 'the present'. Does this undermine the uni-linear nature of temporal development, as Rosa claims (2013, p. 102)? We would prefer to say more modestly that we inhabit a social world characterized by the pluralization of temporalities, on the one hand, and the complexification of technological systems for the coordination of temporality, on the other.

Certainly, the range of interlocking forces pushing the social world towards ever greater temporal coordination – often locally felt as acceleration – is formidable: competitive economic pressures, cultural pressures, and socio-structural pressures, each of them intensifying one or more moments in the underlying 'circle' of seeming social acceleration. That 'circle' itself, according to Rosa, can be broken down into three elements: technical acceleration, acceleration of the pace of life, and acceleration of social change and the perception of social change. The key point is that the circle of influences that *reinforce* the experience of social acceleration is 'largely immune to individual attempts to interrupt it' (Rosa, 2013, p. 153). Put another way, time is involved not just in the relations through which figurations, and figurations of figurations, are built, but also, more widely, in the construction and sustaining of a wider *figurational order* (see Chapter 4) which is *not* directly accessible to individual adjustment. Figurational order (to recall Chapter 1) involves large-scale *ways of organizing things in time* (*meta*-processes), which no actor can challenge without undermining the practicality of cooperation itself (something no one wants to undermine). Media and information infrastructures therefore achieve more than 'technical acceleration', the accelerated transmission of information: they actually shape the figurations through which these intensified relations of interdependence are enacted, and so the possibilities of social order *through* figurations.

The outcome can seem to be a dramatic temporal dislocation: a world in which the demands of work and system, reliant on mediated systems of communication, spill out far beyond the normal boundaries on which everyday habits seem to be built. There are serious issues for work-related inequalities here, and more generally the result, some writers argue, is to damage the fabric of life itself. Media devices are one of the most vivid embodiments of the push towards constraint connectivity and 24/7 living. In Japan, rules of instant response around the friend-focused platform Mixi have taken the 'culture of instantaneity' (Tomlinson, 2007, p. 74) and the principle of constant connectivity (found in many cultures today)[9] to a high pitch of intensity: as a result, many young people sleep with their phones on or under their pillow (Takahashi, 2014, p. 188, 190, 194). Jonathan Crary writing from New York generalizes this phenomenon into a paradoxical '24/7' way of living which, because it can never be realized (human beings *have* to sleep in the end, or die), imposes an impossible injunction whose effectiveness 'lies in the *discrepancy* between [any actual] human life-world and the evocation of a switch-on universe for which no off-switch exists' (2013, p. 30, added emphasis). The crucial point however is that these processes are not simply processes of acceleration; they are instead intensifying figurations of *meaningful interdependence* whose medium is technologically based platforms of communication. That is why our sense of being 'harried' (under continuous pressure of time) is associated not so much with having less time, but with the problems of coordinated performance linked to the 'density of social practices' (Southerton and Tomlinson, 2005, p. 229).

Yet it is only apparently a paradox that these developments are described, and not just by marketers, as a form of freedom. For, if we understand freedom as a complex social achievement of collaborative interdependence, then as Claus Offe once noted, 'the more options we open up for ourselves, the less available as an option is the institutional framework itself with the help of which we disclose them' (Offe, 1987, p. 9). The injunction towards constant connectivity is part of that 'institutional framework'. Because in democratic societies, at least, we start by resisting the idea that we are unfree, it requires considerable work to expose this authoritarianism to view, as something we must confront and change (Cohen, 2011, pp. 188–189). Elias' concept of figurations however helps us see this infrastructure as a process of emerging interdependence that actively shapes our very possibilities for action and imagination. At the core of such processes of interdependence are changing forms of media and communications.

Media and the Changing 'Speed' of Social Development

Before we elaborate that broader point, let's make a more basic point about how we understand the mediated construction of time. Time-relations are socially constructed. The point is not just that what counts as time is socially constructed (Durkheim, 1995 [1912], p. 9), but that what is measured together as *continuous* time is also constructed. According to Roberto Cipriani, '[t]he question of time is centred on a series of relations' in terms of how two or more events are conceived as constituting some sort of series (2013, p. 14). Cipriani quotes Elias: 'clocks certainly help us to measure something: nevertheless, this something is not exactly time, which is invisible, but something which is very tangible like the length of a working day or the eclipse of the moon, or the speed of an athlete who runs the 100 meters.' The spatial extensions of our social world through social media platforms also change the durations and sequences that are considered measurable (the 'time' of a Facebook newsfeed is one very recent, but now pervasive, construction of sequence).

In addition, the individual experience of time is constructed through the figurations in which we are involved. With the change of media and information infrastructures these figurations have also changed, transforming the temporal dimension of the social world and the positioning of the individual in it. Media, through their role in enabling new, ever more stretched-out, figurations of figurations, have changed the ways in which (the *gearing* through which) particular forms of accelerated process are interlinked with other forms. This affects the overall speed at which our social sense of time seems to be transformed.[10]

In Elias' analysis, a new tempo of the social world developed historically over several generations, emerging gradually through felt contradictions between prior habitus and emerging social pressures: such a contradiction might occur over time, over the life course of each individual, but the social response only takes shape in new cultural guidelines that require generations to develop (Dolan, 2010, p. 9). But with the embedding of norms from social media platforms into daily life we may be witnessing a faster transformation, over a single decade, with implications for *intra*generational as well as *inter*generational relations (Rosa, 2013, p. 110).

Not that those changes are felt evenly across space; everything depends on the organization of practice. As some sociologists note, 'temporal scales are institutionalized through the production and reproduction of [. . .] practices', for example in organizations and professional environments, generating distinctive 'temporal orientations' (Karasti et al., 2010, p. 384). In the next section on media's detailed consequences for changing forms of temporal order, we need to bear in mind both universalizing pressures and how people are differentiated precisely in terms of their time practices, and their relative resources for controlling those practices.

6.2 Losing Time and Making Value

So far our comments have been generalized, designed to get into view some features of contemporary populations' relations with time through media. As noted in Chapter 5, there is no way of offering a general account of infrastructure from an abstract 'nowhere', since infrastructures of connection work very differently in different places, and the consequences for time are no exception. Indeed time is itself an infrastructure socially constructed from many different sources.

In this section, we want to consider in more detail the changing practices whereby people are *in time*, and media's role in sustaining those temporal relations. We should bear in mind the consequences for the social world of the shift in the balance in communication from the face to face to the spatially dispersed and non-synchronous. The same shift might also be expressed in terms of a transition (Ellison, 2013) from a world dominated by 'thick' time in which actions are embedded in contextual sequences that have clear relations to each other and to specific time-sequences, versus a world in which 'thin' time is more prominent, that is, an organization of time which provides fewer clear coordinates for action. As Ellison puts it: 'increasing instantaneity and simultaneity [. . .] can be associated [. . .] with a concept of thin time. [. . .] Owing to the complex ways in which time becomes packeted in the digital universe, individuals have to become accustomed to processing, communicating and acting on information across a wide range of "fields" literally "instantaneously" and "simultaneously"' (2013, p. 58). For sure, the consequences of accelerated communication are more complex than just a supplement or enhancement. As an Australian father of two young children interviewed by Melissa Gregg put it: '[we are] spending *less* awake time chatting to each other. We are *separate*' (2011, p. 135, added emphasis).

Time Deficits

In some media cultures there is a growing sense in everyday experience of a deficit of time: not ever having enough time to do what one has to do. The problem is much more than technological acceleration: it is a matter of the changing *interrelations* between economic, cultural and social practices, affecting actors of all sizes and on every level, and media and information infrastructures' changing involvement in *all* those interrelations. Indeed, because the internet is a *connective* space – its potential to connect is effectively unlimited – it amplifies this problem, without limit.

The individual actor may sense a contraction of the present. What we call 'the present' is not an objective measure of time, but our delineation of the everyday as a sphere of action and planning during which we are *entitled* to assume 'no further change'. Accelerated communications change the 'present' because they create pressures to bring forward the moment after which further change must be accommodated. This is the consequence not just of the acceleration of communications, but also an 'accelerated transformation' in 'the context of communication and action' (Rosa, 2013, p. 350 n8). Only within 'the present' can we draw conclusions based on experience 'to date' and so securely orient our actions; when the volume of signals incorporated into 'the present' increases, perhaps to an arbitrarily high level, social actors may have a problem, and may lose the capacity to react to communications.

An important way in which this happens is through 'multi-tasking'. The changing distribution of work across space increases possibilities for 'still doing' multiple tasks even if one has moved away from the location originally associated with that task. But if multi-tasking is facilitated by intensified communication-at-a-distance, it has a profound impact on our sense of 'the present'. It imports the time-signals and time-related obligations from multiple activities into a *single* time-flow. Little wonder then that one of Southerton and Tomlinson's UK respondents speaks wistfully of 'the most relaxing part of the day [when] I only have to do one thing' (2005, p. 235).

Absolute comparisons of speed of transmission and interaction are therefore only a small part of the story we need to consider. After all, speed only affects us if it requires an *adjustment* in our practice, and such a requirement is only registered at all if it appears within the matrix of practices in which we are engaged. Many increases of absolute speed are of no phenomenological concern to us, because they are black-boxed within our experience, or occur in domains of activity where we are not direct actors (for example, the increased speed of electricity distribution or of weapon launching). Where acceleration does concern us, our feeling for it depends on at least two things: the intensity of activity required from us and – depending on the first – the intensity of others' interactions with us that result. Since however our activities are generally meshed together within confined domains of, 'time–space packing' (Hagerstrand, 1975, discussed by Giddens, 1984, pp. 111–118) imposes *limits* upon the resulting acceleration of interactions, and may act as a break on how much faster accelerated possibilities for interaction actually *feel* to social actors.

While there are only so many bodies of a certain size that can fit into a finite space – there are certain natural limits to spatial packing, beyond which the attempt to pack just has to stop (otherwise, bodies get crushed) – the same is not true in time: there is *literally no limit* to how many messages, each sent in a non-synchronous mode, can 'be there together' in one's inbox, each requiring response 'now' across a range of communicative platforms. The situation is very different with white noise, where countless signals cancel each other out so that nothing distinct can be heard. The challenge of communication overload is that each message *can* be heard – as the carrier of a distinct meaning – yet it cannot be attended to, since the time required for doing so is lacking. In this way, contemporary arrangements for communication tend to generate *time-packing* demands on individuals, from moment-to-moment, which along with the related of communicative obligations they can never, in principle, fulfil.

Such multiple and impossible demands might not be problematic in 'thin time' where there is no wider normative framework for ordering action-sequences relative to each other. But they are deeply problematic in 'thick' time, or what Robert Hassan (2003, p. 233) calls 'network time', that is, 'digitally compressed clock-time' in which the temporal calibration of obligations within particular figurations is intensified. The contemporary workplace and the social relations of those periods of intense change in one's social networks (such as adolescence or early adulthood) are likely to be periods of 'thick time' when the burden of communicative obligations left unfulfilled due to time-deficits is felt more strongly (Turkle, 2011). Problems of coordination in periods of 'thick time' become potential problems for any wider figurational order.

Practices in Response

So far our analysis has been on a general level, but we need to approach these possibilities also from the perspective of particular practices. A number of practices (simple and complex) offer entry-points into such transformations.

One practice in everyday life, which seems to point in the opposite direction from time-deficits, is 'time-*deepening*'. By referring to time as 'deep', we mean here not to assert an actual dimension of time – time is not literally deep – but rather the experience, generated by the progressive acceleration of our obligations to interact, of having more to do, more ways in which we must be 'adequate', and more conflict between those increased obligations and our ability to meet them in the available time.

One digital media practice relevant here is *archiving*. We are, through digital infrastructures, archiving all sorts of information, images and other traces of life-processes more easily. As a result, photography becomes embedded as a social practice in new ways (van Dijck, 2007; Bowker, 2008; Christensen and Røpke, 2010). The wider implications are complex: greater *institutional* capacities of memory require improved means for interpreting and sorting the now vast piles of information that accumulate. Meanwhile, the difficulty of ruling out the possibility that some past incident will have been stored in some more or less embarrassing form – so that it can be released by someone at *some* future point – increases the risks for individuals and institutions of managing that uncertainty.

We may also feel time-related obligations to each other of a more complex sort. Think of today's frequent expectation of individuals that they will *keep all channels open* (Couldry, 2012), already hinted at in the discussion above of the problems of constant connectivity. We can now, if we wish, be permanently open (and potentially responsive) to content from all directions. Many writers see the practice (or even compulsion) of continuous connectivity as characteristic of the media generation that grew up with digital media (Bolin, 2014; Hepp et al., 2014, pp. 22–31; Palfrey and Gasser, 2008). Enabling us to be open on all channels in this way is part of the marketing promise of new portable interfaces such as the smartphone. While it is impossible to be open to everything, the demand to 'be available' shapes an emerging practice that is different from earlier modes of media consumption based on intermittent communication and a clear distinction between mass media and interpersonal media. Keeping all channels open means permanently orienting oneself to the world beyond one's private space, and the media circulated within it. It is against the background of this (previously impossible) standard that some people seek to *limit* their openness to communication, at least for certain purposes

In response to the new intensity of time-challenges received through media, we are developing practices of selection: processes by which we peremptorily *stop* doing certain things we always used to do; processes by which we drastically *select from* the environment with which we must interact in order to make it more manageable. Sherry Turkle's striking account (Turkle, 2011) of some of the drastic ways in which young people select *out* (*de*-select) the activity of *just talking* with their friends, because of the acute time–space-packing problems they face, is just one example of how the texture of everyday life may change quite drastically through indirect pressures of selection. In response to such pressures, we seek ways of 'selecting out' from our communication environment while maintaining the illusion that we are still fully connected. Selecting out is increasingly delegated to technological interfaces such as the smartphone, which offer gateways to media that are the result of intense prior selection. By choosing from a vast range of 'apps', people screen out much of the infinite media environment and create a 'chosen' interface that is both manageable and seemingly personal: this is the double level of the 'media manifold' in action. There is the potential here for our experiences to become fragmented,[11] but new forms of linking across disparate sites of experience are also developing. We are now sharing aspects of experience – images of special meals we have just eaten, selfies that record our presence at a location or with a person as we travel – in ways we did not do before.

One important selection practice is 'hiding out'. 'Hiding out' (being online while trying to disguise this from others, or avoiding using the phone for its primary use, speaking) is increasingly common in the USA. Sherry Turkle quotes a 21-year-old college student: 'I don't use my phone for calls any more. I don't have *the time* to just go on and on' (2011, p. 146, added emphasis). This, as Turkle sees, creates a paradox: infrastructures for enhancing interpersonal communication, through their built-in tendency to accelerate interaction, create time-deficits so severe that people have to *stop* communicating, at least directly (face to face), deferring 'full' communication so as to manage their time-deficit better. Hiding out then is part of a wider set of 'practices of demarcation', where people mark off space–times when they will *not* be connected to certain individuals, collectivities or organizations (Hepp et al., 2014, pp. 185–191): on holidays of course, but also other 'slots' in the daily flow of patterned time (Burchell, 2015). Such demarcations impose further adjustments on others: the costs of those adjustments may be absorbed within a wider system of managing mutual availability, or their disruption may fall unequally on particular individuals or particular classes.

Time and Social Order

There is also a broader point about coordination. The problem is not just one of lacking time for reaction to communications, but lacking time for *interpretation*, that is, for making *narrative sense* of what one is supposed to be up-to-date with. The problem may not be amenable to direct adjustment. We reach here a wider problem of figurational order: of 'configuration', as the phenomenological philosopher Paul Ricoeur put it. In Ricoeur's work, the relationship between time and narrative is explicit: 'narrative' is only 'meaningful to the extent that it portrays the features of temporal experience', while 'time' only 'becomes human time to the extent that it is organized after the manner of a narrative' (1984a, p. 3). The possibility of narrative for Ricoeur always requires acts of 'configuring', a temporal synthesis which grasps together a variety of heterogeneous elements. Narrative offers a different way of being in time, since the plot 'extracts a configuration from a [mere] succession' (1984a, p. 66), the mere succession from moment to moment. There is always, for Ricoeur, a paradoxical relation in human life between the possibility of configuration and the reality of mere succession.

Ricoeur's reflections on time and narrative were developed principally for a philosophical and literary context: social ordering was not Ricoeur's priority. But they remain a useful reference-point for thinking sociologically about our lived experiences of media and information infrastructures, and in particular for the problems of 'configuring' the much intensified form of these infrastructures that we now experience: extracting a configuration (of possible narratives) from an endless stream of mere succession. Ricoeur himself was well aware of the *historicity* of the narrative structures within which we operate:

> perhaps, in spite of everything, it is necessary to have confidence in the call for concordance that today still structures the expectations of readers and to believe that new narrative forms, which we do not yet know how to name, are already being born [. . .] For we have no idea of what a culture would be where no one any longer knew what it meant to narrative things. (1984b, p. 28)

Ricoeur intuits a future vulnerability of culture with respect to time, which we are only now, and in particular cultures, beginning to register in practice: the possibility of a new 'culture' which *resists* narrative and creates conditions where the configuring of individual experience is only partly possible.

Problems of figurational order – or of 'configuration' in Ricoeur's term – through which the interrelations in which we are enmeshed make sense to us *as an order* are an expression of the growth of new figurations, and figurations of figurations, that constitute those interrelations. And figurational problems felt at the level of individual actors are a manifestation of the emergence of new forms of *generalized order* by which the world can be governed in new ways. We saw in the last chapter how a growing complexity of spatial reach, made possible by new technologies of transmission, enables new worlds of interaction, such as the trading floors of global stock markets. In this chapter's final section, we explore other ways in which order might be emerging in time across today's increasingly densely woven mesh of social figurations.

6.3 The Rearrangement and Derangement of Social Time

In thinking further about figurational order, let's consider first media-derived transformations in the social domains of work.

Time and Work

Time is important for work since 'work is done in time: it is a temporal act, done by actors' (Lee and Sawyer, 2010, p. 8). The management of time within the bounded spaces of organizations is one of the key dimensions and problems of organizational life (Zerubavel, 1981). But work environments may differ markedly in how they are organized in time. Lee and Sawyer draw a key distinction between monochronic and polychronic work environments:[12]

> Individuals working polychronically place less value on temporal order, accept events as they arise and are likely to engage in multiple activities simultaneously. In contrast, people working monochronically seek to structure activities and plan for events by allocating specific slots of time to each event's occurrence. (Lee and Sawyer, 2010, p. 9)

Most organizations, because they focus on common systems and goals, assume a monochronic way of working, even if individuals operating within them also operate polychronically: that intensifies the normalizing pressures of time structures. Maintaining a common time-environment for working becomes more difficult in distributed work that, in turn, is facilitated at a general level by technologies of communication-at-a-distance. Sarker and Sahay (2004) discovered this when they studied the work of virtual teams developing information infrastructure projects in the USA and Norway. Their research was focused on the role of time and space in shaping the practices of individual team members, and what they found was interesting:

> Key problems related to time appear to be arising from mismatches in psychological and social clocks of team-members, complexities in accounting for time zones, negative interpretations of time lapses, and difficulty in comprehending temporally disordered sequences of chat and threaded messages. (Sarker and Sahay, 2004, p. 4)

Such work involves developing effective forms of coordination and collaboration between people who may not have worked together before, or even seen each other before. A particular issue is 'suspicion', that is, the 'difficulty in physically verifying the actions of remote members' (Sarker and Sahay, 2004, p. 10). In response, people may overcompensate, as evidenced by a study of Australian home workers:

> I feel if I don't answer an email someone thinks I'm purposely ignoring them instead of I haven't read it yet. It's a concern and it's also just how I see myself as a professional. I want people to know I am looking after things. (quoted in Gregg, 2011, p. 15)

A further problem is communicative 'silence': a time-period without communication in what was supposed to be continuous communication. People at a distance tend to interpret communicative silence negatively, as caused by 'incompetence or a lack of commitment', sometimes leading to 'a breakdown of even functional relationships' (Sarker and Sahay, 2004, p. 15). Ways of dealing with this include minimizing the dependences between locations – scaling back the degree of collaboration over distance – or developing new norms of communication (for example, an assumed 24-hour response period). To sum up, 'while ICTs act as key enablers of distributed work' within a technologically mediated space–time, 'they by themselves do not guarantee "location transparency"' (Sarker and Sahay, 2004, p. 16). Translocal communication creates complexities of *managing* the temporal sequence of communications that may undermine the *mutual substitutability of perspectives* that Schutz regarded as necessary for effective social interaction. The pressures towards reliance on translocal cooperation meanwhile accumulate, meaning that the costs of such imperfect working conditions, at the individual level, can be high.

Consider also the organizations that make the information packages, which form much of the background of our shared time: the 'news'. Recent research with major global news producers shows that a change in the inputs to news is affecting those producers' relation to time. Schlesinger and Doyle (2014) argue that, whereas the temporality of news-making was once clear (focused on 'breaking news' and its onward, outward transmission), a changing economic model has meant that news producers must increasingly adapt to the inward flow of audience response and commentary (for example, what is trending on Twitter and Facebook). This leads, they argue, to real-time adjustments in production routines which potentially introduce time-conflicts into the practice of news-making (Schlesinger and Doyle, 2014, p. 9, 15): do you spend time checking or identifying a source for a new story, or do you spend time checking social media reactions to your last story?

Such paradoxes of time-relations through media affect informal types of work too. Think of those outside conventional organizations who are trying to change the economic system: protesters for social change. As anthropologist Veronica Barassi (2015) points out, protesters, like others, have to deal with 'the temporality of immediacy': that means face-to-face interactions and activities must regularly be interrupted by incoming electronic messages, and the need to send out new messages. Barassi's fundamental point, similar to ours, is that it is 'through the organization of our everyday human practices that we construct specific temporalities' (2015, p. 104). It is not just a question of the personal cost of being continuously available on one's mobile, but also of the *trumping*, for everyone, of certain time-consuming types of activity by others which seem more 'immediate'. The *quality* of political practice, especially practice aimed at producing social change through extensive deliberation, may thereby be damaged, as this activist interviewed by Barassi notes: 'I feel that you cannot create a real discussion [on social media]. The communication is too fast, there is no depth. It is also difficult to establish a history of events and thoughts.' Or as another activist puts it, 'we need also to propose our alternatives. The problem is that these complex analyses need to be developed properly, we need *time and space* to do that' (Barassi, 2015, p. 112). Other researchers of social movements note the cost for activists of being locked into 'an [accelerating] event-oriented dynamic' that focuses on the following up, and responding to, social media trends (Poell and van Dijck, 2015). The apparent obligation to 'stay connected' creates hidden time-deficits that, in turn, generate costs for the wider practices in which actors are engaged, without denying however that digital media also facilitate practices of memory and archiving in political movements (Cammaerts, 2015).

Broader Social Orderings through Time

What general principles can we draw from these disparate cases? First, there is a tendency for the temporal dynamics of *communication* systems to override the temporal dynamics of *other* processes in which the actors receiving the outputs of those systems may be involved. Social media platforms seem to carry their own sense of time and time-related obligation, as a number of commentators have noted (Fuchs, 2014; Kaun and Stiernstedt, 2014; Weltevrede, Helmond and Gerlitz, 2014). Political activists may feel a pressure to follow only the spikes in social media (what is 'trending', for example, according to Twitter's algorithms), rather than register a steady growth in interest in their activities, even though it is the latter that may be more useful and sustainable (Poell and van Dijck, 2015, quoting Lotan, 2011). The fact that this message is 'right now' on one's phone – and therefore immediately *available* to be responded to – seems to trump other possible uses of the time required to respond. There are parallels in the world of general social interaction: the fact that a message from an assumed close consociate on the Mixi platform generates a requirement for a young person in Japan to respond immediately (Takahashi, 2014), rather than perform some other action. Because responding immediately, while doing many other things, can be difficult, an overarching requirement may emerge to sustain a state of constant readiness to respond *whenever* a message comes in, even while one is asleep. There is something paradoxical when *technological system* imperatives, in the temporal mode, trump other major needs; for example, for continuous periods of non-responsiveness (usually called 'sleep'). How system imperatives are integrated, well or badly, into everyday reality becomes crucial for the quality of that life.

The problem here for analysis is arguably more difficult than that of grasping the order of complex social domains (such as global trading rooms) built on many interlocking figurations oriented to shared communication and data flows. For those domains carry *their own* narratives of order and, although its reality must be lived by those workers, we can make sense of the idea that such domains operate within boundaries that sustain their effectiveness. More difficult to analyse are cases where system imperatives linked to generalized communications infrastructures bleed out into daily life for individuals, and where narratives to make sense of the resulting disruptions are unavailable. This is the largely uncharted area that Elias captured through his notion of 'tempo'.

In Elias' terms, a dramatic *recalibration* of the social world's tempo – considered from the perspective of some actors relative to others – is under way, and from the perspective of deep mediatization social media platforms are driving it. Elias says that 'tempo' works as 'a function situated at a junction of so many chains of action [which] demands an exact allocation of time; it makes people accustomed to subordinating momentary inclinations to the overriding necessities of interdependence; it trains them to eliminate all irregularities from behaviour and to achieve permanent self-control' (1994 [1939], p. 457). The normative *force* of tempo doesn't derive from anyone's intentions: it accumulates through interlocking mutual relations of many figurations, and figurations of figurations, which over time result in what seem to actors to be 'overriding necessities of interdependence'. The assumed reason for this 'overriding' is that cooperation will break down without them. When one type of call on our time is trumped by another, this has consequences: if this trumping becomes routine, this may cause us *permanently* to direct scarce time away from the uses that have been trumped, opening the gates to an exponential growth in the time-use that generates the trumping. This is one important engine for the *progressive reshaping of everyday life in time through media*. To the extent that we lack ways of making sense of this change (of *configuring* it with our other ways of making sense of the social world), a problem of figurational order arises.

Here we see at work one aspect of deep mediatization that is driven not by any 'logic' inherent to media contents or forms, but by the *dynamics* of the intensified interdependences of meaning and sociality that media make possible. Yet this is only one dimension of how social media platforms are working with deep mediatization. Also important are new modes of *evaluating* others, *commenting on* what they have just said or will shortly do, *imitating* others, all of which have temporal aspects, and so contribute to increased temporal interrelatedness. The possibility that our relations with time are changing through what we do on digital platforms has been noticed by various writers (Weltevrede et al., 2014; Kaun and Stiernstedt, 2014). We are in the middle, potentially, of a major transformation in social ordering whose outcome will depend on more than temporal calibration. As Elias understood so well, questions of tempo cannot be separated from questions of value.

The Transforming 'Here and Now'

One hundred and fifty years ago, a speeding up of the movement of bodies and things (railways) disrupted society's 'traditional space–time continuum' (Schivelbusch, 1986, p. 33), leading to the loss of the 'spatial distance created between localities [which] was the very essence of their "here and now", their self-assured and complacent individuality' (1986, p. 35). It is too early to tell whether the 'consciousness' (as Schivelbusch put it) associated with the here and now of everyday locations, as it was understood *before* the advent of continuous and media-based connection, will be lost completely, but we should not underestimate the convergent forces pointing in that direction.

A banal, indeed parochial, example can speak to the *sort* of problems emerging in many places. In the UK in September 2015 it was reported (*Guardian*, 4 September) that an unnamed 14-year-old boy who flirted with a girl by sending her a naked picture of himself is now recorded in a police crime database, and will remain so for at least a decade. He sent the image, presumably not thinking of its archived after-life (he might not have expected that the recipient would be quick enough to circulate the image on to others). Nor did he expect the image to come to the notice of a police officer based at the school who recorded the 'crime' in the database, although without making any charges. The result of this 'negligence' (and the original no doubt foolish and offensive act) is however an ongoing penalty that seems wholly disproportionate. Something in the figurational order seems out of joint when communicative practices in space (circulation) and in time (archiving) generate consequences whose scale is radically at odds with those anticipated by actors themselves.[13]

An additional force at work is the huge investments involved in converting the interconnected space–time of everyday communications into a domain for profit: however uneven access to communications remains, the *push* to 'connect' a very large proportion of the world's population, for example, by cheap 'smart' phones or 'free' internet provision such as Facebook's Free Basics platform, is real.[14] As Jose van Dijck (2013) explains in her masterly survey of the growth of so-called 'social media' platforms, it is impossible to separate this trajectory and its purported transformation of 'social life' from the development of software which organizes the 'data' of our interactions into a space *of appearances* for us as social users. There would *be* no 'social media' platforms without that process of organizing data, which is not to deny that data processes in themselves already have social consequences. One consequence of the embedding of data-based processes in everyday life may be to shape the reference-points by which we organize action. Those who design data-processes are particularly interested in prediction. When the predictive results of such data-gathering are fed back into *our* own streams of experience ('personalized' adverts, differentiated prices when we buy something, newsfeeds on our social media page, prompts to take action, commendations on our Twitter performance), social actors' own *sense of time* – the various linked time-horizons towards which their actions are oriented – may get changed in the process.

We will return to these questions of order, and their implications for questions of value, in Chapters 10 and 11. We need however in the next chapter to consider more closely a theme that has emerged across Chapters 5 and 6: that is, the implications of 'data' for phenomenology's account of how the social world is constructed.

7

Data

In the two previous chapters, we have stretched classic phenomenological accounts of the construction of the social world by attending to the consequences of mediated communications for the space and time of everyday social interaction. But we have not so far encountered anything that fundamentally disrupts the approach to the sociology of knowledge offered by Berger and Luckmann. They understood social knowledge as built up through the accumulation of 'ordinary' members of society's knowledge acquired through everyday 'thoughts and actions' (1966, p. 33). However, we have noted that data-based infrastructures of computer-mediated communications now play a key role in social interaction and that this *might* be shifting how we acquire social knowledge. In this chapter, we take that issue head on: we will be concerned with the deep enfolding in everyday life of automated data-gathering and data-processing which, in their underlying operations, are very far from everyday 'thought and action'.

What are the implications of 'data' – as acquired, processed, configured and re-presented by computer-based systems – for social knowledge? We use the term 'systems' here in a descriptive, not theoretical, sense to refer to configurations of computing resource that enable the performance of large-scale information processing, operating to a large extent without direct human intervention, through 'automating mediation' via 'software agents' (Mansell, 2012, pp. 108–115). We do not intend the word 'system' to suggest any allegiance to a *theory* of 'social systems': indeed, we reject any such theories.[1] That definitional point aside, this chapter is a turning-point in our argument. This is the point at which a materialist phenomenology starts to diverge substantially from classic phenomenology. As anticipated in Chapter 1, this is also the point where the apparently irreversible breach between the phenomenological tradition (once cast in properly materialist form) and apparently anti-phenomenological (because materialist) accounts of knowledge such as Foucault's (1970, p. xiv) can be repaired.

The strength of Berger and Luckmann's work, and the wider tradition of phenomenology, was to move away from a concern with the social contexts in which 'ideas' are generated (a sociological supplement to traditional 'history of ideas') towards an interest in 'everything that passes for "knowledge" in society', that is, with 'common-sense knowledge' (1966, p. 26). But Berger and Luckmann bracketed out the question, previously raised by Schutz, of the 'social distribution of knowledge' (1966, p. 28), in order to try to develop a 'single body of reasoning' about social knowledge in the style of Talcott Parsons (1966, pp. 28–29). That is why they were comfortable also with bracketing out from their sociology broader questions of epistemology, as if they had no bearing on everyday life. Both decisions now seem problematic. The growth of 'data' is part of a major *re*-distribution of knowledge production: any account today of what we know in the social world must confront a *conflict* (or at least a *plurality*) in what passes for social knowledge and in everyday epistemology. We come face to face with that plurality every day. This gives a new prominence to the sociology of knowledge,[2] but on terms very different from those supposed by Berger and Luckmann.

The classic thesis of the 'social construction of reality' assumed that one could build an account of common-sense knowledge simply by bringing together overlapping perspectives on how knowledge arises for human actors in their everyday 'social contexts' (Berger and Luckmann, 1966, p. 15). Our thesis in this book – the *mediated* construction of reality – considers media's implications for such an account of common-sense knowledge, but what if the workings of 'media' are not understandable exclusively within our accounts of particular bounded social contexts? Data's role in media's operations pushes us further in this direction.

'Data' is the symbolic rough material out of which, through processes of accumulation, sorting and interpretation, 'information' is generated for use by particular actors with particular purposes (Kallinikos, 2009a). Although, casually, we talk about 'raw data', in reality no data is 'raw'. 'Raw data is an oxymoron' (Bowker, 2008, p. 184; Gitelman and Jackson, 2013, p. 13; Kitchin, 2014, p. 20), which means that data always materializes within a particular practice and structure of collection: at its simplest, a data*base*. We can leave the details of that to one side for now. Our point, more basically, is that 'data' and 'information' generated by systems of computers are today a precondition for everyday life; the *selections* from the wider 'world' (Boltanski, 2011) made by data processing are consequential for social life. That much was already grasped by Anthony Giddens in the 1980s (1984, p. 309, quoted in Gandy, 1993, p. 13), although Giddens' particular focus was the state's role in gathering information, not the wider processes of state *and* corporate monitoring we see today. Another pioneering account of the social role of data processing by both markets and states was James Beniger's (1986) description of nineteenth-century modernization, but this did not prioritize phenomenological issues.[3]

The challenge to phenomenology from contemporary data practices stems from three developments subsequent to Giddens' observations. First, the collection of data is now continuous in many processes of social action and interaction, generating volumes of data whose processing is unmanageable without automation. In many rich countries, basic acts, such as booking a train or plane ticket, or keeping in touch with friends, now have as their precondition the unimpeded operation of networked systems of data-gathering and data-processing. Such automated processes are not a special case, or reserved for large institutions such as government departments: they are becoming, for many, the *general background of everyday life*. Second, the largest proportion of data processing now lies in the hands of the 'corporate private sector' (Gandy, 1993, p. 13), that is, organizations whose goals cannot be equated with the general social interest, since they are aimed at private competitive advantage. Those goals are necessarily *external* to the model of social knowledge developed by classic phenomenology, and there is at least an attempt to implement them on a global, not merely national or regional, scale (Mosco 2014). Third, the outcomes of such data processing include the generation, prima facie, of *social knowledge itself*, at least in an instrumental sense: information put to use in the management of social interaction. Social actors are sorted in relation to particular action-outcomes on the basis of how data relating to them is categorized and processed. Data processing is, as Oscar Gandy (1993, p. 15), a pioneer of its sociological study, put it, 'a discriminatory technology' that works through 'three integrated functions': 'identification' (the collection of data of administrative relevance), 'classification' (the resulting assignment of individuals to pre-formulated groups), and 'assessment' (the assignment of individuals to particular action-outcomes based on comparing how they are classified).

In the term 'data' we include all the processes and underlying infrastructures for gathering, sorting, collecting, evaluating and acting upon data. Data comprise today a substantial proportion of the 'socially available stock of knowledge' (Berger and Luckmann, 1966, p. 61). Data production is inherently *asymmetrical*, in a way not envisaged in classic phenomenology's model of social knowledge: it is oriented to the purposes of the institutions – private or governmental – that use the data. True, individual social actors are themselves involved in mutual data-gathering, and may act in ways that adapt to data-gathering processes (we return to this), but this does not change the fact that the primary drivers of data processes as forms of social knowledge are institutions external to the social interactions in question. A large proportion of such data is produced automatically, relying on processes of aggregation and algorithmic calculation that are driven by the needs of those external institutions. True, we could also argue that the growing interdependency of everyday life and media technologies (what we have called deep mediatization) is itself a key driver of data production – at least from the perspective of *today's* version of digital infrastructure: we can surely imagine other versions that are not dependent on continuing data-gathering. That would raise wider issues about the particular types of figurational order that are today becoming dominant, a point to which we will return in Chapter 10. For now, we ask only the basic question: what are the consequences of the deep social embedding of data processing for social phenomenology?

7.1 Data and the Premises of Classic Social Phenomenology

Berger and Luckmann were right to make explicit a key organizing dynamic in social experience, that is, how social actors 'apprehend the reality of everyday life as an *ordered* reality' (1966, p. 35). There is still force to that idea: states of affairs where we *cannot* apprehend our everyday reality as ordered are deeply distressing and disruptive of basic human processes (times of social and civic breakdown, political terror, deep forms of social victimization). But the issues raised by data-processing already confront us with conflicts about *how* reality is ordered, and *what* its order is. Schutz saw the 'how of the individual situation in the lifeworld' (Schutz and Luckmann, 1973, p. 105) as fundamental to social knowledge, but conflicting accounts of that 'how' now circulate: data processes generate many of those accounts. The economy of data collection and processing is now a crucial dimension of the wider market economy, as well as the operations of the state. The collection of data does not operate through the give-and-take – the mutual acknowledgement – of social interaction, but rather through processes of automated extraction exterior to any possible reflexive human action. Social actors may seek sometimes to resist this, but the resistance can only be partial since so many forms of action seem to have, as their precondition, such prior processing and the categorizations on which such processing depends.

As a result, the two premises of Berger and Luckmann's phenomenology of the social world are challenged: first, that 'everyday life presents itself as a reality *interpreted by men* [sic] and subjectively meaningful *to them as a coherent world*'; and, second, that the world of everyday life is not only taken for granted as reality by the ordinary members of society, but 'it is a world that *originates* in their thoughts and acts, and *is maintained as real by these*' (1966, p. 33, emphases added). We are not arguing that in everyday life social actors no longer try to generate common-sense knowledge in their thoughts and acts, just because *automated processes* of data-processing are deeply embedded in their daily lives. For sure, 'common-sense knowledge' of the social world remains 'the knowledge shared with others, the normal, self-evident routines of everyday life' (Berger and Luckmann, 1966, p. 37). But there are other forms of knowledge of the social world now in play,[4] not always self-evident to social actors, over which they have no control and yet which *impact them* deeply, and we need now to integrate this fact into our understanding of what we do and think every day.[5]

Berger and Luckmann were certainly aware of the reliance of social actors on wider patterns of knowledge and institutional knowledge production. They acknowledged the role of language in 'transcending the "here and now"' (1966, p. 54), and they had an account of how, more widely, institutions work to underwrite the hierarchy of knowledge that underlies social order, making legitimation not just a normative but a cognitive fact (1966, p. 111). But their account of how this works fits poorly with the role of automated data processing in everyday life today. Their examples of the role of 'system' in knowledge production were different in kind from today's data-processing systems, and much less consequential for the content of social knowledge: the background role of the telephone system in everyday transmission of communication, the bureaucracy that arranges one's new passport (1966, pp. 56–57). Berger and Luckmann simply could not have anticipated the role of data and information systems in generating *knowledge* for contemporary life, that is, their role in supporting and shaping the *ontology* of everyday interaction. For Berger and Luckmann, 'institutionalization', though broadly defined, depends in the end on a fitting together of how *human agents themselves* act in, and make sense of, the world: 'institutionalization occurs whenever there is reciprocal typification of habitualized actions by types of actors' (1966, p. 72). However bewildering the scale of such institutional forms of sense-making and knowledge production may seem to the individual actor, the institutional world that appears to the individual *remains* 'a humanly produced, constructed objectivity' (1966, p. 78).

How well does this account of the sociology of knowledge fit with data's role in everyday life today? For sure, our reliance on data in the social world already seems a *social* necessity. The internet evolved as an information space connecting, potentially, every computer and computer-based device on the planet, and every file found there. That huge expansion of scale, if it is within our cognitive reach, requires automated processes. The infinity of images and texts, people and events that we now regard as being 'there for us' online could not be 'there *for us*', as human actors with limited processing capacities, if it were not for the automated processes of search engines ('apps'). For this reason, it is important to think about the wider infrastructure of contemporary communications – including their data aspects – as a crucial dimension of what Berger and Luckmann call objectivation whereby 'the externalized products of human activity attain the character of objectivity' (Berger and Luckmann, 1966, p. 78), and so social reality is constructed. But this 'objectivation' operates by rather different rules from those envisaged by classic phenomenology.[6]

The problem is not merely one of increased complexification and delegation. Berger and Luckmann had already anticipated this, arguing that the resulting pressure against overarching order was overcome by 'establishing a stable symbolic canopy for the whole society' (1966, p. 103) which arranged even realities very distant from social actors' experience within a relational hierarchy (1966, p. 110). Data processes are disruptive not just because they are distant, but because they involve the *unimaginably large-scale and automated* repetition of processes of counting, sorting and configuring data (generating new forms of cognition). More generally, a large proportion of what now passes for social knowledge is held not by persons, but within an impersonal 'reserve' of accumulated text and images (the internet) that is available to us not directly (it is too large for that) but indirectly via *automated search* (Halavais, 2009) and automated processing of other sorts. Under these new conditions, Berger and Luckmann's once unobjectionable statement is jarring:

> Knowledge of how the socially available stock of knowledge is distributed, at least in outline, is an important element of that same stock of knowledge. I know, at least roughly, *what I can hide from whom, who* I can turn to for information on what I do not know, and generally *which types of individuals* may be expected to have which types of knowledge. (1966, p. 61, added emphasis)

And yet Berger and Luckmann remain right when they argue that the pressures for things to hang together are strong, and the need to optimize the convergence of 'relevance' is high (1966, pp. 81–82). The *impression of* 'meaningful reciprocity' (1966, p. 82) among social actors is still important, even if there can be no reciprocity (in the sense Berger and Luckmann intended) between humans and the automated processes which accumulate, count and configure data for and about them.

What then if sociology of knowledge acknowledges, in the midst of the social world, *other* forms (indeed forces) of 'social' knowledge than those generated by social actors? The result need not be 'reification', defined by Berger and Luckmann as the forgetting of the human role in the construction of reality, so that 'the objectivated world loses its comprehensibility as a human enterprise' (1966, p. 106): data processes, after all, are themselves the mediated result of any number of social, cultural and political processes, involving humans at some level. But there is something significant in the fact that 'data' involves processes that exceed the direct capacities of human agents, whether to perform or to model:[7] in this sense, data involves a certain kind of *materialization* (via media and their infrastructure) that brings, in turn a particular *institutionalization* of knowledge. The goals, norms and 'knowledges' of those processes are necessarily different in kind from those of human actors. The relations of 'social' knowledge therefore to questions of legitimacy, value and social order become less straightforward than they appeared to Berger and Luckmann. Let us now attempt to explore this in some specific areas.

7.2 New Institutions for 'Social' Knowledge

Like all infrastructures, the infrastructure of 'data' *sinks* inside social arrangements (Star and Ruhleder, 1996): if it did not, it would not be doing its work of enabling our lives to run their ordinary course. But since the data infrastructure is a structure for social *knowledge*, we must bring it to explicit reflection, if we are to have a satisfactory account of how the social world is constructed.

The process of institutionalizing knowledge through data has many components: it operates via the materialization of a network of networks so complex that it makes no sense to regard it as animated by one single logic or 'dominant shaping force' (in that, it is similar to all technology: MacKenzie and Wajcman, 1999, p. 18). That said, its point is, so far as possible, to act *as* an infrastructure, *as* a practical system. *That*, in broad terms, is what someone expects when s/he trusts our credit card, phone or laptop will work when getting off a plane the other side of the world, or indeed a train the other side of a country. And such expectations, on the part of social actors, are inseparable from the goals of countless businesses to achieve a seamless *plane of interoperability* between their products and services and those of other businesses. Such corporate ambitions have become unthinkable without data tracking: as Armand Mattelart puts it, 'the tracking grid now provides meaning on a planetary scale' (Mattelart, 2010, p. 2). The importance of this infrastructure for wider forms of political and social order is undeniable: 'technological innovations are similar to legislative acts or political foundings that establish a framework for public order [. . .] in tangible arrangements of steel and concrete, wires and transistors, nuts and bolts' (MacKenzie and Wajcman, 1999, p. 33) – and, we might now add, code.

Databases and Social Classifications

Crucial to this transformation is the database; 'the ability to order information about entities into lists using classifications [is] a contemporary key to both state and scientific power' (Bowker, 2008, p. 108). The database has a distinctive type of power which Bowker defines as 'jussive', an ordering power based on an 'exclusionary principle' that determines what can and cannot be stored in a particular form (2008, p. 12). The consequences of database operations are in this sense final: 'what is not classified gets rendered invisible' (2008, p. 153). The point of database operations is to fix the *starting-point* (the base) from which data operations – counting, aggregating, sorting, evaluation – begin. In that sense, by being placed in a database, 'data' becomes 'unmoored' from the underlying materials from which it was gathered (Kitchin, 2014, p. 72). It makes no difference to this process that some of the processes developed on the base of the underlying data architecture may themselves go on adapting in response to emerging patterns in data, provided the structure of the underlying database remains the same.[8] Such adaptations are in any case driven not by some independent 'will' present in the processes from which data are gathered but by the emergence of features that, from the perspective of the data process, are defined as significant enough to trigger such adaptations. In all such cases, the 'knowledge' that is produced cannot be separated from the purposive selections out of which the database is formed, or subsequently adapted. Insofar as the outcomes are treated as *direct* knowledge about the processes re-presented by the data, they are misleading. As Bowker put it, 'our memory practices [are] the site where ideology and knowledge fuse' (2008, p. 228). We have already in Chapter 3 suggested that these developments can be seen as a potential new fourth wave of mediatization, through which our interdependencies progressively *deepen* through infrastructures for the continuous production and exchange *of data*: the emerging wave of datafication, within the wider wave of digitalization.

Most data involved in the organization of social life are 'made from the raw material of human experience' (Gandy, 1993, p. 53) and used for social *classification*. The purpose of data-gathering is not neutral, but precisely discriminatory, that is, 'to coordinate and control [people's] access to the goods and services that define life in the modern capitalist economy' (Gandy, 1993, p. 15). This discrimination requires a massive pooling of computational resources: a single database is not sufficient. It is essential to aggregate separate databases into massively larger ones, enabling the matching of patterns across countless sites of data collection, from which predictions can be made (Gandy, 1993, pp. 71–84). From the development of 'distributed relational databases' in the 1990s and 2000s to the work of today's growing data sector, including global businesses on the scale of Google, Expedia, Acxiom (Kallinikos, 2009b, p. 232; Nissenbaum, 2010, pp. 41–45), the aggregation-for-value of data originally collected from specific locations and in specific contexts now comprises a basic fact of social life.

It is naive to ignore the consequences that the principles of selection underlying such data-gathering may have for particular distributions of power, and for the long-term organization of the social world. As Theodore Porter put it in a broader context, 'quantification is a technology of distance', motivated not by a 'truth to nature' but by 'the exclusion of judgement' (1995, p. ix) that makes particular types of judgement possible and efficient through a reshaping of the social world itself: 'the quantitative technologies used to investigate social and economic life work best if the world they aim to describe *can be remade in their image*' (Porter, 1995, p. 43, added emphasis). Indeed, because large-scale institutions necessarily act at a great distance from the realities they seek to influence, the operation of data processes plays a crucial role in *making* a distant, intractable 'world' *into* an ordered, calibrated reality that can be interpreted and governed: as anthropologist James Scott put it, 'legibility' [. . .]. is a central problem in statecraft', requiring a 'politics of measurement' (1998, p. 2, 27). But, as some legal theorists have noted, we must extend this analysis to the whole surveillance apparatus of the contemporary commercial and information technology environment (Cohen, 2012; Pasquale, 2015).

We miss the social form of this complex process, unless we connect up the abstractions inherent in data functions to the *experiential processes* in which those functions have become embedded (Cohen, 2012, p. 20), and so register the potential violence of data-based 'processes of [. . .] representation and classification' (2012, p. 24). For this, phenomenological reference-points are essential.[9] But a core feature of data infrastructures is deeply at odds with the assumptions of classic phenomenology. That is its *opacity*:[10] 'the configuration of networked space [. . .] is increasingly opaque to its users' (Cohen, 2012, p. 202). Data's continuous processes of selection and comparison have a generalizing force across an infinite domain that guarantees a larger asymmetry *in social knowledge*. As Christine Alaimo and Jannis Kallinikos (2015, pp. 15–16) put it, 'it is exactly because of the abstract nature of data and the simplicity of the logic of encoding that the social can be represented in all of its (now compatible) highly pliable forms [. . .] *Once the social gets engraved into data, it ceases to be related to established categories and habits. It is transposed onto and thus enacted according to the very same logic*' by which it was generated. Or, as Jose van Dijck put it more succinctly, 'it is easier to encode sociality into algorithms than to decode algorithms back into social action' (2013, p. 172). The translation of social life into 'data' therefore casts a large shadow: the domain of descriptors that *fail* to get captured by data processes (Balka, 2011).

The result is a change – a potentially profound change – in our relations to infrastructure. Infrastructures are, at root, tools for human action, operating at the highest level of complexity, a black-boxed substrate of 'ordinary' human action. In the digital world, our infrastructural tools (for example, our pages on a social media platform) are increasingly entangled in *powerful* and *distant* processes, which we cannot unpick or challenge. All tools involve mechanisms whose details we forget when we use them, or perhaps never knew: we may guess how a hammer has been put together, even if most know little about how the modern car is constructed, yet both hammer and car are tools of everyday living and our ignorance of their workings (their black-boxedness) is not crucial to the quality of our use. But many of today's 'digital tools', as we use them, are black-boxes of a different sort, black-boxes that *are also in the act of using us*.[11] They track our actions algorithmically, not to enable the tool to work better for us, but to generate data for the *toolmaker's* use: that is, to enable us to be better targeted by advertisers and marketers (Turow, 2011). This is indeed the very rationale of the much-hyped 'Internet of Things', yet its transformation of our usual relations to infrastructure seems not to have been noticed.

The result is a social relationship to abstraction very different from that envisaged by Schutz. Schutz saw artefacts as comprising the extreme end of the spectrum of ways in which *humans typify* (abstract from) their world (Schutz, 1967, p. 201). But today's data-based *artefacts* now themselves operate to *typify humans* mostly for commercial ends and surveillance, to construct a seamless world for commerce and control. We might call this *tool reversibility*. Tool reversibility is not immediately apparent when we use data-based tools, but it becomes apparent through our practices of use and the obstructions those practices encounter: whevever we use a data-based tool, it is already using us. This is one of the deeper cultural and social implications of the embedding of algorithms in everyday life (Napoli, 2014).

Categorization

Data processes rely, in turn, on categorization. Categories have been important in social theory for more than a century. For Durkheim and Mauss (1969 [1902]), categories (as outputs of a system of classification in so-called 'primitive societies') were derivatives of the actual divisions of society itself, and of the very idea of society itself. In most subsequent accounts, the order of causality is reversed with categories contributing to 'the built information environment of a society' (Bowker and Star, 1999, p. 5): 'typification' playing a similar role in classic phenomenology. But to grasp the degree of abstraction involved in data-based categories, we need to look more specifically at their features.

As David Berry explains, no process of computer-based categorization (and so no sorting, combination or evaluation based on it) can operate unless an 'object' has been created: 'in cutting up the world in this pattern, information about the world necessarily has to be discarded in order to store a representation within the computer [. . .] those subtractive methods of understanding reality [. . .] produce new knowledges and methods for the control of reality' (2011, pp. 14–15). So, in order to compose the *objects* in a database, such abstraction, first, needs to have occurred. As already noted, there is no raw data, but only 'data [. . .] produced through measuring, abstracting and generalizing techniques that have been conceived to perform a task' (Kitchin, 2014, p. 19). Second, where large numbers of objects are to be processed by automated functions or algorithms, processing requires prior organization, the design of a database *structure* 'to extract the data located in them as rapidly and as effectively as possible'; in this sense, 'a data structure forms a sort of intermediate level, an abstraction mechanism, in the process of addressing machine memory' (Fuller and Goffey, 2012, p. 84, 85). Third, the more complex the operations to be completed, the greater the need to *combine* data levels and so enable more complex processing, what Fuller and Goffey call 'abstraction layers': 'the more that different functions of a process [. . .] or software can be integrated by one layer of implementation, the wider it circulates and coalesces. The more generality an abstraction is capable of, the greater its degree of usefulness; and the greater its tenacity in self-stabilization, the more activity is arrayed around it' (2012, pp. 88–89). In this way, more and more of what was once heterogeneous information can be processed together, but at the price of ever-greater levels of abstraction. Fourth, the processes of *calculation* performed on data must be automated through the use of algorithms. Algorithms are often identified, casually, with the whole process of data-based transformation of everyday experience, but as 'encoded processes for transforming input data into a desired output, based on specified calculations' (Gillespie, 2014, p. 167), algorithms are merely one of many elements in a sequence of progressive abstraction, if an essential one.

Alongside the relations between data processes (involving categories that do social work), we also need to consider what happens when the outputs of those data processes are *played back to social actors. That* they are played back (Isin and Ruppert, 2015, p. 113) is another factor, which a soci-ology of knowledge that takes data seriously must grasp. Categorization[12] is fundamental to all forms of organization, including social organization. Without it, effective (or at least non-random) interaction with the world would be impossible. Yet in the social realm, categorization has a distinc-tive feature neglected in phenomenology's account of typification and not even conceivable in Durkheim and Mauss's society-driven model. As Ian Hacking pointed out, classifications of human objects are 'interactive' in a way that, arguably, classifications of non-human objects are not:[13]

> Ways of classifying human beings interact with the human beings who are classified. [. . .] classifications do not exist only in the empty space of language but in institutions, practices, material interactions with things and other people [. . .]. people are aware of what is said about them, thought about them, done to them. They think about and conceptualize themselves. Inanimate things are, by definition, not aware of themselves in the same way. (Hacking, 1999, pp. 31–32)

Hacking's insight has particular importance for the digital age when actors and actions are relentlessly categorized in countless ways for various purposes.

Our ways of interacting with categories are not easy to disentangle. They occur not randomly but in a highly structured context linked to the purpose for which data is being gathered in the first place. The simplest example is the social media platform. As Daniel Neyland notes, algo-rithms do not have a simple or automatic recursive effect on the social world, but involve a 'configuration through which users and/or clients are modelled and then encouraged to take up various positions in relation to the algorithm at work' (Neyland, 2015, p. 122). What is striking about the configurations of social media platforms is that we act on and through them, largely as if there were *no* such configuration: indeed the very idea of 'platform' is a constructed space where the interface between everyday interaction and commercial transaction *appears* natural, a seamless data-flow (Gillespie, 2010). Through our underlying desire to maintain our social commitments across the newly configured spaces where they seem to migrate, there emerges a 'growing *social* commitment to functionality' (Plantin, Sandvig et al., forthcoming). This has major implications for how the social world is constructed.

Translating Data into Practice

There are at least five fundamental ways in which data abstracted from social experience can translate into frameworks for social practice. These connect with the dimensions in terms of which the other chapters of Parts II and III are organized.

The first relates to the organization of *space*.[14] As Kitchin and Dodge (2011) analyse extensively, many spaces (physical, organizational, informational) are now 'coded'. Their operations are structured through the software that processes data inputs of various sorts: the highly controlled space of the airport security queue is one clear example (2011, Chapter 7), entry into which is impossible without having met various data-related conditions in a prescribed sequence. This is an aspect of the rise, more generally, of the automated management of social processes. Unlike traditional surveillance, this form of control allows no gaps, since it operates through 'a grammar of action', that is, 'a systematic means of representing aspects of the world [. . .] and an organized language for processing those representations' (Kitchin and Dodge, 2011, p. 80, drawing on Agre, 1994). Under these conditions, the spaces Kitchin and Dodge call 'code/spaces' are *figurations* (in our term) of a particular, highly organized sort, driven by today's complex forms of interdependency.[15] Social media platforms *feel* like 'spaces' where, quite simply, we encounter others, but their existence is shaped by the underlying operation of platform software and its calculative infrastructure. Insofar as they create publics, these are 'calculative publics' (Gillespie, 2014, pp. 188–191), not that calculability itself is new: Weber (1978, p. 975) already saw this a century ago as 'the peculiarity of modern culture', but it has a *constitutive* role today that is unprecedented.

A related point can be made about the *time* of online media. Online media encourage us to operate in a distinctive time of required reactions related to the 'expected' rhythms of platform interaction: the Facebook timeline, the Twitter hashtag stream (Weltevrede et al., 2014). This time is not natural but the result of configuring *time-sequenced* data in a particular array designed to stimulate ever more interaction. We relate to this array as if it were a natural production by the human parties involved in the exchange, yet without the data-based presentation of the platform, there would be no mutual orientation in space–time, and so no 'interaction'. Many platform devices (such as email reminders) are designed to train people to rejoin the flow of what has been called 'social media time' (Kaun and Stiernstedt, 2014), should they slip out of it. This helps stabilize new data-based figurations that can function as 'social metronomes' (Neverla, 2010, p. 183).

The third translation operates at the level of the *self*. Each of us is familiar with the need to operate as a self under various descriptions: difficulties arise when contradictory descriptions of ourselves converge on a single interaction, and this much is familiar from social phenomenology. Unfamiliar from that classic work is the idea that each of us has not just a self-based identity (*vis-à-vis* the state or corporation with which we must deal), but a constantly updated 'data double' that is the resultant of the vast data stream that each of us generates continuously across various sites of data-tracking (Ruppert, 2011, p. 223, drawing on Lyon, 2003). The 'data double', with its built-in relation to multiple interdependent systems of data capture, depends entirely on the 'standardizing [of] classification systems so that they are comparable and databases can be joined up' (Ruppert, 2011, p. 221). It poses sometimes difficult challenges for individuals whose overall data stream may generate undesired or conflicting data, and, as already noted, the 'data double' is cut off from the shadow body of data that does not – perhaps cannot – feed into the relevant processes of calculation (Balka, 2011; Gillespie, 2014, pp. 173–174).[16]

The fourth translation operates at the level of *collectivities*. Data classifies, and so data processes not only work to specify individuals uniquely, but also generate countless groupings to which individuals are treated as belonging (groupings have 'aggregative power'; Ananny, 2015, p. 8). Whether these groupings correspond to anything that might be recognized by social actors as collectivities outside the process of data generation is an open question, but we are familiar with cases where the insistent use of data labels generates a type of action. Think of Facebook 'friends': some of these will have been friends before but many others are likely to be those one has acquired through the practice of receiving and making friend requests on the platform. As Taina Bucher puts it, 'friends have become a primary means through which *the production and occlusion of information* can be programmed' (Bucher, 2013, p. 49). In everyday actions and adjustments, actors become attuned to maximize such data-based groups (another example would be numbers of Twitter followers). Collectivities are sites where, through data processes, new norms of action and reaction emerge. We already know however that data processes are creating new entities for governments and civil society actors to deal with. So when, during Brazil's Junior Masterchef competition in October 2015, offensive and abusive sexual comments emerged online about a 12-year-old girl contestant, an NGO worker created a hashtag #primeiroassédio, which quickly generated more than 80,000 similar stories across multiple platforms (Gross, 2015). The importance of open hashtags as attractors to form political action has been noted for a number of major global protests, for example the rise of the 15-M and indignados movements in Spain in 2011 (Postill, 2014).

The final translation operates at the level of *organizations and order* and flows directly from the third. A problem for governments and corporations from the vast proliferation of continuous data streams is monitoring what counts as 'risk'. According to geographer Louise Amoore, governments are increasingly relying not on judgement or deliberation (no longer possible perhaps in the face of such a vast mountain of 'information') but on an 'ontology of association' that 'draw[s] into association an amalgamation of disaggregated data, inferring across the gaps [. . .] to derive a new form of data derivative' (2011, p. 27). According to Amoore, this new 'politics of possibility' involves a fundamental abstraction *operating on the flow of time itself*: it is oriented to the predicted future, to 'a population yet to come'. 'Data' must be rendered 'actionable' (2011, p. 29), which means selecting and excluding, 'rul[ing] out, render[ing] invisible, other potential futures' (2011, p. 38). These practices of exclusion become the basis for governing and ordering whole territories, a point to which we return in Chapter 10.

In all these ways, the domains of the social world, their practices and knowledge are reconfigured, in part, through processes of categorization based on data. The distributed complexity of these processes is a key contemporary example of the figurations of figurations and other large-scale relations between figurations that we argued a materialist phenomenology must understand. The emerging figurational order that results from this transforms the basis on which, in specific social domains such as the family and school, we are bound into figurations of interaction. It also operates, potentially, to change the very stuff of the social domain that powerful actors such as governments see themselves *as acting upon*. In the next section, we consider some implications of this for how individuals and collectivities act in the social world.

7.3 How We Are in a Social World with Data

Online media present us with appearances which are highly consequential and with which we spend increasing amounts of our time. But these appearances are not 'social facts' in Durkheim's sense, emerging from the flow of interpersonal interactions: rather, they are shaped, at least in part, by the economic and other external imperatives of the platforms through which they appear. When involved in online media, we interact on the basis of habits adapted to these platforms with others whose habits are similarly adapted. This is different from the entanglement people have always had with objects and infrastructures, and for two basic reasons. First, because, being rooted in everyday sociality and knowledge, online media comprise a space governed by *norms*, including expectations of legitimacy (van Dijck, 2013, p. 174). Second, because those norms emerge in relation to actions shaped by particular infrastructures of interaction and exchange, infrastructures already motivated by the corporate goals to *produce* and *stimulate* certain types of effects. This is not, of course, to deny agency, but simply to emphasize that, when we consider how we are in the world 'with' data, the 'facts' of what we do online, like all datafied 'facts', must be weighed carefully by reference to the motivated context in which they occur (boyd and Crawford, 2012): the goal of measuring what goes on in *any* online context as data for evaluation, and the constant stimulation of performance that yields *more* such data for measurement. You do not have to have been active for long on a platform such as Twitter to understand what Burrows and Savage (2014) mean by the 'metricization of social life'.

Monitoring

Although online platforms themselves direct surveillance, the new monitoring affordances of digital communication technologies involve us all: from the basic question ('why hasn't s/he texted yet?'), to Googling others before we meet them, to more persistent forms of mutual monitoring, via multiple forms of 'social media' which include not only social networking sites, but also sites for posting 'user-generated content', 'trading and marketing sites', and 'play and game sites'.[17] For that reason, legal theorist Helen Nissenbaum avoids the term 'surveillance' because of its strong pejorative associations with the state, and proposes the more open term 'monitoring' (2010, p. 22). Indeed the 'digital trail' is a major factor in the life of children, who in a country such as the USA are subject to continuous monitoring by their parents (Schofield Clark, 2013, p. 213). *Self*-monitoring and *self*-tracking (Klauser and Albrechtslund, 2014) is another important part of the picture, sometimes with specific goals (a sick person willingly accepting a measuring device that can warn a local hospital of symptoms of an impending heart attack), but often for more diffuse purposes. Emerging here in everyday practice is what Jose van Dijck calls 'the ideology of dataism [. . .] a widespread belief in the objective quantification and potential tracking of human behaviour and sociality through online media technologies' (2014, p. 2). In some institutionalized fields such as health, practices of continuous monitoring are a new and urgent trend; in others, like education, they build on decades of increased measurement and surveillance in schools (Selwyn, 2015, pp. 74–75). Indeed a consequence of the increasing capacity to combine vast database networks with huge calculative power is that 'the more data there is, the less any of it can be said to be private, since the richness of that data makes pinpointing people "'algorithmically possible"' (Tucker, 2013, quoting Princeton computer scientist Arvind Narayanan, see Narayanan and Felten, 2014). The result over time may be a certain fatalism. We may come to accept a social world characterized by continuous and enhanced mutual monitoring as our *starting-point* for thinking about the social. If so, this is a new and clear example of what we have called *deep* mediatization.

Berger and Luckmann's principle that 'human "knowledge" is developed, transmitted and maintained *in social situations*' (1966, p. 15) – that is, situations where human beings, by virtue of their mutual dependence on shared resources, must *come together* to act and think – now carries a very different implication. The wave of digitalization (Chapter 3) has created a continuous plane of interaction based in technologies of mediated communication where, in principle, any actor, wherever located, can reach, and be reached by, the communications of any other. The temporality of social situations (Chapter 6) has also been transformed in more subtle ways, giving access to aspects of the flow of daily life that were previously lost, once experienced. The resulting enrichment of experience is inseparable from a new degree of *institutionalization of social form*. As Jose van Dijck (2013, pp. 6–7, added emphasis) puts it: 'through social media, these casual speech acts [of previous everyday life] have turned into *formalized inscriptions* which, once embedded in the larger economy of wider publics, take on a different value'. Let us think a little more about the implications of this.

Datafication

Social situations, through their increasing involvement in ecologies of measurement and counting, are deeply implicated in data's status as a source of economic value. While many aspects of the metricization of social space are hidden to social actors, this cannot stop data-processing becoming entangled in the emotions of everyday life: 'more than mere tools, algorithms are also stabilizers of trust, practical and symbolic assurances that their evaluations are fair and accurate, and free from subjectivity, error, or attempted influence' (Gillespie 2014, p. 179). Translated into the language of classic phenomenology, algorithms and other aspects of the data infrastructure become a form of 'objectivation', part of 'the process by which the externalized products of human activity attain the character of objectivity' (Berger and Luckmann, 1966, p. 78). That is why an exposé of the *searcher*-sensitive features of the search engine results in which we trust is shocking (Pariser, 2011).

For Berger and Luckmann, institutionalization depended on 'the generality of the relevance structures' achieved in the production of knowledge (1966, p. 97). The interoperable metricized space of social media platforms and online interaction generally are coming to comprise, with little resistance, a new structure for generating social knowledge. According to a recent survey, of the US parents who use social media, 75 per cent go there for advice about how to solve parenting problems (Duggan, et al., 2015). Put another way, in the language of US pragmatism, the 'generalized other' (Mead, 1967 [1934]) that regulates social action is now increasingly sustained by a commercially encouraged flow of online exchange. Gillespie notes that 'algorithms impinge on how people seek information, how they perceive and think about the contours of knowledge, and how they understand themselves in and through public discourse' (2014, p. 183). If the algorithms associated with particular platforms, sites and practices have acquired legitimacy, anyone and any organization that depends for its power on legitimacy must deal with the consequences of 'what appears' *somewhere* in the unbounded, linked space of the internet. The management of this 'new visibility' (Thompson, 2005b; see Brighenti, 2007, and Heinich, 2012) becomes an all-consuming challenge, creating new challenges for the self: 'being spotted "by accident" against one's will is not an option; missing out on purposeful display becomes a predicament' (Izak, 2014, p. 362).

An interesting example in the private corporate sector is the transformation of the hospitality industry, and its relations with customers and employees, through data-based systems for collecting customer reactions. As Orlikowski and Scott (2014) note, the *force* of platforms such as TripAdvisor (popular at the time of writing) is striking. In an industry whose principal asset is customer anticipation of a good service, a new mechanism of legitimacy in the 'space of appearances' is a profound shift, especially when the results of such recommendations are now distributed ever more efficiently as data within the corporate sector (Hayward, 2015). For political organizations that must sustain legitimacy through a narrative of control of their past but also their ability to manage a whole society's future, the dynamics of legitimacy and information are even more complex (Bimber, 2003). New forms of interdependency are emerging here, based not on digitalization but on datafication, and the link of datafication to categorization. 'People put things into categories and learn from those categories how to behave' (Bowker and Star, 1999, p. 311). Whether or not social actors are aware of the many levels of data processing that work to shape their contexts of action, they interact with data-based contexts such as social media platforms *as if* they were sites for social categorization and normalization.

It might seem, therefore, as if a hurricane is blowing through the domains of the social world and our knowledge of them, threatening to overturn every reference-point and previously bounded context of knowledge production. Two important factors constrain this chaos, although they do not in the process protect the social from datafication, and from the potential normative problems that it generates. First, there is the stabilizing force that, as Berger and Luckmann put it, 'institutions do tend to "hang together"' (1966, p. 81): meanings or (as they put it) 'relevances' overlap between contexts and institutional settings, constraining divergent interpretation, establishing norms of comparison, and (we would add) generating criteria for ensuring things do *not* appear. Arguably, this will work to entrench processes of datafication *into* social reality through a contemporary version of the circular feedback between structuring forces and structured outcomes that Bourdieu called 'habitus'.[18] Second, there is the ongoing and irreducible tension between the grain of social experience and the forms in which it appears online. Social actors are likely to devote increasing efforts to contesting this tension with varying degrees of success.[19] We return to the implications of these struggles for social order in Chapter 10.

Data and its Challenge to Social Knowledge

If we take seriously the possibility that the automated digital tools that measure behaviour and activity online are now a key part of everyday life's background, then phenomenology has been complicated irreversibly. A materialist phenomenology must register how everyday actors are involved in bringing the workings of those tools into their everyday awareness. All are processes of categorization. As Bowker and Star note, categories create a 'social and moral order' (1999, p. 3), but in the case of data-related categories, it is unlikely to go uncontested.

The figurations of figurations that make up the distributed data industries and the domains that rely upon them are transforming the space of social action. In this chapter, we have given key emphasis to the role of data in social media platforms. There is a reason for this: this is precisely where the process of constructing social reality is *remoulded* in detailed forms. As Kallinikos and Constantiou (2015, p. 73) say, 'social media platforms elaborate architectural arrangements through which communal interaction and daily living are transformed into data ready to enter the circuits of calculation and so-called personalization'. But social media platforms are only one area where data processes are becoming deeply embedded in the building-blocks of social action. Others are the growth of data-generating 'wearable' devices in the health sector, and this is just part of the wider 'Internet of Things', whose consequences for the texture of the social world are, at this point, uncertain.

We can put all this in a broader philosophical perspective. The philosopher John McDowell (1994, p. 84) considers how our 'mindedness' (our unfolding conscious relation to the world as human beings) becomes embodied in forms of interaction and resource, as part of what he calls our 'second nature' (the evolving set of social institutions which humans are disposed to develop alongside their first, biological 'nature'). For McDowell, the forms that embody the 'possibility of an orientation to the world' have a history (McDowell, 1994, p. 125),[20] and this history is constantly open to revision. This formulation enables us to frame with particular clarity the problem that data pose for the social world as conceived by classic phenomenology.

Berger and Luckmann assume that the forms of our 'mindedness' evolve *only* from the accumulation of sense-making by *human* social actors, but what if today there is an *alternative* 'embodiment of mindedness' (McDowell, 1994, p. 124)? What if 'data', in all their direct and indirect forms, are being installed as an alternative *and exterior* cognitive infrastructure through which not only do *we* become minded, but the world becomes *mindful of us*, and everything we do? Since the data processes discussed in this chapter are part of an informational infrastructure that is being spread globally at huge speed, this amounts to a further stage in the deepening of mediatization. The very scale and scope depends upon the *delegation* of knowledge generation and knowledge application to automated processes. Once delegated, those processes become exterior to the process of social knowledge as classical phenomenology conceived it: they become what we might call, building on McDowell, a '*third nature*', driven by the economic imperatives of the data industries and all the wider goals of capitalist expansion that, in turn, drive those industries. This 'third nature', if it is to order social life, requires social actors to adapt to it in a process that, following Agamben (2009, p. 15), we can call 'subjectification': the production of entities that can function *as subjects* within this new type of social order. One achievement of materialist phenomenology is to remind us that we *are* those entities – unless, that is, we refuse to be.

In sum, in the wave of datafication, new means for producing social knowledge have emerged with two key features. First, they produce ostensibly social knowledge through automation that is necessarily exterior to everyday processes of human sense-making. Second, they are oriented to goals, driven by wider economic forces, that are different in type from the goals that embodied actors are able to have, unless, that is, they give up on their autonomy entirely. The result is the emergence, unevenly at this stage, of a new kind of sociality – call it 'computed' or 'platformed' (Kallinikos and Tempini, 2014; van Dijck, 2013, p. 5) – that changes the starting-points for everyday reflexivity and sociological reflection. Social order (which classic social phenomenology set out to explain) is now, through its very conditions of formation, inhabited by a form of already '*rationalized* reason' (Bernstein, 2002, p. 239, added emphasis),[21] which cannot be comfortably integrated into the reflection of individual social actors. Positive readings of this world (what Papacharissi calls its 'algorithmically rendered materiality': 2015, p. 119) are possible, but they cannot cover over the fissure developing within the production of social knowledge itself. Not surprisingly, in response, some call for the 'right to disconnect'.[22] The only repairs to this fissure must lie in the agency of social life on various levels, to which we turn in Part III.

Part III

Agency in the Social World

8

Self

Our previous chapters have laid the foundations for exploring more broadly how agency in the social world is changing. This is the theme of Part III. But why start this section on agency with a chapter on the self? Because we look out on the social as selves: to focus on how we do so is as good a place as any to grasp how the construction of the social world is now enacted in various forms of agency, and how that agency is being transformed by media and communications, including data processes.

Indeed, in the twenty-first century's second decade, the change in how social knowledge is produced, discussed in Chapter 7, has generated a different role *for the self*, resulting in new mechanisms of socialization. The connected space of the web moved in the mid 2000s from being a domain of static websites to being a tissue of platforms (Gillespie, 2010) that invite, even require, the active *input* of individuals, datafied individuals. The past ten years, as part of the emergence of a new wave of datafication within the overall wave of digitalization, have seen a change in the *basic* conditions for any social actor to exist *as such*: the self is expected in many societies to be available for interaction through digital platforms and even feels a certain pressure to represent itself on these platforms in the 'culture of connectivity' (van Dijck, 2013).

Anything less than *performing itself* in the connected, archived space of the web amounts, it seems, to a failure of the self. Mobile phones provide a basic example. Not only is mobile phone usage almost universal in most countries across the world, but using one's mobile phone not for 'phoning' (speaking) but for connection to online networks of peers ('social media') is becoming a dominant usage, as corporations push to expand smartphone usage. One respondent to a multi-country survey of university students said, 'I constantly check my phone for messages even though it does not ring or vibrate [. . .] I cannot help it. I do it all the time every day' (quoted in Mihailidis, 2014, p. 64). Media have consequences for more strategic types of self-performance too, for example attempts to find employment.

As a South African university careers guide puts it: 'have a personality: use different platforms to *show* different aspects of your personality'.[1] The result is to implicate the self's performance in processes of the operations of social media platforms (another example of deep mediatization).

The same careers guide goes on: 'But don't overshare.' In a world where selves are required to *manage themselves* online – yet who knows where, or when, your online profile or online activities will get picked up and evaluated, and by whom? – the self faces new types of risk *and* opportunity. The *risks* are not so much being too generous or too friendly, but rather (in management terms) failing to calibrate well the optimal balance between 'self-sharing' (for presentational benefit) and 'self-exposure' (exposing aspects of the self to unknown others with risks that cannot be calculated). Selves have always faced risks in the act of presenting themselves, as they moved from one encounter to the next. 'Face work' is an ongoing challenge of human life in a complex social space (Goffman, 1967 [1955], pp. 5–9, 41–45). But the massively increased interconnectivity of the internet transforms such risks into features of a continuous space–time without reliable or complete boundaries. The *opportunities* are the new possibilities of organizing our lives as selves through media technologies, through digital devices that help the self cope better with the multiple expectations of contemporary life and new possibilities of self-representation, of which the 'selfie' is only one recent example (Senft and Baym, 2015). And at a basic level, the individual simply has a greater scale of action across space and time on which to pursue and achieve her needs.

This spatial and temporal transformation, discussed already in Chapters 5 and 6, changes what it is to *maintain* a self. Being 'someone' shifts from being associated with a certain quality the self and others can abstract from the stream of everyday habitual action, to being a continuously managed 'project', that is, an 'external' responsibility of the self *towards* the social world. The self is now 'in' social space–time in a different way. Data, discussed in Chapter 7, are a crucial dimension of how this repositioning of the 'self' in space and time changes power-relations, and changes the sorts of trace that digital selves can have; it changes also the nature of the self's reflexivity. The *site of the self* is being transformed, and this may be the most important shift in how communications shape social reality in the past decade.[2]

This deep transformation is the reason, over and above the many layers of neoliberal incitement and economic force, why it does *not* seem entirely strange today, in a country such as the USA, to talk about the 'branded' self (Banet-Weiser, 2013). Consider, for example, this advice about how to 'manage your online brand' from the university careers guide quoted earlier:

> Personal branding is about *identifying* and *communicating* what makes you unique, *relevant* and *differentiated*. Your online brand (digital footprint) is established through: photos, blogs, articles, comments, recommendations, reviews, likes, favourites, retweets, etc. Managing your online brand [. . .] can enhance both your *personal and* professional brand.

Even more bluntly: 'If you don't have an active LinkedIn profile, you may as well be dead (to the world of work).'[3] Reducing this discourse to an ideology of neoliberal performance misses much of what is important here. First, it talks about the online *brand*, and that is inseparable from the abstraction of your 'digital traces': that is, the totality of 'digital footprint' that you have left online. Second, what the individual has to modulate is not her uniqueness – that much can be assumed – but rather her unique *value* to an exterior world, her 'relevance' and 'differentiatedness' (from others in a particular space of valuation). Third, alongside the obvious and perhaps unobjectionable idea of a professional brand, is the accompanying need for a 'personal' brand, because that will be judged too. Fourth, it is never enough just to identify a difference; it must be *communicated*, and its digital traces lodged in a relevant space of evaluation (such as LinkedIn).

Therefore, in an age of deep mediatization, the self is constructed through new figurations that are highly mediated. What would once have been called unproblematically the 'socialization' (here of early adulthood) becomes, under these conditions, as much a matter of system-calibration as of contextual learning. The self's recorded performance becomes its own data: data to be protected, edited and managed. As the quoted careers guide puts it, 'use "Vanity search" (Google yourself) to aggregate social mentions and delete unflattering content'. Online tools are now marketed to optimize this process, with vivid names such as Socioclean. We are back to the topic that Marcel Mauss announced eighty years ago – the social *construction* of the self:

> It is plain [. . .] that there has never existed a human being who has not been aware, not only of his body, but also at the same time of his individuality, both spiritual and physical [. . .] My subject is entirely different and independent of this. It is one relating to social history [. . .] how it slowly evolved – not the sense of 'self' – but the notion or concept that men have formed of it. (Mauss, 1980 [1938], p. 3)

Modern institutions have, for some time, put very distinctive pressure on the self as a site where various conflicts of value and worth must be resolved (Illouz, 2012). We are now living through a deepening of those conflicts under new infrastructural conditions, that is, deep mediatization.

Analysing the changing figurations, and figurations of figurations, in which social actors are routinely now involved provides a way into understanding these conflicts. Digital media platforms now install self-*projection* and self-*promotion* as part of the basic means of the self to be deployed across the managed continuity of online space and time. These means are worked out through a series of performances and anticipations within particular figurations. The resulting *re*configuration of what selves do online has changed how individuals *are in the world* and, in the course of this, recalibrated individuals' potential relations to social institutions.

It is worth emphasizing two points about our analysis in this chapter. First, we are not presuming a pre-existing independent self of the sort assumed in conventional 'liberal individualism'. Rather, we mean by 'the self' only the viewpoint on the social world associated with a particular embodied consciousness. But this viewpoint and speaking position only emerges in the course of an individual's intermeshing with many other individuals and with a social world of institutions and individuals: this is the basic insight of Elias' notion of 'figurations' (Elias, 1978, p. 132). This notion of self is inherently dialogical: 'the self is brought into being by the communicational processes established with others and with oneself', a process of continually 'negotiating meaning with others' (Salgado and Hermans, 2005, p. 11). Because this process of intermeshing is never complete and involves endless new frictions and opportunities, it is impossible to see the self as static. As Elias (1978, p. 18) puts it, 'a person is constantly in movement; he not only goes through a process, he *is* a process'. It is essential therefore to *dereify*[4] the notions of individual and society, and understand their evolving *networked* relations.

The second point applies the first: not only is the self always processual, but a special attention must be paid to the material processes of forming and sustaining the self. The figurations and underlying infrastructures whereby individuals come to be in relations with others are themselves changing with deep mediatization. There is a special value at such times in what Durkheim called 'social morphology': a type of analysis that 'observes [the social substratum] as it is evolving in order to show how it is being formed' (Durkheim, 1982 [1895], p. 242). The self is a good site to see at work this changing social morphology, driven in part by large corporate interests in *their* search for new sources of economic value. We will develop this, by considering, in turn, socialization, the changing resources of the self, and the self's digital traces.

8.1 Socialization

When Elias introduces his account of social life as 'networked phenomena', his first example is the process of 'socialization' (1991 [1939], pp. 26–27). We use this term with some caution, since it can suggest a functionalist account in which society's values are unproblematically passed on to its youngest members, who in turn reproduce them. No functionalist model is assumed here: by 'socialization', we mean merely the heterogeneous attempts and claims to pass on certain legitimate norms within social life (whether successful or not). When Elias wrote, it would have been absurd to argue for any role of media institutions in this building-up of basic relationships; even if (unknown to the child) some commercial branding and media processes had lain behind some of the toys with which the child played (see Wachelder, 2014), there was no question then of media entering into how children sustain relationships with significant others. But, by the 1960s and 1970s, when as authors we spent our early childhoods, the continuous presence of television and radio in most family homes in Europe meant that media played a significant role in the *imagined* world of the child, as an important influx from outside the home: television programmes produced for children, cartoons and films, live sports broadcasts. Insofar as those sources sometimes generated reference-points for play and performance (cartoon characters, sporting heroes), there is no doubt that the role of media deserved already some emphasis (Kress, 1986), an emphasis completely absent in Berger and Luckmann's account of 'socialization', either in its primary (parental and family) or secondary (institutional, especially educational) phases (Berger and Luckmann, 1966, pp. 149–166).[5] In this world, as children were growing up, media did nothing to mediate the relations of primary or secondary socialization. Indeed at that time the situations in which parents, teachers and school peers passed on norms and values were still very likely to be face to face.

Today the situation is very different for many children, at least in richer countries. Their parents (and peers) are able to main a consistent 'presence' to them through mobile phones and other devices. Everyday play for the child may involve what we might call the 'depth of field' of complex media interfaces such as the tablet. Books (a form of media too, of course) have played this role at least from the nineteenth century, but only recently have children possessed media that offer *manipulable interfaces* with the world (Ito et al., 2010, pp. 1–28). One of us was recently standing on the 100th floor of Shanghai's tallest skyscraper, the Financial District Tower, and, along with everyone else, marvelling at the view: at our feet was a young child (around two years old) who had her back turned to the view and was playing, completely absorbed, with a tablet. Meanwhile, tablets have become commonplace in schools, for reasons as much to do with the corporatization of the school as an environment (Selwyn, 2014, pp. 120–124) as with the new capacities of contemporary media generations (Bolin, 2014). The 'class', as Sonia Livingstone and Julian Sefton-Green (2016) call it, is nowadays a deeply mediatized space, in which 'personal autonomy and control' (2016, p. 236) in relation to media have great value: a key question there becomes whether teachers can have access to students' social platforms' profiles (and vice versa).

Two important steps are involved here. First, the child increasingly depends from her early awareness on a media infrastructure, in order to be present to and with her parents. Such basic forms of initial socialization once did not involve media, but now increasingly they do. Since, as Berger and Luckmann rightly say, the child generally knows their parents not just as one set of parents among others, but 'as *the* world, the only existence and only conceivable world' (1966, p. 154), mediated connection is now installed from early on as an operating condition of 'the world' itself. Second, media infrastructure is intrinsic to the space of play: it is a mediated space–time (of games, database searching, talking, seeing photos, playing with images) *into which the child reaches* when she reaches out to play, whether with or without her parents. This transformation has spread far beyond elites, at least in rich countries.[6] Fleer (2014) provides an example of the use of video-editing via tablet in play among the under-fives in Australia, while Sun Systems' John Gage expresses nicely the general transformation under way, albeit not from an objective standpoint:

> Today a child, anywhere in the world, linked to the Internet, can reach across the network to access databases of images, bring them to the screen and fly across the face of the earth, zooming down the streets and homes or up over mountain peaks and down river valleys. Today, a child can see planes on runways at San Francisco International Airport, visit the hospital inside the Imperial Palace in Tokyo, float above cars and trucks on the streets of Kabul, circle Mount Everest, or examine the bottom of the Grand Canyon. (Gage, 2002, p. 6)

In that sense, mediated connectivity becomes an operating condition of the child's imagined world, as well as, later on, its secondary institutions of socialization.

Talk about media and doing things with media becomes a basic part of socialization. The media environment, and the computer-based infrastructure of information on which that environment is based, is today part of the interactional world about which the child starts to reflect, as she gets older. A facility for interacting fluently with that world becomes part of how a child grows into that world *well*. This happens in different ways in different cultures and under different conditions of wealth and poverty (Banaji, 2015), but that this mediated dependency is a *potential* feature of socialization everywhere is undeniable. The conditions of socialization have in other words changed. *Socialization, in its basic aspects, has become mediatized.*

A sign of this is that parents' working definitions of literacy may be changing from traditional book literacy to include a facility for using digital technologies in everyday life, resulting in a growing disconnect between the home environment and school environment – assuming schools restrict access to tablets for the under-fives, but parents encourage them.[7] There is much more to be discovered, for sure, about media's potential to *enhance* skills through play. Some argue for a new pedagogic framework of 'participatory learning' and 'media literacies' (Jenkins et al., 2016, pp. 90–119) which explicitly recognizes the role of cross-media interfaces: first, in deepening the ways in which children can construct worlds in play and then communicate about those worlds; second, in facilitating children's memory-structure within play via the archiving and editing features of digital devices; and third, through enhancing children's awareness of the multiple ways of expressing the same idea in different media (Alper, 2011, pp. 184–188). Particularly interesting is the notion of 'distributed cognition', that is, 'forms of reasoning that would not be possible without the presence of artefacts or information appliances' (Jenkins, 2006a, pp. 65–66). The potential that digital devices have to augment human cognitive capacities, and so the cognitive dimension of socialization, is important (Mansell, 2012, pp. 188–190). Media contents' *transferability* in multi-media contexts has become intrinsic to practical ways of learning and thinking (Drotner, 2009). At the same time, the world of early learning may no longer involve any barrier between contexts of literacy and contexts of commercial consumption, a point made forcefully by cultural sociologist Dan Cook:

> the world of consumption and marketplaces represents a key and absolutely necessary site for the study of childhood – as well as for social action – precisely because it disrupts even the most generous of conceptions of children and the locus of power. To keep consumption, popular culture and media culture separate and distant from children and childhood in our studies and undertakings is to reaffirm a vision of social life disconnected from lived experience. (Cook, 2005, p. 158)

If so, the encouragement towards a new type of mediated literacy is ambiguous, to say the least. There is much more to be said here, for example, on children's early skills of searching online, taking pictures for exchange, sharing things online, chatting online, and commenting on each others' digital skills. The main point for the generations growing up with deep mediatization is that they become socialized *into* a world in which the media manifold is a matter of course. While that doesn't imply a new generation has homogeneous patterns of media and communications practice – a misunderstanding we find in discussion about 'digital natives' (Hepp et al., 2014, pp. 22–31) – the range of young people's media and communications practices will have in common a basis reaction to a transformed media environment which for them is 'natural' and provides the basis for their positioning in the social world.

Equally important however are children's expectations from an early age that they will leave digital traces. We both grew up in an age when, while the camera was not rare, it was relatively cumbersome (to use and to have its images developed) and the taking of photographs or videos was an occasional event, performed always with considerable emphasis: on holiday, at major family events, and so on. This is very different from today's world, in rich countries at least, of continuous image-swapping and posting. What family occasion is *not* now accompanied by someone taking a picture, usually on their mobile phone, and later exchanging it so that absent others can see it and comment on it? A well-known expression of this is the 'selfie'. It is today *banal* for the child to have her actions associated with the possibility of later commentary: 'that looked nice!', 'you looked so pretty that day!', 'did you have a good time (I saw the pics on Facebook)?' This is the result not of the technologies themselves – a technologically determinist approach would precisely miss the work of social construction going on here – but of our practices with and around digital technologies which builds a *tissue* of media resource and media-based reflection around much of everyday growing up. As children, we grew up leaving few trails of connection as we moved from day to day, situation to situation. That is not true for the contemporary child: the *texture* of everyday life during childhood has changed, and that texture is woven, primarily, *out of* mediated materials, *out of* the basic platforms for externalization and exchange that media devices and infrastructures provide (Christensen and Røpke, 2010, p. 251; van Dijck, 2007).

We can talk validly then of the mediatization of socialization. This plays out in multiple ways for early adulthood: teenagers who are still in education, and young adults – whether or not teenagers, since the average age of entering work varies radically from country to country – who have recently entered the world of work and are starting to form key emotional partnerships outside the family. Early adulthood is in between what Berger and Luckmann (1966, p. 150) called 'primary socialization' by which the child becomes a member of society (through relations with parents and increasingly peers), and 'secondary socialization', in which the socialized individual is introduced to new domains of the social world (centres of further education, clubs and workplaces).

Young adults' primary socialization with peers exhibits even more dramatic evidence of mediatization than early childhood. We have already discussed the role of media in mediating children's interface with parents: this continues through teendom, with the mobile phone texting and calling, and online chat streams accessible via smartphones, playing a key role in linking parents and teenagers together as they move across space (Schofield Clark, 2013). In addition, mediated spaces and platforms have become for countless adolescents *the* space where they 'hang out' away from parents and other sources of authority. As danah boyd (2008) noted in an important essay on young people growing up in the USA, free speech and relatively unregulated behaviour are impossible for them in their homes or in public spaces or shopping malls, schools and the like, so social media provide a crucial space in which to be *in* the world. In that sense, social networking sites are not a lifestyle or fashion choice, but a response to *necessity* whose configuration depends precisely on the spatial features of the internet:

> What is unique about the internet is that it allows teens to participate in unregulated publics while located in adult-regulated physical spaces such as homes and schools [. . .] they do so [not to turn their backs on adults but] because they seek access to adult society. Their participation is deeply rooted in their desire to engage publicly. (boyd, 2008, pp. 136–137; see also boyd, 2014, pp. 19–20)

This space *to be* is of particular importance for those whose identities are marginalized or stigmatized in adult society, for example sexual minorities (Gray, 2012). From this basic point, however, certain consequences flow for how primary socialization with peers now works. The basic structure of platforms and their commercial imperatives create certain distinctive conditions that affect how teenagers and young adults can exist in public. Unlike face-to-face meetings, such public existence is 'searchable', leaving a permanent trail of digital traces, which is also easily replicable, and so may start *chains of signification* across multiple contexts and actions beyond the control of the initial actor. These longer-term consequences play out, in part, in front of audiences who the initial actor doesn't, and cannot, know: what danah boyd calls 'invisible audiences'. As she points out: 'in unmediated spaces, structural boundaries are assessed [by young people] to determine who is in the audience and who is not [. . .] In mediated spaces, there are no [spatial] structures to limit the audience; search collapses all virtual walls' (boyd, 2008, p. 132). That does not mean young people cannot find ways, over time, to deal with these consequences, and boyd's later work (2014) charts ways in which at least US teenagers may do exactly that. But it does mean that, as they grow up, young people face uncertainty about 'where' and 'when' they act, and so whether they, or someone or something else, is ultimately in control, as they perform ordinary actions.

Online performance is however only one aspect of how, in the course of growing up, young adults are now being required to reflect on and make choices about how they want to be mediated. Sherry Turkle's book *Alone Together* (Turkle, 2011) comments on how young people of school age, again in the USA, are increasingly rationing the real-time media-based communications they have with others, because of the pressures and risks attached to open-ended communication (for example, on the phone or on online chat): for example, a 16-year-old school pupil who told Turkle that she preferred SMS text to phone calls 'because in a call "there is a lot less boundness to the person"' (Turkle 2011, p. 146). Digital media put young people in view of, and in contact with, such a large potential group of peers and others that it is not surprising they are developing ways of screening people out. But as Turkle notes, this may lead to an instrumentalization of personal communication that is unhealthy. Philosopher Immanuel Kant's injunction that one should always treat people as 'ends not means' (Kant 1990 [1795]) is not, without considerable adjustment, even *compatible* with a time when, in the ordinary course of early life, one acquires hundreds of Facebook friends and thousands of Twitter followers. The question Turkle poses is whether the continuous availability of today's mediated relationships enhances togetherness and community-building, or rather creates a sheath of superficial connection: continuous involvement with no depth. When it comes to socialization, Turkle understands face-to-face conversation as important but under pressure from the new forms of what she calls '(quantified) self-reports' via social platforms and the resulting sense of oneself as an 'algorithmic self' (Turkle, 2015, pp. 79–99). Data processes here enter the fabric of the self's reflexivity.

A further version of these pressures may occur when an individual starts paid work, and encounters for the first time new institutions of secondary socialization in the form of employers, but under conditions where the individual is particularly liable to be shaped, indeed trained, in a certain way. Dave Eggers' novel *The Circle* (2013) offers a brilliant fable on these issues. It follows the trajectory of a keen new employee, Mae Holland, at a technology company whose goal is to build a complete interface for all interactions, transactions and data accumulation online. The important point of the commercial imperatives behind such business models is that they depend on the individual's commitment to *input* data constantly from 'natural' social intercourse, so that it can be aggregated and processed, contributing to wider value-generation: as Eggers imagines, towards the ever more complete achievement of the 'circle' of knowledge. In the course of submitting to this imperative, Mae Holland finds that she risks dismantling the boundaries – around her informal self, and those of her friends and parents too – on which her everyday functioning as a social self had implicitly relied. The walls, not just of particular situations but also of her social self, collapse, and for a while she cannot go on. An older character reacts to the pressures of constant connectivity even more drastically by committing suicide 'live' (that is, in view of social networks). What Eggers dramatizes is a situation, increasingly recognizable in many societies, where the pressure to be part of a 'pervasive sociality' – curated not out of love or affection, but for profit – conflicts with the self's need for freedom, for a 'scope for movement' and 'breathing room' (Cohen, 2012, p. 149).

These issues affect not just young adults, but all adults. They impinge however with particular intensity on those in the early stages of adulthood who are *building* their work- and friend-networks outside the family for later life (Marwick, 2015). Presence on social media platforms necessitates submission to external judgement by peers as well as by non-peers (such as potential employers). As one participant in a focus-group study of Norwegian students put it, 'on Facebook, you judge each other's lives. That's what you do' (quoted in Storsul 2014, p. 24).[8] This is the significance of the many contemporary stories of young adults suddenly finding that the regulatory pressures of the adult work-world intervene in their socializing activities with peers. When employers can search back into the present *and past* social media archive of their potential employees, to look for misdemeanours and indiscretions, or signs of undesirable opinions, but without of course any access to the context that gave those earlier traces their meaning, a fundamental rupture has emerged in the fabric of socialization. Processes of healthy experimentation with social roles, or with social boundaries – simply through the way the internet's architecture works: its ability to archive everything without undifferentiation – get converted into 'evidence' (at some arbitrary point in the future) of something problematic. This damages the very *movement* of socialization which allows early periods of reduced accountability when young adults prepare for the fully accountable domain of adulthood. Deep assumptions about the *contextual integrity* on which the functioning of everyday life depends (Nissenbaum, 2004, 2010) are here overridden by archival fiat. The young adult self increasingly finds itself in a new, hyperlinked *situation* of uncertain spatial and temporal span: the expanded 'situation' is part of what young selves must increasingly reflect upon.

This contemporary transformation of the *modalities* of socialization in childhood and early adulthood finds a striking, if distant, parallel in Norbert Elias' 1930s reflections on the conditions for the emergence of the modern state:

> the whole apparatus which shapes the individual, the mode of operation of the social demands and prohibitions which mould his social makeup, and above all *the kinds of fear* that play a part in his life are decisively changed. (Elias, 1994 [1939], p. xv, added emphasis)

Fear is a key force in socialization; it moulds our sense of the spaces and contexts in which we are safe, and of the relations to time, which are comfortable, or not comfortable, to us. Fear generates the need for new rules, new primers of behaviour. In the early European Renaissance, leading philosophers such as Erasmus advised young people on how to manage their body.[9] Today, young adults – and increasingly even children too – are required to manage not just their physical bodies, but also their 'data bodies'. A modern Erasmus would surely need to include a chapter on how to comport oneself on social media platforms. For, as one employer in the previously quoted careers guide comments about a potential employee's social media trail: 'it's the first thing I look at'. A phenomenology of the social world must register this changing social morphology.

8.2 The Changing Resources of the Self

So far we have argued that media and communications are transforming how selves are 'in' the social world, and the processes through which they come to be social actors (socialization). But this transformation cannot be separated from changes in the *nature* of the self.

The self, understood not as a substance, but as a process, is hugely complex. An important strand in social psychology has emphasized that the self is not formed in opposition to the external 'social' world, or to particular 'others' within it, but in continuous dialogue with that world and its others (Hermans, 2004). Recognizing the complex processual nature of the self – always changing and developing, always reflecting on and transforming itself, never complete – is quite consistent with recognizing that the self uses many means, including media, for interfacing with the world. But it is important not to assume that the expansion of media platforms through which the self now faces the social world do not in themselves imply any *change to the self* in its fundamental nature. Framing things *that* way – through, for example, a claim that our self is simply now 'extended' or 'distributed' by its technological practices (Belk, 1998, 2013; Helmond, 2010) – misses precisely the tensions that flow from the attempt to maintain the self's freedom and integrity as a project (Touraine, 1981) under these new and highly challenging conditions. It is not the self that is extended but, rather, the space–time *across which* the self is now exposed, managed and governed.

A positive aspect of this transformation is that the self now has new resources available to it for sustaining its integrity as a reflexive project for action (Martuccelli, 2002). Let us now examine some of the new resources available to the self through media and especially digital information-infrastructures: we will turn in the next section to the particular issues that arise for resources derived from data infrastructures.

The self relies at all times on resources acquired in the processes of socialization and daily life. By 'resource', we mean material structures (whether institutions, spaces, tools, facilities, capital),[10] which enhance the ability of the self to act in various ways: from the analysis of this chapter so far, it is clear that media are today part of the resources of the self. We can think about those resources as forming three distinct types: first, *resources for self-narration* (identity maintenance through narrative); second, *resources for self-representation* (or presenting); and third, *resources for self-maintenance*, that is, for keeping the self as a functioning social actor. In conducting its battles, the self always carries an account of itself born out of a desire to narrate the particularity of its path through the world (Cavarero, 2000). Only in certain societies and cultural contexts however have individuals had the practical means, resources and status to circulate an account of the particularities of their life. The ability to create and continuously revise a narrative (text, images, sound, archive) that came with digital media is a significant chapter in the history of the self that supplements the earlier history of the diary, and so on. First, the blog and more recently the time-line on social media platforms have become banal, expected whenever someone works abroad for a year, goes on a special journey, experiences a life-changing challenge (e.g. cancer). But this increasing frequency should not mask what is far from banal about these developments: the extended spatiotemporal reach of self-narratives, which is distinctive to the age of digitalization. 'My blog', to quote one respondent to Korean researchers Jinyoung Min and Hweseok Lee, 'is where my thoughts meet the world' (Min and Lee, 2011, pp. 23–47).

Depending on the structure of one's society, and in particular its hierarchies of voice, this interface between self and world can be transformative, as for example with the Middle Eastern (especially Saudi) women bloggers analysed by Guta and Karolak (2015). If speaking up in a public space is deeply restricted (as for women in many Middle Eastern countries), the blog is a liminal site where otherwise silent selves enter public existence, even if still a restricted one (it is impossible for Saudi women to post selfies online: Guta and Karolak, 2015, p. 122).

Once we move beyond the *basic* innovation of opening one's thoughts to the social world, an interesting underlying structure emerges. Consistently maintaining a blog or an active platform page involves maintaining a 'presence' (Couldry, 2012, pp. 33–58) under conditions that are, inherently, much less controllable than in the face-to-face performances analysed by Erving Goffman. Through its desire to exhibit itself (Hogan, 2010, pp. 381–382), the blogging self sustains its narrative presence, but becomes reliant on a third-party curator or platform (one's blog post, after all, can always be taken down, or the platform discontinued). Unlike with face-to-face performance, the online exhibition is always filtered by the platform used and the platform's algorithmic practice (Litt, 2012); equally, through the open-ended architecture of the web, it is available through search engines, to become read in new, unpredictable contexts.

Self-narratives have always been focused around a sense of *some* possible audience, even if, as with the paradigmatic case of Anne Franks' diary, it was a reader in some unknowable future. That follows from the inherently social nature of narrative as an anticipated exchange (MacIntyre, 1981; Couldry, 2010, p. 7). But, with offline narratives, it was possible to lock the diary in a drawer or other secret place, or to restrict its readership to one or two trusted friends. Such degree of control is however incompatible with the means by which we externalize self-narrative today. As Andreas Kitzmann puts it:

> Before electronic media, the place of the diary was a private place [. . .] for the Web diary writer [. . .] the audience is not only anticipated, but expected, and this influences the very manner in which the writer

articulates, composes and distributes the self-document. (Kitzmann, 2003, p. 56).

For that reason, self-disclosure in the digital age is always in part 'non-directed' (Jang and Stefanone, 2011). Depending on the exact balance between expected and unexpected components within the audience, the expectations, even norms, of distant audiences can start to shape not just the writing, but even the *life-process* on which the writing was meant to report, as one travel-blog writer suspects (Magasic, 2014). This is all the more likely when the practice of blogging becomes overlaid with the motivation of data measurement: a desire for 'likes' and other validating interactions with an unseen audience (Bucher, 2012a; Magasic, 2014; Papacharissi and Easton, 2013). People can no doubt live with a considerable degree of complexity here, inhabiting the 'privately public' or the 'publicly private' (Lange, 2007), and a processual understanding of the self must acknowledge this. But if self-maintenance today necessarily involves the risk of reaching an *undesirable* audience (risk once reserved for broadcasting institutions who scatter their messages across space: Peters, 1999), then the processes of self-maintenance have been unsettled in an important way.[11]

Another practice, which has appeared to challenge our sense of the boundaries around the self, is the selfie. It is too easy to dismiss this as simple narcissism, curious though the sight is of someone walking through a remarkable location, selfie-stick in hand, and taking regular pictures of themselves, hardly focusing on the look of the location. But what is a selfie? Multiple interpretations have been offered: as an attempt to visualize an insecure self into existence (Fausing, 2014); as a practice of place-making (Losh, 2014); as a gesture (Senft and Baym, 2015); or as an embryonic bid for attention and capital (Marwick, 2015). But two Korean researchers Yoo Jin Kwon and Kyoung-Nan Kwon have perhaps best captured the basic meaning: the selfie is a practical means for sustaining a *continuous* narrative of the self that can be taken as 'natural' (Kwon and Kwon, 2015). Once we grasp this *banal* purpose, we can acknowledge its often deeply paradoxical nature, captured in this example from Israel: 'D, a 16-year-old boy from Tel Aviv [who] is intensely involved in photography. He takes many photos on a regular basis in sundry situations: at school, with friends, with girls, or alone. However he is not particularly interested in photography as such. In an interview, he describes his range of subjects as extremely narrow: "only myself"' (Schwarz, 2010, p. 163).

The selfie stamps the marker of 'the self' onto whatever things a person wants to record as a way of increasing its value. But why should *that* have become so important recently? There are no doubt many overlapping factors at work here including the changing affordances of smartphones, but one background factor, we want to suggest, is the increasing *devaluation of introspection*: that is, reflecting, comparing, building the basis of a memory through organized thought that remains 'internal' (still unshared). Introspection, in the habit of taking selfies, gets overridden by the 'higher' value of generating an exchangeable trace of one's 'experience' whose form is tailored exactly to the data-based needs of social media platforms.

The selfie is, in other words, a repeated gesture of *externalization*, whose insistence is striking, though not without precedent. In the late eighteenth century it was fashionable for a while to carry a convex mirror (the 'Claude glass') as one walked in the countryside which would enable one to compress a beautiful vista into a small focused image whose likeness to a painting that one might have seen would thereby become clearer: the 'picturesque' needed a technique to produce itself reliably (Andrews, 1989, pp. 67–73). So too today, the selfie-stick with camera attached produces a reliable *self*-tagged image of one's passage through the world – not for immediate consumption but for deferred value that will come from its circulation via social media. The selfie integrates the deferred possibility of online circulation perfectly into the present, so confirming Sage Elwell's point that 'we no longer "go online", rather the Internet is of a piece with the infosphere where we already are and of which we are increasingly a part' (Elwell, 2013, p. 235).

To say this is not to deny the possibility of more intense and less banal forms of self-externalization through media technologies. Media are, without question, enabling new forms of intimacy towards loved ones: sending images of or comments upon things just seen (Villi, 2012); or continuous phatic communication as in the 'telecocoon' of young lovers (Habuchi, 2005). And clearly such intensified externalization – so different in intensity and regularity from the sparse generation of self-images in everyday life just twenty years ago – brings risks, since one cannot be in full control of the storage or distribution of this volume of symbolic material (Schwarz, 2011).

Here the deepening of mediatization becomes clear. For those who live in a world of constant 'connectivity', the self faces new pressures to perform itself online in order *just to function* as a social being. These pressures go far beyond the expression of identity, an optional supplement to everyday existence, which – as Bev Skeggs (1994) argued – attracts individuals very differently, depending on class and gender. The transformation of resource we are discussing here is more basic: a requirement just to be present on particular platforms and in particular exchanges, and the preconditions for being cognitively equipped for the world. The needs of basic social recognition and basic practical functioning converge on the production of one's 'data double'. The self becomes increasingly *dependent* on digital infrastructure for its survival and integrity.[12] The operating conditions of digital infrastructures become part of the functioning conditions of the self.

We have noted one consequence already in the problem of *too much* social memory: the need, that is, to forget, in order to have the possibility of forgiving actions in a distant past (Bannon, 2006; Dodge and Kitchin, 2007). But this is only one (temporal) dimension of the wider transformation of the self's place within the social: can there then be excessive connectivity? Ben Agger approaches this through the notion of what he calls 'iTime': 'it is non-trivial that people are always available as they exist in iTime [. . .]. One cannot hide in iTime. Boss, colleagues, family expect one to be available' (Agger, 2011, p. 123). Across all these contexts, a consistency of performance seems required (van Dijck, 2013), yet perhaps is unattainable. Before we just succumb to the requirement of consistency, it is worth remembering that in the ancient classical world, the problem was rather different. Remember the saying of Roman philosopher Seneca: 'Believe me, it is a major achievement to act as one person' (quoted in Hermans, 2001, p. 276). Two millennia later, in an age where family, friendship and work are performed in a continuous set of linked spaces,[13] we ask a different question: how much *inconsistency* is a self now allowed?

In the next section, we turn to one particular version of these tensions and potentials: the self's increasing ability, perhaps necessity, to generate meaning from its 'digital traces', and the infrastructural dependencies that follow from this.

8.3 The Self's Digital Traces and Their Infrastructure

A prominent characteristic of the self in the age of deep mediatization is the *digital traces s/he leaves*: whatever we do, we leave 'footprints' of our digital media use that build digital traces. We do this consciously for example by uploading photographs or writing comments on the 'timelines' of digital platforms. More often we do this unaware, as an unintended side-effect of our activities in a media-based domain, for example using our smartphones' or cars' navigation systems (and leaving a 'trace' of where we are); doing our shopping and leaving 'traces' of our transaction when we pay by credit card, smartphone or discount card. But digital traces even go further: they are made not just by us but also by *others* when they interact online with reference to us, for example when they synchronize their address books with our digital addresses, tag pictures, texts or other digital artefacts with our name, and so on. It can even be argued that digital traces now begin before birth with the 'mediatization of parenthood' (Damkjaer, 2015): pregnancy is accompanied by an ongoing flow of communication via apps and platforms that produce digital traces of the child growing in the womb. Some argue that nowadays 'we cannot *not* leave digital traces' (Merzeau, 2009, p. 4, added emphasis).

Putting Digital Traces in Context

But how can we understand digital traces in detail? Digital traces are more than just (big) data: they are a form of digital data which becomes meaningful only when a sequence of 'digital footprints' is related to a certain actor or action, typically (of) a person but in principle also a collectivity or organization. It is the *tie* of data to the unique individual that underlies why marketers and other institutions of data processing are highly interested in collecting and aggregating data. Such data is not just any information, but always information linked to processes of counting, as reflected in the French expression for digital traces, *traces numériques*. Digital traces are numerically produced correlations of disparate kinds of data that are generated by our practices in a digitalized media environment. Because of the tie that such correlations always have to a certain entity or process in the social world, digital traces are a major, but not the only, reference-point for how a social entity acquires its 'digital identity'.

This deep mediatization of the self has, unsurprisingly, generated much debate about how sociology can, any more, stay in touch with what selves are and do.[14] Some academics go one step further and argue that the self's digital traces amount to more than traces of a self that still (in principle) can be reached through other routes (observation, listening). They argue that such traces offer for the first time a *direct* access to ongoing processes of social construction. Maybe the most prominent example is Bruno Latour's integration of the investigation of digital traces into his overall approach to social analysis (Latour, 2007). A 'digital traceability' (Venturini and Latour, 2010, p. 6) then becomes a possibility for analysing processes of social construction *in situ*: 'being interested in the construction of social phenomena implies tracking each of the actors involved and each of the interactions between them' (Venturini and Latour, 2010, p. 5). This approach attempts to move beyond the old micro/macro divide (a classic topic in sociology)[15] by arguing that statistical methods allow us to get at 'macro' phenomena *directly* by an analysis of the individuals' online activities. With digital traces, they claim, we have a direct access that allows us to witness processes of assembling in the moment they take place (Latour et al., 2012; Venturini, 2012).

This argument is, in our view, fundamentally mistaken: it misunderstands the nature of digital traces in relation to the self. The error begins with misinterpreting the social world as 'flat' and so accessible to analysis simply through an aggregation of trace-patterns registered in the various data domains that are underpinned by media infrastructure. Such patterns may well have some value, but this move reduces the complexity of the contemporary social world to a flat plane without differentiated levels, so replicating on a large scale the problem with the concept of assemblages that we have critiqued already in Chapter 4. Second, and even more fundamentally, such an approach misunderstands digital traces as something 'neutral', offering us a 'direct access' to the social world. However, they are not 'neutral phenomena' but rely on the technical procedures of *governing institutions* that produce this kind of information. The construction of the self's traces therefore already, through its very process, inscribes certain *interests* as well as *visions* of society: we find here a strange echo of Jacques Derrida's (1973, p. 85) insistence on how subjectivity ('the self of the living present') is always 'a trace' that links to a 'temporalization' and 'spacing' that carries beyond itself. Digital traces do not offer access to the social world 'as it is' but an access to the procedures whereby powerful organizations attempt to *construct a world on which they can act*.

A materialist phenomenology must therefore take a rather different approach to the self's digital traces. Far from treating them as direct 'traces' of what is, it insists on approaching them from two directions: first, in terms of their *consequences* for the everyday world of the individual and, second, in terms of their *origins* in the world-making strategies of governing institutions. Because all social classifications are 'interactive' (Hacking, 1999, pp. 30–31), these two aspects overlap in the flow of practice, but at no point do they converge into the possibility that the self's data traces provide direct access to the social. This complicates our evaluation of contemporary movements that attempt to transform reflexivity through processes based precisely on datafication, to which we turn next.

Self-Quantification

Quite how big an adjustment data practices demand of sociology's traditional approach to the self emerges when we return to the original thoughts of Berger and Luckmann on self-consciousness. As they put it:

> The world of everyday life is not only taken for granted as reality by the ordinary members of society in the subjectively meaningful conduct of their lives. It is a world that *originates* in their thoughts and actions, and is *maintained as real* by these. [. . .] we must attempt to clarify the foundations of knowledge in everyday life [. . .] [in] the objectivation of subjective processes (and meanings) by which the *inter*subjective common-sense world is constructed. (1966, pp. 33–34, first two emphases added)

To some extent at least, this starting-point is uncontestable, but in certain key respects it is now in tension with a new notion of self-consciousness and self-knowledge that is emerging through the automated collection of data. Gary Wolf is a key proselytizer of the 'quantified self' movement: while aware of the tensions and potential strangeness of the idea that 'self-knowledge [comes] through numbers' (Wolf, 2009), he also provides some of the key arguments in apparent support of this proposition. For example, the idea that 'our ordinary behaviour contains obscure quantitative signals that can be used to inform our behaviour, once we learn to read them' (Wolf, 2010, p. 4), which of course builds on the practical starting-point discussed throughout this chapter that 'social media made it seem *normal* to share everything' (ibid., added emphasis). The process is self-fuelling: 'the more [people] want to share, the more they want to have something to share' (2010, p. 6). This is an explicitly collaborative form of mediated construction that, as it grows in regularity and intensity, produces alongside each concrete individual a 'data double' (Haggerty and Ericson, 2000) which – from certain perspectives like those of the quantified self movement, but also perhaps some contemporary governments (Ruppert, 2011) – contains more 'truth' than an individual's own self-reflections. We are witnessing here innovations in relation to the fundamental languages for describing and measuring the self: we cannot therefore imagine them to be innocent of power. On the contrary, what is under way is a transformation *of* social and political power: as Julie Cohen (2015) puts it, 'we are witnessing the emergence of a distinctly Western, democratic type of surveillance society, in which surveillance is conceptualized first and foremost as a matter of efficiency and convenience'.

The case of self-quantification in the health domain is particularly illuminating. More and more people are using tracking devices to generate continuous data about themselves (for example, heart-rate, metabolic rate and so on). As Deborah Lupton points out, this is more than just another 'technology of the self' (Foucault, 1988): it is a way of embedding the self, and its 'data practices', in a much wider infrastructure of data generation, aggregation and analysis, which potentially might transform the distribution of resources in the health industries away from cure and towards continuous activities of prevention. Aside from the installation of self-measurement into the basic processes of everyday life (a 'personal Taylorism' (Lupton, 2014, p. 8), this changes what *counts as* self-awareness, with so-called self-quantifiers using 'data to construct the stories that they tell themselves about themselves' (Lupton, 2014, p. 8, quoting Davis, 2013), and the norms that orient reflexive self-awareness.[16]

So far these practices are the preserve of a small movement of enthusiastic first-adopters, but they have behind them a considerable momentum and leverage.[17] Some in the health industries see patients' continuous sharing of their health data as part of an (increasingly obligatory) practice of 'self-management' (Hawn, 2009, p. 365). Though sometimes disguised as a game, as a sort of play, self-monitoring 'enrolls people into self-governance by using their highest aspirations and capacities, that of self-case and self-development' (Whitson, 2013, p. 170): once we acknowledge the gaps in our normal memories, why not supplement them with the 'more objective' materials generated automatically by continuous data collection (Whitson, 2013, p. 175)? Yet, the price of playing along is acceptance of a data collection and data-sharing infrastructure whose rules are non-negotiable (Whitson, 2013, p. 175). There are of course problems like tracking devices, which may generate too much information to be interpreted (Choe et al., 2014). But those concerns may easily be overridden by more powerful claims: for example, that data collection tools enable subjects to *become conscious* of their otherwise unconscious behaviours and behavioural patterns (Kido and Swan, 2014); that this is how individuals *take responsibility* for preventive medicine (Swan, 2012); or more generally that this is how individuals *optimize* their 'performance' along various dimensions (Swan, 2013).

Positive readings of these developments are readily available: as a protective 'technology blanket' wrapped around the self (Swan, 2012, p. 97); as an 'improved "higher quality" self' (Swan, 2013, p. 93); as a form of collaborative memory (Frith and Kalin, forthcoming) or 'macroscope' (Wolf, 2009); or even, according to one leading proselytizer, Kevin Kelly, as a form of an 'exoself' (Kelly, 2012; see Bostrom and Sandberg, 2011). There is no doubt of the serious commercial intent to build such a comprehensive layer of data-tracking around the individual, at least in the context of the richest societies and their highly resourced health and personal development industries. To speak of such developments as a transformation of the 'self', however, precisely begs the key question: whether such quantification practices are compatible with other senses of the self and, even if so, whether the price they exact is too high. Once we leave aside the more crass rhetoric (for example of a 'people-powered health' at the Nesta web page),[18] the notion of every person carrying an 'algorithmic skin' is closely tied to the futures of 'commercial, governmental and medical research' (Williamson, 2015, p. 139), and mobilizes a discourse about self-awareness for distinctively institutional ends. As Williamson puts it:

> Self-quantification produces a 'calculable public', a public that is presented back to itself through the data organized and coordinated by algorithmic approximations of its traceable health activities. (Williamson, 2015, p. 143)

So strong is the drive towards greater self-awareness and more sustainable self-improvement that it is easy to lose track of the potential damage that is being done here to our everyday notions of self-consciousness which have never, until now, needed to resort to external data-gathering infrastructures to validate their claims about self, others and the social world. There is a risk already, even before we consider the biases that the process of metrification and datafication introduce into daily life.

Towards the Institutionalization of the Self

We have explored in this chapter a self that, through the operations of the media manifold, increasingly interacts in extended domains of the social world – which in turn act back on the self, increasingly through processes of datafication. This self is a site of tension between its own claims to awareness and new notions of 'enhanced' self-awareness derived from new automated data-gathering techniques. These potential new transformations carry a price. While apparently enhancing the freedom of the self, they build into the fabric of the self an infrastructural dependency: a process of *institutionalization* and *materialization* that, because of the asymmetrical power-relations at work in the media domain involved, introduces a dimension of *unfreedom* that today's selves must confront (Cohen, 2012).

Deep mediatization – that is, the integration of media-based processes and relations into the very elements from which the self sustains its project *as a self* – introduces therefore a new friction into daily life. We will consider this problem more fully in Chapter 10. Undeniably however, if the site of the self is transformed by mediatization, then so too is the site of the 'we' that comes together through the grouping of selves. The risk that we mimic each other in certain ways and so converge artificially in our behaviours on online platforms, becoming 'partial analogues of others', has been noted for a while (Agha, 2007). We need in the next chapter to explore more broadly how the construction of 'collectivity' operates in an age of deep mediatization.

9

Collectivities

We discussed in the last chapter what deep mediatization means for the self. We ask in this chapter the same question for what we will call 'collectivities'. That term is just the latest in a line of concepts used historically to describe groupings of various sorts: from 'masses' and 'crowds' to 'citizen publics' and 'communities'.[1] With digitalization, further types of collectivity-building and other, 'smaller' media-related collectivities gain importance. Even more recent is the phenomenon of collectivities created by automated calculation based on the 'digital traces' that individuals leave online. While our descriptive concepts change, one fundamental point remains: media are conceived as an essential means for bringing complex collectivities into being, and as a consequence changes in media transform the dynamics of collectivities. We therefore need a more detailed analysis of the various forms of collectivities and the contexts in which they are typically formed.

We define as a collectivity *any figuration of individuals that share a certain meaningful belonging that provides a basis for action- and orientation-in-common*. The form of such meaningful belonging can differ. It can be a feeling of a 'common we', as with traditional face-to-face communities (Knoblauch, 2008). It can be based on a 'shared organized situational action', as in the case of smart mobs (Rheingold, 2003). Or it can be based on processes of datafication like the collectivities of 'numeric inclusion' (Passoth et al., 2014). And also when we consider questions surrounding community, a change of perspective might be helpful to grasp community not as a given entity but as an ongoing process of community-making: that is, in Weber's term, 'communitization' (*Vergemeinschaftung*).[2] Across all these specific cases, the key characteristic of collectivities remains their *meaningful* character for the actors involved – and media play an important role in supporting the construction of such meaning. This understanding of collectivity is much more specific than the concept of 'collectives' used in recent writing about assemblages (Falb, 2015, pp. 273–342; Latour, 2013, pp. 296–325; and see Chapter 4), which has recently been adopted in media and communication research (Stäheli, 2012). Referring back to Tarde (2000 [1899], p. 35), we find there an emphasis on the 'repetition' that results in the emergence of 'collectives' (Latour, 2007, p. 14). Such collectives are assemblages of humans and non-humans that have a certain form of joint agency.[3] These reflections allow us to think about the close media-relatedness of our collectivities (Schüttpelz, 2013, pp. 3–18), but it is unhelpful to confuse any linkage of human actors and media whatsoever with a collectivity. That fails to demarcate those groupings that are more than just an assemblage, because they involve the construction of meaningful 'boundaries' through communication.[4]

How can we understand the ways in which collectivities are transformed in an era of deep mediatization? What are their characteristics and particular features? First, we will explain the fundamental processes of collectivity-building within groups, and then explore collectivities purely based on imagination and datafication.

9.1 Groups, Collectivities and Deep Mediatization

While older forms of 'community' entail stability, coherence and embeddedness, tied to shared experience or common history, social relations based on 'network sociality' less 'narrational' than 'informational', involving primarily 'an exchange of data and on catching up' (Wittel, 2008, p. 157). For many writers, network sociality is associated with the *loss* of community, and is enabled by 'communication technology, transport technology and technologies to manage relationships' (Wittel, 2008, p. 177).[5] Similarly analyses are offered of 'networked individualism' (Castells, 2001, p. 131; Wellman et al., 2003, p. 3), which involves translocal mediated communications not constructed any more by reference to a single place.[6]

Accounts like these are however problematic since they reduce these transformations to a switch within a simplified binary ('network' versus 'community' (Postill, 2011, p. 102). They also reduce media-related changes to a single line of transformation. But we can hardly locate any *one* single way in which collectivities are being transformed: various forms of collectivities diverge from each other while others have their boundaries blurred. It is also inadequate to describe these collectivities simply as 'networks': rather, they build complex figurations with a certain constellation of actors, and it is the latter *constellation* that we can describe as a network. However, collectivities remain phenomena constructed through processes of meaning; they have a meaningful boundary even if they are locally situational, like smart mobs. On the contrary, the variety of collectivities has expanded through the use of media technologies.

It is useful nonetheless to distinguish analytically between two basic kinds of collectivity because media and their infrastructures play different roles in these figurations. There are collectivities for which media are *constitutive* in the sense that those collectivities cannot exist without media, for example online groups. These collectivities constituted by media emerged with mediatization, and we therefore call them 'media-based collectivities'. And then there are collectivities (for example, families) for which media are not constitutive but are increasingly *constructed through and moulded by* media-related communications: we call these 'mediatized collectivities'.

Media-Based Collectivities

Media can constitute collectivities in two ways. First, they can offer *by their content* a frame of relevance for constructing such collectivities. Second, they can offer the *space of communication* in which these collectivities get constructed, regardless of the actual content that meet their specific frames of relevance. In the first case, media are constitutive in the sense of constructing the meaningful boundaries of these collectivities. In the second case, media are constitutive in the sense of supporting the communications practices through which these collectivities always get constructed. Each type has its specific dynamics that requires a more detailed analysis, but both need the label 'media-based collectivity'.

The clearest examples of media-based collectivities are those that gather around particular media content (Friemel, 2012). An example for this, often discussed in media and communications research, is 'audiences', especially for exceptional media events (Dayan and Katz, 1992; Hepp and Couldry, 2010; Scannell, 2002): people who follow television sports games, ceremonies, extraordinary popular shows or comparable 'events' that are communicated as a source of collective identification. Later we will discuss in more detail to what extent processes of constructing 'imagined collectivities' (of the nation or of other kinds) are at work here. The point we want to make is that, even if these people do not necessarily feel themselves to be part of a community, they may still build a more loosely connected collectivity as the spectators of a particular media spectacle (Kellner, 2010, p. 76).

With reference to certain forms of media content, we can also witness the emergence of more stable collectivities for which 'fan communities' or 'fan cultures' are a prominent example (Fiske, 1989, pp. 146–151; Jenkins, 1992; Winter, 2010). Media are important here in a double sense: first, they define the relevance-frames for such figurations; second, they are important as means for keeping these collectivities together. With digital media the possible influence of these collectivities increased as new 'politics of participation' became possible 'not simply through the production and circulation of new ideas (the critical reading of favourite texts) but also through access to new social structures (collective intelligence) and new models of cultural production (participatory culture)' (Jenkins, 2006a, p. 246). The digitalization of photography and the rise of platforms for the easy sharing of images (those created digitally, and digitized archival images) have enabled new collectivities to focus on sharing memories in new ways (MacDonald, 2015; van Dijck, 2007): as one participant in Richard MacDonald's study put it, 'I've shown [my photos online] because it might jog someone's memory' (quoted in Macdonald, 2015, p. 28). While we have to be careful not to romanticize these collective cultures (Carpentier, 2011; Cordeiro et al., 2013; Jenkins and Carpentier, 2013), it is evident that digitization has expanded their scale, scope and regularity. Importantly, some media-based collectivities may now operate translocally, joining together Taiwanese fans of, for example, Japanese and other foreign television programmes, usually watched live through various unofficial online means (Tse, 2014). But we have to be aware that using the word 'community' to describe them is not necessarily helpful. Quite early on there was a discussion about how far 'interpretive communities' (Grossberg, 1988; Lindlof, 1988; Radway, 1984) necessarily constitute groups of people who know each other and have a self-understanding as a group, or whether they might actually be much more loosely attached collectivities. Such a discussion regains relevance as the 'new digital environment increased the speed of fan communication, resulting in [. . .] 'just in time fandom' (Jenkins, 2006b, p. 141), partly experienced through digital platforms and 'second screens' in parallel to other forms of media use. The figurations of these fan collectivities become more diverse and ever more deeply related to media technologies. Therefore, instead of understanding each and every fan culture necessarily as *a single* community, we might do better to understand it as a complex figuration of figurations that links up different local groups in a range of interdependent activities.

Other media-based collectivities include various sorts of 'online groups', and again it is an open question how far they are communities. The owners of digital platforms especially have a tendency to call themselves 'communities' and understand by this rather a kind of forum function

(Deterding, 2008; Yuan, 2013). However, we should be careful not to mix such 'technological definitions of "community"' (Baym, 2015, p. 83) with sociological ones. Basically, online groups are figurations that are built with reference to a certain platform and the topic of communication there. But it is an empirical question *whether* and *how far* these collectivities make progress towards becoming a community (Weber's question about 'communitization'). Contemporary digital platforms offer possibilities for creating a *variety* of different online groups on one platform, each of them based on various topics of interest, and various software add possibilities for online group-building; for example, multi-user online games where game-related collectivities like 'guilds' play against each other and whose construction is supported by the game software in various ways (Williams et al., 2006). The 'guilds' may be built, for example, by text- or video-chat in parallel to the game played: such game-related collectivities may derive from or result in offline relationships, or remain solely online (Domahidi et al., 2014). The *degree* of community involved depends on the individual case and its meaning.

Media-based collectivities can also be local and situated; for example, 'flash' or 'smart mobs'. A 'flash mob' can be defined as a large group of people who gather by the support of digital media in some predetermined location, perform some brief action, and then quickly disperse (McFedries, 2003, p. 56). The term 'smart mob' (Rheingold, 2003, p. xii) originally having a more specific political focus, although the distinction has become blurred (Houston et al., 2013, p. 237). Whatever exact term we use, such mobs are forms of collectivity that have (digital) media as a pre-condition of their existence, and are a figuration tied to particular local gatherings or situations. In this they are similar to other new forms of situational collectivities, like 'mobile clubbing' (groups of people who go from bar to bar while connected by mobile media (Kaulingfreks and Warren, 2010, p. 211), or 'mobile gaming' (Frith, 2013, p. 251), or 'urban swarms' of protesters (Brejzek, 2010, p. 110). Whatever their duration, these figurations, in their close relations to media, are typical of an era of deep mediatization.

Mediatized Collectivities

Even collectivities whose existence and formation are *independent* of media can form what we can call 'mediatized collectivities': families, peer groups, migrant groups or groups of excluded people nowadays are collectivities whose forms of meaningful belonging are, in part, *constructed through* the use of media. Here we find what Nancy Baym calls 'networked collectivism': 'groups of people now network throughout the internet and related mobile media, and in-person communication, creating a shared but distributed group identity' (Baym, 2015, p. 101).

When it comes to families, the appropriation of media – especially of television – was and still is important for maintaining them as a collectivity (Hirsch, 1992; Morley, 1986; Peil and Röser, 2014). However, the crucial point here is that keeping up family life became a cross-media endeavour (Hasebrink, 2014). When family photos are shared on online platforms and through that a family memory is constituted (Lohmeier and Pentzold, 2014; Pentzold et al., 2016, p. 2), or when family relationships are articulated by digital media use (Cardoso et al., 2012, pp. 49–70), it is the whole media ensemble that is involved. Such a mediatization of the family enables new forms of the figuration of the family, especially families that are spread across long distances and at the same time keep up a close relation to their family members (Greschke, 2012; Madianou and Miller, 2012, pp. 128–135): their ensemble of *different* media (mobile phones, internet-based visual telephony, email, texting, digital platforms) makes it possible to keep up family roles like that of 'mothering' across long distances. But media change the 'feel', 'texture' and 'meaning' of a family's relationships: the relationships between parents and children, for example, if constructed by video conferences, telephone calls and mobile phone surveillance, remain more distanced than one constructed mainly in face-to-face interaction (Madianou and Miller, 2012, pp. 103–123).

Similarly with peer groups. While nothing new, peer groups, especially of young people, are nowadays moulded to a significant degree through their use of media, not least because mediated popular culture provides them with a relevant point of reference. Indeed, an increasing portion of young peer-groups' communication *as a group* takes place via media: mobile phones, digital platforms, chat apps (Buckingham and Kehily, 2014). Members of peer groups feel under pressure to appropriate media and to fulfil the rules of communication specific to them (Hepp et al., 2014, pp. 175–198). Group membership becomes *defined by* access to particular media ensembles so that failure to use certain media may result in group-exclusion. Put differently, in the age of deep mediatization, membership of a peer group is *enacted through* appropriating its media ensemble.

Further evidence for the mediatization of collectivities comes from migrant groups. Nowadays the very act of migrating is already highly intertwined with media: the 'image' of the place to which one is migrating as well as the possible migration network is built up via the internet *before* the act of migration (see Braune, 2013). Migration itself is organized by digital platforms and smartphones, which together allow detailed navigation, ongoing information, as well as documentation of the migration process. The relevance these media have is closely related to the 'information precarity' (Wall et al., 2015, p. 2) of refugees in large camps: without technological and social access to relevant information, with irrelevant, sometimes dangerous, information prevalent, unable to control the circulation of their own images, and under continuous risk of surveillance by state authorities. The 'connected migrant' (Diminescu, 2008, p. 568) is involved in various mediatized collectivities during his or her journey, building mediatized groups of support along the way, and maintaining at the same time contact with family, friends and others at the place of origin. Media have always enabled migrants to maintain links to their wider migrant group through various, mainly 'smaller media' (Dayan, 1999, p. 22). But with digitalization these possibilities significantly increase (Leurs, 2015, pp. 103–242).

Deep mediatization may also transform the experience of intensely marginalized groups. One striking example is homeless people. For a long time, media have been relevant as sources of entertainment and opportunities for communitization in shelter homes and elsewhere (Fiske, 1993, pp. 3–5). With the spread of digital media, homeless people in media-saturated societies become regular users of digital technology, especially of smartphones (see for the USA, Pollio et al., 2013). Beside organizational matters, they use these technologies to maintain contact with friends and families and for collectivity building (Woelfer and Hendry, 2012, pp. 2828–2831). Their media use goes beyond self-representation as with homeless persons' newspapers (Koch and Warneken, 2014). It is much more about keeping contact with and remaining part of ongoing collectivities while still living on the street.[7]

Some Emerging Principles

It is obvious that the specificities and possible transformations of the collectivities discussed so far cannot be related solely to media. Other processes are driving forces too: individualization (Beck and Beck-Gernsheim, 2001; Burzan, 2011), globalization (Tomlinson, 1999; Slater, 2013; Waisbord, 2013a), commercialization (Lash and Lury, 2007; Lupton, 2013). But having these further meta-processes of change in mind and comparing 'media-based' and 'mediatized collectivities', it becomes evident that collectivity-building does not dissolve into a single form of individualized network. Collectivities remain a meaningful unit of human life in times of deep mediatization, but through mediatization become transformed in a range of ways. Three points are striking.

1. *Media contents become important resources for defining collectivities* when media contents become the 'topic' around which those collectivities are constructed. This is especially evident in media-based collectivities such as fan cultures that are predominantly defined by a shared enthusiasm for a certain media content (a series, a genre, etc.). But it applies, too, to mediatized collectivities – families, peer groups – that appropriate various kinds of media in constructing their moralities, rules, boundaries and joint experiences. While such content a decade ago was typically communicated by mass media (print, film, radio, television), and access to it was more limited, today a huge variety of symbolic resources is accessible via online distribution. Therefore, the spectrum of *possible* collectivities has increased fundamentally.

2. *Media are means for constructing collectivities*, especially for online groups that constitutively rely on their online space of communication, but also for those peer groups and families that become related to the use of media like smartphones. Actor-constellations may be sustained across long distances and collectivity experienced synchronically at a distance, even under circumstances of intense mobility, whether of individuals or the whole collectivity. New textures of collectivity emerge through a variety of media ensembles as well as very different opportunities for constructing collectivities. Together a collectivity's specific features and the communicative capacities of its media ensemble define its possibilities of transformation.

3. *Media trigger dynamics in collectivities*. It is less the single medium that matters here than the whole media ensemble,[8] the dynamics of which can however vary hugely: having access to certain media may become fundamental for becoming a member of this collectivity, or media may affect the communication that takes place within collectivities (online groups, for example, are well known for their practices of 'flaming', rooted in the lack of co-presence between their members). Even in mediatized collectivities, the degree to which members are 'always on' has consequences for the quality of their communications.

Elaborating the original ideas of Hubert Knoblauch (2008), we can call a shift from 'collectivities of *pure* co-presence' to 'collectivities of *multimodal* communication'. By this we mean that, before the spread of today's communications media, human collectivities involved co-presence, in which everyone knew each other, practices typically were shared, and core knowledges were distinctive of the whole collectivity. This is the conception of community found in classic writings about communities (Tönnies, 2001 [1935]). But, with mediatization's successive waves of mechanization, electrification and digitalization, further kinds of collectivities gained relevance that we can call 'collectivities of multi-modal communication'. Based on and shaped by a diverse media ensemble, less rooted in direct experience but in shared processes of mediated communication, these 'collectivities of multi-modal communication' become communities when they build up a 'common we' as well as long-term structures. However, an important characteristic of deep mediatization is the *variable intensity* of such collectivities, and the role that choices *between* media modalities (media options within the media manifold) play in the formation of distinctive collectivities (what makes them 'multi-modal'). Far from a general switch-over to purely 'personal' networks, in an age of deep mediatization we see a more *differentiated range* of collectivities, in part because even older collectivities of co-presence have now become mediatized.

9.2 The Political Project of Imagined Collectivities

So far we have discussed collectivities whose members are in interaction with each other. But we also need to consider collectivities that are constructed through certain ways of *representing* that collectivity. Thereby, a number (smaller or larger) of people who are not in personal contact with each other are nonetheless addressed simultaneously. Historically we can relate imagined collectivities to religious communities, and later the nation as an 'imagined community', constructed by print media and electronic mass media like radio and television. The actors who constructed these collectivities were typically powerful: churches, political state institutions and their representatives. However, with deep mediatization, the 'imagining' of collectivity has became an increasingly contested field.

Imagined Political Communities

Originally, the nation as an 'imagined community' involved the idea of national public media as crucial to the construction of this imagined community. In his enlightening analysis, Benedict Anderson emphasized 'the novel and the newspaper' as 'the technical means for "re-presenting" the kind of imagined community that is the nation' (Anderson, 1983, p. 25). In such a perspective the 'development of print-as-commodity' is the key to understanding the construction of a communicative space that offers the possibilities to imagine a 'national consciousness' (Anderson, 1983, p. 37). Electronic media later supplemented this process – mainly radio and television – which gave 'print allies unavailable a century ago' (Anderson, 1983, p. 135). In this way, processes of communication that allowed the construction of the nation were intensified.

However, it would be a mistake to understand this mediated representation of the nation as an *explicit* discourse about the nation as a political unit. Rather, it is a 'banal nationalism': a habitual representation of the nation as a point of identification in a 'mundane way' (Billig, 1995, p. 6). This process of construction works through how, in media, a 'homeland' is articulated as a 'here' and the group of the people living in this homeland as a 'national we'. Contests and conflicts with other people become a competition of 'nations', and even the weather is something that is automatically related to a national territory. This 'constant flagging' of the nation ensures that, 'whatever else is forgotten in a world of information overload, we do not forget our homelands' (Billig, 1995, p. 127). And even today this process of constructing the world as a world of nations continues, for example in online platforms that are not necessarily bound to a national territory (Hepp et al., 2016, pp. 112–121; Skey, 2014). For various kinds of political actors – politicians, parties, governments, and journalists – the imagined community of the nation remains the point of reference for constructing social order. This keeps the imaginary of the nation as a 'quasi-natural' unit of living and identification: 'It is a form of life in which "we" are constantly invited to relax, at home, within the homeland's borders' (Billig, 1995, p. 127).

With globalization in general and globalization of the media in particular, however, such social imaginaries became weaker (Hepp, 2015, pp. 10–34; Taylor, 2004). *Besides* the 'project' of constructing the nation as a collectivity, other kinds of 'projects' of imagining collectivity became more widespread. One prominent example for this is the 'community of Europeans' that can be understood in parallel to the nation as a 'community of communication' (Risse, 2010, p. 157): it is imagined through collective processes of communication. Here, the underlying communicative space is a *transnational* and *multi-lingual* public sphere that emerges from the increasing discussion of European issues across borders as well as an increasing monitoring of European political affairs in Brussels (Koopmans and Statham, 2010, pp. 63–96; Risse, 2015, pp. 144–153; Wessler et al., 2008, pp. 40–54). While on the level of everyday experience this kind of imagined collectivity has not the 'natural' character of the nation, we can see under way an ongoing construction of a 'banal', however contested, Europeanness (Hepp et al., 2016, pp. 217–231).

Alternative Ways of Imagining Collectivity

But such alternative territorially related communities are only one way of imagining collectivity. With deep mediatization we have a variety of other publics and imagined collectivities that partly conflict with each other and partly connect to each other (Baym and boyd, 2012, p. 321). This starts with 'personal publics' (Schmidt, 2013, p. 121) or 'private spheres' (Papacharissi, 2010, p. 161) grouped around certain individuals, and ends with the 'networked publics' (Benkler, 2006, p. 11; boyd, 2008, p. 61) of digital platforms that are characterized by a particular communicative architecture which enables these spheres of communication (Loosen and Schmidt, 2012, p. 6). Around some topics, situational 'issue publics' (Lippmann, 1993 [1925]; Marres, 2007) emerge across various digital media, including the mobile phone itself (see Wasserman, 2011, on mobile phones and political participation in Africa). What we can notice here is a massive differentiation and multiplication of the different spaces of political communication, shaped in particular by underlying inequalities of socio-economic resources. This makes essential a 'context-centered model' of media's role in the formation of collectivities (Wasserman, 2011, p. 150). We do not even know therefore the full variety of imagined collectivities that such publics support, but we know they expand far beyond the confines or reference points of national states or confederations.

To explore this more closely it is helpful to consider the case of online blogging. What is called the 'blogosphere' (Schmidt, 2007, p. 1409) is an online space of bloggers who are more or less closely interrelated. Typically, these relations become visualized as networks of technical (Bruns, 2007; Reese et al., 2007) or semantic links of (mutual) personal references (Tække, 2005; Vicari, 2015). The main question here is what kinds of collectivities are built by these bloggers. Partly, they are understood as a kind of 'community of practice' (Wenger, 1999), being preoccupied with a certain topic, referring more or less to each other, and so building up an arena of discourse.[9] However, we need again to ask how far the term 'community' is helpful, or whether this collectivity is defined simply by the shared interest of the involved bloggers. The situation becomes even more complicated if we consider the bloggers' readers. The 'intense affective unification' (Stage, 2013, p. 216) of blogging on a certain topic can result in 'online crowds' with their own dynamics: members of this collectivity come together on certain online sites, imagining themselves as a kind of collectivity of political interest and expressing their political position in affective ways.[10] With such 'online crowding' we are witnessing the unification and relative synchronization of publics in relation to certain political issues through shared affective practices (Stage, 2013, p. 216) and through a structure of feeling (Papacharissi, 2015, p. 116, drawing on Williams, 1958).

The multiplication of possible publics also multiplies the possibilities for constructing types of imagined collectivities. The most prominent examples of this are social movements. While social movements have a long-term history of imagining collectivity – the most prominent example for this is the international socialist movement – so-called 'new' social movements' (Porta, 2013; Rucht and Neidhart, 2002) like the environmental or alter-mondialization movement are characterized by their *global* imaginations of collectivity that move beyond any national or supra-national political units. With the support of media, these movements aim at transformations on a global scale (Klein, 2000), offering new imaginations of collectivity based around shared 'project identities' (Castells, 1997, p. 421) and offering 'networks of hope' (Castells, 2012). However, there are good arguments to be cautious about such claims. Social movements certainly have better resources for collectivity building today than before digitalization: a prominent recent example for this was the 'occupy movement'.[11] Yet, at the same time, the internet also offers political elites many opportunities to intensify and diversify the ways in which they sustain themselves in positions of power (Chadwick, 2006, p. 202). Therefore, the transformative potential of new political collectivities might be far more limited than their own imaginaries suggest. However, with digitalization the actual character of social movements changes. There emerges a tension between more loosely connected, individualized forms of political action on the one hand, and new ways of actually constructing political collectivity on the other. While the two seem contradictory at first glance, a second look shows that both are an expression of the changing figurations of social movements and their imaginations of collectivity.

In an important book W. Lance Bennett and Alexandra Segerberg describe this shift in social movements as being from a 'logic of collective action' to a 'logic of connective action' (Bennett and Segerberg, 2013, p. 27). With digital media platforms, they argue, we can distinguish three kinds of social movement figurations: first, there is 'collective action' which takes place in figurations of 'organizationally brokered networks', characterized by a strong organizational coordination of action. Media technologies are used to manage participation and coordinate the organizational goals as well as the communication of other aims. Second, there is 'connective action' realized by organizationally enabled networks with a looser coordination of action: media technologies support communicative practices that enable more personalized forms of action. And third, there is 'connective action' that is supported by crowd-enabled networks with little or no formal organizational coordination. Here, we have a large-scale personal access to multi-layered media technologies and communication centred on emergent personal action. While this threefold distinction is certainly idealized, it addresses the diverse consequences of digital media for the structure of social movements today: digital platforms support *both* hierarchically organized social movements *and* a highly individualized political engagement that is more 'me-centric' (Langlois et al., 2009, p. 418; see also Fenton and Barassi, 2011, p. 180).

But we have to be very careful not to confuse this possible shift with a disappearance of imaginations of collectivity. Even much looser figurations remain dedicated to the construction of imagined (political) collectivities. In a careful analysis, Anastasia Kavada (2015) demonstrated this for the Occupy movement, which involved protests without formal organization, supported by a very open figuration of activists linked by protest and media-based communications practices. In such an open figuration 'social media followers formed an outer ring while the inner ring included activists who were participating regularly in the physical occupations' (Kavada, 2015, p. 879). Through the use of digital media platforms, it became possible to construct two kinds of collectivities: first, the collectivity of the group protesting in the streets and parks, and second, a collectivity that followed the events (a kind of imagined collectivity of supporters). Occupy became a movement with transnational impact in part because it offered *symbolic* resources for imagining oneself as part of such a wider collectivity, and in so doing supported its own spread beyond the figurations of local protests. Such more open structures of organizing protest do not result in a default to 'me-centric protest' but rather in a more varied imaginary of 'protest collectivity' (see Kavada, 2015, p. 883). All can find a place within this collectivity of those who define themselves as part of the '99 percent' movement against global capitalism.

Collectivities for Media Change

Social movements are now aware how important media technologies are for social processes in general and for collectivity building in particular. As a result, they consider media and media infrastructures themselves increasingly as an *object of* political engagement. Roots of this can be found in the 'alternative' and 'radical' media movements of the 1970s (Atton, 2002; Downing, 1984; Rodriguez, 2001) that aimed to achieve 'alternative' forms of public spheres (Negt and Kluge, 1993, p. 94, 127). With reference to network infrastructure and digital media, important examples are the 'hacker movement' and the 'open source movement'. The hacker movement's political aim was to make the implications of the increasing omnipresence of computers and datafication publicly known and thereby politically negotiable (Levy, 1984). The focus of the 'open source movement' was first to foster a certain form of non-proprietary software development; later it became a political movement intertwined with a general political engagement in 'open access' to information: the 'open data movement' (Baack, 2015). A remarkable hybrid example is the Chaos Computer Club, one of the world's largest and Europe's oldest hacker organizations (Kubitschko, 2015). More recent examples include the technologically driven 'repair movement', combining hackers' competences with an engagement for sustainability and a zero growth economy (Kannengießer, forthcoming). Collectivities like these not only *use* media and their infrastructure to support their engagement for particular political aims; they consider media and their infrastructure *as themselves an issue* of political engagement.

This focus of certain movement collectivities on contesting *media* is a general characteristic of an era of deep mediatization: in such an era, media, and ways of reflecting on media, become part of the stuff out of which the social world is built and so, for example, larger collectivities come together *as such*. Prominent recent examples are the 'media-related pioneer communities' (Hepp, 2016) like the 'quantified self movement' (Boesel, 2013; Lupton, 2015; Nafus and Sherman, 2014) or the 'makers movement' (Anderson, 2012; Hyysalo et al., 2014; Toombs et al., 2014).[12] While they call themselves 'movements', these collectivities are instead hybrids between social movements and think tanks. Like social movements, pioneer communities have informal networks, a collective identity, and a shared aim for action. More particularly, they come very close to 'technology-oriented and product-oriented movements' (Hess, 2005, p. 516), like the open-source movement (Tepe and Hepp, 2008). However, pioneer communities are generally not involved in conflict-driven relations with identifiable opponents as social movements are: indeed, they are more open to forms of entrepreneurship and policymaking, lending them an affinity with think tanks (McGann and Sabatini, 2011; Shaw et al., 2014; Stone et al., 1998). Pioneer communities here share with think tanks an ability to produce ideas, and an effort to influence both public and policymakers.

The imaginaries that characterize *all* these collectivities are oriented to media technologies. The 'quantified self movement' imagines better forms of healthcare through collective self-measurement and the accumulation of personal and collective data. The 'makers movement' imagines that new technologies will allow decentralized forms of production and new collectivities of value creation that will supplant traditional forms of (industrial) production. Such pioneer communities spread their imaginaries transculturally.[13]

We could continue our analysis and discuss many further examples, whether religious collectivities[14] or transnational political violence, which have become more and more based on building collectivity through media.[15] But again the point we want to make is a more general one: that we are experiencing *a shift in how collectivities are imagined for political ends*. While the imagining of collectivity through media was for a long time predominantly related to imagining the nation, we are nowadays confronted with much more diverse and conflicting processes of imagination that can no longer easily be integrated into the container of well-integrated 'national projects'. Looking back, the project of imagining the nation depended on a close fit with the waves of mechanization and electrification and with the nationally based media infrastructure on which they were based, whether we turn to France, the USA, or colonial Nigeria (Flichy, 1995; Larkin, 2008; Starr, 2005). The high point of the communicative construction of the nation was in the second half of the twentieth century. With deep mediatization, and its more diversely configured media infrastructures, political projects for imagining collectivities become themselves more diverse, even contradictory.

Two points are striking. First, the communicative spaces of constructing these imagined collectivities are increasingly detached from territorial borders. This does not mean that the project of imagining national communities has come to an end. But such imaginations are increasingly confronted with mediatized 'old' and 'new' imaginations of collectivity: *supranational* imaginaries jostle for prominence with national imaginaries, while social movements offer new imaginations of transnational and transcultural political belonging, and new types of media-oriented collectivity emerge. A characteristic of deep mediatization is the existence *in parallel* of these conflicting imaginations of collectivity and the unresolvable diversity of political values and political projects that results.

Second, the close relation between our imaginaries of collective life and media becomes taken-for-granted. First steps in such a direction are the various social movements that focus on media and their infrastructures as a political issue. Maybe more characteristic for deep mediatization are the media-related pioneer communities which call themselves 'movements' but are more closely tied to existing power centres. Their imaginings of collectivity involve ideas of living better together, through and by media technologies: those imaginings are effected not just by circulating media, but by a much broader range of practices focused on media that constitute what Hilde Stephansen calls the 'social foundations' of publics (Stephansen, 2016). In our terminology, media-related practices enable new types of publicly significant figurations to be formed. With deep mediatization these imaginings become concrete political projects, based in the material infrastructure of media and commUnciations.

9.3 Collectivity without Communitization

There is one further characteristic of contemporary collectivity that must be discussed. By this we mean collectivities whose construction involves various forms of mediated communication and datafication, but without *communitization*. Such 'collectivities without communitization' are frequently driven by corporate interests, and relate in particular to 'digital work': that is, kinds of labour that are undertaken in the sphere of digital media, often without the individuals involved understanding this *as* work. Such collectivities take various forms.

'Working' for Brands and the Data Economy

We can trace this development back to the idea of 'brand communities'. At first sight these are very close to the features of fan cultures, being collectivities built around certain (media) products or even (think of Apple) the producing companies themselves. However, it is worth looking more closely at this phenomenon. In their original sense brand communities were specialized, non-geographically bound communities, based on a structured set of social relationships among admirers of a brand (Muniz and O'Guinn, 2001, p. 412). They were 'largely imagined communities' (Muniz and O'Guinn, 2001, p. 419) insofar as their horizon was not just the artefact of a certain kind of product (a computer or a car) but the brand that this artefact represents. The fundamental point about brand communities is that they cannot be 'made' by companies but are rooted in the everyday practices of those who use these brands (Pfadenhauer, 2010, p. 363). Nowadays, such collectivities go beyond the companies' own strategies of marketing and encompass the mediated communication of the members of the community. Such brand communities are not 'sub' or 'fan cultures' because their members see themselves not as something 'special' or 'marginal' but as general consumers with an interest for a certain kind of *accepted* brand (Muniz and O'Guinn, 2001, p. 414); even so, as with fan communities, the community-building itself takes place by interaction either at physical meetings or online (Bagozzi and Dholakia, 2006, pp. 46f.).

Building up brand *communities* became, paradoxically, a top-down strategy of marketing, which resulted in 'brand collectivities' with a far lower level of communitization. The possibilities of digital platforms stimulated companies to experiment with 'online groups' of consumers in order to foster relationships between and to them (Andersen, 2005, pp. 41f.; Arnone et al., 2010, p. 97). The parallel relationship that consumers have to a common brand creates already a figuration, albeit one characterized by an intense asymmetry. The hope of corporations is often to support the development of more reliable consumer relationships (Tsimonis and Dimitriadis, 2014, pp. 333–336), but, when they do so, something different takes place: the construction of a visible and therefore meaningful collectivity of 'followers' who do not necessarily perceive this figuration as involving 'community'. There is a big difference between those who just 'like' the web pages of certain brands on digital platforms, and the brand-related groups on these platforms founded by the users themselves (Zaglia, 2013, p. 221). The first group shares only a positive view of a brand, but is *represented* as a collectivity through data accumulation. In the second case there is an interaction from the bottom up between people who not only share an interest for this brand and its products, but also develop a joint discourse about it, and potentially a relation to each other (Habibi et al., 2014). Only the latter is close to the original idea of 'brand communities'.

With deep mediatization and the expansion of mediated interdependence that it brings, this first kind of brand collectivity becomes more widespread, especially in the corporate sector. But companies increasingly want to encourage forms of collective practice that create value in more tangible ways: online 'collectivities of work' which involve people outside formal employment or organizational membership, in the interactive production of data-flows and activity-streams from which commercial value can be extracted. Let's leave aside the intense debate about the status of this sort of labour or 'playbor' (Mejias, 2013),[16] and focus on the *underlying* sociological question: what *sort of* collectivities does such 'work' construct on a massive scale? Take the case of so-called 'brand volunteering' (Cova et al., 2015, p. 16). It is performed by a complex set of figurations: the figurations of local brand communities ('clubs' with an interest for a certain brand) become linked to the figurations of online platforms and marketing campaigns to build up a certain collectivity of work. One study researched brand volunteering around a car company: anything like community only emerged at the local brand groups or during face-to-face events (Cova et al., 2015). 'Brand volunteering' is marked by many tensions; mistrust by the supporters for the overall strategy of the company; feelings of being exploited. Nevertheless, the *interest in* the brand which motivates some members of brand communities to become 'brand volunteers' requires that the figuration built around the brand, and the broader context in which this 'invitation to work' occurs, is strong enough at least to encourage people to devote their scarce time to 'collective' projects oriented towards a reference-point that is abstract, a *representation* of a value.

For other 'collectivities of work' not even this is the case. They are built around online platforms to which individuals contribute 'work' as a collectivity of 'online workers' with little or no possibility of direct interaction with each other (they are not in this sense a 'community'): for example, platforms which integrate individual contributions (rating platforms for people, restaurants, locations etc.) or platforms that link services that individuals offer (accommodation, rides etc.). In both cases these platforms are typically marketed as 'cost saving' and 'democratizing', but they are just as plausibly seen as forms of unpaid exploitation. The basic idea of rating platforms is that a company offers an online infrastructure to evaluate certain services. The unpaid work individuals do is to contribute their assessment to a public forum, with the assumed bonus that other users are paying attention to reviewers' opinions. Such platforms then function as 'a reflexive feedback loop' (Zukin et al., 2015, p. 3), both reflecting popular sentiments about specific services and helping to form those sentiments. From this perspective the actors and roles in this figuration are clearly defined by the supposed 'benefit' for all involved. The providers of this platform *financially* benefit by selling the information produced by this platform: the review-writers supposedly benefit by having the opportunity to express their opinion, and the readers, presumably, think they benefit by getting the latest information.

There is no communitization in this collectivity of (unpaid) work, whose outputs are sold by the platform operators. On the contrary, it can be argued that such collectivities of work have the side-effect of undermining community. See for example Zukin, Lindeman and Hurson's (2015) research on a rating platform for restaurants and clubbing locations that undermined existing community structures through the way it reinforced symbolic and other forms of privilege embedded in the practices of its 'workers'. Far from being communitization, the side effects of this 'collectivity of work' may work to undermine actual processes of community building elsewhere. Similar dynamics operate in platforms that link together services that individuals offer (accommodation, car rides etc.). Such brokerage platforms are part of a 'sharing economy' (Zervas et al., 2014, p. 5). The model of such platforms is to offer a convenient interface that matches supply and demand in trusted ways (see Rosen et al., 2011).[17] Such platforms have had far-reaching success in such varied areas as accommodation, car rides or jobs (Guttentag, 2015; Irani, 2015; Yannopoulou, 2013; Zervas et al., 2014).[18] We can understand the collectivities structured around these platforms as 'collectivities of work' insofar as their members offer their hospitality, transport service or data labour for financial gain. But again such figurations are structured primarily around corporate platforms in order to make profit, with disturbing side-effects: for example, patterns of race segregation on accommodation platforms, including differential rates of remuneration driven by the automated collection of ethnicity data generated from the pictures users post of themselves (see Edelman and Luca, 2014). We do not deny that, in some civil society platforms based on 'sharing economy' – including those close to social movements such as OpenStreetMaps (Lin, 2011) – the work is much less individualized and based on social movements and local groups with specific interests in such alternative platforms. Our point however concerns the general trend, which is dominated by the commercially successful platforms that follow a different kind of dynamic.

Other platforms produce a 'crowd' of low-skilled digital labourers who perform vast numbers of minor data tasks and are paid small amounts of money for this 'microwork' (Irani 2015, p. 721). Such platforms organize digital workers to fit the needs of datafication. Service requesters post a 'task' that then can be performed by the 'microworkers', in accordance with the requirements of the programming or digital industries. On this model 'humans (are) made into modular, protocol-defined computational services' (Irani, 2015, p. 731), working on a large scale and in a fully monitorable way. Here, we start to see how the vast data infrastructure on which deep mediatization is based generates *its own costs* in terms of hidden forms of exploitative labour. Meanwhile, those forms of labour are themselves only possible on the basis of new types of figurations: collectivities *without* community. Through these forms of labour, individuals literally become *part of* the datafication process: 'humans-as-a-service' (Irani, 2015, p. 724).

Collectivities Through Numbers

There is a second way in which today's data infrastructure generates new types of collectivity: 'numeric inclusion' (Passoth et al., 2014, p. 282). There is nothing new about quantifying media audiences (Ang, 1991) or national populations (Porter, 1995). But with datafication, precise measurement at one data-point can be calibrated, almost in real time, to information stored (or simultaneously gathered) in myriad other databases to produce instant categorization and 'appropriate' action. Based on the digital traces we all leave online, groupings of people who share certain characteristics are continuously produced to support the advertising industry's aim of reaching individuals with customised advertising (Couldry and Turow, 2014; Turow, 2011). This accumulation of data is subsequently communicated back to the individuals: by online shops that produce lists of the other goods people making the same purchase bought; by online radio stations that produce charts, access statistics and rankings with reference to certain tastes of their users; by news pages that offer further information based on the previous reading choices of other users etc. Processes of 'numeric inclusion' therefore work to construct collectivities that 'would not be possible without the measurement and activity assessments delegated to algorithms and statistical programs' (Passoth et al., 2014, p. 282). What is constructed here is an *accumulation* of individuals who are treated as sharing characteristics within networked processes of 'big data' processing.

'Numeric inclusion', however, when embedded back into daily practice, stimulates the construction for instrumental purposes of a meaningful horizon – mainly of taste, interest and orientation[19] – within which individuals *may* come to position themselves as members of a certain collectivity:[20] those categorized as liking the same band, or the same type of book, or any other categorized feature. But such collectivities based on 'numeric inclusion' are generated without (or with very limited) communitization: indeed, there is no reference-point whatsoever for any affective relation to the collectivity's other members, who remain hidden from each other, except via the *assumption* that they too were categorized the same way. Nevertheless, these collectivities are potentially influential: they represent large numbers of persons who have been constructed for important purposes as *part of the same category,* and who may orient their actions accordingly. To that extent, these collectivities too are an incipient contribution to an emerging social order.

Remaking Our Collectivities

At this stage it is an open question how much such collectivities formed by 'numeric inclusion' – that is, by datafication – might have in common with the media-based and mediatized local collectivities discussed at the beginning of this chapter. They would seem to be at opposite ends of the expanded spectrum of mediated collectivity in an age of deep mediatization. Are there practices emerging that might link up these different types of collectivity, and so transform the nature of communitization still further?

One important such practice is the embedding into everyday life of robotics, or rather 'social robotics': the 'placement of robots in human social spaces' (Sandry, 2015, p. 335). At present, the most widespread forms of these 'social robots' are not physical artefacts but 'assistant apps' that can be associated with our smartphones (Barile and Sugiyama, 2015, p. 407; Turkle, 2015, p. 339). Such apps are presented to us as quasi-human interaction partners with whom (through voice-recognition software) we can communicate using our natural voice. In reality, however, such 'assistants' are interfaces to large computer networks that process the questions we might ask and give 'answers' by reference to their comparability to an available dataset of questions and answers, combined with the data we have inputted. Through such a relationship we become a living, interactive member of a collectivity without community.

We can easily imagine face-to-face communities of people in such 'relationships' who come together to compare their experience of them. This may be only one of many entry-points for social robotics into the domain of social interaction: there has been much discussion of care-giving robots, or the robot puppets in dementia care,[21] but just as relevant are 'smart' living environments and 'smart' self-driving cars and trains. Already, key aspects of smartphones and smart watches train us to communicate with systems of this sort.

There is of course no simple global story of how such new technologically mediated ways of constructing collectivity are everywhere transforming 'the world', 'our world' or 'anyone's world': such stories remain *rhetorics* which mask hugely uneven processes that, in turn, are deeply implicated in underlying inequalities of socio-economic resource, which indeed they help deepen.[22] Such rhetorics, even if already normalized in pioneer communities and the like, rely on very particular notions of 'centre' and 'periphery' that reduce most sites of everyday life across the globe to 'sites *of replication* of a future invented prior and elsewhere', as a recent analysis of IT practices in Peru notes (Chan, 2013, p. x, added emphasis).

Our aim in registering some of the practices entangled with such rhetorics has absolutely *not* been to reproduce those rhetorics. But it would be equally dangerous not to acknowledge such pressures towards transformation, since they amount to nothing less than an attempt to transform our models of the social, a deeply motivated adjustment in the very basis of collectivity. As Sherry Turkle (2015, p. 338, added emphasis) puts it: 'even before we make the robots, *we remake ourselves as people* ready to be their companions'. If this is so, we have no choice but, in important ways, to remake our collectivities and potentially our socialities too. But what are the wider costs? What are the consequences for the possibility of social order? These are the questions to which we turn in the book's last two chapters.

10

Order

We now reach the double question on which this book has been converging: what sort of *order* does contemporary social life have? And what is the role of media, in the broadest sense, in constructing and sustaining that order?

We propose here only a minimal, basic notion of 'social order'. By 'order', we mean a relatively stable pattern of interdependences between not just individuals, groups and institutions, but also (at a higher dimension) between the numerous types of relation involved in social life that all depend on larger stabilities of resource and infrastructure. We do *not* mean by 'order' here two familiar notions: one is a functionalist notion of social life, on whatever scale, seen as a homeostatic and self-sustaining order in which countless processes, values and actions all seamlessly contribute to the wider end of social functioning (see Couldry, 2006); the other is a social order operating solely at the level of 'national containers' called 'societies' (see Beck, 2000a, b). Indeed, at no point has our argument depended on the assumption that we live in societies that constitute 'distinct, discrete entities forming coherent wholes or systems' (Wrong, 1994, p. 8), or that indeed media form corresponding discrete and coherent systems. Instead, we insist on the plurality of social 'centres', indeed on the regular contestation over the construction and definition of social life, and the plurality of competing values that underlie such contests (Boltanski and Thévenot, 2006). But this position is perfectly consistent with acknowledging that *some* degree of order, in the basic sense we propose, is necessary if social life is to be livable at all: for if *every* level of human activity and interrelations were the subject of endless and explicit contestation, there would be an unlivable chaos, captured by Hobbes' Leviathan. In every way of life therefore that is minimally successful, there is a degree of social 'order', and identifying and analysing this is, as Dennis Wrong (1994) argued twenty years ago in *The Problem of Order*, the fundamental question of social theory.

Our key theme throughout has been *interrelatedness* as the basic feature of the social world, and the importance of analysing interrelatedness on all scales through the arrangements of particular figurations, based on a distinctive organization of material resource. Interrelatedness already points us *towards* the question of order, since as Elias himself noted in relation to civilization (his term), this 'happened by and large unplanned, but it did not happen without a specific type of order' (1994, p. 443). In this chapter therefore our question becomes: what does *deep* mediatization (the penetration of mediated processes into how the very elements of social life are formed and sustained) contribute specifically to the *type* of order that today is possible? Our understanding here of social order – as basically, the higher-dimensional 'settlement' that enables a minimal level of stability under particular conditions – leaves open two further questions, both carrying normative implications.

The first question concerns the *relative benefits of the various types of order possible under the same basic material conditions*. As Dennis Wrong points out, there are various readings of how social order is possible in social and political theory: force, mutual self-interest, and norms. Since few would assume that mutual self-interest is sufficient to found social order, the key choice is between 'force' and 'norms'. Since in this book we reject functionalist readings of social order in which the causal role of norms is dominant (the Parsonian reading of a norm-based integrative social order), our starting-point is always to give some explanatory role to 'force'. But when we consider deep mediatization, a new question arises. Media certainly provide a way of reinforcing and focusing norms that are already in circulation, and perhaps of inventing new norms. Media also provide a cognitive background against which selves (and collectivities of selves) can pursue their interests. What then is the relation between media infrastructures and force? Is one consequence of today's data infrastructure perhaps, as foreshadowed in Chapter 7, to install *a new type of force* into social life, an authoritarian structure of compulsion linked to our increasing dependence on that infrastructure for the conditions of basic life? If so, how orderly can the social results of such force be long-term, especially if its operations become increasingly divorced from certain important norms that ground institutional legitimacy in various ways? That is a key question raised by radical changes in how social interrelatedness today works that appear to flow from *deep* mediatization. Is it possible that the *balance* of pressures that constitute social order is today changing, and that the interrelations constituted and underpinned by media infrastructures are important to that change? We certainly cannot rule out such change, unless we rely on the Parsonian assumption that social orders are inevitably and broadly stable, which Elias firmly rejected (1978, p. 115). We need, in other words, to take seriously today's potential pressures towards 'disorder' (Wrong, 1994, p. 12) on smaller or larger scales.

The second question is about *value*, and how particular forms of order do, or do not, fit with particular overarching values. 'Order' is something in which, as humans, we have a stake, but not just *any* sort of order: different orders generate different types of benefit, cost and contradiction, and those varying outcomes may be judged positive or negative. The ways in which we are embedded in a 'world' carry a moral and ethical charge *because* they are integral to our resources and horizons of action, both spatial and temporal. It is only insofar as the social world 'hangs together' to a certain degree that we *can become* fully embedded in it, but each form of order brings distinctive costs that affect people unevenly. Here a critical phenomenology has a distinctive contribution to make. We have argued that, under conditions of deep mediatization, the role of media is precisely to mould *how* the social world hangs together at every level, to mould key elements *from which* it is constituted. This is very different from the view of classic social phenomenology, that the social world's hanging together is the upshot, in large part, of *human beings'* 'mindedness' (McDowell, 1994, p. 84). What if, as suggested already in Chapter 7, pressures towards datafication – new planes of action generated through automated processes of data collection and processing – constitute an *externally* generated type of 'mindedness' that is radically different from that of the pre-digital age? We already register this when we legal theorists point out that the system-based 'mindedness' of vast calculative capacity, when let loose on large amounts of anonymous data, can easily de-anonymise identity (Ohm, 2010), so that individuals become recognizable and retrievable via algorithms, in ways completely contrary to the intention of the human actors involved in the original data collection. What implications does this have for the type of social order that is today emerging, and for whether it fits with values such as recognition and freedom? In generating such questions, phenomenology becomes a *critical* science, a register of potential ethical and political challenges emerging within our ways of life with media.

Crucial to phenomenology, understood this way, is recognizing the power that may accrue to the institutions that, as Luc Boltanski put it, determine 'the whatness of what is' (2010, p. 75). The deep embedding of data processes in everyday life, for example, gives new force to the interactivity of social classifications and has the potential to mould social reality itself; as Espeland and Sauder (2007) put it in the title of their article, 'public measures recreate social worlds'. But datafication is just one aspect of the normative consequences of the emerging social order. There are also the increasing pressures deriving from the sheer complexity of today's web of interdependences that media have served to intensify. Once again, Elias provides a useful perspective. Late in his career, reviewing the increasing complexity of figurations in large societies, Norbert Elias reflected on the possibility of general 'fluctuations in what might be called "social pressure", in particular the "internal pressure" in a society' (1991, p. 145). Can this perhaps be relevant today? As linked infrastructures of communications grow in scope and intensity, and as the figurations – and figurations of figurations – built on the back of those infrastructures create stable connections between larger and larger domains of action, creating new *forms* of coordinated social action – so the 'pressure' that can materialize at any one nodal point, and for the actors associated with that point, increases exponentially. Time-pressures are a particularly clear, if not the only, way into registering this increase in general pressure, and the costs it generates; those costs affect actors unevenly, creating new forms of inequality regarding time and other resources. At the same time, such intensified patterns of interdependence create new opportunities for coordinated complex action.

These are some of the aspects of social order under conditions of deep mediatization that we will try to unpack in this chapter. If we manage to do so, we will complete our survey of the mediated construction of reality, but this involves taking our argument to a still more complex level: a level that seems abstract but in reality directly affects the fabric of our personal lives. We are encouraged by Elias' defence of complexity in *What is Sociology?*

> The indices of complexity set out here may perhaps help to make everyday matters appear rather strange. This is necessary if one is to understand why sociology's field of investigation – the processes and structures of interweaving, the figurations formed by the actions of interdependent people, in short, societies – is a problem at all. (1978, p. 103)

Building on the earlier chapters of this Part, we will approach this difficult question of order, first from the point of view of 'selves' and 'collectivities', and then from the point of view of 'organizations' as particular figurations of order, before turning for the first time to the even more complex level of 'government'. We will turn explicitly to the questions of value generated by this analysis in the next, concluding chapter.

10.1 Materialist-Phenomenology as Deep Hermeneutics

Before we consider in detail how deep mediatization might affect the types of social order that are now possible, we need to make as explicit as possible the hermeneutic approach to social understanding that underlies our argument in this chapter and book, and underlies materialist phenomenology, indeed all phenomenologies. In the contemporary social world, the production of social knowledge has reached a paradoxical point: where it denies itself as knowledge, where those who claim to 'know' about the social claim routes to such knowledge which have nothing in common with how social knowledge has been produced in the past. Yet this is not accidental, but derives from particular forms of symbolic power linked to the data infrastructure on which deep mediatization depends. We are in the middle of a 'changing relationship between ways of knowing and forms of power' (Andrejevic, 2013, pp. 5–6), indeed an attempt to create a 'global culture of knowing' data processing (Mosco, 2014, p. 2), which is intimately linked to particular corporate ambitions. Under these circumstances, a hermeneutic approach to the social becomes all the more important.

Some writers see this transformation as the signal that a revolution in the human and social sciences is needed to integrate data-processing techniques, a necessary 'rupture' that 'accepts the digital imperative' (Wieviorka, 2013, p. 60). But this goes much too far, since it ignores the long conflict between theories of communication which see information as just 'bits' that must be transmitted freely and without friction (Shannon and Weaver, 1959) and an approach that considers the 'meaning of information from an interpretative point of view' (Mansell, 2012, p. 47). While big data approaches to social knowledge do not depend on any theory of communication, they do depend on *ignoring* the contextual nature of information, its need to be interpreted, and indeed its source in a world that is *situated and interpretative*. It is essential therefore to insist on just this aspect of knowledge if we are to have any grasp of what is at stake in battles to define the contemporary social order.

Influential claims on behalf of big data-processing techniques as a new, radically *improved* form of social knowledge (Anderson, 2008) aim to outlaw older projects of interpreting social reality from the perspective of situated human beings. Social reality – indeed the reality known by the physical sciences too – is simply too complex, Anderson claims, for interpretation, theory or taxonomy. Though controversial, derided even in some quarters, what matters about such claims is that they offer a blueprint for claims to 'knowledge' that legitimize completely new types of knowledge producer, knowledge institution and mechanism for funding knowledge production: a new *social order* of knowledge, we might say. This social order of knowledge is, as we saw in Chapter 9, embedded in various practices: those for example of 'pioneer communities' that are gaining influence on individuals and institutions in the health sector. We should not underestimate the force of the processes whereby new types of 'knowledge' production based on collecting, aggregating and processing data across countless sites get normalized. There is no more effective way for a new method of knowledge production to become installed into social order than through banal repetition. As Schutz and Luckmann wrote, our everyday lives depend on a large degree of order: 'so long as the structure of the world can be taken to be constant, as long as my previous experience is valid, my ability to operate upon the world in this and that manner remains in principle preserved' (1973, p. 7). When the nature of that order changes, the foundations of social life change too.

The casualty, potentially, in this shift to a new social order of knowledge is the hermeneutic perspective on which Schutz and Luckmann's whole understanding of the social depends. Their book *The Structures of the Life World* starts out from a definition of 'the everyday lifeworld' as 'the region of reality in which man can engage himself and which can change while he operates in it by means of his animate organism' (1973, p. 3). They understand the lifeworld (which we prefer to call 'social world') as the sphere in which human beings act through engagement with that world, that is, by exercising their ability *to interpret it*. This hermeneutic approach to the nature of knowledge is so fundamental that we find it shared by the early twentieth-century biologist Jakob von Uexküll who around the same time as Schutz developed the notion of *Umwelt*, but in this case to understand the worlds of animals in general, not just humans. A key part of each animal's Umwelt, or 'environment', was for von Uexküll the signs that it contained *for* that animal, signs that denote, according to von Uexküll's translator, 'the way in which the subject organizes its Umwelt through selective *perception of* those features' (von Uexküll, 2010 [1934/1940], p. 36, added emphasis). In case there is any doubt that this is a hermeneutic approach to animal lifeworlds, von Uexküll himself writes that 'the question *as to meaning* must therefore have priority in all living beings' (2010, p. 151, added emphasis).

This hermeneutic reading of social order is itself under challenge from a particular direction of social life: the approach to self-knowledge and social knowledge that van Dijck calls 'dataism'. By this, she means an ideological

reshaping of datafication into 'a widespread belief in the objective quantification and potential tracking of all kinds of human behaviour and sociality
through online media technologies' (2014, p. 28), which enables continuous recording and accumulation of data that can be translated readily into
numbers. What can never be translated into numbers is the perspective
of the interpreter herself, her situated position in a field of past action and
interpretation that informs any new action and interpretation. So dataism
is directly *opposed* to a phenomenological approach to knowledge, including social knowledge: indeed it is an 'anti-hermeneutic' whose emergence
in contemporary social life needs itself to be interpreted and understood
(Couldry, 2014a). Dataism denies not only a crucial aspect of how we interpret the social world, but a capacity of human beings in general to develop
what philosopher Hans-Georg Gadamer called 'historically effected consciousness' (2004 [1975], p. 301). This consciousness derives from our particular way of being embedded in the social world and builds out from each
interpreter's *'situation'* in the social world: hermeneutics as interpretative
knowledge are based in the individual's and group's 'action of being in the
world' (2014, p. 309, 310–312). But Gadamer also recognizes the possibility
of 'the alienation of the interpreter from the interpreted' through 'a false
objectification' (2014, p. 312). Writing forty years ago, Gadamer attributed
this to the influence of natural science methods, but dataism is a strong
contemporary version of such alienation that paradoxically claims to be a
new type *of* social knowledge (Couldry, 2014a; Mosco, 2014).

While the supposed benefits of such datafied knowledge are open to
debate, the costs are absolutely clear: a social fabric built out of continuous mutual surveillance. The price of datafication is beautifully captured
in Dave Eggers' novel *The Circle* in the paradoxical image of a system for
integrating the cameras worn by millions of people across the world called
'SEECHANGE': 'this is ultimate transparency. No filter. See everything.
Always.' (Eggers 2013, p. 69). Yet the philosophy of 'dataism' provides
no foundation whatsoever for grasping the social order which has generated its deeply limited perspective on social knowledge. To do so we
must start somewhere else; we must return to the questions of materialist
phenomenology.

10.2 Institutionalized Selves and Collectivities

We considered in Chapters 8 and 9 various ways in which the practices of
the self and of collectivities change with deep mediatization. In this chapter
we return to this perspective, but ask a different question: what do such

changed practices (at the level of selves and collectivities) imply about how *social order* is today constituted in and through media? At the core of this lie the implications for changing forms of social order of the increasing *institutionalization* of individual and group life.

At the start of the book we noted the early medieval precedent for how fundamental changes in media practices – new practices of literacy and reading, storing and transporting texts – were associated with a newly individuated self (Illich, 1996, p. 25). We are too early in the transformations of the wave of digitalization to see established any clear shifts in the nature of the self, as we saw in Chapter 8, but there are certainly visible some shifts in the relation between self-maintenance and wider social order.

The self is a temporal project, unfolding in time. But as Hartmut Rosa (2013, p. xxxvi, xxxvii) shows, for complex reasons including the massive acceleration in the transmission of communications, the self's social domains have been transformed, affording a new 'horizon of possibility' for the individual actor, that in turn brings a divergence between her 'horizon of expectation' (the time she can anticipate and which orients her) and her 'space of experience' (her sphere of immediate action). Indeed, each actor's social domains have also been extended considerably. As a result, actors, through their technologically mediated interface with others, regularly have to balance competing demands and expectations across long time-scales: in other words, simply to function as a self, the individual actor has to coordinate with larger numbers of people over longer periods of time, and with more fine-grained coordination (Lahire, 2007, pp. 11–41). The result is a greater *intensity of interdependence* between social actors, whether or not they know each other well (as in families and friendships), and a *greater dependence* of each individual *on media and their infrastructures* that sustain the possibilities of such coordination. In both ways, the entanglement of individuals in wider order, and their ability to contribute to it negatively or positively, are increased. In addition, the increasing ability to receive communications and informational resources from a distance, to manage relationships at a distance through technologically mediated communications, and indeed to travel physically over long distances, shifts the relation between space and action, so that according to Rosa 'space has lost its property of immutable givenness, of being an unchangeable background condition' (2013, p. 101). In this respect too, the individual may find her firm anchoring in everyday routines challenged and disrupted, as the relation between assumed foreground and assumed background in social life becomes transformed. In this context, social media platforms – and their ability to *sustain* relations with a large group of close and distant consociates – are no trivial contribution to the order of everyday life than otherwise.

In such a context of intensified translocal communications, new 'relations between people and vast arrangements of technologies and conventions' have become banal, as Isin and Ruppert note, including 'tweeting, messaging, friending, emailing, blogging, sharing' (2015, p. 2). By becoming banal and habitual, these once strange activities lose, as Schutz and Luckmann put it, 'their character of acts' (1973, p. 7), entering the domain of the natural. In various ways, individuals now participate in the wider task in which corporations are also engaged: the task of *managing continuity* between people, situations, locations and contexts. In what Gerlitz and Helmond (2013) call the 'like economy', the traces of what social actors do on social media platforms are distributed across the web in ways that further integrate it within an economic functionality. Writing of Facebook's 'introduction of social Plugins and the Open Graph' earlier in the decade, they note: 'Facebook activities such as liking, commenting and sharing are no longer confined to the platform but are distributed across the web and enable users to connect a wider range of web content to their profiles' (2013, p. 7).

Once again Dave Eggers' novel *The Circle* offers an insight, when a character criticizes another character for writing an entry about a walk in her manuscript diary:

> my problem with paper is that all communication dies with it. It holds no possibility of continuity [. . .]. It ends with you. Like you're the only one who matters [. . .] but if you'd been using a tool that would help confirming the identity of whatever birds you saw, then anyone can benefit [. . .] Knowledge is lost every day through this sort of shortsightedness. (Eggers, 2013, p. 187)

In Eggers' novel the pressure to 'participate', and so create 'social knowledge', becomes unbearable for various characters for whom the corporate slogans of the Circle – 'sharing is caring' or, more grandly, 'equal access to all possible human experience is a basic human right' (2013, p. 301) – provide little comfort.

The question indeed is access *for whom*. Any access that individuals gain to others' experience must, on this datafied model, always be mediated through the ordering operations of a platform and data infrastructure whose harvest is corporately owned. Participation involves therefore cooperation in something collective, but only in a highly mediated sense: as Ulises Mejias puts it, it is a contribution 'to the social *order*' (2013, p. 8, added emphasis), that is, the social order sustained by and for corporations, a point we will explain more in a later section. If a self needs to sustain certain relations to a data infrastructure in order to sustain herself as a self, this is *an entirely new way of binding selves into a social order.* The individual's place in social relations becomes itself dependent on the good functioning of corporate infrastructure, and of the individual's managed relations with that infrastructure. What van Dijck calls 'the imperative of sharing' (2013, p. 50) matches, on a different level, *'l'impératif numérique'.* Associated with the imperative of sharing is a process of institutionalization: the self, in performing its basic functions, becomes inherently institutionalized, reliant upon, and in part referent to, the goals and demands of external, generally commercial, institutions. Or, as the Canadian novelist Margaret Atwood put in in her review of *The Circle*: 'what happens to us if we must be "on" all the time? Then we're in the twenty-four-hour glare of the supervised prison' (Atwood 2013, p. 8).

Not that 'being outside' of this circle is the answer: indeed it constitutes a new and deep form of exclusion, insofar as it is not voluntary. As in all processes of institutionalization, but to an extent commensurate with the degree of functional integration being attempted here, this process *excludes* a substantial class of people. In 2015, the Unreported Britain project noted a 'digital catch-22' whereby the resources to *get out* of unemployment and other forms of socio-economic exclusion themselves depend on already having the continuous and high-quality online connection that those without jobs cannot have (Armstrong and Ruiz del Arbol, 2015). Whatever the hype, and even in a rich country such as the UK, 14 per cent of households still lack internet access (Office for National Statistics, 2015).

Can we see a broader pattern here? We believe we can. Norms – one of Wrong's three mechanisms for sustaining social order – are particularly important in sustaining what, otherwise, would be an improbably complex and diverse set of relations. At the level of production, platforms have to be maintained within a wider space of 'seamless interoperabilty' (van Dijck, 2013, p. 166) that enables communicative practices to occur, and economic value to be generated without obstacle, across many different platforms and applications: that, in turn, requires an overlapping of system-norms within the various interlinking software packages. At the level of the user, some norms of behaviour are expected in order to encourage a regularity of data flow:

> the power of norms, in the area of sociality, is much more influential than the power of law and order [. . .] in less than a decade, the norms for

> online sociality have dramatically changed from emphasizing connected-
> ness to aligning connectedness with commerciality and using the terms
> interchangeably. (van Dijck 2013, p. 174)

Norms, as embodied by individual actors, contribute to a habitual order
into which also collectivities, institutions and market structures are locked.
The meanings of individual actions within this order are changed by their
economic value (van Dijck, 2013, pp. 6–7), the value that those actions
carry within a wider economy of data processing.

There are three broader consequences for social order of this matrix of
connective practices that are today very common on social media platforms. First, through these interfaces' managed continuity, individuals
– many of whom would not otherwise have been in a 'situation' of shared
action with each other – become so. As Boltanski and Thévenot (2006,
p. 35) point out, in complex societies there are countless relations of 'coexistence', but 'in our everyday experience, coexistence does not always
produce a situation', an encounter for mutual influence. But the managed
continuity of platforms perforce creates *new forms of 'situation'* between
people, which, in turn, create new starting-points for social order. Second,
such situations create *collectivities* of varying significance, as discussed in
Chapter 9. Sometimes the significance is real for the users and, in exceptional circumstances, can be the focus of collective action, although rarely
(without other conditions being met) are these collectivities the focus
of solidarity and risk-taking. Sometimes the significance is minimal for
users, but great for the underlying commercial interests, since they are a
precondition of the generation of economic value. Third, such interfaces
create new forms of closer interdependence with *commercial* sites of power
that once were uninvolved in everyday social life, except when 'invited
in' through the choice of a consumer product. As Ulises Mejias says, 'new
modes of sociabililty emerge' under these conditions, but 'they become
organized under a structure where every aspect of the public is owned,
hosted or powered by private interests' (2013, p. 131). Some go further
and see here, in the way that norms of social performance increasingly
ape norms of market performance, an 'economization of self' as a bundle
of capital that 'must be productively invested' through attracting more
followers, likes, retweets and so on (Brown, 2015, pp. 33–34). Whatever
one's view of that, the *salience* of commercial power in everyday sociality
has been hugely increased, and that has consequences for the overall type
of social order in which we are living.

10.3 Organizations

How do these shifts in the nature of communicative processes for selves and collectivities translate to the level of organizations? Typically, an organization is defined by its orientation to a shared purpose and practices, by a coordinated division of work or responsibility, and by certain rules of membership.[1] If we characterize organizations this way, they can be seen as distinctive institutions focused on specific goals, and offering particular roles in terms of membership and practice. But organizations are not static phenomena: they are rooted in practices and produced through an ongoing process of 'organized sensemaking' (Weick, Sutcliffe and Obstfeld, 2005, p. 410). Organizations are 'discursive constructions' (Fairhurst and Putnam, 2004, p. 22), constructed through a kind of 'metaconversation' (Robichaud et al., 2004, p. 624) about their purposes that evolves through practice.

There are two sides to this organizational sense-making: an internal side (how actors within the organization construct a sense of what the organization means), and an external side (how the organization constructs a sense of the organization in relation to its external environment). But this division between internal and external is itself continually *constructed* as part of the organization's practice, building on the various resources that are available to that organization. In this sense, organizations are a special kind of figuration – or figuration of figurations – in which individuals are implicated in *formal* ways and which, through their ongoing processes of construction and various processes of legal recognition, acquire as 'corporate actors' a certain kind of agency that is very different from the informal agency of collectivities discussed in Chapter 9 (Mayntz and Scharpf, 1995, pp. 49–51). Through this agency, organizations have an ordering power within wider institutional fields like law and the economy (see Thornton et al., 2012, pp. 133–147). There are at least three levels on which organizations and their ordering power are affected by the changing media environment within a context of deep mediatization: organizational orientation, organizing processes, and underlying knowledge production.

Organizational orientation – the overall meaning of an organization – is transformed through relations with media, not only within the organization, but through more general discourses. Meyer and Rowan (1977) long ago introduced the concept of 'rationalized institutional myth': that is, the social construction of myths such as organizational 'efficiency', 'structures' and 'missions', that legitimate organizations *as such* and orientate their practice. Such myths are communicated mainly *through* media. They are what we called in Chapter 4 'meaningful arrangements' of the social world, and have consequences both within and beyond the organization, *'co-constitut[ing]* the public's ideas of organizations' and organizations' ideas of themselves and acting 'not only [as] descriptions of organizations, but [as] descriptions *for* organizations' (Schultz et al., 2014, p. 26; added emphasis). Such myths may be general or specific, but when they become related to particular organizations, they provide ideas *of order*. Think of the well-known myths of 'success' for companies, or of 'efficiency' for bureaucracies, or the myth of 'delivery' used across both organizations and government in neoliberal democracies. The crucial point is *less* that all these organizations always fulfil such expectations. It is rather that such myths provide legitimacy for organizations, and act as a normative basis for organizational practice and its evaluation. Or as Magnus Fredriksson and Josef Pallas put it: 'the way the media monitor and scrutinize [. . .] organizations is of great importance in understanding how the legitimacy and reputation of these organizations are constructed and how they operate' (Fredriksson and Pallas, 2014, p. 235). New myths such as dataism (van Dijck, 2014) can also work *across* different organizations, just as discourses about 'new technologies' of communication have worked throughout the history of 'modernization' (Martín-Barbero, 1993, pp. 182–186). More broadly, as places where people spend much of their waking hours, organizations are powerful *amplifiers* of broader myths about desirable *forms of order*: in that way, they contribute also to the construction of a wider social order, oriented to particular myths.

Media are also involved in the *transformation of organizational processes*. There is a wide literature on how digital media have changed the structures of organizations from top to bottom.[2] The claim is made that major organizational change derives from digital media infrastructures, which make new kinds of 'network organizations' possible. Manuel Castells for example linked the late twentieth-century transformation of the economy to organizational changes that became possible with the internet and the rise of 'network organizations' (Castells, 2000, pp. 163–166). More recently, it has also been argued that 'the global data network exerts institutional force on all contemporary organizations' (Lammers and Jackson, 2014, p. 33). Media and data networks have become a critical infrastructure for most organizations, shaping changes in how they are organized at a micro level and becoming embedded in the ambitions and goals of those working in organizations (Fredriksson and Pallas, 2014).

While deep mediatization plays out differently depending on the organizational and institutional context (Donges, 2011; Fredriksson et al., 2015; Hjarvard, 2014; Øyvind and Pallas, 2014; Thorbjornsrud et al., 2014), there remains a general transformative moulding force of media on organizations. The capabilities of digital media and their infrastructures enable the figurations on which organizations are based to be differently ordered *in space*: they are no longer necessarily organized around physical proximity (see Lammers and Jackson, 2014, p. 41). This does not mean that locality no longer matters, as research on globalized cities has demonstrated: cities remain culturally dense places, and therefore important for many organizations, especially corporate ones (Krätke, 2011; Zook, 2005). But it became easier for organizations to be distributed across different locations, while sustaining an intense practice of internal communication and communicational norms that integrate spatially dispersed actors. The result is to change the *quality and complexity* of how individuals and collectivities relate to organizations. Arguably, 'the dispersion of social networking technologies creates greater familiarity with forming teams and groups' (Noveck, 2009, p. 161). Looking outside the organization, links to the sorts of collectivities of work discussed in the previous chapter can enable the traditional form of organization to extend itself more widely into other social domains. Communicative practices in organizations become themselves moulded by those organizations' ensembles of media: for example, writing emails, sharing documents and conducting video conferences, instead of sending letters and memos, accelerates and intensifies day-to-day communication in the organization, while digital archives can be searched more quickly and in different ways than printed ones. Through the ways in which individual practices are moulded, deep mediatization intensifies the acceleration of communications processes within and between organizations.

In sum, all the media-based changes discussed in Chapters 5 and 6 regarding space and time also matter for organizations and their practice. There is a basic dialectic at work here: some organizational transformations are initiated externally, and indeed whole institutional fields are being transformed, by a changing media environment, while others are transformed internally by their *uses* of their changing media environment – the organization's actualization of the media manifold so as to order *its* ensemble. It is from the working out of this dialectic in the context of particular organizations that wider consequences for social order flow.

Third, there is the *transformation of knowledge production* within organizations, linked to the changing media environment. We already referred to the internet and data networks as important organizational infrastructures which encourage the extension of organizational communications in space and in time. But the more far-reaching point – echoing the arguments made in Chapter 7 – is that datafication, as an automated process, has become part of most organizations' knowledge production. The legal theorist Julie Cohen (2012, p. 188) notes for example with regard to today's standardized data and information infrastructures that they are 'architectures of control [. . .] reflect[ing] a fundamental shift in our political economy, toward a system of governance based on precisely defined, continually updated authorization of access by and to actors, resources, and devices'. There were always of course systems operating within organizations that restricted access to various kinds of information on one basis or another. Our point is that in organizations that have integrated a data-architecture into their operations, their data 'system' – often stored via an external arrangement 'in the cloud' (see next section) – *is* now those organizations' operating and long-term memory. Once again, and in parallel to the transformation of individual and collective life, organizational life becomes dependent on an external layer of *institutionalized* interdependence that affects the wider distribution of power and the nature of social order.

The work of many organizations nowadays integrates algorithmic models in which the norms and ordering processes of these organizations become inscribed. An example discussed in earlier chapters is organizations within the financial market whose models of market operation have become at last partly dependent upon complex computer systems that span the many centres of electronically connected market activity: 'the global market itself is these produced-and-analyzed displays to which traders are attached' (Knorr-Cetina, 2014, p. 40). Only through the 'synthetic situations' constructed by these systems of 'scopic media' can their *organizational* purposes be fulfilled, and only through these situations is 'the market' (the organizational myth around which those organizations are above all focused) itself constructed. 'Synthetic agents' more and more are doing the organizational work, even if supervised by traders. Other types of organization are also in the process of moving in this direction: for example, police authorities and tax agencies are beginning to use accumulated and automated data analytics to solve cases and even *predict* future ones (with the hope of preventing them).[3] And even organizations in the institutional field of education such as schools rely on datafication to calculate the quality of schools and teaching on the basis of data-driven models of student evaluation (Breiter, 2014; Selwyn, 2015). We are however only at the beginning of these changes in organizational knowledge through datafication, not the end.

To summarize, deep mediatization is transforming the 'inner life' of organizations, and by that also changing the terms on which organizations interact with wider power structures, and their implication therefore in social order. At the core of this lies the role that media generally, and datafication in particular, play in the very basis of organizations' processes of ordering in an age of deep mediatization, but also in the way organizational purposes are constructed in wider public discourse. Therefore, if we want to consider the role that organizations have in wider institutionalized fields and how thereby they contribute to social order, we have to take seriously their deep implication in processes of mediation.

10.4 Politics and Government

We have argued that the three basic actors in social life – selves, collectivities and organizations – are being transformed by media and media infrastructures including data and information infrastructures, and in the course of this are becoming implicated in social order in a radically new way. What happens when we extend our argument to consider the seemingly open spaces *beyond* organizations in which government and various other types of power seek to intervene and regulate? These are spaces characterized by multiple actors of varying levels of complexity, so that it is difficult to evaluate overall consequences or directions of change. But, provided we choose well our angle of entry, a number of important developments come into view.

Politics and government have always been complex, relative to the norms of the social domains in which they sought to intervene, but the *increase* in the complexity of communication challenges faced by those involved in early twenty-first-century politics and government is not trivial. It is important to see both positive and negative sides of the changes under way. New forms of communication linkage make possible, as legal theorist and former US government adviser Beth Noveck points out, new ways of involving citizens and experts in effective government: there is, she rightly warns, 'too little diversity in the work of managing society' (Noveck, 2009, p. 16), although there is little evidence so far that the opportunities that digital networks offer to generate decisive change in how democracies function have been taken. Meanwhile, new forms of exclusion from the civic and political process are being forged.

Historical Parallels and Differences

To help us imagine the *possible* scale of changes in politics and government now under way, it is worth dwelling on a historical example when a shift in mediatization was associated with a change in the nature of government. Most accounts of early modernity focus on the invention from the fifteenth century onwards of printing in Europe as decisive for the *later* emergence of the modern nation-state. But more decisive, some historians argue, and more far-reaching in its implications for how modern government would come to be conducted, was the shift to *rule through written document* that M.T. Clanchy (1993) dates much earlier, that is, to the eleventh to thirteenth centuries. The changing modalities of government were a crucial driver in cultural change: 'lay literacy *grew out of bureaucracy*, rather than from any abstract desire for education or literature' (1993, p. 19, added emphasis). The increasing circulation of written documents for everyday purposes – from maps to legal records to royal decrees – and the skills associated with their production and interpretation, transformed how a ruler could interact with his territory. By the time of England's King Edward I, government, in theory at least, 'had access to every place of habitation, however small, and every man, however lowly his status' (1993, p. 47), not through any ease of personal physical access (roads remained very rudimentary), but through the coordinated power of a network of practices based on written documents. The state's leading role in this shift parallels Elias' account of the state's leading role in the 'structure of civilized behaviour' and 'manners' (1994, p. xiv) in the fifteenth and sixteenth centuries in Europe. The increasing shift from modes of government based on norms of personal (face-to-face) command to modes of government based on the deferred force of written description and instruction had other implications too: the growth of *permanently available* written records as reference-points for rule (1993, pp. 153–154); the need to find ways of *ordering* the sudden mass of important records (the invention of the alphabetical index: Clanchy, 1993, pp. 177–179; Illich, 1996, pp. 102–103).[4]

The broad parallels with the profound transformation of government and politics through the explosion of digital records from the 1990s onwards (Bimber, 2003) are striking. So too is the emergence of extreme inequalities of resource associated with both historic and contemporary transformations: just as today the power to build, design and manage digital infrastructures is concentrated in very few rich institutions (Google, Facebook, Amazon: see Chapter 4), so in the early medieval period 'only the king possessed permanently organized writing facilities' (his 'Chancery': Clanchy, 1993, p. 57). The potential for broader shifts in the organization of power and order from shifts in the degree of mediatization were present in the early medieval period, just as they are today. Those shifts operate within nations and between nations, with terms such as the 'digital underclass' (Helsper, 2011) having an ambiguous status as a national *and* transnational phenomenon.

If by contrast we turn back to nineteenth-century America, we can learn also from James Beniger's account of the emergence of modern communications – the telegraph, newspaper, postal services, telephone – in response to the 'crisis of control' created by the mismatch between the communication 'demands' of an expanding social and economic domain and the 'supply' of a rudimentary communications infrastructure. The transformation in modes of communication that emerged across all areas of business and government in the second half of the nineteenth century in expanding capitalist economies was not a matter of inventing a single medium and embedding it in daily life, but involved shifts in the *interdependence* of all aspects of organizational life, what Beniger calls 'the progressive layering of control levels' (1986, p. 292).

How much then can we learn from these earlier precedents for the transformation in social order now under way through the wave of digitalization? One key difference between then and now is the new salience, even dominance, of private corporations, a theme that so far we have approached more generally through our discussion of the *institutionalization* of selves, collectivities and the frameworks in which organizations operate. All the processes we are discussing here have their basis in the institutionally based infrastructure of connection we call 'the internet'. Certainly, the state in various countries was enormously important in the early investments and planning of the internet as a connective infrastructure (Mazzucatto, 2013; Keen, 2015), a contribution that in fact goes back deep into the history of the computer and the nineteenth-century calculative technologies that preceded it (Agar, 2003, p. 41). But today, while the state is a key beneficiary of new forms of digital rule, it is not the main driver of change. As Louise Amoore argues in her history of the new data-based systems of surveillance and tracking movements across borders:

> It is not the advent of a war on terror that ushered in a raft of novel and unprecedented security technologies. In fact, quite the reverse is true: the events of 9/11, and the exceptional measures that were so quickly declared actually cleared space for the sovereign enrolment of mundane, ordinary technologies that had been used in the gathering of everyday transactions of bread and sausages for some eight years. (Amoore, 2013, pp. 41–42)

Amoore details the role of executives from IBM and UK food and clothing retailer Marks and Spencer in developing 'association rules' that would predict consumer behaviour better from the textual traces available to new data mining techniques (2013, pp. 39–41, 50–51). The drive of marketers to track consumers more continuously and predictively (from which states in turn benefited) was part of the expansion of opportunities *for corporate organizations* that derived from the new digital infrastructure. Other pressures towards data mining, however, derived from the increasing problem for advertisers that flowed from the explosion of digital media content in circulation in the late 1990s, which made it increasingly difficult to claim that any one expensive piece of discrete advertising reached its audience more effectively than another (Turow, 2011). Building on this, powerful media players, such as Facebook, are 'reworking the fabric of the web' to make it a space better integrated to their economic goals (Gerlitz and Helmond, 2013, p. 7).

From many directions then, the organizational implications of digitalization are having profound consequences for order and rule. Also important, from the point of view of balances of power, is the shift in control over the computing infrastructure on which the digital world's communications infrastructure relies. Today's economy depends on vast data-processing capacity that has become, in most respects, too expensive for individual corporations *or* national governments to own internally. The rise of 'the cloud' – that is, 'the storage, processing and distribution of data, applications and services for individuals and organizations' (Mosco, 2014, p. 17) – represents a massive shift of control *away from* the nation-state, which until a decade ago had broad control of its information resources (2014, pp. 66–67), and towards the small number of dominant corporations (Apple, Google, Microsoft) which manage the remote computer servers on which 'the cloud' exists. We are not arguing here that the result is necessarily more order, let alone an order that is better attuned to key normative values. Although some classic analyses see the growth of information infrastructure as crucial to how effective social order was achieved in different phases of history (e.g. Beniger, 1986), there are counter-examples, for example the ambiguous status of bureaucracy in the large-scale violence of the twentieth century. We will return to the normative questions in Chapter 11.

A New Type of Politics?

Alerted then to the possibility that the changes in the communications infrastructure constituted by the waves of digitalization (and datafication) may *themselves constitute* a significant shift in the nature of social order, how can we relate this to the stuff of everyday politics and government?

Apparent changes in the nature of politics derived from digital media have attracted most attention. There is no doubt that media platforms for social networking have made short-term political mobilization easier (see Chapter 9), while also intensifying the dynamics of political scandal (Thompson, 2005b). But this is very different from concluding that the nature and balance of politics *overall* has been changed by these new communication tools.

There are at least four strong reasons for caution against rushing to such a conclusion. First, the aspects of politics that would appear to have been transformed by digital communications are principally the *'negative'* *ones*, what Pierre Rosanvallon (2009) calls 'counter-democracy', leaving the implications for other aspects of politics, for example, the long-term building of parties for political transformation, less clear or perhaps even negative (Couldry, 2012, pp. 108–132). Second, the large-scale narratives told of how politics has changed through digital media tend to be *universal stories* built on generalizations from a limited number of cases, most notable the USA and the UK. More careful comparative analyses of digital politics paint a more mixed picture, with very different implications in different political systems (Nielsen, 2012; Stanyer, 2013; Vaccari, 2013). Third, once we begin to grasp the *complexity* of how the wave of digitalization has affected organizations, we cannot underestimate the complexity of how it has affected political organizations such as parties engaged in multi-level conflicts. The combination of increased production and archiving of politically relevant information and more distributed access within and beyond organizational boundaries to that same information probably *reduces* the stability on average of political institutions (Bimber, 2003). Meanwhile, extended networks of communication have enabled organizations, such as political parties working in elections, to join up multiple political actors in what Rasmus Kleis Nielsen calls 'campaign assemblages' for the purposes of organizing *face-to-face* communication with potential voters (Nielsen, 2012). Not only does this reverse the prediction of 1990s campaigners that 'personalized' communication was redundant in modern digital campaigning, but it alerts us to the effectiveness, in the pressured context of elections, of figurations of 'fundamentally and never fully integrated mutually dependent actors who then go their separate ways once the election is over' (2012, p. 179). In such contexts, once again, the balance between political power and commercial power may be surprising: 'your local supermarket is very likely to be more organizationally and technologically sophisticated than your local congressional campaign', notes Nielsen (2012, pp. 183–184).

A final reason for caution, moving in the other direction, is that the general proliferation of politically relevant information (just as with consumer-relevant information) makes it all the more difficult to predict the consequences of political communication by particular organizations. Not only is cultural and historical *context* important, but so too (and just as culturally variable, potentially) are citizens' habits of *selection from* the vast information universe available to them to motivate their political choices (Zolo, 1992). Many fear that information selection regularly locks people in 'bubbles' that are reinforced by the operations of search engines in presenting information to web searchers that fits better with the searchers' past patterns of information use (Pariser, 2011). Against this background, we need to know more about the *figurations of solidarity and expression* in which citizens of particular types at particular locations are, or are not, involved. An excessive emphasis on networked politics at the expense of more detailed research on the social figurations in which network interactions actually matter has so far held back research in this area.[5]

A Different Type of State?

Rather than expect as yet to find clear patterns in how, under conditions of deep mediatization, *particular political conflicts* work themselves out, it may be more promising to examine the changing conditions for *general projects of political order*, that is, for government. As we saw already, governments, the embodiment of the nation-state, are becoming deeply reliant on the private corporate interests that sustain today's data infrastructure. That granted, what are the implications of deep mediatization for rule?

If we think of governments as very large figurations of figurations, then the implications of deep mediatization for organizations apply even more strongly to governments: there are new opportunities for coordination on an extended scale and with increased precision over time, facilitating government *by delegation* to a vast range of authorities. Domains of internal networked communication are fundamental to the expanding work of government. But government, of course, does not work in a vacuum. The requirement of government, particularly in democratic states, to retain a minimal, even high, level of legitimacy before its citizens necessarily exposes governments to the accelerated communication flows of the general media environment. Over a decade ago, German political scientist Thomas Meyer (2003, pp. 40–44) pessimistically argued that the foreshortened time-scales of media narratives in the 24/7 digital news environment accelerated not only the time-scale of government reaction to news events, but also the cycle of *policy generation*, with corrosive impacts on the quality of policy itself. There are certainly accounts from former senior governments that would support that view (Foster, 2005), and the beginnings of comparative empirical work that might give some support to these fears (Kunelius and Reunanen, 2014). But more extensive empirical work is needed.

Meanwhile, far from the locations where policy is developed, citizens go on with their lives, but in a changed relationship to what they still imagine as 'the state', mediated by an increasingly vast data infrastructure. Two authoritative commentators, Engin Isin and Evelyn Ruppert, note that 'although the internet may not have changed politics radically in the fifteen years [between 1998 and 2013], it has radically changed the meaning and function of *being citizens* with the rise of both corporate and state surveillance' (Isin and Ruppert, 2015, p. 7, added emphasis). It is not just a matter of performing a citizen identity in a new range of situations: it is, more fundamentally, a matter of increasingly integrating the rhythms and patterns of individual practice into the demands of the new systems of data collection on which the state increasingly relies. We saw in Chapter 7 the significance for selves of the rise of deep forms of categorization through data processes, in Chapter 8 for collectivities and their imaginary of political communities. But what exactly are the implications for government, and the possibility of social order through governing? We are, once more, too early in this shift to offer a definitive judgement, but some directions of change are becoming clear.

The importance of managing media for government's stability has been clear for decades (Meyrowitz, 1985; Scammell, 1993; Bimber, 2003; Chadwick, 2013), and has always revolved around the management presentation of external realities, such as crises, scandals and natural disasters. But as the project of government shifts in part to *managing* the vast data infrastructure on which its targeted actions-at-a-distance now depend, government-citizen relations *themselves* become increasingly mediated by this infrastructure and its bureaucratic interfaces. As Ruppert puts it:

> What people do in relation to government (transactions) becomes more central rather than what they say they do and who they say they are (subjective identifications) [. . .] through all of this doing, subjects are less able to challenge, avoid or mediate their data double. (2011, p. 227)

We discussed the concept of 'data double' in Chapter 7 in relation to the self, but we must return to it here since it is fundamental to understanding the type of governmental 'order' that is emerging under conditions of deep mediatization. Relations between citizens and governments have never been free from possibilities of alienation. But when governments' actions, *whatever* their democratic intent, become routinely dependent on processes of automated categorization, a dislocation is threatened between citizens' experience and the data trajectory on the basis of which they are judged. Schutz and Luckmann's phenomenology grounded the 'natural attitude of daily life' in the individual's 'stock of previous experience' (1973, p. 7) yet there was more than enough grim experience in the mid twentieth century to show that citizens could not always expect their governments to avoid actions that clashed violently with their stock of experience. But datafication is disturbing in a more banal way, because it is a mode of government that is *never* likely to be responsive to 'what [citizens] say they do and who [citizens] say they are'.[6]

What consequences can we expect, over the longer term, for the core constituents of order and legitimate government: *trust, legitimacy*, the *credibility* of government action, citizens' sense of their own *efficacy* as political actors? As yet, we do not know. But two large-scale and disturbing trends need at least to be registered. First, there is the association of the new datafied social infrastructure with the entrenchment of social economic and ethnic inequality (Gangadharan, 2015). Second, as already noted, there is the increasing importance of force, rather than consensus-based norms, in the constitution of social order. Norms in the area of data collection are, as we have seen, changing: dataism is precisely an attempt to *inculcate* new norms of data generation, that naturalize a certain submission to new relations between corporations and consumers, and citizens and state, based on continuous surveillance and the citizen's active role in the generation of data. Yet the very infrastructure on which our networked digital communications relies is, in an important sense, 'authoritarian' (Cohen, 2012, pp. 188–189), based on 'compliant submission to authority', not consent. Norms in the absence of possible meaningful consent and negotiation become very close to *force*, with potentially dangerous long-term implications for wider institutional legitimacy.

That is our concern: that, under conditions of deep mediatization, an ever more complex infrastructure of interdependent communication installs a datafied social order which relies more on infrastructural *force* (or near-force) than on the openly contestable legitimacy of norms. We need in the next and concluding chapter to consider more fully the normative implications of such large-scale shifts in the construction of the social world and of social order.

11

Conclusion

This book began with a question, which we rephrase here. What are the consequences of the social world being mediated, that is, constructed from, and through, media, that is, technologically mediated processes and infrastructures of communication? We have sought in this book to address that question in stages.

In Part I we analysed the consequences for the basic fabric of the social world when it becomes constructed through mediated communications. In particular, we considered the role of communications in the history of the past six centuries, and the long-term process of successive waves of mediatization that have resulted in the current stage of 'deep' mediatization. Deep mediatization involves all social actors in relations of interdependence that depend, in part, on media-related processes: through these relations, the role of 'media' in the social construction of reality becomes not just partial, or even pervasive, but 'deep': that is, crucial to the elements and processes *out of which* the social world and its everyday reality is formed and sustained. At the same time, and connectedly, media outlets and platforms become themselves increasingly interconnected in both production and usage, creating a many-dimensional space of possibility that we have called the media manifold. A helpful concept for grasping our relations to and within the media manifold is that of figuration, developed from the late work of Norbert Elias. Part II was dedicated to exploring the fundamental dimensions of our social world under these new conditions, and specifically their increasing interrelatedness with media contents and media infrastructures. We examined the dimensions of space and time, and the new dimension of 'data', which more and more is involved in the moulding of what counts as social knowledge. In Part III we addressed agency in the social world: the construction of the self and of collectivities, and the emergence of wider social order under conditions of deep mediatization.

The discussion of order in our last chapter began to raise new questions about how we *evaluate overall* the consequences for human life-in-common of the mediated construction of reality. That is the main focus of this concluding chapter. Our argument throughout has been designed to move beyond the limitations of Berger and Luckmann's classic account of 'the social construction of reality', which failed completely to register the role that mediated communications play in that construction. But registering media seriously within a phenomenological approach requires us not only to develop a fully *materialist* phenomenology (since 'media' are undeniably a complex material infrastructure), but to recognize the particular new type of deep infrastructure for constructing the social world that today's data-driven platforms and patterns of social connection represent. And that recognition provides the basis for a second move beyond Berger and Luckmann, which identifies a level of analysis absent from their argument, a level on which the pressures towards particular types of social order may come into conflict within important human goals and needs. This level of *evaluative critique*, built on phenomenological premises, and inspired in particular by Elias' insights into how social order is built and the pressures it exerts, was not available to Berger and Luckmann, because their analysis retained a primary focus on face-to-face communications and forms of institutionalization that ultimately derive from face-to-face interactions, and ignored the transformative, but tension-laden, role that mediated communications may come to play in the construction of the social world.

It is worth emphasizing that, in what follows, we are not pretending that there are no variations between cultures and societies in the extent to which deep mediatization, in all its aspects, has taken hold there. But, since the aim of this conclusion is to alert readers to the implied *direction* of change linked to deep mediatization, we will put less emphasis here on variability and more on what we see as the key outlines of an emergent trend that is gaining force in many parts of the world *regardless* of uneven access and economic development: a tendency towards a new *type* of social order distinctive to deep mediatization and to datafication. Our aim however is not to predict a universal direction of travel, and, indeed, if resistance to this trend were to halt the tendencies we identify, we would be delighted. Just as important as identifying strong tendencies towards order is to be alert to the possibilities of *agency*, and resistance to order, as we have noted at various points in Part III.

We are concerned with the *social* unfolding of transformations in media infrastructures, that is, the complex consequences of media technologies' embedding in everyday social life. We reject entirely a technological determinist approach, and specifically in the form that argues that new 'media' generate a specific 'logic' that, in some simple way, is rolled out across the social terrain. That is not how technologies make a difference, and it is not how social change occurs. Relatedly, the growth over time of relations of *interdependence* cannot be understood except within a model of non-linear causal complexity.[1] For that reason, it is *incoherent* to think of deep mediatization as involving the unfolding of just *one* 'logic'. Rather, deep mediatization refers to a meta-process involving, at every level of social formation, media-related dynamics coming together, conflicting with each other, and finding different expressions in the various domains of our social world. At the very least, deep mediatization derives from the interaction of two very different types of transformation: a changing media environment characterized by increasing differentiation, connectivity, omnipresence, pace of innovation and datafication (the emergence of the media manifold); and the increasing interdependence of social relations (the complex role in social life of figurations and figurations of figurations, that are based, in part, on a media-based infrastructure, but whose dynamics evolve beyond it).

To set the scene, let us first revisit what broad principles we have learned during the course of this book about deep mediatization. What implications do those principles have for how we *evaluate* the mediated construction of reality?

Deep Mediatization and its Broader Implications

To restate one of the book's fundamental claims: the social world is constructed from interdependencies. Media, as they have expanded through successive stages of their development, introduce their own interdependencies, which become embedded in daily life, generating the overall 'outcome' we label, for convenience, 'mediatization'. But when 'everything is mediated' (Livingstone, 2009, p. 2), mediatization reaches a new point: a phase of *deep* mediatization, when the nature and dynamics of interdependencies (and so of the social world) *themselves become dependent upon* media contents and media infrastructure, to a significant degree. At this point, mediatization can justifiably be called 'deep'.

Deep mediatization emerged out of a particular historic shift in both media infrastructures and the embedding of media in social life. The decisive break occurred with what we called in Chapter 3 the wave of digitalization, and the reason was the increased degree of *interconnectedness between media* that the digitalization of content and the parallel building of an open-ended space of connection (the internet) made possible. That interconnectedness between media brought, inevitably, increasing interdependence between the actors (individual, collective, organizational) that use media for various reasons, not least to connect and interact with each other. The transformation of media provided a starting-point for the transformation of social order. Understanding the consequences of *all this* for social processes and the possibilities of social order is the goal of researching deep mediatization.

Deep mediatization, as just noted, operates in a nonlinear way. We can no longer understand the influence of 'the media' any more as the influence of a separate domain (for example, journalism) *onto* other domains of the social world. It does not matter which part of the social world we consider: its formation is in one way or another related to media. The broader transformations that result are complex, contradictory and likely to create tensions – between actors and institutions and between different levels of organization and resource allocation – that are only partly resolvable. It follows that, if we pay attention to deep mediatization, we become interested in much more than the presence of media processes in all or most social domains of daily life (which is now, as philosophers say, 'trivially true'). We engaged also with how, through social actors' evolving uses of the media manifold, *the nature and quality of social interdependence is itself changing*: the issue, in other words, of agency.

This emerges, for example, in those moments when individuals try to withdraw from the various media interfaces on which the social world now seems to rely. Just as any attempt to pull back from 'social acceleration' into 'oases of deceleration' (for example, through various forms of body and mind maintenance) is paradoxical, because only temporary and provisional (Rosa, 2013, p. 87), so too with mediatization. People who refuse to use certain (digital) media and try to limit their reachability through media, companies that introduce email-free holidays, hotels that offer a room switch 'to block wireless internet signals' (Moore 2015), and so on, to help people 'refuel' and then 'get back on again' – *all* are looking for what, after Rosa, we might call 'oases of de-mediatization' (compare Turkle, 2015, pp. 3–17). Much popular self-help literature reflects on such attempts to slow down the process of mediatization, but they are destined to fail: they are almost certainly a prelude to a return, to a re-absorption into media which in turn acts to confirm the depth of mediatization 'after all'.

There are three fundamental implications of deep mediatization that only become fully clear at this stage of our argument: deep recursivity, expanded institutionalization, and intensified reflexivity.

First, under conditions of deep mediatization, both social and media processes become *deeply recursive*. 'Recursivity' is a term from logic and computer science indicating that rules are reapplied to the entity that generated them (Kelty, 2008). More broadly, this refers to processes that reproduce themselves by replaying all or part of the calculative or other rational process that initially generated them. But in many respects, the social world has always been recursive, at least insofar as it is based on rules and norms: we keep it going, and repair it when problems arise, by replaying once again the rules and norms on which it was previously based.[2] In a social world characterized by interdependencies whose practicality depends on an infrastructure of multiple connected media – the media manifold – recursivity deepens.

Many forms of action now involve the use of software, and software itself involves recursivity (MacKenzie, 2006), that is, 'as symbolic forms coalesce in massively networked code formations, the agential relations in software become involuted and recursive'.[3] Since software must function in the wider space of connection, even apparently simple acts by social actors depend on very many levels of recursion. This deep recursivity becomes the default feature of a social life that is increasingly dependent on digital media, their infrastructure and institutional bases, and our time spent with them. We feel the costs viscerally: when 'our' media break down – we lose internet connection, our password stops working, we are unable to download the latest version of software required by the device or function we want to use – it is *as if* the social infrastructure were itself, in some respect, breaking down: recursivity has been interrupted, ontological security becomes threatened. Deep social recursivity is the corollary of deep mediatization under conditions of ever more interrelated media and data infrastructures.

Under such circumstances, what once seemed radical about some versions of media theory (their focus on the transformations wrought by a single 'medium': Innis, 1951; McLuhan and Lapham, 1994; Meyrowitz, 2009) becomes radically inadequate. While it remains true that we need to emphasize the 'materiality of media' (Gumbrecht and Pfeiffer, 1994), this materiality cannot be grasped any more except by focusing on each medium *in relation to other media* and the forms of *social* interdependence that build around those media interrelations.

Second, deep mediatization (at the level of media interrelations and basic social interrelations) has an implication for wider social order: this is the process of *expanded institutionalization* noted in Chapters 8, 9 and 10. Actors (individual, collective, organizational), and other elements of social life, that could once be considered as discrete, that is, able to act relatively independently, become in the digital age dependent for their basic operations and functioning on a wider media infrastructure that is supplied and controlled by new types of institutional power (search engines, data aggregators, cloud computing suppliers, and so on). Under these conditions, the space of social action is overlain with a skein of connections from which it is almost impossible to escape, because it entangles actors on every scale. Far from being accidental, this transformation is highly motivated: it provides completely new sources of income and profit from the supply of privately owned, commercially driven infrastructure that enable not just aspects of material life (like a postal service or car fuel), but *the material spaces of social life itself.* This *construction* of the social is literally that: a *remaking* of the social. The era of deep mediatization brings with it not so much a deepening of institutionalization (since it is the *lateral* force of these entanglements to ever more distant and opaque institutions that strike us) but its expansion.

Third, deep mediatization brings with it the *intensified reflexivity* of social actors. In this context, it is worth noting the double meaning of 'reflexivity'. First, if we follow Ulrich Beck (1994), reflexivity in an increasingly complex world refers to the increasing number of side-effects of a social process, side-effects that may work against their originating forces, undermining various forms of stable tradition and structure in the process. It remains an open question whether deep mediatization fits within the undermining of structure. But, for sure, it brings with it many complex and unanticipated side-effects, including those of deep recursivity and expanding institutionalization.[4] We have already discussed a number of examples for this kind of reflexivity of deep mediatization. Interestingly, one fundamental characteristic of deep mediatization seems to be that a typical reaction to the negative side-effects of mediatization is not to withdraw, but to solve the anticipated problems by even further introduction of media technologies (Grenz and Möll, 2014), so reinforcing, not undermining, structure. But there is a second sense of reflexivity that was put forward by Anthony Giddens (1994b) who emphasizes the practical *self*-awareness and *self*-directedness of social actors (Giddens, 1990, pp. 36–45). The making and sustaining of media, both content and infrastructure, involves the actions of social actors who are reflexive: whatever pressures it faces – and in Chapter 7 we discussed how much of today's media infrastructure operates in ways opaque to social actors – reflexivity in the latter sense cannot be squeezed out of the social world. But something is changing in the sites of self-directed reflexivity. As the mutual transformations of media and social life intensify along multiple dimensions, they increasingly expose 'edges' that attract concern and anxiety, and push people towards withdrawal, requiring normative repair and invention. Self-reflexivity in a world characterized by the 'mediation of everything' (Livingstone, 2009) becomes increasingly open to anxiety, causing what one of us has called a 'normative turn' in media debates (Couldry, 2016). We pick up some of these anxieties and concerns about the direction of travel in the age of digitalization later in the chapter.

The normative shifts in public debates bring practical changes too. Media as technological means of communication are developed and introduced by some forms of pre-planning and involve reflection. But in times of deep mediatization self-reflexivity goes one step further: at the level of everyday media use, people have a practical awareness of the specificities of different media and select from the media manifold accordingly. Technologies are developed, put on the market, and continuously re-developed and modified in complex processes of interaction between different groups of actors (Grenz, 2015, pp. 104–139). Deep mediatization gets an additional push from this media-related 'self-monitoring', which becomes a permanent characteristic also of 'institutional reflexivity' (Giddens, 1994b, p. 185; see Grenz et al., 2014, p. 82). Datafication, for example, is an aspect of this, offering the chances for new, quantified forms of 'reflexivity' through the ongoing data that individuals produce, but it is an aspect deeply driven by the needs of media and data industries themselves, and brings costs quite different from those previously associated with reflexivity. Once more, we see how complex 'solutions' to problems of interdependence bring with them proposals of yet higher systemic dependence.

Possible Normative Consequences of Deep Mediatization

How then, as media and social theorists, do we start to think about the normative consequences of deep mediatization and its implications for the social world? We need at this point to abstract here from the messy and detailed picture of how reality is constructed through media on the ground to expose a hidden, but disturbing tension, a tension that would, we believe, have also disturbed our intellectual guide through much of this book, Norbert Elias.

At no point in the book have we drawn substantively on Elias' concept of a 'civilizing process': we have drawn instead on the approach to understanding social life – in terms of material relations of interdependencies – that allowed him to formulate the idea of a 'civilizing process' stimulated by the early modern state, and we have drawn in particular on the concept in terms of which, more fully in his later work, he came to understand those interdependencies: figuration. But the wider hypothesis of a civilizing process, controversial though it has been, remains, at the broadest level, important for raising *normative* questions about the large-scale consequences of how many overlapping interdependencies, and the costs or deficits to which they give rise, are lived out and sometimes find 'solutions'. It is with normative questions that we want to close our argument.

Is the tendency of the shift towards the complex media environment and infrastructure and heightened social, economic and political interdependency that we have called deep mediatization overall positive – when considered by reference to the 'quality of life' (Nussbaum and Sen, 1993; Hepp, Lunt and Hartmann, 2015) that it enables – or is it negative?

This is not a question that we can answer definitively here, since so many of the many-levelled transformations we have been considering are in their early stages, and their long-term interaction cannot be predicted. Yet over the past half decade or so, a number of writers have begun to draw conclusions about the direction of travel, and we would like to contribute to that debate.

In doing so, we make good on the normative commitment embedded in the project of materialist phenomenology, the commitment to developing as rich a hermeneutic reading as possible of how the everyday world tends to appear to people under particular material conditions. Elias' concern too with understanding social change was at its core a moral one focused on what is stake for human beings in particular ways of living together. As he wrote towards the end of *What is Sociology?*:

> People often seem deliberately to forget that social developments have to do with changes in human interdependence and with changes in men themselves. But if no consideration is given to *what happens to people* in the course of social change – changes in figurations composed of people – then any scientific effort might as well be spared. (Elias, 1978, p. 172)

As human beings, we cannot adapt some imaginary value-free standpoint in relation to 'what happens to people'.[5] But pretending to go on as if we could, or alternatively building intellectual 'values' from refinements of theoretical speculation detached from 'what happens to people', is all too common, and perhaps part of what Axel Honneth meant when he wrote that 'moral categories have all but disappeared from the theoretical vocabulary of sociology' (Honneth, 2013, p. 98).

What has emerged, throughout all our chapters, is a structural tension within 'what happens to people' under conditions of deep mediatization. We will end by exposing this tension, even though it cannot, for sure, be resolved at this historical moment. In this final move in our argument, we show that a focus on mediatization can precisely foreground the sorts of contradictions that characterize the figurational order (or, perhaps better, 'orders') of social life.

Unresolved Normative Questions

On the one hand, the emergence of the internet as an infinite space of connection and information storage has, through its embedding in everyday life, expanded in countless ways the range and depth of everyday action. What Anthony Giddens calls 'the digital revolution' (Giddens, 2015) has a depth which can be easy to miss, precisely because it represents a change in the ways in which social life *can be deep*, connected, resourceful, reflexive, retentive.

New figurations of connection are without doubt, in various contexts around the world, enabling 'emergent social and cultural systems' (Stokes et al., 2015) that reconfigure people and resources in new ways, and on the basis of new spatial mappings. Mediatization is a meta-concept (Krotz, 2009), and in many respects what it refers to are changes at a 'meta' level: changes in what is thinkable, doable and manageable. How can this expansion of the possibilities for social action not, at some level, be positive, even if the speed of change has created a situation where satisfactory conventions to stabilize and resolve the resulting problems of interdependence have not yet emerged? That indeed is one reading of today's normative turn in social thinking about media and communications, data and information: that we are in the early phase of an epochal shift in the material basis of social life, which will generate its own solutions, reconfiguring social and personal life in the process. Rather than be concerned, we should, some argue (for example, Mark Deuze, 2012), be celebrating the dawn of a new era of ethical invention, the start of a new 'media life' (perhaps a 'data life'?). That is however just one view.

On the other hand, a growing chorus of voices across the public world, and right across the social sciences, is becoming concerned at the direction of change. Let us gather some of those voices. Media analyst Mark Andrejevic calls on us 'to unearth the experience of the withering of experience itself' (2013, p. 162). Legal theorist Julie Cohen is concerned at the 'gap between the rhetoric of liberty' associated with the new information environment and 'the reality of diminished individual control' over her relations in and with that environment (2012, p. 4). Another legal theorist, Paul Ohm, is concerned at the need to find new human and normative solutions to the problem that even the attempt to anonymise personal data can almost always be defeated by algorithmic processes that are resourceful enough (2010, p. 1761). Social theorist Hartmut Rosa is concerned that 'the core of modernization, the acceleration process, has turned against the very project of modernity that originally motivated, grounded and helped set it in motion' (2013, p. 295); this is for the paradoxical reason that modernity's accumulated investment in technologies of communication, and practices of ever more complex coordination, create side-effects of social acceleration that undermine the self-determination of the modern individual. But if these critics are correct, the problems they identify are more than individual problems; they are problems with the *social order* that is emerging through deep mediatization, a problem implicitly also for its normative legitimacy and so its long-term sustainability.

The tensions that surface here are not trivial: they have philosophical resonances. Listen to renowned social psychologist Sherry Turkle (2015, p. 345) lamenting that, with progressing digitalization, the vast proliferation of opportunities (and obligations) to communicate pushes us to turn *other people into machines*, that is, 'even as we treat machines as if they were almost human, we develop habits that have us treating human beings as almost machines'. Yet the requirement *not* to treat others as things was the core of the leading moral philosophy of the Enlightenment, Kant's. That injunction echoes also the fears of philosopher, Axel Honneth. Honneth recently revived the concept of 'reification' to refer to how people treat somebody 'as a thing', that is 'to take him or her as something that lacks all human properties and capacities' (2008, p. 148). Honneth interestingly reflects also on the possibility of '*self*-reification (2008, p. 73), explaining this term in ways that register some of the pressures we have uncovered at various points in our argument:

> the more a subject is exposed to demands for self-portrayal, the more he will tend to experience all of his desires and intensions as arbitrarily manipulable things [. . .] the ways in which users come into contact with each other obliges them to enter their personal characteristics under predetermined and precalibrated rubrics. (2008, p. 83)

However abstractly, we sense something here of the concerns that today's growing processes of datafication are inspiring in citizens of all sorts, and not just philosophers. Such media-based forms of reification are the outcome (Hepp, 2013, p. 59; Chapter 2) of a progressive materialization of media and their infrastructures: when complex technological systems of media are built and stabilized, and related practices of communication become institutionalized, the mediated construction of reality comes to appear 'natural', and, in that way, processes of *mediated* construction become reified.

There is a sense then of tension between emerging infrastructure and inherited norms of social life. Is this tension merely an unfortunate mis-understanding that will gradually be ironed out as we become acclimatized to deep mediatization? Recalling Harold Innis, the great Canadian com-munications scholar of the mid twentieth century and Marshall McLuhan's teacher, reminds us why it is risky to believe so: 'improvements in commu-nication', he wrote, 'tend to divide mankind' (Innis, 2004, p. 95).

Is the problem alternatively that the sheer complexity of our mediated interdependency is now so great that we are struggling to evolve appro-priate conventions that could stabilize our relations and their costs in a normatively and practically satisfying way? Possibly, and it is too early to know for sure, but remember the definition of 'conventions' in the classic philosophical study of the subject: 'conventions are regularities in behaviour, sustained by an interest in coordination and an expectation that others will do their part' (Lewis, 1969, p. 208). David Lewis explained how human life may, and does, become orderly on the basis of minimal infor-mation, *provided* actors have an interest in coordination. But the type of regularity that Honneth in general – and many critics of datafication more specifically – fear is a regularity that derives not from social actors' general 'interest in coordination' among themselves, but from commercial plat-forms' interests in *engineering* the seamless generation of data from others' interactions in the service of their own profit.

This then is the deepest tension: between the necessary *openness* of social life, as the space where human life-in-common develops autonomously, and the motivated (and, in its own domain, perfectly reasonable) *enclosure* for commercial ends of the spaces where social life is today being con-ducted. A problem for any social order that hopes to carry some measure of legitimacy over the longer term comes when our spaces and processes of mutual recognition get themselves blurred with the imperatives of private interests to generate profit *from* those very same spaces and pro-cesses. The problem is not the profit motive as such, but the blurring of its motivated constructions of 'the social' with the forms of life that, as beings who value autonomy, we need ourselves and others to lead.

Under today's mediated conditions, then, the social construction of reality has become implicated in a deep tension between convenience and autonomy, between force and our need for mutual recognition, that we do not yet know how to resolve. This book's attempt to develop a materialist phenomenology of our mediated world has, we hope, helped at least to identify that tension. What collective resources are needed to address it satisfactorily will be the work of a whole generation to discover.

Notes

1 Introduction

1 Nietzsche opens the preface to his greatest work *Beyond Good and Evil* (1990 [1887], p. 32): 'Supposing truth to be a woman – what?' In the profoundly patriarchal society in which he wrote, Nietzsche felt there was no more shocking way of exposing philosophy's core concept of 'truth' than to suppose it 'a woman'. We adapt his question, for a very different context, to disrupt sociology's core concept of 'the social'.

2 See especially Latour (2005).

3 Compare Durkheim (1995) [1912].

4 Compare Kracauer (1995); Boorstin (1961); Brunsdon and Morley (1978); Hall (1980); and Meyrowitz (1985).

5 Compare Scannell (1996) and Douglas (1987).

6 Compare Sewell (2005, p. 329).

7 We have been inspired here by Sewell's formulation (2005, pp. 320–321): we borrow the second term from him, but the first is ours, adjusted from his term 'language-games' which assumes more philosophical background than we need at this stage of our argument.

8 Compare on humanism in research, for example, the late British philosopher Bernard Williams (Williams, 2006).

9 Arguably it never did, which is why Ian Hacking spares from his polemic against social constructionism Berger and Luckmann's 1966 book in whose wake our book, in a sense, follows: paradoxically, given today's much higher standing of Latour's work over Berger and Luckmann's, it is Latour's early sociology of science that comes in for heavy criticism from Hacking for its social constructionism!

10 For a rare and preliminary exploration, see Adoni and Mane (1984).

11 Compare the recent call for a new 'sociology of media and communications' (Waisbord, 2014).

12 Compare Illich (1996, p. 4, added emphasis).

13 Many current developments, such as the growth of software studies, can be interpreted as part of the same 'cognitive' turn in the human and social sciences.

14 In any case, Luhmann says very little about media (although for an exception see Luhmann, 1999). Mansell (2012, ch 5) and Rosa (2013) offer ways of taking the best from systems theory, while leaving behind its limitations.

15 Ian Hacking's blunt but not unsympathetic dismissal of Latour's own rejection of agency is worth recalling here: 'I am, if Latour likes to say so, a new agent when my possibilities for action change. But I am not made a new agent when I simply pick up a gun. The gun is not an agent. There is no hybrid man-gun [. . .] It is possible that cyborgs are hybrids; but that does not imply that everything is a hybrid' (Hacking, review of Latour (1999), Times Literary Supplement, 10 September, p. 13).

16 Compare the analytic philosopher John McDowell (1994, Lecture IV).

17 See for a broadly Aristotelian approach Lovibond (2002); McDowell (1994); and for the Hegelian tradition, Pinkard (2012) and Pippin (2008).

18 McDowell, a philosopher who unusually combines the neo-Aristotelian and Hegelian traditions, proposes the German word 'Bildung' for this, but not only has this word been discredited because of its unfortunate association with certain bourgeois notions of elite knowledge, but also it tends to be used in an individualistic sense, whereas both we and McDowell refer to a form of evolving order which is inherently trans-individual, that is, as Wittgenstein put it, 'part of *our* natural history' (McDowell, 1994, p. 95, quoting Wittgenstein (1978) [1953], p. 12, para. 25, with our added emphasis).

19 Compare Boltanski (2011), Schatzki (1996, p. 202).

20 We explain the concept of the '*media* manifold' in Chapter 3.

2 The Social World as Communicative Construction

1 Compare Giddens' idea that social structures 'recursively organize' social practices' (1984, p. 25).

2 On the latter, we agree with Boltanski and Thévenot (2006, p. 216) that 'we have to give up the idea of associating worlds with groups'.

3 We however avoid that term because it seems disconnected from the sociological specificity of institutions, but come back to the nature of institutionalization later.

4 Boltanski (2011, p. 51) underlines the common ground between his account and that of social phenomenology, by referring explicitly to the work of Alfred Schutz, while at the same time being deeply critical and suspicious of a too consensual reading of the notion of 'institutions' (2011, pp. 51–57).

5 Boltanski calls this wider space 'world', as opposed to (what we take for) '*reality*'. See also discussion in Couldry (2012, pp. 61–62).

6 Boltanski's original phrase is 'la realité de la realité' (2009, p. 62).

7 What we find here is a very early form of the argument that was later brought forward by Benedict Anderson (1983) and John B. Thompson

(1995), namely, that we cannot understand the emergence of the modern nation state without considering the (mass) media.

8 In the original translation of Schutz' 'Der Aufbau der sozialen Welt', the term 'mediacy' is used for the German *Mittelbarkeit* (Schutz, 1967, p. 182). However, we prefer the term 'mediatedness' as it sounds more natural in the English language.

9 Compare Christensen (2009, pp. 444–445), discussing Berger and Luckmann.

10 W. I. Thomas and D. S. Thomas' famous 'theorem' (that 'if men *define* situations as real, they are real in their consequences' (Thomas and Thomas, 1928, p. 571) does not therefore go deep enough.

11 This said, certain kinds of content are communicated more via specific forms of communication than are others. This becomes obvious if we consider institutionalized contexts of communication, for example, in the field of religion. Here, religious contents are communicated via certain forms of communication (the 'prayer',' 'homily', etc.), which we recognize via their *forms* as religious. However, these religious forms can be transferred to other contexts, for example, when a certain form of religious presenting is used to convince someone in a political speech. Examples like these demonstrate that there are certain links between form and content, and that we cannot see them as completely independent. Analytically, though, it is important to make this distinction if we want to understand how communication takes place as both action and practice.

12 As we might say in the terminology of Actor Network Theory, communicative practices are carried out in networks of 'human actors' and 'non-human actants' (Latour, 2007, pp. 54f.).

3 History as Waves of Mediatization

1 Especially the new 'media archaeology' (Huhtamo and Parikka, 2011; Kittler, 2014; Parikka, 2013).

2 Compare for this argument Appadurai, 1996; Chakrabarty, 2001; Fabian, 1983; Nederveen Pieterse, 1995.

3 For an analysis of this, see García Canclini, 1995; Murphy and Rodríguez, 2006; Straubhaar, 2007; Waisbord, 2013a.

4 Luhmann also discusses the role of symbolically generalized 'success media' like, for example, money for the development of what he calls functional systems of society (Luhmann, 2012, pp. 113–238). As technological media of communications are the focus of our analysis we do not focus on this argument in the following.

5 We develop here an idea by Klaus Merten (1994) to visualize the 'evolution of communication' while we do not share his narrow and functionalist interpretation.

6 Our argument has at this point a certain parallel to Finnemann's (2011)

reflections that mediatization has to do with technologically driven changes across all epochs; compare on this also Lammers and Jackson, 2014, p. 34.

7 An excellent example of such an approach is Lev Manovich's book on software as 'the engine of contemporary societies' (Manovich, 2013, p. 6).

8 See Barbrook (2007) on how politics influenced the 'imaginary futures' of the emerging computer era.

9 See Turner (2006) on the move from counterculture to cyberculture.

10 Thanks to Andrew Keen's recent book (Keen, 2015), which, though polemical, sets out these key stages with unusual sharpness.

11 There were alternative protocols, but TCP/IP won out (Agar, 2003, pp. 381–382).

12 It is worth noting however that media forms such as cinema have, to a significant degree, always been converged with other ancillary media (A. Rogers, 2013, p. 14).

13 This was anticipated by Marshall McLuhan (1987 [1964], p. 349).

14 As noted already by Henry Jenkins (Jenkins, 2006a).

15 First suggested in Couldry (2011); see also Couldry, 2012, pp. 16–17 and 44.

16 In September 2015 the Swedish-based company Shortcut Labs announced the development of a device to help us select from the increasing proliferation of apps, an app for apps, as it were: *Guardian* 7 September, p. 26.

17 In developing the concept of media manifold, we acknowledge the usefulness of the widespread idea of media's 'affordances' (Gibson, 1967; Hutchby, 2001). While helpful in considering interrelations with a specific medium, however, it is less useful here, since, in daily practice, in the media manifold new types of 'affordances' continuously overlap and conflict with each other, obscuring the broader relations in which we are interested.

4 How We Live with Media

1 For an attempt to apply Luhmann's systems theory to media's operations, see Qvortrup (2006).

2 For a detailed account, see Hepp and Couldry (forthcoming).

3 We can notice such a reification of the term 'network' for example when Rainie and Wellman write about people who 'work in social networks, not groups' (Rainie and Wellman, 2012, p. 11).

4 Again, for further review, see Hepp and Couldry (forthcoming).

5 Because this book's account of the 'social world' starts from the interrelatedness which *characterizes* the actors that belong to it, our position is perfectly compatible with the idea that, in some broader sense, ontology is 'flat', that is, that all objects are equal insofar as they are 'objects', so resisting 'the idea of a governing principle that unifies all objects' through the supposed 'property' of belonging to '*the* world' (Gabriel 2015, p. 252). As the philosopher Markus Gabriel points out, the notion of 'flat *ontology*'

rather than the 'flat metaphysics' (which is how he interprets Manuel DeLanda's position) is 'based on the idea of [objects'] *mere coexistence* such that *the actual structures of the objects determine their nature* and not the fact that they relate to some more substantial concept' (added emphasis). Since, following Elias, we see interrelatedness between entities as fundamental to social life, to ignore it would be to ignore objects' 'actual structures': there is nothing therefore in our account of structures of interrelatedness that is incompatible with a flat ontology in this broad sense. Gabriel, a prominent contemporary proponent of a 'flat ontology' himself, insists, for example, precisely on the structural differences between 'objects' and 'field' (2015, p. 295), avoiding thereby the trap of a flat metaphysics.

6 We acknowledge however that it is the reason why Latour, in spite of his desire to integrate 'the rich descriptive vocabulary of phenomenology' into an ANT analysis of '"non-intentional" entities' (Latour, 2007, p. 61, 67), must also part ways with phenomenology.

7 At this point there are various deep relations between a figurational approach and approaches of network analysis (see Willems, 2010, pp. 103–107, 256, 260–262).

8 For a detailed discussion of this with reference to figurations, see Hepp et al. (2015, pp. 186–189).

9 Even if certain platforms now offer sixty options for defining one's gender and sexual preferences (Hafner, 2015, p. 7), this does not change the fact that their technologies associate certain gender definitions with certain ways of self-representation.

10 We do not find helpful the suggestion (Marston et al., 2005) that we should abandon 'scale' entirely as a concept, any more than (see above) we find it helpful to say that the social world is 'flat', that is, merely two-dimensional.

11 Remember Latour's (1991, p. 103) famous phrase that 'technology is society made durable'.

12 In the phrase 'hanging together', we are recalling the perspective of practice theory: see Schatzki (1996, p. x).

13 For a comparable approach to rethinking Berger and Luckman's original argument from the perspective of discourse, see Keller (2011, p. 45).

14 See in general Couldry (2003; 2012) and Laclau (1990); for the myth of social media collectivities, see Couldry (2014a); for the myth of big data as a source of social knowledge, see Couldry (2014b); Mosco (2014, p. 5); boyd and Crawford (2012).

5 Space

1 We return to the term 'figurational order' in Chapters 6 and 10.

2 As a result, people may become used to meeting people in new types of space, for example in the social media feeds linked to a popular television

programme: research on Brazil for example provides multiple examples (Campanella, 2012; Drumond, 2014).

3 We are not impressed therefore with anthropologist Tim Ingold's proposal that we drop the notion of 'space' altogether (Ingold, 2011), which seems like an exemplary case of throwing the baby out with the bathwater.

4 In contrast to Marston et al. (2005), see here our criticism in Chapter 4.

5 According to Pew Research Centre (2012), 53 per cent of all adult cellphone owners in the USA have used their phones 'recently' while watching television 'for engagement, diversion or interaction', while Google research reported that 77 per cent of television viewers in the USA also watch television with another device (generally a smartphone, laptop or PC) with them (Google, 2012).

6 For the broader literature here, see Valentine (2006).

7 *Guardian* 19 August 2015, reporting on 2015 Good Childhood report by the Children's Society: https://www.childrenssociety.org.uk/sites/default/files/TheGoodChildhoodReport2015.pdf.

8 *El País* 20 August 2015, page 40: 'Juan y Juana', by Natalia Junquera (translated by us).

9 See Humphreys (2008; 2010) on the early platform Dodgeball in USA.

10 See http://www.megafone.net/BARCELONA, discussed by Cornelio and Ardevol (2011).

11 Here the term 'topology' can, finally, be used in a non-metaphorical way to capture the contrasting continuities and discontinuities of action that characterize differently qualified actors in code/space (contrast the discussion in Chapter 4).

6 Time

1 This point can be extended to the loss and derangement we feel when we face the possibility of an end to human time (Scheffler, 2013), for example, when contemplating environmental catastrophe.

2 Berger and Luckmann make a similar point about 'consciousness': 'temporality' they say 'is an intrinsic property of consciousness' (1966, p. 40): they call this *Bewusstseinsstrom*, flow of consciousness.

3 Compare our discussion in Chapter 3 with Slater's (2013) powerful critique.

4 As Luckmann puts it, 'the temporality of everyday life, as effectively as it may be structured by abstract, socially objectivated categories, *is* the intersubjective temporality of immediate social interaction and *rests on* the synchronization of the rhythms of inner time among men and women' (1991, p. 159, added emphasis).

5 Compare Ling (2012) and Chapter 7.

6 Luckmann was aware of Elias, but moves quickly past his work (1991, p. 152), seeing no general theoretical contribution there.

7 As Kosseleck notes: 'science and technology have stabilized progress as a temporally progressive difference between experience and expectation [. . .] this difference persists only through its constant renewal [indicated by] acceleration' (2004, p. 269).

8 Note that we are not saying that time itself is a technology (as does Ling, 2012, p. 38). Time is socially constructed, and its instantiations depend on social technologies of measurement, but it is also much more than those measures: it is, as we indicated at the start of the chapter, a framework through which life itself is understood. That is important to remember if we want to argue that social life, and the social world, are structured in part by our relations *around* time.

9 Compare the title of one section of Gregg: 'the connectivity imperative' (2011, p. 21).

10 For this reason, we agree with Judy Wajcman (2015) that it is too simple to say that 'everything' is accelerated in late modernity, but disagree with her rejection of Rosa's (2013) thesis that in late modernity there is an increasing problem in our social relations to time.

11 Compare Crary (2013, p. 53) on the 'parcellization and fragmentation of shared zones of experience'.

12 See Neverla (2002) for the concept of polychrony and media.

13 Concern at such out-of-jointness has generated legislative action in various countries, for example the so-called 'eraser bill' passed in California to enable young people to demand the taking-down of posted material from websites and platforms (Caldwell, 2013).

14 For an insightful commentary on the controversy that Free Basics has, rightly, sparked in India, see Lafrance (2016) 'Facebook and the New Colonialism', *The Atlantic*, 11 February.

7 Data

1 See our discussion in Chapter 1.

2 As noted in an authoritative recent essay on algorithms (Gillespie, 2014, p. 169).

3 See especially Beniger (1986, p. 25), where he remarkably anticipated the connective space of the contemporary internet as a process of 'digitalization'.

4 Savage and Burrows (2007) and Burrows and Savage (2014) have alerted sociologists to the emergence of new forms of data-based social knowledge, but their interest is the implications for the methods and goals of professional sociologists. Here we are concerned with the implications for *social actors themselves*, and for the domain of everyday action that classic phenomenology claims to map.

5 For an anticipation of the argument that follows, see Calhoun (1992b).

Calhoun's reference is not Schutz, but the US pragmatist Cooley. Calhoun extends Cooley's account of social relations (in terms of primary, i.e. role-based, and secondary, that is, whole-person-based, relations) to include in the later twentieth century not just 'tertiary' relations (known relations that we have with distant infrastructure), but also, most relevantly, 'quaternary relations' (1992b, pp. 218–219) which operate *automatically* without social actors' awareness, including processes of information processing.

6 We are well aware that, by considering this infrastructure from the perspective of (some extension of) classic phenomenology, we already fly in the face of those who argue that the only starting-point for sociological or social-theoretical analysis today is an already fused process of 'socio-materiality'. Yet, as discussed in Part I, our version of social construction takes for granted the mutual imbrication of social and material and the mutual intertwining of human and material (Pickering, 1995, pp. 15–20). So too did Elias' (and Schutz's) and, less emphatically, Berger and Luckmann's approaches. But to go further and argue that our starting-point should be 'not tasks undertaken by people in roles but material-discursive practices *enacted through apparatus* that simultaneously *constitute and organize phenomena*' (Scott and Orlikowski, 2013, p. 78; see Orlikowski and Scott, 2014) is in our view unhelpful. Nor do we find helpful approaches to 'socio-materiality' inspired by a reading of scientific domains such as quantum mechanics that, by definition, are remote from the conditions of everyday sense-making (Barad, 2007, relied upon by Scott and Orlikowski). As Jonathan Sterne notes, the endless debate between 'materiality' and 'constructivism' has become 'unproductive', once we acknowledge that, in researching technologies of communication, we are interested, *always*, in processes which 'aren't simply material, but have irreducibly material dimensions' (2014, p. 121). But that is exactly the interest of a materialist phenomenology.

7 There is an excess too built into code, as software studies note: 'in saying something, code also does something, but never exactly what it says' (MacKenzie, 2006, p. 177); 'encoded material enactments translate / extend agency, but never exactly' (Introna, 2011, p. 113).

8 For the distinction between database and algorithm, and the different levels on which they act, see Manovich (2001, ch. 5), Gillespie (2014), Kallinikos and Constantiou (2015).

9 Cohen (2012, p. 52) describes her approach as 'postphenomenological', because it insists on attending to our relations to technology, while still drawing on phenomenology. Properly developed however, as we have argued throughout, a phenomenological perspective *must already* address our relations to technology.

10 Again, classic phenomenology raised the question of opacity of the social world, but saw it as a feature of the relative degrees of social knowledge,

and our shared lack of knowledge about the future (Schutz and Luckmann, 1973, p. 168). For Schutz, there is here no unresolvable problem: 'the life-world is experienced as only relatively [. . .] intransparent, but in principle transparent' (1973, p. 169). Data processes, arguably, however, create a world which is *in principle and always already* opaque.

11 This is the force of Frank Pasquale's critique of the 'black-box *society*' (Pasquale 2015).

12 Isin and Ruppert (2015, ch. 7) prefer the term 'closings' to encompass the acts of categorization and sorting, but also a range of other acts that limit possibilities of interpretation. We prefer the term 'categorization' because of its link directly back to social theory.

13 Some challenge the idea that the classification of non-human objects is non-interactive (Knorr-Cetina, 2014), but that is not our concern here.

14 See also our discussion in Chapter 5.3.

15 What Kitchin and Dodge call 'an ongoing relational problem' (2011, p. 78).

16 Compare Mejias (2013) on how, in general, networks, as structures of nodes, exclude by definition the 'paranodal', that is, the not-networked, not-sorted domain that lies 'to the side of' nodes and so 'to the side of' network flows.

17 The typology is drawn from van Dijck (2013, p. 8).

18 See Papacharissi (2015, pp. 122–123) from whom we take the interesting reworking of the habitus concept for the age of datafication.

19 This is the area of 'social analytics' on which one of us has written (Couldry, Fotopoulou and Dickens, 2016): that is, the study of how social actors make use, and reflect upon, data-driven measurements of their own practice to better fulfil their own social ends, possibly drawing on values other than those linked to datafication. For a somewhat similar topic, see Nafus and Sherman (2014) and Knapp (forthcoming).

20 See also Chapter 1's conclusion.

21 J. M. Bernstein (2002) offers an interesting reading of McDowell which places the latter's fiercely abstract work in the context of critical theory and particularly Adorno's account of the disenchantment of reason.

22 Evgeny Morozov writes: 'the only autonomy that will be worth fighting for will be one which flourishes in opacity, ignorance, and disconnection' (2015, our translation). This basic idea was already anticipated by Gilles Deleuze a quarter of a century earlier: 'the key thing may be to create vacuoles of noncommunication, circuit-breakers, so we can elude control' (1995, p. 175).

8 Self

1 *University of Cape Town Careers Service Guide* 2015, p. 30. We quote this guide as a model of its kind: its clarity and explicitness are what make it

interesting as evidence. Many thanks to Nawaal Boolay of UCT's Careers Service for providing us with a copy.

2 Although they develop it within a wider critique of changing forms of labour and alienation under capitalism, some Italian autonomist Marxists make this essential point: 'both simple executing workers and entrepreneurial managers share the vivid perception that they depend on a constant flow that cannot be interrupted and from which they cannot step back save at the price of being marginalized' (Berardi, 2009, pp. 88–89). Crucially this new flow, as in our analysis, depends on a spatial and temporal change – 'the digital network is the sphere where the spatial and temporal globalization of labor is made possible'; 'the infinite vastness of the Infosphere' (Berardi, 2009, p. 89, 101) – although the establishment of that network is analysed in terms of a device (the mobile phone) that connects up to his network (Berardi, 2009, p. 89; see Agamben, 2009, p. 21), rather than the overall infrastructure of the contemporary internet.

3 *University of Cape Town Careers Service Guide 2015*, page 30, added emphasis.

4 Sewell (2005, p. 369), and compare Elias, 1991, p. 9; Martuccelli, 2002; Lahire, 2007.

5 Media first occur in Berger and Luckmann's account of socialization when they imagine an adult travelling to work on a suburban train, reading and seeing others read the *New York Times*, but as a reference to 'the farthest extent of the public world: [the NYT] of course reaffirms the widest coordinates of the individual's reality. From the weather report to the help-wanted ads it assures him that he is, indeed, in the most real world possible' (1966, p. 169).

6 By October 2014, more than sixty per cent of UK children used a tablet in the home (Gibbs 2014, drawing on an Ofcom survey).

7 This is the suggestion of a four-country comparative study of under-5s in England, Greece, Malta and Luxembourg (Palaiologou, 2014, p. 1).

8 There may still however be implicit limits here: an app floated in September 2015 called Peeple, whose entire purpose was to enable people to rate others they knew on a fixed scale, generated criticism, notwithstanding its founder's claim that it was 'a positivity app for positive people' (quoted in Hunt, 2015).

9 See Erasmus' early modern bestseller *De civilitate morum puerilium*, 1530.

10 For a rare detailed account of these processes, see Martuccelli (2002).

11 For this reason it is problematic to see blogs as a simple space of free expression. Precisely because of these uncertainties people may feel a disincentive to say what they think (Storsul, 2014; see Couldry, 2014a on the new 'spiral of silence').

12 There is a large literature here: boyd, 2014; Cohen, 2012; Mansell, 2012; Marwick 2015.

13 See for example Agger (2011) and Vaast (2007)
14 See for example Savage and Burrows (2007); Ruppert et al. (2013, p. 22); R. Rogers (2013).
15 See Knorr-Cetina and Cicourel (1981).
16 As a celebratory account of self-tracking's benefits for 'self-optimization' unwittingly brings out when it states that 'tracking devices [. . .] promote new frameworks for approaching normalities and pathologies in everyday life' (Ruckenstein, 2014, p. 81). That is precisely the problem.
17 For a trenchant account of these developments, see Andrejevic (2013).
18 See http://www.nesta.org.uk/project/people-powered-health

9 Collectivities

1 For a historical discussion of these concepts, see Briggs, 1985; Butsch, 2013, p. 93; Butsch, 2008, pp. 1–19; Ginneken, 1992; Lunt and Livingstone, 2013; Schnapp and Tiews, 2006; Williams, 1976.
2 Already 100 years ago Max Weber in his original writings preferred the term *Vergemeinschaftung* which means 'communitization' in a literal translation (Weber, 1972 [orig. 1918/19], p. 21).
3 At this point, there is for Latour no difference between 'former times' and 'modernity' beside the technological character non-humans nowadays have which results in a deeper entanglement between humans and non-humans within collectives (Keller and Lau, 2008, pp. 319–320; Kneer, 2008, pp. 295–302). As Latour puts it, 'the modern collective is the one in which the relations of humans and non-humans are so intimate, the transactions so many, the mediations so convoluted, that there is no plausible sense in which artefact, corporate body, and subject can be distinguished' (Latour, 1999, p. 197; see also Latour, 2013, pp. 296–325).
4 Or, expressed in our preferred terminology: not every figuration is a collectivity. For example, customers of an online store who simply belong to the set of those who have bought there are not connected by any meaningful form of relatedness and so cannot be described as a collectivity.
5 This 'loss of community' is also discussed as a general change of society, related to individualization (Sennett, 1998).
6 In such a perspective the character of contemporary communities is a very specific one: networked individualism supposes that people's involvement in multiple networks often limits their involvement in and commitment to any one network; their collectivities become more and more 'communities of "limited liability"' (Rainie and Wellman, 2012, p. 124). Typical for networked individualism is the experience that even 'weak ties can provide a sense of community' (Rainie and Wellman, 2012, p. 132) and that networked individuals have '"sparsely knit" personal communities' (Rainie and Wellman, 2012, p. 135), which means that most of the network

members are not directly connected with one another. Put another way, 'communities continue to exist, except as spatially dispersed and differentiated personal networks rather than neighbourhoods or densely knit groups' (Rainie and Wellman, 2012, p. 146).

7 Such an inclusion can be important for homeless people as it provides some measure of ontological security while living on the street (Hepp et al., 2015, pp. 186–189).

8 An ensemble of media can, as Charles Hirschkind notes (for the pre-digital context of the cassette sermons very popular in Egypt at least till the mid 2000s), have an 'effect on the human sensorium, on the affects, sensibilities and perceptual habits of [a] vast audience', changing 'practices of public sociability' (2006, pp. 2–3).

9 See Ekdale et al., 2010, pp. 218–220; Schmidt, 2007, pp. 1411–1418.

10 See Olofsson, 2010, pp. 770–772; Striphas, 2015, pp. 401–403.

11 See Crane and Ashutosh, 2013; Juris, 2012; Kreiss and Tufekci, 2013; Penney and Dadas, 2014; Salvo, 2013.

12 These pioneer communities belong to a longer tradition of collectivity building through internet-based media; see for example Rheingold, 1995, on 'virtual communities', Castells, 2001 (pp. 36–63), on the 'virtual communitarian culture' within 'internet culture', or Turner, 2006, on so-called 'new communalists' which turned 'away from political action toward technology and the transformation of consciousness as the primary sources of social change' (p. 4). Compare generally Streeter, 2010.

13 The quantified self and the makers movement both started in the US Bay area, but quickly tried to extend their influence across North America, Europe and other parts of the world. For details, see Hepp, 2016.

14 See especially Hoover, 2006; Hjarvard, 2011; Lundby, 2013; Clark, 2011; and the contributions to the special issue 1 / 2016 of *Media, Culture and Society* on Media and Religion.

15 For this discussion see Freedman and Thussu, 2012; Seib and Janbek, 2011; Weimann, 2004; and most recently Berger, 2015; Gates and Podder, 2015; and Zelin, 2015.

16 See Ritzer and Jurgenson, 2010; Burston et al., 2010, p. 214; Fuchs, 2014, p. 120; see also the articles in Scholz, 2013.

17 It is astonishing to what extent these platforms are discussed as a model even to solve the financial problems of the American middle classes confronted with impoverishment (see Sperling, 2015).

18 At the time of writing, the most prominent examples of these platforms are Airbnb (accommodation), Uber (car rides) and Amazon's Mechanical Turk (data labour). However, our point concerns not these specific offerings but the collectivities of work formed around them whose figurations share fundamental similarities.

19 Barile and Sugiyama (2015, p. 413) put emphasis especially on the role of

'taste'; we want to argue however that such collectivities can also be related to interest and overall orientation.

20 Compare what Nicholas Carah (2015, p. 13) has called 'algorithmic branding'. The key point goes beyond the data-driven production of collectivities with reference to brands; it is rather the data-based *imagination* of certain collectivities with reference to certain 'styles' and 'tastes', which may or may not relate to brands.

21 Here the robots are used as means to create an occasion for conversation or even a whole communication setting focused on the artefact (Pfadenhauer and Dukat, 2015, pp. 401f.).

22 For important work on the links between new media use and social stratification in China, see Pan et al. (2011); Zhou (2011).

10 Order

1 With this understanding of organization we refer back to Kühl, 2011, pp. 9–22; Meier and Schimank, 2012, p. 26, and Weick, 1979, p. 13.

2 Compare as an overview of the present discussion for example the chapters in Pallas, Strannegard and Jonsson (2014) or the various chapters on organizations in a recent handbook on mediatization, edited by Knut Lundby (2014).

3 See for example Gernert (2015); and more generally Ruppert (2011); Amoore (2013).

4 There is another side to this, which we do not have time to consider: the role of technologies of writing in the emergence of modern accounting in early medieval Europe (Bisson, 2009, pp. 336–349).

5 See Couldry (2014b) for fuller argument.

6 Compare Amoore's (2013, p. 61) account of government focused on data-driven risks management: 'risk in its derivative form is not centred on who we are, nor even on what our data say about us, but on what can be imagined and inferred about who we might be – on our very proclivities and potentialities'.

11 Conclusion

1 The appreciation of *causal complexity* is starting to become widespread in discussions of mediatization in various domains, as scholars acknowledge a *variety of different* 'logics' underlying media influence (Strömbäck and Esser, 2014a, p. 19; also Strömbäck and Esser, 2014b), or reject the idea of a universal media logic resulting in all-embracing media dependence of politics' (Schulz, 2014, p. 61), and emphasize instead different '*modes* of mediatization' (Lundby, 2014, p. 19f, added emphasis) and their interrelations.

2 This is the core of Giddens' structuration theory, although, as William

Sewell pointed out, it is much more plausible for the 'rules' aspect of social structure than material 'resources' (Sewell, 2005, c. 4). See also section 2.2. of Chapter 2 above.

3 True, MacKenzie (2006) argues that 'the concepts of signification and meaning [. . .] lack purchase on the structures, patterns, relations and operations that constitute code objects' (p. 15), but he is emphasizing the discontinuities and instabilities in the actual workings of code in the world, and we do not need to emphasize that in our broad context, although we acknowledge it. Overall MacKenzie defines 'software formally as a set of permeable distributions of agency between people, machines and contemporary symbolic environments carried as code. Code itself is structured as a distribution of agency' (p. 19).

4 We acknowledge here Margaret Archer's very different view that intensified 'reflexivity' is not opposed to, but integral to, the evolution of social structure and culture (Archer, 2012, pp. 3–4).

5 Or, as Robert Bellah put it, 'without a reference point in traditions of ethical reflection the very categories of social thought would be empty' (Bellah, 2006, p. 394). See generally on the risk of neglecting value in the social sciences, Sayer (2011).

References

Adoni, H. and Mane, A. (1984) 'Media and the Social Construction of Reality', *Communication Research*, 11(3): 323–340.

Agamben, G. (2009) *What is an Apparatus? And Other Essays*. Stanford, CA: Stanford University Press.

Agar, J. (2003) *The Government Machine: A Revolutionary History of the Computer*. Cambridge, MA: MIT Press.

Agger, B. (2011) 'iTime: Labor and Life in a Smartphone Era', *Time and Society*, 20(1): 119–136.

Agha, A. (2007) 'Recombinant Selves in Mass Mediated Spacetime', *Language & Communication*, 27(3): 320–335.

Agre, P. (1994) 'Surveillance and Capture', *Information Society*, 10(2): 101–127.

Alaimo, C. and Kallinikos, J. (2015) 'Encoding the Everyday: Social Data and its Media Apparatus', in Sugimoto, C., Ekbia, H. and Mattioli, M. (eds.) Big Data is Not a Monolith: Policies. Unpublished paper.

Albion, R. G. (1932) 'The "Communication Revolution"', *American Historical Review*, 37(4): 718–720.

Allen, J. (2011) 'Powerful Assemblages?', *Area*, 43(2): 154–157.

Alper, M. (2011) 'Developmentally Appropriate New Media Literacies: Supporting Cultural Competencies and Social Skills in Early Childhood Education', *Journal of Early Childhood Literacy*, 13(2): 175–196.

Altheide, D. L. and Snow, R. P. (1979) *Media Logic*. Beverly Hills, CA: Sage.

Amin, A. (2002) 'Spatialities of Globalisation', *Environment and Planning A*, 34(3): 385–400.

Amoore, L. (2011) 'Data Derivatives', *Theory, Culture & Society*, 28(6): 24–43.

Amoore, L. (2013) *The Politics of Possibility*. Durham, NC: Duke University Press.

Ananny, M. (2015) 'Towards an Ethics of Algorithms', *Science, Technology & Human Values*, doi: 10.1177/0162243915606523.

Andersen, P. H. (2005) 'Relationship Marketing and Brand Involvement of Professionals Through Web-enhanced Brand Communities', *Industrial Marketing Management*, 34(3): 39–51.

Anderson, B. (1983) *Imagined Communities*. New York: Verso.

Anderson, C. (2008): 'The end of theory: The data deluge makes the scientific method obsolete', *Wired Magazine*, 23 June 2008.

Anderson, C. (2012) *Makers: The New Industrial Revolution*. New York: Random House.

Andrejevic, M. (2008) *I-spy*. Lawrence, KS: University of Kansas Press.

Andrejevic, M. (2013) *Infoglut*. London: Routledge.

Andrejevic, M. (2014) 'Becoming Drones: Smart Phone Probes and Distributed Sensing', *The ICA Annual Conference*, Seattle, WA, 22–26 May.

Andrews, M. (1989) *The Search for the Picturesque*. Aldershot: Scolar.

Ang, I. (1991) *Desperately Seeking the Audience*. London: Routledge.

Appadurai, A. (1996) *Modernity at Large*. Minneapolis, MN: Minneapolis University Press.

Archer, M. (2012) *The Reflexive Imperative in Late Modernity*. Cambridge: Cambridge University Press.

Armstrong, S. and Ruiz del Arbol, M. (2015) 'Digital Catch-22', *The Guardian*, 10 April.

Arnone, L., Colot, O., Croquet, M., Geerts, A. and Pozniak, L. (2010) 'Company Managed Virtual Communities in Global Brand Strategy', *Global Journal of Business Research*, 4(2): 76–112.

Arthur, W. B. (2009) *The Nature of Technology*. Harmondsworth: Penguin.

Atton, C. (2002) *Alternative Media*. London: Sage.

Atwood, M. (2013) 'When Privacy is Theft'. *New York Review of Books*. 21 November.

Austin, J. L. (1962) *How to do Things with Words*. Oxford: Clarendon Press.

Averbeck-Lietz, S. (2014) 'Understanding Mediatization in "First Modernity"', in Lundby, K. (ed.) *Mediatization of Communication*. Berlin: de Gruyter, pp. 109–130.

Baack, S. (2015) 'Datafication and Empowerment', *Big Data & Society*, 2(2). Available at: http://bds.sagepub.com/content/spbds/2/2/2053951715594 634.full.pdf.

Baecker, D. (2007) *Studien zur nächsten Gesellschaft*. Frankfurt am Main: Suhrkamp.

Bagozzi, R. P. and Dholakia, U. M. (2006) 'Antecedents and Purchase Consequences of Customer Participation in Small Group Brand Communities', *International Journal of Research in Marketing*, 23(1): 45–61.

Balbi, G. (2013) 'Telecommunications', in Simonson, P., Peck, J., Craig, R. and Jackson, P. (eds.) *The Handbook of Communication History*. London: Routledge, pp. 209–222.

Balka, E. (2011) 'Mapping the Body Across Diverse Information Systems', *The Annual Meeting for the Society for Social Studies of Science*, Cleveland City Center Hotel, Cleveland, OH, 2–5 November.

Banaji, Shakuntala (2015) 'Behind the high-tech fetish: children, work and media use across classes in India', *International Communication Gazette*, 77 (6): 519–532.

Banet-Weiser, S. (2013) *Authentic™*. New York: New York University Press.

Bannon, L. J. (2006) 'Forgetting as a Feature, Not a Bug: The Duality of Memory and Implications for Ubiquitous Computing', *CoDesign*, 2(1): 3–15.

Barad, K. (2007) *Meeting the Universe Halfway: Quantum Physics and the Entanglement of Matter and Meaning*. Durham, NC: Duke University Press.

Barassi, V. (2015) *Activism on the Web*. London: Routledge.

Barbrook, R. (2007) *Imaginary Futures*. London: Pluto Press.

Barile, N. and Sugiyama, S. (2015) 'The Automation of Taste', *International Journal of Social Robotics*, 7(3): 407–416.

Barker, C. (1997) *Global Television: An Introduction*. London: Blackwell.

Barnouw, E. (1990) *Tube of Plenty*. New York: Oxford University Press.

Bausinger, H. (1984) 'Media, Technology and Daily Life', *Media, Culture & Society*, 6(4): 343–351.

Baym, N. K. (2015) *Personal Connections in the Digital Age*. 2nd edn. Cambridge, MA: Polity.

Baym, N. K. & boyd, d. (2012) 'Socially Mediated Publicness', *Journal of Broadcasting & Electronic Media*, 56(3): 320–329.

Beck, U. (1994) 'The Reinvention of Politics', in Beck, U., Giddens, A. and Lash, S. (eds.) *Reflexive Modernization*. Cambridge: Polity, pp. 1–55.

Beck, U. (2000a) 'The Cosmopolitan Perspective', *British Journal of Sociology*, 51(1): 79–105.

Beck, U. (2000b) *What is Globalization?*. London: Blackwell Publishers.

Beck, U. (2006) *Cosmopolitan Vision*. Cambridge, MA: Polity.

Beck, U. and Beck-Gernsheim, E. (2001) *Individualization*. London: Sage.

Behringer, W. (2006) 'Communications Revolutions', *German History*, 24(3): 333–374.

Belk, R. (1998) 'Possessions and the Extended Self', *Journal of Consumer Research*, 15(2): 139–168.

Belk, R. (2013) 'Extended Self in a Digital World', *Journal of Consumer Research*, 40(3): 477–499.

Bellah, R. (2006) 'The Ethical Aims of Social Inquiry' in Bellah, R. and Tifton, S. (eds.) *The Robert Bellah Reader*. Durham, NC: Duke University Press, pp. 381–401.

Bellingradt, D. (2011) *Flugpublizistik und Öffentlichkeit um 1700*. Stuttgart: Franz Steiner.

Bengtsson, S. (2006) 'Framing Space: Media and the Intersection of Work and Leisure' in J. Falkheimer and A. Jansson (eds.) *Geographies of Communication*. Göteborg: Nordicom, 189–204.

Beniger, J. (1986) *The Control Revolution*. Cambridge, MA: Harvard University Press.

Benjamin, W. (1968) 'The Storyteller', in Arendt, H. (ed.) *Illuminations*. New York: Schocken Books, pp. 83–110.

Benkler, Y. (2006) *The Wealth of Networks*. New Haven, CT: Yale University Press.

Bennett, W. L. and Segerberg, A. (2013) *The Logic of Connective Action.* Cambridge: Cambridge University Press.

Berardi, F. (2009) *The Soul at Work.* New York: Semiotext(e).

Berger, J. M. (2015) 'The Metronome of Apocalyptic Time', *Perspectives on Terrorism*, 9(4): 61–71.

Berger, P. L. (2002) 'The Cultural Dynamics of Globalization', in Berger, P. L. and Huntington, S. P. (eds.) *Many Globalizations.* Oxford: Oxford University Press, pp. 1–16.

Berger, P. L. and Luckmann, T. (1966) *The Social Construction of Reality.* London: Penguin.

Berker, T., Hartmann, M., Punie, Y. and Ward, K. (2006) *Domestication of Media and Technology.* London: Open University Press.

Bernstein, J. M. (2002) 'Re-enchanting Nature', in Smith, N. (ed.) *Reading McDowell.* London: Routledge, pp. 217–245.

Berry, D. (2011) *The Philosophy of Software.* Basingstoke: Palgrave Macmillan.

Billig, M. (1995) *Banal Nationalism.* London: Sage.

Bimber, B. (2003) *Information and American Democracy.* Cambridge: Cambridge University Press.

Bird, S. E. (2003) *The Audience in Everyday Life.* London: Routledge.

Bisson, T. (2009) *The Crisis of the Twelfth Century: Power, Lordship and the Origins of European Government.* Princeton, NJ: Princeton University Press.

Blumer, H. (1954) 'What is Wrong with Social Theory?', *American Sociological Review*, 19(1): 3–10.

Boden, D. and Molotch, H. (1994) 'The Compulsion of Proximity', in Friedland, R. and Boden, D. (eds.) *Nowhere: Space, Time and Modernity.* Berkeley, CA: University of California Press, pp. 257–286.

Boesel, W. E. (2013) 'What is the Quantified Self Now?', *The Society Pages.* Available at: http://thesocietypages.org/cyborgology/2013/05/22/what-is-the-quantified-self-now/

Bolin, G. (2014) 'Media Generations', *Participations*, 11(2): 108–131.

Boltanski, L. (2009) *De La Critique: Précis de Sociologie de L'émancipation.* Paris: Gallimard.

Boltanski, L. (2011) *On Critique.* Cambridge, MA: Polity.

Boltanski, L. and Thévenot, L. (2006) *On Justification.* Princeton, NJ: Princeton University Press.

Bolter, J. D. and Grusin, R. (2000) *Remediation.* Cambridge, MA: MIT Press.

Boorstin, D. (1961) *The Image: Or, Whatever Happened to the American Dream.* London: Weidenfeld & Nicolson.

Bösch, F. (2015) *Mass Media and Historical Change.* Oxford: Berghahn.

Bostrom, N. and Sandberg, A. (2011) 'The Future of Identity', *United Kingdom Government Office for Science.* Oxford: Future of Humanity Institute. Available at: http://www.nickbostrom.com/views/identity.pdf

Bourdieu, P. (1991) *Language and Symbolic Power.* Cambridge: Polity.

Bourdieu, P. (1993): *The Field of Cultural Production*. Cambridge: Polity.

Bowker, G. (2008) *Memory Practices in the Sciences*. Cambridge, MA: MIT Press.

Bowker, G. and Star, S. (1999) *Sorting Things Out*. Cambridge, MA: MIT Press.

boyd, d. (2008) 'Why Youth ♥ Social Network Sites', in Buckingham, D. (ed.) *Youth, Identity and Digital Media*. Cambridge, MA: MIT Press, pp. 119–142.

boyd, d. (2014) *It's Complicated: The Social Lives of Networked Teens*. New Haven, CT: Yale University Press.

boyd, d. and Crawford, K. (2012) 'Critical Questions for Big Data', *Information, Communication and Society*, 15(5): 662–679.

Braune, I. (2013) 'Our Friend, the Internet: Postcolonial Mediatization in Morocco', *Communications – The European Journal of Communication*, 38(3): 267–287.

Brecht, B. (1979) 'Radio as a Means of Communication', *Screen*, 20(3/4): 24–28.

Breiter, A. (2014) 'Schools as Mediatized Organizations from a Cross-cultural Perspective,' in Hepp, A. and Krotz, F. (ed.) *Mediatized Worlds*. London: Palgrave, pp. 288–303.

Brejzek, T. (2010) 'From Social Network to Urban Intervention', *International Journal of Performance Arts & Digital Media*, 6(1): 109–122.

Briggs, A. (1985) 'The Language of Mass and Masses in 19th Century England', in Briggs, A. (ed.) *Collected Essays of Asa Briggs, Vol I: Words, Numbers, Places, People*. Urbana, IL: University of Illinois Press, pp. 34–54.

Briggs, A. and Burke, P. (2009) *A Social History of the Media*. 3rd edn. Cambridge: Polity.

Brighenti, A. (2007) 'Visibility: A Category for the Social Sciences', *Current Sociology*, 55(3): 323–342.

Brock, G. (2013) *Out of Print: Newspapers, Journalism and the Business of News in the Digital Age*. London: Kogan Page.

Brooker-Gross, S. (1983) 'Spatial Aspects of Newsworthiness', *Geografisker Annaler*, 65(B): 1–9.

Brown, W. (2015) *Undoing the Demos*. New York: Zone Books.

Bruns, A. (2005) *Gatewatching*. New York: Peter Lang.

Bruns, A. (2007) 'Methodologies for Mapping the Political Blogosphere', *First Monday*, 12(5). Available at: http://firstmonday.org/ojs/index.php/fm/article/view/1834/1718

Brunsdon, C. and Morley, D. (1978) *Everyday Television:"Nationwide"*. London: BFI.

Bucher, T. (2012a) 'Want to be on the top? Algorithmic power and the Threat of Invisibility on Facebook', *New Media & Society*, 14 (7): 1164–1180.

Bucher, T. (2012b) 'The Friendship Assemblage: Investigating Programmed Sociality on Facebook', *Television & New Media*, 14 (6), S: 479–493.

Buckingham, D. and Kehily, M. J. (2014) 'Rethinking Youth Cultures in the Age of Global Media', in Buckingham, D., Bragg, S. and Kehily, M. J. (eds.)

Youth Cultures in the Age of Global Media. Basingstoke: Palgrave Macmillan, pp. 1–18.

Burchell, K. (2015) 'Tasking the Everyday: Where Mobile and Online Communication Takes Time', *Mobile Media & Communication*, 3(1) pp. 36–52.

Burrows, R. and Savage, M. (2014) 'After the Crisis? Big Data and the Methodological Challenges of Empirical Sociology', *Big Data & Society*, 1(1). Burston, J., Dyer-Witheford, N. and Hearn, A. (2010) 'Digital Labour', *Special Issue, Ephemera: Theory and Politics in Organization*, 10(3/4): 214–221.

Burzan, N. (2011) 'Zur Gültigkeit der Individualisierungsthese./The Validity of the Individualization Thesis.', *Zeitschrift für Soziologie*, 40(6): 418–435.

Bush, V. (1945) 'As We May Think', *Atlantic Monthly*, July.

Butsch, R. (2008) *The Citizen Audience*. London: Routledge.

Butsch, R. (2013) 'Audiences', in Simonson, P., Peck, J., Craig. R. T. and Jackson, J. P. (eds.) *The Handbook of Communication History*. New York: Routledge, pp. 93–108.

Caldwell, C. (2013) 'The right to hide our youthful mistakes', *Financial Times*, 27 September.

Calhoun, C. (1992a) *Habermas and the Public Sphere*. Cambridge, MA: MIT Press.

Calhoun, C. (1992b) 'The Infrastructure of Modernity', in Haferkamp, H. and Smelser, N. (eds.) *Social Change and Modernity*. Berkeley, CA: University of California Press, pp. 205–236.

Calhoun, C. (2007) *Nations Matter*. London: Routledge.

Calhoun, C. (2010) 'Beck, Asia and Second Modernity', *British Journal of Sociology*, 61(3): 597–619.

Cammaerts, B. (2015) 'Technologies of Self-Mediation', in Uldam, J. and Vertergaard, A. (eds.) *Civic Engagement and Social Media*. Basingstoke: Palgrave Macmillan, pp. 97–110.

Campagnolo, G. M., Pollock, N. and Williams, R. (2015) 'Technology as we do not Know it: The Extended Practice of Global Software Development', *Information and Organization*, 25(3): 150–159.

Campanella, B. (2012) *Os Olhos do Grande Irmã: Uma Etnographia dos Fãs do Big Brother Brasil*. Porto Alegre: Editora Sulina.

Carah, N. (2015) 'Algorithmic Brands', *New Media & Society*, doi: 10.1177/1461444815605463.

Cardoso, G., Espanha, R. and Lapa, T. (2012) 'Family Dynamics and Mediation', in Loos, E., Haddon, L. and Mante-Meijer, E. (eds.) *Generational Use of New Media*. Farnham: Ashgate, pp. 49–70.

Carey, J. (1989) *Communications as Culture*. Boston, MA: Unwin Hyman.

Carpentier, N. (2011) 'The Concept of Participation', *CM-časopis za upravljanje komuniciranjem*, 6(21): 13–36.

Castells, M. (1996) *The Rise of the Network Society. The Information Age: Economy, Society and Culture. Vol. 1.* Oxford: Blackwell.

Castells, M. (1997) *The Power of Identity: The Information Age: Economy, Society and Culture. Vol. 2.* Oxford: Blackwell.

Castells, M. (2000) *The Rise of the Network Society. The Information Age: Economy, Society and Culture. Vol. 1.* 2nd edn. Oxford: Blackwell.

Castells, M. (2001) *The Internet Galaxy.* Oxford: Oxford University Press.

Castells, M. (2009) *Communication Power.* Oxford: Oxford University Press.

Castells, M. (2012) *Networks of Outrage and Hope.* Cambridge: Polity.

Castells, M., Monge, P. and Contractor, N. (2011) 'Prologue to the Special Section Network Multidimensionality in the Digital Age', *International Journal of Communication,* 5(1): 788–793.

Cavarero, A. (2000) *Relating Narratives.* London: Routledge.

Chadwick, A. (2006) *Internet Politics.* Oxford: Oxford University Press.

Chadwick, A. (2013) *The Hybrid Media System.* Oxford University Press.

Chakrabarty, D. (2001) *Provincializing Europe.* Princeton, NJ: Princeton University Press.

Chan, A. (2013) *Networking Peripheries.* Cambridge, Mass.: MIT Press.

Chesley, N. (2005) 'Blurring Boundaries? Linking Technology Use, Spillover, Individual Distress and Family Satisfaction', *Journal of Marriage and Family,* 67(5): 1237–1248.

Choe, E. K., Lee, N. B., Lee, B., Pratt, W. and Kientz, J. A. (2014) 'Understanding Quantified-selfers' Practices in Collecting and Exploring Personal Data', *The Proceedings of the 32nd Annual ACM Conference on Human Factors in Computing Systems,* Metro Toronto Convention Center, Toronto, Canada, 26 April–1 May.

Chow, K.-W. (2003) *Publishing, Education, and Cultural Change in Late Imperial China.* Stanford, CA: Stanford University Press.

Christensen, T. H. (2009) '"Connected Presence" in Distributed Family Life', *New Media & Society,* 11(3): 433–451.

Christensen, T. and Røpke, I. (2010) 'Can Practice Theory Inspire Studies of ICTS in Everyday Life?', Brauchler, B. and Postill, J. (eds.) *Theorising Media and Practice.* New York: Berghahn Books, pp. 233–256.

Cipriani, R. (2013) 'The Many Faces of Social Time: A Sociological Approach', *Time & Society,* 22(1): 5–30.

Clanchy, M. T. (1993) [1979] *From Memory to Written Record: England 1066–1307.* Oxford: Blackwell.

Clark, L. S. (2011) 'Considering Religion and Mediatisation Through a Case Study of the J K Wedding Entrance Dance', *Culture and Religion,* 12(2): 167–184.

Clark, L. S. (2013) *The Parent App.* Oxford: Oxford University Press.

Clarke, A. E. (2011) 'Social Worlds', in Ritzer, G. and Ryan, J. M. (eds.) *The Concise Encyclopedia of Sociology.* Oxford: Wiley-Blackwell, pp. 384–385.

Cohen, J. (2012) *Configuring the Networked Self.* New Haven, CT: Yale University Press.

Cohen, J. (2015) 'Code and Law Between Truth and Power', *Lecture delivered at the London School of Economics and Political Science,* 11 March.

Contractor, N., Monge, P. and Leonardi, P. M. (2011) 'Multidimensional Networks and the Dynamics of Sociomateriality', *International Journal of Communication,* 5(1): 682–720.

Cook, D. (2005) 'The Dichotomous Child in and of Commercial Culture', *Journal of Consumer Culture,* 12(2): 155–159.

Cooley, C. (1902) *Human Nature and the Social Order.* New York: Charles Scribner's Sons.

Cordeiro, P., Damasio, M., Starkey, G., Botelho, I., Dias, P., Ganito, C., Ferreira C. and Henriques, S. (2013) 'Networks of Belonging: Interaction, Participation and Consumption of Mediatised Content', in Carpentier, N., Schrøder, K. and Hallet, L. (eds.) *Generations and Media: The Social Construction of Generational Identity and Differences.* London: Routledge, pp. 101–119.

Cornelio, G. S. and Ardevol, E. (2011) 'Practices of Place-Making Through Locative Media Artworks', *Communications,* 36(3): 313–333.

Couldry, N. (2003) *Media rituals.* London: Routledge.

Couldry, N. (2006) 'Transvaluaing Media studies; or, beyond the myth of the mediated centre', in J. Curran and D. Morley (eds.) *Media and Cultural Theory.* London: Routledge, pp. 177–194.

Couldry, N. (2008) 'Mediatization or Mediation? Alternative Understandings of the Emergent Space of Digital Storytelling', *New Media & Society,* 10(3): 373–391.

Couldry, N. (2010) *Why Voice Matters.* London: Sage.

Couldry, N. (2011) 'More sociology, more culture, more politics'. *Cultural Studies,* 25 (4–5): 487–501.

Couldry, N. (2012) *Media, Society, World.* Oxford: Polity.

Couldry, N. (2014a) 'A Necessary Disenchantment: Myth, Agency and Injustice in a Digital World', *Sociological Review,* 62(4): 880–897.

Couldry, N. (2014b) 'The Myth of Us: Digital Networks, Political Change and the Production of Collectivity', *Information Communication and Society,* 18(6): 608–626.

Couldry, N., Fotopoulou, A. and Dickens, L. (2016) 'Real Social Analytics: A Contribution Towards a Phenomenology of a Digital World', *British Journal of Sociology,* 67(1): 118–137.

Couldry, N. and Hepp, A. (2012) 'Comparing Media Cultures', in Esser, F. and Hanitzsch, T. (eds.) *The Handbook of Comparative Communication Research.* New York: Routledge, pp. 249–261.

Couldry, N. and Hepp, A. (2013) 'Conceptualising Mediatization', *Communication Theory,* 23(3): 191–202.

Couldry, N. and McCarthy, A. (2004) 'Introduction', in Couldry, N. and McCarthy, A. (eds.) *MediaSpace*. London: Routledge, pp. 1–18.

Couldry, N. and Turow, J. (2014) 'Advertising, Big Data and the Clearance of the Public Realm', *International Journal of Communication*, 8(1): 1710–1726.

Cova, B., Pace, S. and Skalen, P. (2015) 'Brand Volunteering', *Marketing Theory*, doi: 10.1177/1470593115568919.

Crane, N. J. and Ashutosh, I. (2013) 'A Movement Returning Home? Occupy Wall Street After the Evictions', *Cultural Studies <=> Critical Methodologies*, 13(3): 168–172.

Crary, J. (2013) *24/7*. London: Verso.

Da Matta, R. A. (1985) *A Casa e a Rua: Espaço, Ciudidania, Mulher e Norte no Brasil*. São Paulo: Brasiliense.

Damkjaer, M. S. (2015) 'Becoming a Parent in a Digitized Age', *Normedia 2015, TWG: Media Across the Lifecourse*, Aarhus, Aarhus University, 13–15 August.

Dant, T. (1999) *Material Culture in the Social World*. Milton Keynes: Open University Press.

Davis, J. (2013) 'The Qualified Self', *Cyborgology*. Available at: http://thesocietypages.org/cyborgology/2013/03/13/the-qualified-self/

Dayan, D. (1999) 'Media and Diasporas', in Gripsrud, J. (ed.) *Television and Common Knowledge*. London: Routledge, pp. 18–33.

Dayan, D. and Katz, E. (1992) *Media Events*. Cambridge, MA: Harvard University Press.

de Angelis, M. (2002) 'Hayek, Bentham and the Global Work Machine', in Dinerstein, A. and Neary, M. (eds.) *The Labour Debate*. Aldershot: Ashgate, pp. 108–134.

DeLanda, M. (2006) *A New Philosophy of Society*. London: Continuum International Publishing.

Deleuze, G. (1995) *Negotiations*. New York: Columbia University Press.

Deleuze, G. and Guattari, F. (2004) [1980] *A Thousand Plateaus: Capitalism and Schizophrenia*. London: Continuum International Publishing.

Dennis, K. (2007) 'Time in the Age of Complexity', *Time & Society*, 16(2/3): 139–155.

Derrida, J. (1973) *Speech and Phenomena*. Evanston, IL: Northwestern University Press.

Deterding, S. (2008) 'Virtual Communities', in Hitzler, R., Honer, A. and Pfadenhauer, M. (eds.) *Posttraditionale Gemeinschaften*. Wiesbaden: VS, pp. 115–131.

Deuze, M. (2012) *Media Life*. Cambridge: Polity.

Dijck, J. V. (2013) *The Culture of Connectivity*. Oxford: Oxford University Press.

Diminescu, D. (2008) 'The Connected Migrant', *Social Science Information*, 47(4): 565–579.

Dodge, M. and Kitchin, R. (2007) '"Outlines of a World Coming into Existence":

Pervasive Computing and the Ethics of Forgetting', *Environment and Planning B*, 34(3): 431–445.

Dolan, P. (2010) 'Space, Time and the Constitution of Subjectivity', *Foucault Studies*, 8(1): 8–27.

Domahidi, E., Festl, R. and Quandt, T. (2014) 'To Dwell Among Gamers', *Computers in Human Behavior*, 35(1): 107–115.

Donges, P. (2011) 'Politische Organisationen als Mikro-Meso-Makro-Link,' in Quandt, T. and Scheufele, B. (eds.) *Ebenen der Kommunikation*. Wiesbaden: VS, pp. 217–232.

Douglas, S. (1987) *Inventing American Broadcasting 1899–1922*. Baltimore, MD: The Johns Hopkins University Press.

Downing, J. (1984) *Radical Media*. Boston, MA: South End Press.

Drotner, K. (2009) 'Children and Digital Media', in Qvortrup, J., Corsaro, W. and Honig, M. (eds.) *The Palgrave Handbook of Childhood Studies*. Basingstoke: Palgrave Macmillan, pp. 360–375.

Drumond, R. (2014) 'VEM VER #NOVELA, @VOCÊ TAMBÉM: Recepção Televisa e Interações em Rede a Partir do Twitter', *The 23rd Annual Meeting of COMPOS*, Belém, Brazil, 27–30 May.

Duggan, M., Lenhart, A., Lampe, C. and Ellison, N. (2015) 'Parents and Social Media', *Pew Research Center*. Available at: http://www.pewinternet.org/2015/07/16/parents-and-social-media

Dunning, E. and Hughes, J. (2013) *Norbert Elias and Modern Sociology*. London: Bloomsbury.

Durkheim, É. (1982) [1895] *The Rules of Sociological Method and Selected Texts on Sociology and its Method*. New York: Free Press.

Durkheim, É. (1995) [1912] *The Elementary Forms of Religious Life*. New York: Free Press.

Durkheim, É. and Mauss, M. (1969) [1902] *Primitive Classification*. London: Routledge.

Edelman, B. G. and Luca, M. (2014) 'Digital Discrimination: The Case of Airbnb.com', *Harvard Business School NOM Unit Working Paper*, 14–054.

Eggers, D. (2013) *The Circle*. London: Allen Lane.

Eisenstein, E. (2005) *The Printing Revolution in Early Modern Europe*. Cambridge: Cambridge University Press.

Ekdale, B., Namkoong, K., Fung, T. and Perlmutter, D. D. (2010) 'Why Blog? (Then and Now)', *New Media & Society*, 12(2): 217–234.

Elias, N. (1978) *What is Sociology?*. London: Hutchinson.

Elias, N. (1991) [1939] *The Society of Individuals*. London: Continuum International Publishing.

Elias, N. (1994) [1939] *The Civilizing Process*. Oxford: Blackwell.

Elias, N. (2003) 'Figuration und Emergenz', in Schäfers, B. (ed.) *Grundbegriffe der Soziologie*. Stuttgart: Leske + Budrich, pp. 88–91.

Elias, N. and Scotson, J. L. (1994) [1965] *The Established and the Outsiders*. London: Sage.

Ellison, N. (2013) 'Citizenship, Space and Time', *Thesis Eleven*, 118(1): 48–63.

Elwell, J. S. (2013) 'The Transmediated Self: Life Between the Digital and the Analog', *Convergence*, 20(2): 233–249.

Engelke, M. (2013) *God's Agents*. Berkeley, CA: University of California Press.

Erasmus (1530) *De Civilitate Morum Puerilium*. London: W. de Worde.

Espeland, W. and Sauder, M. (2007) 'Rankings and Reactivity', *American Journal of Sociology*, 113(1): 1–40.

Esser, F. and Strömbäck, J. (2014b) *Mediatization of Politics*. Houndsmills: Palgrave Macmillan.

Evans, E. (2011) *Transmedia Television: Audiences, New Media, and Daily Life*. London: Routledge.

Fabian, J. (1983) *Time and the Other: How Anthropology Makes its Object*. New York: Columbia University Press.

Fairhurst, G. T. and Putnam, L. (2004) 'Organizations as Discursive Constructions', *Communication Theory*, 14(1): 5–26.

Falb, D. (2015) *Kollektivitäten: Population und Netzwerk als Figurationen der Vielheit*. Bielefeld: Transcript.

Fausing, B. (2014) 'SELF-MEDIA: The Self, the Face, the Media and the Selfies', *The International Conference on Sensoric Image Science*, Sassari, Italy, 24 July.

Featherstone, M. (1995) *Undoing Culture*. London: Sage.

Fenton, N. and Barassi, V. (2011) 'Alternative Media and Social Networking Sites', *The Communication Review*, 14(3): 179–196.

Ferreux, J. (2006) 'Un Entretien avec Thomas Luckmann', *Sociétés*, 93(1): 45–51.

Fickers, A. (2013) 'Television', in Simonson, P., Peck. J, Craig, R. T. and Jackson, J. (eds.) *The Handbook of Communication History*. London: Routledge, pp. 238–256.

Finnemann, N. O. (2011) 'Mediatization Theory and Digital Media', *European Journal of Communication*, 36(1): 67–89.

Fischer, C. (1992) *America Calling*. Berkeley, CA: University of California Press.

Fiske, J. (1989) *Understanding Popular Culture*. London: Unwin Hyman.

Fiske, J. (1993) *Power Plays – Power Works*. London: Verso.

Fleer, M. (2014) 'The Demands and Motives Afforded Through Digital Play in Early Childhood Activity Settings', *Learning, Culture and Social Interaction*, 3(1): 202–209.

Flichy, P. (1995) *Dynamics of Modern Communication*. London: Sage.

Foster, C. (2005) *British Government in Crisis*. Oxford: Hart Publishing.

Foucault, M. (1970) *The Order of Things*. New York: Random House.

Foucault, M. (1988) *The History of Sexuality: The Care of the Self*. New York: Vintage.

Fredriksson, M. and Pallas, J. (2014) 'Media Enactments', in Pallas, J.,

Strannegard, L. and Jonsson, S. (eds.) *Organisations and the Media*. London: Routledge, pp. 234–248.

Fredriksson, M., Schillemans, T. and Pallas, J. (2015) 'Determinants of Organizational Mediatization', *Public Administration*, doi: 10.1111/padm.12184.

Freedman, D. and Thussu, D. K. (2012) *Media and Terrorism*. London: Sage.

Friedland, R. and Alford, R. R. (1991) 'Bringing Society Back In: Symbols, Practices and Institutional Contradictions', in Powell, W. W. and DiMaggio, P. J. (eds.) *The New Institutionalism in Organizational Analysis*. Chicago: University of Chicago Press, pp. 232–263.

Friemel, T. N. (2012) 'Network dynamics of television use in school classes', *Social Networks*, 34(3): 346–358.

Frith, J. (2013) 'Turning Life into a Game', *Mobile Media & Communication*, 1(2): 248–262.

Frith, J. and Kalin, J. (forthcoming) 'Here, I Used to Be: Mobile Media and Practices of Place-based Digital Memory', *Space and Culture*. Available at: http://www.academia.edu/7240819/Here_I_Used_to_Be_Mobile_Media_and_Practices_of_Place-based_Digital_Memory

Fuchs, C. (2014) 'Digital Prosumption Labour on Social Media in the Context of the Capitalist Regime of Time', *Time & Society*, 23(1): 97–123.

Fuller, M. and Goffey, A. (2012) *Evil Media*. Cambridge, MA: MIT Press.

Gabriel, M. (2015) *Fields of Sense: A New Realist Ontology*. Edinburgh: Edinburgh University Press.

Gadamer, H.-G. (2004) [1975] *Truth and Method*. London: Continuum.

Gage, J. (2002) 'Some Thoughts on How ICTs Could Really Change the World', in Kirkman, G., Cornelious, P., Sachs, J. and Schwab, K. (eds.) *The Global Information Technology Report 2001–2002*. Oxford: Oxford University Press, pp. 4–9.

Gandy, O. (1993) *The Panoptic Sort: A Political Economy of Personal Information*. Boulder, CO: Westview Press.

Gangadharan, S. P. (2015) 'The Downside of Digital Exclusion: Expectations and Experiences of Privacy and Surveillance among Marginal Internet Users', *New Media & Society*. Available at: http://nms.sagepub.com/content/early/2015/11/06/1461444815614053.full.pdf+html.

García Canclini, N. (1995) *Hybrid Cultures: Strategies for Entering and Leaving Modernity*. Minneapolis, MN: Minnesota University Press.

García Canclini, N. (2014) *Imagined Globalization*. Durham, NC: Duke University Press.

Gates, S. and Podder, S. (2015) 'Social Media, Recruitment, Allegiance and the Islamic State', *Perspectives on Terrorism*, 9(4): 107–116.

Georgiou, M. (2013) *Media and the City*. Cambridge: Polity.

Gerlitz, C. and Helmond, A. (2013) 'The Like Economy', *New Media & Society*, doi: 10.1177/1461444812472322.

Gernert, J. (2015) 'Er Wird, er Wird Nicht, er Wird', *Taz, Gesellschaft*, Oktober (24/25): 18–20.

Gibbs, S. (2014) 'Table Computers Replace Television as Children's Top Gadget', *Guardian*, 10 October.

Gibson, J. (1967) 'Theory of Affordances', in Shaw, R. and Bransford, J. (eds.) *Perceiving, Acting, Knowing*. New York: Erlbaum, pp. 67–82.

Giddens, A. (1984) *The Constitution of Society*. Cambridge: Polity.

Giddens, A. (1990) *The Consequences of Modernity*. London: Polity.

Giddens, A. (1994a) *Modernity and Self-Identity*. Cambridge: Polity.

Giddens, A. (1994b) 'Risk, Trust, Reflexivity', in Beck, U., Giddens, A. and Lash, S. (eds.) *Reflexive Modernization*. Cambridge: Polity, pp. 184–197.

Giddens, A. (2015) 'The Digital Revolution', *Lecture delivered at the London School of Economics and Political Science*, 10 November.

Gillespie, T. (2010) 'The Politics of "Platforms"', *New Media & Society*, 12(3): 347–364.

Gillespie, T. (2014) 'The Relevance of Algorithms', in Boczkowski, P., Foot, K. and Gillespie, T. (eds.) *Media Technologies*. Cambridge, MA: MIT Press, pp. 167–194.

Ginneken, J. V. (1992) *Crowds, Psychology, and Politics, 1871–1899*. Cambridge: Cambridge University Press.

Gitelman, L. and Jackson, V. (2013) 'Introduction', in: Gitelman, L. (ed.): '*Raw Data' is an Oxymoron*. Cambridge: MIT Press, pp. 1–13.

Gitlin, T. (2001) *Media Unlimited*. New York: Metropolitan Books.

Goffman, Erving (1967) [1955] *Interaction Rituals*. New York: Garden City.

Gómez Garcia, R. and Treré, E. (2014) 'The #YoSoy132 Movement and the Struggle for Media Democratization in Mexico', *Convergence*, 20(4): 1–15.

Google (2012) 'The New Multi-Screen World'. Available at: https://think. withgoogle.com/databoard/media/pdfs/the-new-multi-screen-world-study_research-studies.pdf

Governance, C. O. G. (1995) *Our Global Neighbourhood*. Oxford: Oxford University Press.

Graham, S. (2005) 'Software-Sorted Geographies', *Progress in Human Geography*, 29(5): 562–580.

Graham, S. and Marvin, S. (2001) *Splintered Urbanisms*. London: Routledge.

Gray, M. (2012) *Out in the Country*. Chicago, IL: University of Chicago Press.

Green, N. (2002) 'On the Move: Technology, Mobility and the Mediation of Social Time and Space', *The Information Society*, 18(4): 281–292.

Gregg, M. (2011) *Work's Intimacy*. Cambridge: Polity.

Grenz, T. (2015) 'Mediatisierung als Organisationale und Außerorganisationale Konstruktion', Doctor of Philosophy Thesis. KIT (unveröff. Manuskript).

Grenz, T. and Möll, G. (2014) 'Zur Einleitung: Mediatisierung von Handlungsfeldern', in Grenz, T. and Möll, G. (eds.) *Unter Mediatisierungsdruck*. Wiesbaden: VS, pp. 1–15.

Grenz, T., Möll, G. and Reichertz, J. (2014) 'Zur Struktuierung von Mediatisierungsprozessen', in Krotz, F., Despotovic, C. and Kruse, M. (eds.) *Mediatisierung von Vergemeinschaftung und Gemeinschaft.* Wiesbaden: VS, pp. 73–91.

Greschke, H. M. (2012) *Is There a Home in Cyberspace? The Internet in Migrants' Everyday Life and the Emergence of Global Communities.* London: Routledge.

Gross, A. S. (2015) 'Explicit Tweets to Junior MasterChef Star in Brazil Spark Campaign Against Abuse', *Guardian.* Available at: http://www.theguardian.com/global-development/2015/nov/11/brazil-explicit-tweets-junior-masterchef-star-online-campaign-against-abuse-sexual-harassment

Grossberg, L. (1988) 'Wandering Audiences, Nomadic Critics', *Cultural Studies,* 2(3): 377–391.

Gumbrecht, H. U. and Pfeiffer, K. L. (1994) *Materialities of Communication.* Stanford, CA: Stanford University Press.

Gunaratne, S. A. (2010) 'De-westernizing Communication/Social Science Research', *Media, Culture & Society,* 32(3): 473–500.

Guta, H. and Karolak, M. (2015) 'Veiling and Blogging: Social Media as Sites of Identity Negotiation and Expression Among Saudi Women', *Journal of International Women's Studies,* 16(2): 115–127.

Guttentag, D. (2015) 'Airbnb: Disruptive Innovation and the Rise of an Informal Tourism Accommodation Sector', *Current Issues in Tourism,* doi: 10.1080/13683500.2013.827159.

Habermas, J. (1984) [1981] *The Theory of Communicative Action.* Boston, MA: Beacon Press.

Habermas, J. (1989) *The Structural Transformation of the Public Sphere.* Cambridge, MA: MIT Press.

Habibi, M. R., Laroche, M. and Richard, M.-O. (2014) 'Brand Communities Based in Social Media', *International Journal of Information Management,* 34(2): 123–132.

Habuchi, I. (2005) 'Accelerating Reflexivity', in Ito, M., Okabe, D. and Matsuda, M. (eds.) *Persona, Portable, Pedestrian.* Cambridge, MA: MIT Press, pp. 165–182.

Hacking, I. (1983) *Representing and Intervening.* Cambridge: Cambridge University Press.

Hacking, I. (1999) *The Social Construction of What?.* Cambridge, MA: Harvard University Press.

Hafner, G. (2015) 'Zurück ins Paradies? Die neue, alte Uneindeutigkeit', *Der Freitag,* 31(7).

Hagerstrand, T. (1975) 'Space, Time and Human Conditions', in Karlqvist, A., Lundquist, L. and Snickars, F. (eds.) *Dynamic Allocation of Urban Space.* Farnborough: Saxon House, pp. 1–14.

Haggerty, K. and Ericson, R. (2000) 'The Surveillant Assemblage', *British Journal of Sociology,* 51(4): 605–622.

Halavais, A. (2009) *Search Engine Society*. Cambridge: Polity.

Hall, S. (1980) 'Encoding/ Decoding', in Hall, S., Hobson. D., Lowe, A. and Willis, P. (eds.) *Culture, Media, Language*. London: Unwin Hyman, pp. 128–138.

Hartmann, B. J. (2015) 'Peeking Behind the Mask of the Prosumer', *Marketing Theory*, doi: 10.1177/1470593115581722.

Harvey, D. (1990) *The Condition of Postmodernity*. Oxford: Blackwell.

Harvey, P. (2012) 'The Topological Quality of Infrastructural Relation', *Theory, Culture & Society*, 29(4/5): 76–92.

Hasebrink, U. (2014) 'Die Kommunikative Figuration von Familien', in Rupp, M., Kapella, O. and Schneider, N. F. (eds.) *Zukunft der Familie. Tagungsband zum 4. Europäischen Fachkongress Familienforschung*. Opladen: Verlag Barbara Budrich, pp. 225–240.

Hasebrink, U. and Domeyer, H. (2012) 'Media Repertoires as Patterns of Behaviour and as Meaningful Practices', *Participations: Journal of Audience & Reception Studies*, 9(2): 757–783.

Hasebrink, U. and Hölig, S. (2013) 'Conceptualizing Audiences in Convergent Media Environments', in Karmasin, M. and Diehl, S. (eds.) *Media and Convergence Management*. Berlin: Springer, pp. 189–202.

Hassan, R. (2003) 'Network Time and the New Knowledge Epoch', *Time & Society*, 12(2/3): 225–241.

Hawn, C. (2009) 'Take Two Aspirin and Tweet Me in the Morning: How Twitter, Facebook and Other Social Media are Reshaping Health Care', *Health Affairs*, 28(2): 361–368.

Hayles, N. K. (1999) *How We Became Posthuman*. Chicago, IL: University of Chicago Press.

Hayward, T. (2015) 'The Recommendation Game', *Finance Times*, 21 August. Available at: http://www.ft.com/cms/s/2/94c55f50–46af-11e5–af2f-4d6e0e5eda22.html

Heath, C. and Hindmarsh, J. (2000) 'Configuring Action in Objects', *Mind, Culture, and Activity*, 7(1/2): 81–104.

Heinich, N. (2012) *De La Visibilité*. Paris: Gallimard.

Helmond, A. (2010) 'Identity 2.0', *The Proceeding of Mini-Conference Initiative*, Amsterdam: University of Amsterdam, 20–22 January.

Helsper, Ellen (2011) *The Emergence of a Digital Underclass*. LSE Media Policy Project Series, Broughton Micova, Sally, Sujon, Zoetanya and Tambini, Damian (eds.) Media Policy Brief 3. Department of Media and Communications, London School of Economics and Political Science, London, UK.

Hepp, A. (2004) *Netzwerke der Medien*. Wiesbaden: VS.

Hepp, A. (2013a) *Cultures of Mediatization*. Cambridge: Polity.

Hepp, A. (2013b) 'The Communicative Figurations of Mediatized Worlds: Mediatization Research in Times of the "Mediation of Everything"', *European Journal of Communication*, 28 (6): 615–629.

Hepp, A. (2015) *Transcultural Communication*. Malden, MA: Wiley-Blackwell.

Hepp, A. (2016) 'Pioneer Communities. Collective Actors in Deep Mediatization', *Media, Culture & Society*, forthcoming.

Hepp, A., Berg, M. and Roitsch, C. (2014) *Mediatisierte Welten der Vergemeinschaftung*. Wiesbaden: VS.

Hepp, A. and Couldry, N. (2010) 'Media Events in Globalized Media Cultures', in Couldry, N., Hepp, A. and Krotz, F. (eds.) *Media Events in a Global Age*. London: Routledge, pp. 1–20.

Hepp, A., Elser, M., Lingenberg, S., Mollen, A., Möller, J. and Offerhaus, A. (2016) *The Communicative Construction of Europe*. Basingstoke: Palgrave Macmillan.

Hepp, A. and Hasebrink, U. (2014) 'Human Interaction and Communicative Figurations: The Transformation of Mediatized Cultures and Societies', in Lundby, K. (ed.), *Mediatization of Communication*. Berlin and New York: de Gruyter, pp. 249–272.

Hepp, A., Lunt, P. and Hartmann, M. (2015) 'Communicative Figurations of the Good Life', in Wang, H. (ed.) *Communication and 'The Good Life'*. Berlin: Peter Lang, pp. 181–196.

Hermans, H. (2001) 'The Dialogical Self', *Culture & Psychology*, 7(3): 243–281.

Hermans, H. (2004) 'Introduction: The Dialogical Self in a Global and Digital Age', *Identity*, 4(4): 297–320.

Hess, D. J. (2005) 'Technology- and Product-Oriented Movements', *Science, Technology & Human Values*, 30(4): 515–535.

Hickethier, K. (1998) *Geschichte des Deutschen Fernsehens*. Stuttgart: Metzler Verlag.

Hillier, B. and Hanson, J. (1984) *The Social Logic of Space*. Cambridge: Cambridge University Press.

Hirsch, E. (1992) 'The Long Term and the Short Term of Domestic Consumption', in Silverstone, R. and Hirsch, E. (eds.) *Consuming Technologies*. London: Routledge, pp. 208–226.

Hirschkind, C. (2006) *The Ethical Soundscape: Cassette Sermons and Islamic Counterpublics*. New York: Columbia University Press.

Hitzler, R. (2010) *Eventisierung*. Wiesbaden: VS.

Hjarvard, S. (2011) 'The Mediatisation of Religion', *Culture and Religion*, 12(2): 119–135.

Hjarvard, S. (2013) *The Mediatization of Culture and Society*. London: Routledge.

Hjarvard, S. (2014) 'Mediatization and Cultural and Social Change', in Lundby, K. (ed.) *Mediatization of Communication*. Berlin: de Gruyter, pp. 199–226.

Hjorth, L. and Gu, K. (2012) 'The Place of Emplaced Visualities', *Continuum*, 26(5): 699–713.

Hogan, B. (2010) 'The Presentation of Self in the Age of Social Media', *Bulletin of Science, Technology & Society*, 30(6): 377–386.

Honneth, A. (1995) *The Fragmented World of the Social*. New York: SUNY Press.
Honneth, A. (2008) *Reification: A New Look at an Old Idea*. New York: Oxford University Press.
Honneth, A. (2013) *The I in We*. Cambridge: Polity.
Hoover, S. (2006) *Religion in the Media Age*. London: Routledge.
Horst, H. A. (2013) 'The Infrastructures of Mobile Media', *Mobile Media & Communication*, 1(1): 147–152.
Houston, J. B., Seo, H., Taylor-Knight, L. A., Kennedy, E. J., Hawthorne, J. and Trask, S. L. (2013) 'Urban Youth's Perspectives on Flash Mobs', *Journal of Applied Communication Research*, 41(3): 236–252.
Hugill, P. J. (1999) *Global Communications Since 1844*. Baltimore, MD: The Johns Hopkins University Press.
Huhtamo, E. and Parikka, J. (2011) *Media Archaeology*. Berkeley, CA: University of California Press.
Humphreys, L. (2008) 'Mobile Social Networks and Social Practice', *Journal of Computer-Mediated Communication*, 13(1): 341–360.
Humphreys, L. (2010) 'Mobile Social Networks and Urban Public Space', *New Media & Society*, 12(5): 763–778.
Humphreys, L. (2012) 'Connecting, Coordinating and Cataloguing', *Journal of Broadcasting and Electronic Media*, 56(4): 494–510.
Hunt, E. (2015) 'App lets you rate people you know, even if they don't ask', *Guardian*, 2 October.
Hutchby, I. (2001) 'Technologies, Texts and Affordances', *Sociology*, 35(2): 441–456.
Hyysalo, S., Kohtala, C., Helminen, P., Mäkinen, S., Miettinen, V. and Muurinen, L. (2014) 'Collaborative Futuring with and by Makers', *CoDesign*, 10(3/4): 209–228.
Illich, I. (1996) *In the Vineyard of the Text*. Chicago, IL: University of Chicago Press.
Illouz, E. (2012) *Why Love Hurts*. Cambridge: Polity.
Ingold, T. (2011) *Being Alive*. London: Routledge.
Innis, H. A. (1950) *Empire and Communications*. Oxford: Clarendon Press.
Innis, H. A. (1951) *The Bias of Communication*. Toronto: Toronto University Press.
Innis, H. A. (2004) *Changing Conceptions of Time*. Boulder, CO: Rowman and Littlefield.
Introna, L. D. (2011) 'The Enframing of Code', *Theory Culture & Society*, 28(6): 113–141.
Irani, L. (2015) 'The Cultural Work of Microwork', *New Media & Society*, 17(5): 720–739.
Isin, E. and Ruppert, E. (2015) *Being Digital Citizens*. Boulder, CO: Rowman and Littlefield.
Ito, M., Baumer, S., Bittanti, M., boyd, d., Cody, R., Herr-Stephenson, B.,

Horst, H. A., Lang, P. G., Mahendran, D., Martinez, K. Z., Pascoe, C. J., Perkel, D., Robinson, L., Sims, C. and Tripp, L. (2010) *Hanging Out, Messing Around, and Geeking Out: Kids Living and Learning with New Media*. Cambridge, MA: MIT Press.

Izak, M. (2014) 'Translucent Society and its Non-fortuitous Design', *Culture and Organization*, 20(5): 359–376.

Jang, C.-Y. and Stefanone, M. A. (2011) 'Non-Directed Self-Disclosure in the Blogosphere', *Information, Communication & Society*, 14(7): 1039–1059.

Jansson, A. (2013) 'Mediatization and Social Space', *Communication Theory*, 23(3): 279–296.

Jenkins, H. (1992) *Textual Poachers: Television Fans and Participatory Culture*. London: Routledge.

Jenkins, H. (2006a) *Confronting the Challenges of Participatory Culture*. Chicago, IL: MacArthur Foundation.

Jenkins, H. (2006b) *Convergence Culture*. New York: New York University Press.

Jenkins, H. and Carpentier, N. (2013) 'Theorizing Participatory Intensities', *Convergence*, 19(3): 265–286.

Jenkins, H., Ford, S. and Green, J. (2013) *Spreadable Media*. New York: New York University Press.

Jenkins, H., Ito, M. and boyd, d. (2016) *Participatory Culture in a Networked Era*. Malden, MA: Polity.

Jensen, K. B. (2010) *Media Convergence*. London: Routledge.

Jessop, B., Brenner, N. and Jones, M. (2008) 'Theorizing Sociospatial Relations', *Environment and Planning D: Society and Space*, 26(3): 389–401.

Johnson, K. (2000) *Television and Social Change in Rural India*. New Delhi: Sage.

Juris, J. (2012) 'Reflections on #Occupy Everywhere', *American Ethnology*, 39(2): 258–279.

Kallinikos, J. (2009a) 'On the Computational Rendition of Reality', *Organization*, 16(2): 183–202.

Kallinikos, J. (2009b) 'The Making of Ephemeria', *The International Journal of Interdisciplinary Social Sciences*, 4(3): 227–236.

Kallinikos, J. and Constantiou, I. (2015) 'Big Data Revisited', *Journal of Information Technology*, 30(1): 70–74.

Kallinikos, J. and Tempini, N. (2014) 'Social Data as Medical Facts', *Information Systems Research*, 25(4): 817–833.

Kannengießer, S. (forthcoming) 'Repair Cafés', in Milstein, T., Pileggi, M. and Morgan, E. (eds.) *Pedagogy of Environmental Communication*. London: Routledge.

Kant, I. (1990) [1795] *Groundwork of the Metaphysic of Morals*. London: Routledge.

Karasti, H., Baker, K. and Millerand, F. (2010) 'Infrastructure Time', *Computer Supported Cooperative Work*, 19(3/4): 377–415.

Kaulingfreks, R. and Warren, S. (2010) 'SWARM: Flash Mobs, Mobile Clubbing and the City', *Culture and Organization*, 16(3): 211–227.

Kaun, A. and Stiernstedt, F. (2014) 'Facebook Time: Technological and Institutional Affordances for Media Memories', *New Media & Society*, 16(7): pp. 1154–1168.

Kavada, A. (2015) 'Creating the Collective', *Information, Communication & Society*, 18(8): 872–886.

Keen, A. (2015) *The Internet is not the Answer*. London: Atlantic Books.

Keller, R. and Lau, C. (2008) 'Bruno Latour und die Grenzen der Gesellschaft', in Kneer, G., Schroer, M. and Schüttpelz, E. (eds.) *Bruno Latours Kollektive*. Frankfurt am Main: Suhrkamp, pp. 306–338.

Kellner, D. (2010) 'Media Spectacle and Media Events', in Couldry, N., Hepp, A. and Krotz, F. (eds.) *Media Events in a Global Age*. London: Routledge, pp. 76–91.

Kelly, K. (2012) 'The Quantified Century'. *Quantified Self Conference*, Stanford University, Palo Alto, CA, 15–16 September, 2012. Available online at http://quantifiedself.com/conference/Palo-Alto-2012

Kelty, C. M. (2008) 'Geeks and Recursive Publics: How the Internet and Free Software Make Things Public'. Available online http://kelty.org/or/papers/unpublishable/Kelty.RecursivePublics-short.pdf

Kido, T. and Swan, M. (2014) 'Know Thyself: Data-Driven Self-Awareness for Understanding Our Unconscious Behaviors', *AAAI Spring Symposium Series*. Available at: https://www.aaai.org/ocs/index.php/SSS/SSS14/paper/view/7678

Kitchin, R. (2014) *The Data Revolution*. London: Sage.

Kitchin, R. and Dodge, M. (2011) *Code/space: Software and Everyday Life*. Cambridge, MA: MIT Press.

Kittler, F. (2014) *The Truth of the Technological World*. Stanford, CA: Stanford University Press.

Kitzmann, A. (2003) 'The Different Place: Documenting the Self Within Online Environments', *Biography*, 26(1): 48–65.

Klauser, F. and Albrechtslund, A. (2014) 'From Self-Tracking to Smart Urban Infrastructures', *Surveillance & Society*, 12(2): 273–286.

Klein, N. (2000) *No Logo. Taking Aim at the Brand Bullies*. London: Flamingo.

Knapp, D. (forthcoming) 'Living with Algorithms: Reclaiming Agency Under Conditions of Data-Driven Surveillance', PhD thesis undertaken at London School of Economics and Political Science.

Kneer, G. (2008) 'Hybridität, Zirkulierende Referenz, Amoderne? Ein Kritik an Bruno Latours Soziologie', in Kneer, G., Schroer, M. and Schüttpelz, E. (eds.) *Bruno Latours Kollektive*. Frankfurt am Main: Suhrkamp, pp. 261–305.

Knoblauch, H. (2008) 'Kommunikationsgemeinschaften.', in Hitzler, R., Honer, A. and Pfadenhauer, M (eds.) *Posttraditionale Gemeinschaften*. Wiesbaden: VS, pp. 73–88.

Knoblauch, H. (2013a) '"Alfred Schutz" Theory of Communicative Action', *Human Studies*, 36(3): 323–337.

Knoblauch, H. (2013b) 'Communicative Constructivism and Mediatization', *Communication Theory*, 23(3): 297–315.

Knorr-Cetina, K. (2014) 'Scopic Media and Global Coordination', in Lundby, K. (ed.) *Mediatization of Communication*. Berlin: de Gruyter, pp. 39–62.

Knorr-Cetina, K. and Bruegger, U. (2002) 'Inhabiting Technology: The Global Lifeform of Financial Markets', *Current Sociology*, 50(3): 389–405.

Knorr-Cetina, K. and Cicourel, A. (1981) *Advances in Social Methodology*. London: Routledge and Kegan Paul.

Koch, G. and Warneken, B. J. (2014) 'Über Selbstrepräsentationen von Obdachlosen in verschiedenen Medien', *Hamburger Journal für Kulturanthropologie*, 2014 (1): 51–62.

Koopmans, R. and Statham, P. (2010) *The Making of a European Public Sphere*. Cambridge, Cambridge University Press.

Kosseleck, R. (2004) [1979] *Futures Past*. New York: Columbia University Press.

Kovarik, B. (2011) *Revolutions in Communication*. London: Continuum International Publishing.

Kracauer, S. (1995) *The Mass Ornament*. Cambridge, MA: Harvard University Press.

Krätke, S. (2011) *The Creative Capital of Cities*. Malden, MA: Wiley-Blackwell.

Kress, G. (1986) 'Language in the Media: The Construction of Domains of Public and Private', *Media, Culture & Society*, 8(4): 395–419.

Kreiss, D. and Tufekci, Z. (2013) 'Occupying the Political', *Cultural Studies <=>Critical Methodologies*, 13(3): 163–167.

Krotz, F. (2009) 'Mediatization: A Concept with Which to Grasp Media and Societal Change', in Lundby, K. (ed.) *Mediatization*. New York: Peter Lang, pp. 19–38.

Kubitschko, S. (2015) 'The Role of Hackers in Countering Surveillance and Promoting Democracy', *Media and Communication*, 3(2): 77–87.

Kühl, S. (2011) *Organisationen*. Wiesbaden: VS.

Kunelius, R. and Reunanen, E. (2014) 'Transparency Discourse and Mediatized Governance', *Mediatization of Politics and Government Conference*, The London School of Economics and Political Science, London, 25–26 April.

Kwon, Y. J. and Kwon, K.-N. (2015) 'Consuming the Objectified Self: The Quest for Authentic Self', *Asian Social Science*, 11(2): 301–312.

Laclau, E. (1990) 'The Impossibility of Society', in Laclau, E. (ed.) *New Reflections on the Revolution of Our Time*. London: Verso, pp. 87–90.

Lafrance, A. (2016) 'Facebook and the New Colonialism', *The Atlantic*. 11 February.

Lahire, B. (2007) *The Plural Actor*. Cambridge: Polity.

Lammers, J. C. and Jackson, S. A. (2014) 'The Institutionality of a Mediatized Organizational Environment', in Pallas, J., Strannegard, K. and Jonsson, S. (eds.) *Organisations and the Media*. London: Routledge, pp. 33–47.

Lange, P. G. (2007) 'Publicly Private and Privately Public', *Journal of Computer-Mediated Communication,* 13(1): 361–380.

Langlois, G., Elmer, G., McKelvey, F. and Devereaux, Z. (2009) 'Networked Publics: The Double Articulation of Code and Politics on Facebook', *Canadian Journal of Communication,* 34(1): 415–434.

Larkin, B. (2008) *Signal and Noise: Media, Infrastructure, and Urban Culture in Nigeria.* Durham, NC: Duke University Press.

Lash, S. and Lury, C. (2007) *Global Culture Industry.* Cambridge: Polity.

Latour, B. (1991) 'Technology is Society Made Durable', in Law, J. (ed.) *A Sociology of Monsters: Essays on Power, Technology and Domination.* London: Routledge, pp. 103–131.

Latour, B. (1999) *Pandora's Hope: Essays on the Reality of Science Studies.* Cambridge, MA: Harvard University Press.

Latour, B. (2005) *Reassembling the Social.* Oxford: Oxford University Press.

Latour, B. (2007) 'Beware, Your Imagination Leaves Digital Traces', *Times Higher Literary Supplement,* 6(4). Available at: http://www.bruno-latour. fr/sites/default/files/P-129-THES-GB.pdf

Latour, B. (2013) *An Inquiry into Modes of Existence.* Cambridge, MA: Harvard University Press.

Latour, B., Jensen, P., Venturini, T., Grauwin, S. and Boullier, D. (2012) 'The Whole is Always Smaller than its Parts: A Digital Test of Gabriel Tardes' Monads', *British Journal of Sociology,* 63(4): 590–615.

Leal, O. F. (1995) 'Popular Taste and Erudite Repertoire', in Jackson, S. and Moores, S. (eds.) *The Politics of Domestic Consumption.* London: Prentice Hall, pp. 314–320.

Lee, H. and Sawyer, S. (2010) 'Conceptualizing Time, Space and Computing for Work and Organizing', *Time & Society,* 19(3): 293–317.

Lefebvre, H. (1991) *The Production of Space.* Oxford: Blackwell.

Lemos, A. (2009) 'Mobile Communication and New Sense of Places', *Revista Galáxia,* 16(1): 91–108.

Leurs, K. (2015) *Digital Passages.* Amsterdam: Amsterdam University Press.

Levinson, S. C. (1983) *Pragmatics.* Cambridge: Cambridge University Press.

Levy, S. (1984) *Hackers: Heroes of the Computer Revolution.* New York: Doubleday.

Lewis, D. (1969) *Convention: A Philosophical Study.* Cambridge, MA: Harvard University Press.

Licoppe, C. (2004) '"Connected" Presence', *Environment and Planning D,* 22(1): 135–156.

Lin, Y.-W. (2011) 'A Qualitative Enquiry into OpenStreetMap Making', *New Review of Hypermedia and Multimedia,* 17(1): 53–71.

Lindlof, T. R. (1988) 'Media Audiences as Interpretive Communities', *Communication Yearbook,* 11(1): 81–107.

Ling, R. (2012) *Taken for Grantedness.* Cambridge, MA: MIT Press.

Lippmann, W. (1993) [1925] *The Phantom Public*. Edison, NJ: Transaction Publishers.

Lissack, M. R. (1999) 'Complexity: The Science, its Vocabulary, and its Relation to Organizations', *Emergence*, 1(1): 110–126.

Litt, E. (2012) 'Knock Knock. Who's There? The Imagined Audience', *Journal of Broadcasting and Electronic Media*, 56(3): 330–345.

Livingstone, S. (2004) 'The Challenge of Changing Audiences', *European Journal of Communication*, 19(1): 75–86.

Livingstone, S. (2009) 'On the Mediation of Everything', *Journal of Communication*, 59 (1): 1–18.

Livingstone, S. and Sefton-Green, J. (2016) *The Class. Living and Learning in the Digital Age*. New York: New York University Press.

Lohmeier, C. and Pentzold, C. (2014) 'Making Mediated Memory Work: Cuban-Americans, Miami Media and the Doings of Diaspora Memories', *Media, Culture & Society*, 36(6): 776–789.

Loosen, W. and Schmidt, J. (2012) '(Re-)discovering the Audience', *Information, Communication & Society*, 15(6): 867–887.

Losh, E. (2014) 'Beyond Biometrics: Feminist Media Theory Looks at Selfiecity', *Selfiecity*. Available at: http://selfiecity.net/

Lotan, G. (2011) 'Data Reveals that "Occupying" Twitter Trending Topics is Harder than it Looks!', *SocialFlow*. Available at: http://blog.socialflow.com/post/7120244374/data-reveals-that-occupying--twitter-trending-topics-is-harder-than-it-looks

Lovibond, S. (2002) *Ethical Formation*. Cambridge, MA: Harvard University Press.

Luckmann, B. (1970) 'The Small Life-worlds of Modern Man', *Social Research*, 37(4): 580–596.

Luckmann, T. (1991) 'The Constitution of Human Life in Time' in Bender, J. and Wellbery, D. (eds.) *Chronotypes*. Stanford, CA: Stanford University Press, pp. 151–166.

Luhmann, N. (1994) [1968] 'Die Knappheit der Zeit und die Vordringlichkeit des Befristeten', in Luhmann, N. (ed.) *Politische Planung*. Opladen: Westdeutscher Verlag.

Luhmann, N. (1999) *The Reality of the Mass Media*. Cambridge: Polity.

Luhmann, N. (2012) *Theory of Society. Volume 1*. Stanford, CA: Stanford University Press.

Lundby, K. (2009) 'Introduction: "Mediatization" as a Key', in Lundby, K. (ed.) *Mediatization*. New York: Peter Lang, pp. 1–18.

Lundby, K. (2013) 'Media and Transformations of Religion', in Lundby, K. (ed.) *Religion Across Media*. New York: Peter Lang, pp. 185–202.

Lundby, K. (2014) 'Mediatization of Communication', in Lundby, K. (ed.) *Mediatization of Communication*. Berlin: de Gruyter, pp. 3–35.

Lunt, P. and Livingstone, S. M. (2013) 'Media Studies' Fascination with the Concept of the Public Sphere: Critical Reflections and Emerging Debates', *Media, Culture & Society*, 35(1): 87–96.

Lupton, D. (2013) 'The Commodification of Patient Opinion: The Digital Patient Experience Economy in the Age of Big Data', *Sociology of Health and Illness*, 36(6): 856–869.

Lupton, D. (2014) 'You are Your Data'. Available at: http://papers.ssrn.com/sol3/papers.cfm?abstract_id=2534211

Lupton, D. (2015) *Digital Sociology*. London: Routledge.

Lury, C., Parisi, L. and Terranova, T. (2012) 'Introduction: The Becoming Topological of Culture', *Theory, Culture & Society*, 29(4/5): 3–35.

Lyon, D. (2003) 'Surveillance as Social Sorting', in Lyon, D. (ed.) *Surveillance as Social Sorting*. London: Routledge, pp. 13–30.

MacDonald, R. (2015) '"Going Back in a Heartbeat": Collective Memory and the online circulation of family photographs', *Photographies* 8(1): 23–42.

MacIntyre, A. (1981) *After Virtue*. London: Duckworth.

MacKenzie, A. (2006) *Cutting Code*. New York: Peter Lang.

MacKenzie, D. and Wajcman, J. (1999) *The Social Shaping of Technology*. Milton Keynes: Open University Press.

Madianou, M. (2014) 'Polymedia Communication and Mediatized Migration', in Lundby, K. (ed.) *Mediatization of Communication*. Berlin: de Gruyter, pp. 323–348.

Madianou, M. and Miller, D. (2012) *Migration and New Media*. London: Routledge.

Madianou, M. and Miller, D. (2013) 'Polymedia', *International Journal of Cultural Studies*, 16(2): 169–187.

Magasic, M. (2014) 'Travel Blogging', *First Monday*, 19(7). doi: 10.5210/fm.v19i7.4887.

Malvern, J. (2015) 'Vinyl Junkies Send Records Racing Back Up the Charts', *The Times*. Available at: http://www.thetimes.co.uk/tto/arts/music/article4409436.ece

Manheim, E. (1933) *Die Träger der öffentlichen Meinung*. Brünn: Verlag Rudolf M. Rohrer.

Manovich, L. (2001) *The Language of New Media*. Cambridge, MA: MIT Press.

Manovich, L. (2013) *Software Takes Command*. New York: Bloomsbury.

Mansell, R. (2012) *Imagining the Internet*. Oxford: Oxford University Press.

Mansell, R. and Silverstone, R. (1998) *Communication by Design*. Milton Keynes: Oxford University Press.

Marres, N. (2007) 'The Issues Deserve More Credit: Pragmatist Contributions to the Study of Public Involvement in Controversy', *Social Studies of Science*, 37(5): 759–780.

Marston, S., Jones, J. and Woodward, K. (2005) 'Human Geography without Scale', *Transactions of the Institute of British Geographers*, 30(4): 416–432.

Martin, L. and Secor, A. J. (2014) 'Towards a Post-Mathematical Topology', *Progress in Human Geography*, 38(3): 420–438.

Martín-Barbero, J. (1993) *Communication, Culture, and Hegemony*. London: Sage.

Martín-Barbero, J. (2006) 'A Latin American Perspective on Communication/ Cultural Mediation', *Global Media and Communication*, 2(3): 279–297.

Martuccelli, D. (2002) *Grammaires de L'Individu*. Paris: Gallimard.

Marwick, A. E. (2015) 'Instafame: Luxury Selfies in the Attention Economy', *Public Culture*, 27(1 75): 137–160.

Massey, D. (1992) 'Politics and Space/Time', *New Left Review*, I(196): 65–84.

Mattelart, A. (1994) *Mapping World Communication*. Minneapolis, MN: Minnesota University Press.

Mattelart, T. (2009) 'Audio-visual Piracy', *Global Media and Communication*, 5(3): 308–326.

Mattelart, A. (2010) *The Globalization of Surveillance*. Cambridge: Polity.

Mattoni, A. and Treré, E. (2014) 'Media Practices, Mediation Processes, and Mediatization in the Study of Social Movements', *Communication Theory*, 24(3): 252–271.

Mauss, M. (1980) [1938] 'A Category of the Human Mind', in Carruthers, M., Collins, S. and Lukes, S. (eds.) *The Category of the Person*. Cambridge: Cambridge University Press, pp. 1–26.

Mayntz, R. and Scharpf, F. W. (1995) 'Der Ansatz des Akteurszentrierten Institutionalismus', in Mayntz, R. and Scharpf, F. W. (eds.) *Gesellschaftliche Selbstregelung und Politische Steuerung*. Frankfurt am Main: Campus, pp. 39–72.

Mazzucatto, M. (2013) *The Entrepreneurial State*. London: Anthem Books.

McDermott, J. P. (2006) *A Social History of the Chinese Book*. Hong Kong: Hong Kong University Press.

McDowell, J. (1994) *Mind and World*. Cambridge, MA: Harvard University Press.

McFedries, P. (2003) 'Mobs R Us', *IEEE Spectrum*, 40(10), p. 56.

McGann, J. G. and Sabatini, R. (2011) *Global Think Tanks: Policy Networks and Governance*. London: Routledge.

McLuhan, M. (1962) *The Gutenberg Galaxy*. Toronto: University of Toronto Press.

McLuhan, M. (1987) [1964] *Understanding Media*. London: Ark Paperbacks.

McLuhan, M. and Lapham, L. H. (1994) *Understanding Media*, MA: MIT Press.

McLuhan, M. and Powers, B. R. (1992) *The Global Village*. Oxford: Oxford University Press.

Mead, G. H. (1967) [1934] *Mind, Self and Society*. Chicago, IL: Chicago University Press.

Meier, F. and Schimank, U. (2012) *Organisation und Organisationsgesellschaft*. Hagen: Fernuniversität Hagen.

Mejias, U. (2013) *Off the Network*. Minneapolis, MN: Minnesota University Press.

Merten, K. (1994) 'Evolution der Kommunikation', in Merten, K., Schmidt, S. J. and Weischenberg, S. (eds.) *Die Wirklichkeit der Medien. Eine Einführung in die Kommunikationswissenschaft*. Opladen: Westdeutscher Verlag, pp. 141–162.

Merzeau, L. (2009) 'Présence Numérique: Les Médiations de L'identité', *Les Enjeux de L'information et de la Communication*, 1(1): 79–91.

Mesjasz, C. (2010) 'Complexity of Social Systems', *Acta Physica Polonica-Series A General Physics*, 117(4), p. 700.

Meyer, B. and Moors, A. (2006) *Religion, Media, and the Public Sphere*. Bloomington, IN: Indiana University Press.

Meyer, J. W. and Rowan, B. (1977) 'Institutionalized Organizations', *American Journal of Sociology*: 340–363.

Meyer, T. (2003) *Media Democracy*. Cambridge: Polity.

Meyrowitz, J. (1985) *No Sense of Place*. New York: Oxford University Press.

Meyrowitz, J. (1995) 'Medium Theory', in Crowley, D. J. and Mitchell, D. (eds.) *Communication Theory Today*. Cambridge: Polity, pp. 50–77.

Meyrowitz, J. (2009) 'Medium Theory: An Alternative to the Dominant Paradigm of Media Effects', in Nabi, R. L. and Oliver, M. B. (eds.) *The Sage Handbook of Media Processes and Effects*. Thousand Oaks, CA: Sage, pp. 517–530.

Mihailidis, P. (2014) 'A Tethered Generation: Exploring the role of mobile phones in the daily life of young people'. *Mobile Media and Generation*, 2(1): 58–72.

Min, J. and Lee, H. (2011) 'The Change in User and IT Dynamics', *Computers in Human Behaviour*, 27(6): 2339–2351.

Mitchell, M. (2009) *Complexity: A Guided Tour*. Oxford: Oxford University Press.

Moon-Year, P. (2004) 'A Study on the Type Casting, Setting and Printing Method of "Buljo-Jikji-Simche-Yoyrol"', *Gutenberg-Jahrbuch*, 79(1): 32–46.

Moore, M. (2015) 'German hotel group offers ultimate luxury – check in to check out of web'. *Financial Times*, 26 June.

Moores, S. (2004) 'The Doubling of Place: Electronic Media, Time–space Arrangements and Social Relationships', in Couldry, N. and McCarthy, A. (eds.) *MediaSpace*. London: Routledge, pp. 21–36.

Morley, D. (1986) *Family Television*. London: Comedia.

Morley, D. (2000) *Home Territories: Media, Mobility and Identity*. London: Routledge.

Morozov, E. (2015) 'El Derecho a Desconectarse', *El País*. Available at: http://elpais.com/elpais/2015/04/05/opinion/1428258905_239072.html

Mortensen, M. (2013) 'War', in Simonson, P., Peck, J., Craig, R. and Jackson, P. (eds.) *The Handbook of Communication History*. London: Routledge, pp. 331–346.

Mosco, V. (2014) *To the Cloud: Big Data in a Turbulent World*. Boulder, CO: Paradigm.

Muniz, A. M. and O'Guinn, T. C. (2001) 'Brand Community', *Journal of Consumer Research*, 27(4): 412–432.

Murphy, P. D. and Rodríguez, C. (2006) 'Introduction: Between Macondo and McWorld: Communication and Culture Studies in Latin America', *Global Media and Communication*, 2(3): 267–277.

Nafus, D. and Sherman, J. (2014) 'This One Does Not Go Up to 11: The Quantified Self Movement as an Alternative Big Data Practice', *International Journal of Communication*, 8(11): 1784–1794.

Napoli, P. M. (2014) 'Automated Media', *Communication Theory*, 24(3): 340–360.

Narayanan, A. and Felten, E. W. (2014) 'No silver bullet: De-identification still doesn't work', unpublished manuscript, http://randomwalker.info/publications/no-silver-bullet-de-identification.pdf

Neddermeyer, U. (1998) *Von der Handschrift zum gedruckten Buch. Quantitative und qualitative Aspekte. 2 Teile (Text und Anlagen)*. Wiesbaden: Harrassowitz.

Nederveen Pieterse, J. (1995) 'Globalization as Hybridization', in Featherstone, M., Lash, S. and Robertson, R. (eds.) *Global Modernities*. London: Sage, pp. 45–68.

Negt, O. and Kluge, A. (1993) *Public Sphere and Experience*. Minneapolis, MN: University of Minnesota Press.

Neverla, I. (2002) 'Die Polychrone Gesellschaft und Ihre Medien', *Medien & Zeit*, 17(2): 46–52.

Neverla, I. (2010) 'Medien als Soziale Zeitgeber im Alltag', in Hepp, A. and Hartmann, M. (eds.) *Die Mediatisierung der Alltagswelt*. Wiesbaden: VS, pp. 183–194.

Neyland, D. (2015) 'On Organizing Algorithms', *Theory, Culture & Society*, 32(1): 119–132.

Nielsen, R. K. (2012) *Ground Wars: Personalized Communication in Political Campaigns*. Princeton, NJ: Princeton University Press.

Nicolini, D. (2007) 'Stretching Out and Expanding Work Practices in Time and Space', *Human Relations*, 60(6): 889–920.

Nietzsche, F. (1990) [1887] *Beyond Good and Evil*. Translated by R. J. Hollingdale. Harmondsworth: Penguin.

Nissenbaum, H. (2004) 'Privacy as Contextual Integrity', *Washington Law Review*, 79(1): 119–158.

Nissenbaum, H. (2010) *Privacy in Context*. Stanford, CA: Stanford University Press.

Noveck, B. (2009) *Wikigovernment*. Washington, DC: Brookings Institution Press.

Nowotny, H. (1994) *Time: The Modern and Postmodern Experience*. Cambridge: Polity.

Nussbaum, M. and Sen, A. (1993) *The Quality of Life*. Oxford: Oxford University Press.

Offe, C. (1987) 'The Utopia of the Zero-Option: Modernity and Modernization as Normative Political Criteria', *Praxis International*, 7(1): 1–24.

Office for National Statistics (2015) 'Internet Access – Households and Individuals 2015', *Great Britain*. Available at: http://www.ons.gov.uk/ons/dcp171778_412758.pdf

Oggolder, C. (2014) 'When Curiosity met Printing', in Butsch, R. and Livingstone, S. M. (eds.) *Meanings of Audiences*. London: Routledge, pp. 37–49.

Ohm, P. (2010) 'Broken Promises of Privacy', *UCLA Law Review*, 57(1): 1701–1777.

Olofsson, J. K. (2010) 'Mass Movements in Computer-Mediated Environments', *Information, Communication & Society*, 13(5): 765–784.

Ong, W. J. (2002) *Orality and Literacy*. London u. a.: Routledge.

Orlikowski, W. J. (2010) 'The Sociomateriality of Organisational Life: Considering Technology in Management Research', *Cambridge Journal of Economics*, 34(1): 125–141.

Orlikowski, W. J. and Scott S. V. (2014) 'The Algorithm and the Crowd', *MIS Quarterly*, 39(1): 201–216.

Øyvind, I. and Pallas, J. (2014) 'Mediatization of Coorporations', in Lundby, K. (ed.) *Mediatization of Communication*. Berlin: de Gruyter, pp. 423–442.

Palaiologou, I. (2014). 'Children Under Five and Digital Technologies', *European Early Childhood Education Research Journal*, doi: 10.1080/1350293X.2014.929876.

Palfrey, J. and Gasser, U. (2008) *Born Digital*. Revd edn. New York: Basic Books.

Pallas, J., Strannegard, L. and Jonsson, S. (eds.) (2014) *Organisations and the media*. London and New York: Routledge.

Pan, Z., Yan, W., Jung, G. and Zheng, J. (2011) 'Exploring Structured Inequality in Internet Use Behavior', *Asian Journal of Communication*, 21(2): 116–132.

Papacharissi, Z. (2010) *A Private Sphere*. Cambridge: Polity.

Papacharissi, Z. (2015) *Affective Publics*. Oxford: Oxford University Press.

Papacharissi, Z. and Easton, E. (2013) 'In the Habitus of the New' in Hartley, J., Burgess, J. and Bruns, A. (eds.) *A Companion to New Media Dynamics*. Chichester: Wiley, pp. 171–184.

Parikka, J. (2013) *What is Media Archaeology?* Cambridge: Polity.

Pariser, E. (2011) *The Filter Bubble*. New York: Viking/Penguin.

Parks, L. and Schwoch, J. (2012) *Down to Earth: Satellite Technologies, Industries and Cultures*. New Brunswick, NJ: Rutgers University Press.

Parsons, T (1966) *Societies*. Prentice-Hall, Inc., Englewood Cliffs, New Jersey.

Pasquale, F. (2015) *The Black Box Society*. Cambridge, MA: Harvard University Press.

Passoth, J.-H., Sutter, T. and Wehner, J. (2014) 'The Quantified Listener', in

Hepp, A. and Krotz, F. (eds.) *Mediatized Worlds*. London: Palgrave, pp. 271–287.

Peil, C. and Röser, J. (2014) 'The Meaning of Home in the Context of Digitization, Mobilization and Mediatization', in Hepp, A. and Krotz, F. (eds.) *Mediatized Worlds*. London: Palgrave, pp. 233–249.

Penney, J. and Dadas, C. (2014) '(Re)Tweeting in the Service of Protest', *New Media & Society*, 16(1): 74–90.

Pentzold, C., Lohmeier, C. and Hajek, A. (2016) 'Introduction: Remembering and Reviving in States of Flux', in Hajek, A., Lohmeier, C. and Pentzold, C. (eds.) *Memory in a Mediated World*. Basingstoke: Palgrave Macmillan, pp. 1–12.

Peters, J. D. (1999) *Speaking into the Air*. Chicago, IL: Chicago University Press.

Pew Research Centre (2012) 'The Rise of the "Connected Viewer"', http://www.pewinternet.org/2012/07/17/the-rise-of-the-connected-viewer/

Pfadenhauer, M. (2010) 'Artefakt-Gemeinschaften?! Technikverwendung und Entwicklung in Aneignungskulturen', in Honer, A., Meuser, M. and Pfadenhauer, M. (eds.) *Fragile Sozialität*. Wiesbaden: VS, pp. 355–370.

Pfadenhauer, M. (2014) 'On the Sociality of Social Robots', *Science, Technology & Innovation Studies*, 10(1): 135–153.

Pfadenhauer, M. and Dukat, C. (2015) 'Robot Caregiver or Robot-Supported Caregiving?: The Performative Deployment of the Social Robot PARO in Dementia Care', *International Journal of Social Robotics*, 7(3): 393–406.

Phillips, J. (2006) 'Agencement/Assemblage', *Theory, Culture & Society*, 23(2/3): 108–109.

Phillips, J. W. (2013) 'On Topology', *Theory, Culture & Society*, 30(5): 122–152.

Pickering, A. (1995) *The Mangle of Practice*. Chicago, IL: Chicago University Press.

Pinkard, T (2012) *Hegel's Naturalism*. Oxford: Oxford University Press.

Pippin, R. (2008) *Hegel's Practical Philosophy*. Cambridge: Cambridge University Press.

Plantin, J.-C., Sandvig, C. (forthcoming) 'Beneath It All: Infrastructure Studies Meet Platform Studies in the Age of Google and Facebook', *New Media & Society*.

Poe, M. T. (2011) *A History of Communications*. Cambridge: Cambridge University Press.

Poell, T. and Van Dijck, J. (2015) 'Social Media and Activist Communication', in Atton, C (ed.) *The Routledge Companion to Alternative and Community Media*. London: Routledge, pp. 527–537.

Pollio, D. E., Batey, D. S., Bender, K., Ferguson, K. and Thompson, S. J. (2013) 'Technology Use Among Emerging Adult Homeless in Two US Cities', *Social Work*, 58(2): 173–175.

Porta, D. D. (2013) 'Bridging Research on Democracy, Social Movements and

Communication', in Cammaerts, B., Mattoni, A. and McCurdy, P. (eds.) *Mediation and Protest Movements*. Bristol: Intellect, pp. 21–38.

Porter, T. (1995) *Trust in Numbers: The Pursuit of Objectivity in Science and Public Life*. Princeton, NJ: Princeton University Press.

Postill, J. (2011) *Localizing the Internet*. New York: Berghahn.

Postill, J. (2014) 'Democracy in an Age of Viral Reality: A Media Epidemiography of Spain's Indignados Movement', *Ethnography*, 15(1): 51–69.

Pred, A. (1990) *Making Histories and Constructing Human Geographies*. Boulder, CO: Westview Press.

Qiu, J. L. (2009) *Working-class Network Society: Communication Technology and the Information Have-less in Urban China*. Cambridge, MA: MIT Press.

Qvortrup, L. (2006) 'Understanding New Digital Media Medium Theory or Complexity Theory', *European Journal of Communication*, 21(3): 345–356.

Radway, J. (1984) 'Interpretive Communities and Variable Literacies', *Daedalus*, 113(3): 49–73.

Rainie, L. and Wellman, B. (2012) *Networked: The New Social Operating System*. Cambridge, MA: MIT Press.

Rantanen, T. (2009) *When News Was New*. Malden, MA: Wiley-Blackwell.

Reese, S. D., Hyun, K. and Jeong, J. (2007) 'Mapping the Blogosphere', *Journalism*, 8(3): 235–261.

Rheingold, H. (1995) *The Virtual Community*. London: Minerva.

Rheingold, H. (2003) *Smart Mobs: The Next Social Revolution*. Cambridge, MA: Perseus Publishing.

Ricoeur, P. (1980) 'The Model of the Text', in Ricoeur, P. and Thompson, J. B. (eds.) *Hermeneutics and the Human Sciences*. Cambridge: Cambridge University Press, pp. 197–221.

Ricoeur, P. (1984a) *Time and Narrative*. Volume 1. Chicago, IL: Chicago University Press.

Ricoeur, P. (1984b) *Time and Narrative*. Volume 2. Chicago, IL: Chicago University Press.

Risse, T. (2010) *A Community of Europeans?* New York: Cornell University Press.

Risse, T. (2015) 'European Public Spheres, the Politicization of EU Affairs, and its Consequences', in Risse, T. (ed.) *European Public Spheres*. Cambridge: Cambridge University Press, pp. 141–164.

Ritzer, G. and Jurgenson, N. (2010) 'Production, Consumption, Prosumption', *Journal of Consumer Culture*, 10(1): 13–36.

Robichaud, D., Giroux, H. and Taylor, J. R. (2004) 'The Metaconversation: The Recursive Property of Language as a Key to Organizing', *Academy of Management Review*, 29(4): 617–634.

Rodriguez, C. (2001) *Fissures in the Mediascape*. Creskill, NJ: The Hampton Press.

Rogers, A. (2013) *Cinematic Appeals*. New York: Columbia University Press.

Rogers, E. M. (2003) *Diffusion of Innovations*. 5th edn. New York: Free Press.

Rogers, R. (2013) *Digital Methods*. Cambridge, MA: MIT Press.

Rosa, H. (2013) *Social Acceleration*. New York: Columbia University Press.

Rosanvallon, P. (2009) *CounterDemocracy*. Princeton, NJ: Princeton University Press.

Rosen, J. (2006) 'The People Formerly Known as the Audience'. Available at: http://journalism.nyu.edu/pubzone/weblongs/pressthink/2006/06/27/ppl_frmr_p.html

Rosen, D., Lafontaine, P. R. and Hendrickson, B. (2011) 'CouchSurfing', *New Media & Society*, 13(6): 981–998.

Rucht, D. and Neidhart, F. (2002) 'Towards a "Movement Society"?', *Social Movement Studies*, 1(1): 7–30.

Ruckenstein, M. (2014) 'Visualized and Interacted Life', *Societies*, 4: 68–84.

Ruppert, E. (2011) 'Population Objects: Interpassive Subjects', *Sociology*, 45(2): 218–233.

Ruppert, E., Law, J. and Savage, M. (2013) 'Reassembling Social Science Methods', *Theory, Culture & Society*, 30(4): 22–46.

Salgado, J. and Hermans, B. (2005) 'The Return of Subjectivity', *E-Journal of Applied Psychology: Clinical Section*, 1(1): 3–13.

Salvo, J. (2013) 'Reflections on Occupy Wall Street', *Cultural Studies <=> Critical Methodologies*, 13(3): 143–149.

Sandry, E. (2015) 'Re-evaluating the Form and Communication of Social Robots', *International Journal of Social Robotics*, 7(3): 335–346.

Sarker, S. and Sahay, S. (2004) 'Implications of Space and Time for Distributed Work: An Interpretive Study of US–Norwegian Systems Development Teams', *European Journal of Information Systems*, 13(1): 3–20.

Sassen, S. (2006) *Territory, Authority, Rights*. Princeton, NJ: Princeton University Press.

Savage, M. and Burrows, R. (2007) 'The Coming Crisis of Empirical Sociology', *Sociology*, 41(5): 885–899.

Sayer, D. (2011) *Why Things Matter to People*. Cambridge: Cambridge University Press.

Scammell, M. (1993) *Designer Politics*. Basingstoke: Palgrave Macmillan.

Scannell, P. (1989) 'Public Service Broadcasting and Modern Public Life', *Media, Culture and Society*, 2(11): 135–166.

Scannell, P. (1996) *Radio, Television and Modern Life*. Oxford: Blackwell.

Scannell, P. (2002) 'Big Brother as Television Event', *Television & New Media*, 3(3): 271–282.

Scharpf, F. W. (1997) *Games Real Actors Play: Actor-centered Institutionalism in Policy Research*. Boulder, CO: Westview Press.

Schatzki, T. (1996) *Social Practices*. Cambridge: Cambridge University Press.

Scheffler, S. (2013) *Death and the Afterlife*. New York: Oxford University Press.

Schimank, U. (2010) *Handeln und Strukturen, 4. Auflage*. Weinheim: Juventa.

Schivelbusch, W. (1986) *The Railway Journey*. Berkeley, CA: University of California Press.

Schlegloff, E. A. (2002) 'Beginnings in the Telephone', in Katz, J. E. and Aakhus, M. (eds.) *Perpetual Contact*. Cambridge: Cambridge University Press.

Schlesinger, P. and Doyle, G. (2014) 'From Organizational Crisis to Multi-Platform Salvation?', *Journalism*, 16(3): 305–323.

Schmidt, J. (2007) 'Blogging Practices', *Journal of Computer-Mediated Communication*, 12(4): 1409–1427.

Schmidt, J.-H. (2013) 'Persönliche Öffentlichkeiten und Privatsphäre im Social Web', in Halft, S. and Krah, H. (eds.) *Privatheit*. Passau: Karl Stutz, pp. 121–137.

Schnapp, J. T. and Tiews, M. (2006) *Crowds and Collectivities in Networked Electoral Politics*. Stanford, CA: Stanford University Press.

Scholz, T. (2013) *Digital Labor: The Internet as Playground and Factory*. New York: Routledge.

Schrøder, K. C. and Kobbernagel, C. (2010) 'Towards a Typology of Cross-media News Consumption', *Northern Lights*, 8(1): 115–137.

Schultz, F., Suddaby, R. and Cornelissen, J. P. (2014) 'The Role of Business Media in Constructing Rational Myths of Organizations', in Pallas, J., Strannegard, L. and Jonsson, S. (eds.) *Organisations and the Media*. London: Routledge, pp. 13–32.

Schulz, W. (2014) 'Mediatization and New Media', in Esser, F. and Strömbäck, J. (eds.) *Mediatization of Politics*. Houndmills: Palgrave Macmillan, pp. 57–73.

Schüttpelz, E. (2013) 'Elemente Einer Akteur-Medien-Theorie', in Thielmann, T. and Schüttpelz, E. (eds.) *Akteur-Medien-Theorie*. Bielefeld: Transcript, pp. 9–67.

Schütz, A. (1964) 'The Well-informed Citizen', in Schütz, A. and Brodersen, A. (eds.) *Collected Papers, Volume II: Studies in Social Theory*. The Hague: Martinus Nijhoff, pp. 120–134.

Schütz, A. (1967) [1932] *The Phenomenology of the Social World*. Evanston, IL: Northwestern University Press.

Schütz, A. and Luckmann, T. (1973) *The Structures of the Life World. Volume II*. Evanston, IL: Northwestern University Press.

Schwanen, T. and Kwan, M.-P. (2008) 'The Internet, Mobile Phone and Space-Time Constraints', *Geoforum*, 39(3): 1362–1377.

Schwarz, O. (2010) 'On Friendship, Boobs and the Logic of the Catalogue', *Convergence*, 16(2): 163–183.

Schwarz, O. (2011) 'Who Moved my Conversation? Instant Messaging, Intertextuality and New Regimes of Intimacy and Truth', *Media, Culture & Society*, 33(1): 71–87.

Scott, J. (1998) *Seeing Like a State*. New Haven, CT: Yale University Press.

Scott, S. and Orlikowski, W. (2013) 'Sociomateriality – Taking the Wrong

Turning? A Response to Mutch', *Information and Organization*, 23(2): 77–80.

Searle, J. R. (1969) *Speech Acts*. Cambridge: Cambridge University Press.

Searle, J. R. (1995) *The Construction of Social Reality*. Harmondsworth: Penguin.

Searle, J. R. (2011) *Making the Social World*. Oxford: Oxford University Press.

Seib, P. M. and Janbek, D. M. (2011) *Global Terrorism and New Media*. New York: Routledge.

Selwyn, N. (2014) *Distrusting Educational Technology*. New York: Routledge.

Selwyn, N. (2015) 'Data Entry: Toward the Critical Study of Digital Data and Education', *Learning, Media and Technology*, 40(1): 64–82.

Senft, T. M. and Baym, N. K. (2015) 'What Does the Selfie Say?', *International Journal of Communication*, 9(1): 1588–1606.

Sennett, R. (1998) *The Corrosion of Character: Personal Consequences of Work in the New Capitalism*. New York: W. W. Norton & Company.

Sewell, W. H. (2005) *Logics of History*. Chicago, IL: University of Chicago Press.

Shannon, C. E. and Weaver, W. (1959) 'The Mathematical Theory of Communication', *The Bell System Technical Journal*, 27(3): 379–423.

Shaw, S. E., Russell, J., Greenhalgh, T. and Korica, M. (2014) 'Thinking about Think Tanks in Health Care', *Sociology of Health and Illness*, 36(3): 447–461.

Shibutani, T. (1955) 'Reference Groups as Perspectives', *American Journal of Sociology*, 60(6): 562–569.

Sibley, D. (1988) 'Survey 13: Purification of Space,' *Environment and Planning D: Society and Space*, 6(4): 409–421.

Silverstone, R. (2005) 'The Sociology of Mediation and Communication', in Calhoun, C., Rojek, C. and Turner, B. (eds.) *Sage Handbook of Sociology*. London: Sage, pp. 188–207.

Silverstone, R. (2006) 'Domesticating Domestication', in Berker, T., Hartmann, M., Punie, Y. and Ward, K. (eds.) *Domestication of Media and Technology*. London: Open University Press, pp. 229–248.

Silverstone, R. and Hirsch, E. (1992) *Consuming Technologies*. London: Routledge.

Simmel, G. (1971) *On Individuality and Social Forms*. Chicago, IL: Chicago University Press.

Simmel, G. (1992) [1908] *Soziologie. Untersuchungen über die Formen der Vergesellschaftung*. Frankfurt am Main: Suhrkamp.

Skeggs, B. (1994) *Becoming Respectable: Formations of Class and Gender*. London: Sage.

Skey, M. (2014) 'The Mediation of Nationhood: Communicating the World as a World of Nations', *Communication Theory*, 24(1): 1–20.

Slater, D. (2013) *New Media, Development and Globalization*. Cambridge: Polity.

Sloss, R. (1910) 'Das Drahlose Jahrhundert', in Brehmer, M. (ed.) *Die Welt in Hundert Jahren*. Reprint 2013, Berlin: Verlagsanstalt Buntdruck, pp. 27–48.

Smith, N. (1990) *Uneven Development: Nature, Capital and the Production of Space*. Oxford: Blackwell.

Southerton, D. (2003) 'Squeezing Time', *Time & Society,* 12(1): 5–25.

Southerton, D. and Tomlinson, M. (2005) '"Pressed for Time" – The Differential Impacts of a "Time Squeeze"', *The Sociological Review,* 53(2): 215–239.

Sperling, G. (2015) 'How Airbnb Combats Middle Class Income Stagnation', *Airbnb.* Available at: http://publicpolicy.airbnb.com/new-report-impact-airbnb-middle-class-income-stagnation/

Spitulnik, D. (1993) 'Anthropology and Mass Media', *Annual Review of Anthropology,* 22(1): 293–315.

Spitulnik, D. (2010) 'Personal News and the Price of Public Service', in Bird, S. E. (ed.) *The Anthropology of News and Journalism: Global Perspectives.* Bloomington, IN: Indiana University Press, pp. 182–193.

Stage, C. (2013) 'The Online Crowd: A Contradiction in Terms? On the Potentials of Gustave Le Bon's Crowd Psychology in an Analysis of Affective Blogging', *Distinktion: Scandinavian Journal of Social Theory,* 14(1): 211–226.

Stäheli, U. (2012) 'Infrastrukturen des Kollektiven', *Zeitschrift für Medien- und Kulturforschung,* 2(1): 99–116.

Stanyer, J. (2013) *Intimate Politics.* Cambridge: Polity.

Star, S. L. and Ruhleder, K. (1996) 'Steps Toward an Ecology of Infrastructure', *Information Systems Research,* 7(1): 111–134.

Starr, P. (2005) *The Creation of the Media.* New York: Basic Books.

Stephansen, H. (2016) 'Understanding Citizen Media as Practice', in Baker, M. and Blaagaard, B. (eds.) *Citizen Media and Public Spaces.* London: Routledge.

Sterne, J. (2014) '"What Do We Want?" "Materiality!" "When do We Want it?" "Now!"' in Boczkowski, P., Foot, K. and Gillespie, T. *Media Technologies.* Cambridge, MA: MIT Press, pp. 119–128.

Stokes, B., Villanueva, G., Bar, F. and Ball-Rokeach, S. (2015) 'Mobile Design as Neighbourhood Acupuncture', *Journal of Urban Technology,* 22(3): 55–77.

Stone, D., Denham, A. and Garnett, M. (1998) *Think Tanks Across Nations.* Manchester: Manchester University Press.

Storsul, T. (2014) 'Deliberation or Self-presentation?: Young People, Politics and Social Media', *Nordicom Review,* 35(2): 17–28.

Straubhaar, J. D. (2007) *World Television.* London: Sage.

Strauss, A. (1978) 'A Social World Perspective', *Studies in Symbolic Interaction,* 1(1): 119–128.

Streeter, T. (2010) *The Net Effect.* New York: New York University Press.

Striphas, T. (2015) 'Algorithmic Culture', *European Journal of Cultural Studies,* 18(4/5): 395–412.

Strömbäck, J. and Esser, F. (2014a) 'Introduction', *Journalism Practice,* 8(3): 245–257.

Strömbäck, J. and Esser, F. (2014b) 'Mediatization of Politics', in Esser, F.

and Strömbäck, J. (eds.) *Mediatization of Politics*. Houndmills: Palgrave Macmillan, pp. 3–28.

Swan, M. (2012) 'Health 2050: The Realization of Personalized Medicine through Crowdsourcing, the Quantified Self, and the Participatory Biocitizen', *Journal of Personalized Medicine*, 2(3): 93–118.

Swan, M. (2013) 'The Quantified Self', *Big Data*, 1(2): 85–99.

Tække, J. (2005) 'Media Sociography on Weblogs', *The Sixth Annual Media Ecology Association Convention*, New York: Fordham University, Lincoln Center Campus, 22–26 June 2005.

Takahashi, T. (2014) 'Youth, Social Media and Connectivity in Japan', in Sergeant, P. and Tagg, C. (eds.) *The Language of Social Media*. Basingstoke: Palgrave Macmillan, pp. 186–207.

Tarde, G. (1901) *L'opinion et la Foule*. Paris: Presses Universitaires de France.

Tarde, G. (2000) [1899] *Social Laws*. Kitchener: Batoche Books.

Taylor, C. (2004) *Modern Social Imaginaries*. Durham, NC: Duke University Press.

Tazanu, P. (2012) *Being Available and Reachable*. Doctor of Philosophy Thesis. Bamenda: Langaa RPCIG. Available at: http://www.africanbookscollec tive.com/books/being-available-and-reachable

Tenbruck, F. H. (1972) 'Gesellschaft und Gesellschaften', in Bellebaum, A. (ed.) *Die Moderne Gesellschaft*. Freiburg: Herder, pp. 54–71.

Tepe, D. and Hepp, A. (2008) 'Digitale Produktionsgemeinschaften', in Lutterbeck, B., Bärwolff, M. and Gehring, R. A. (eds.) *Open Source Jahrbuch*. Berlin: Lehmanns Media, pp. 171–187.

Thomas, W I. and Thomas, D. S. (1928) *The Child in America*. New York: Knopf.

Thompson, E. P. (1967) 'Time, Work-discipline and Industrial Capitalism', *Past & Present*, 38(1): 56–97.

Thompson, J. B. (1995) *The Media and Modernity*. Cambridge: Cambridge University Press.

Thompson, J. B. (2005a) *Books in the Digital Age*. Cambridge: Polity.

Thompson, J. B. (2005b) 'The New Visibility', *Theory Culture & Society*, 22(6): 31–51.

Thompson, J. B. (2010) *Merchants of Culture*. Cambridge: Polity.

Thorbjornsrud, K., Figenschou, T. U. and Ihlen, Ø. (2014) 'Mediatization in Public Bureaucracies', *Communications*, 39(1): 3–22.

Thornton, P., Ocasio, W. and Lounsbury, M. (2012) *The Institutional Logics Perspective*. Oxford: Oxford University Press.

Thrift, N. (2008) *Non-Representational Theory*. London: Routledge.

Thrift, N. and French, S. (2002) 'The Automatic Production of Space', *Transactions of the Institute of British Geographers*, 27(3): 309–335.

Tomlinson, J. (1999) *Globalization and Culture*. Cambridge: Polity.

Tomlinson, J. (2007) *The Culture of Speed*. New Delhi: Sage.

Tönnies, F. (2001) [1935] *Community and Civil Society*. Cambridge: Cambridge University Press.

Toombs, A., Bardzell, S. and Bardzell, J. (2014) 'Becoming Makers: Hackerspace Member Habits, Values, and Identities', *Journal of Peer Production*. Available at: http://peerproduction.net/issues/issue-5–shared-machine-shops/peer-reviewed-articles/becoming-makers-hackerspace-member-habits-values-and-identities/

Touraine, A. (1981) *Return of the Actor*. Chicago, IL: Chicago University Press.

Treré, E. (2015) 'The Struggle Within: Discord, Conflict and Paranoia in Social Media Protest', in Dencik, L. and Leistert, O. (eds.) *Critical Perspectives on Social Media and Protest*. Boulder, CO: Rowman and Littlefield, pp. 163–180.

Tse, Y.-K. (2014) 'Television's Changing Role in Social Togetherness in the Personalized Online Consumption of Foreign TV', *New Media & Society*. Available at: http://nms.sagepub.com/content/early/2014/12/18/1461444814564818.abstract.

Tsimonis, G. and Dimitriadis, S. (2014) 'Brand Strategies in Social Media', *Marketing Intelligence & Plan*, 32(3): 328–344.

Tuan, Y-F. (1977) *Space and Place: The Perspective of Experience*. London: Edward Arnold.

Tucker, I. and Goodings, L. (2014) 'Mediation and Digital Intensities', *Social Science Information*, 53(3): 277–292.

Tucker, P. (2013) 'Had Big Data Made Anonymity Impossible?', *MIT Technology Review*. Available at: http://www.technologyreview.com/news/514351/has-big-data-made-anonymity-impossible/

Turkle, S. (1996) *Life on the Screen*. London: Weidenfeld & Nicolson.

Turkle, S. (2011) *Alone Together: Why We Expect More from Technology and Less from Each Other*. New York: Basic Books.

Turkle, S. (2015) *Reclaiming Conversation*. New York: Penguin.

Turner, F. (2006) *From Counterculture to Cyberculture*. Chicago, IL: University of Chicago Press.

Turow, J. (2011) *The Daily You: How the New Advertising Industry is Defining Your Identity and Your Worth*. New Haven, CT: Yale University Press.

Vaast, E. (2007) 'The Presentation of Self in a Virtual but Work-related Environment', in Crowston, K. (ed.) *Virtuality and Virtualization*. Boston, MA: Springer, pp. 183–199.

Vaccari, C. (2013) *Digital Politics in Western Democracies*. Baltimore, MD: Johns Hopkins University Press.

Valentine, G. (2006) 'Globalizing Intimacy', *Women's Studies Quarterly*, 34(1/2): 365–393.

van Dijck, J. (2007) *Mediated Memories in the Digital Age*. Stanford, CA: Stanford University Press.

van Dijck, J. (2013) *The Culture of Connectivity*. Oxford: Oxford University Press.

van Dijck, J. (2014) 'Datafication, Dataism and Dataveillance', *Surveillance and Society*, 12(2): 197–208.

Venturini, T. (2012) 'Building on Faults: How to Represent Controversies with Digital Methods', *Public Understanding of Science*, 21(7): 796–812.

Venturini, T. and Latour, B. (2010) 'The Social Fabric', *Proceedings of Future En Seine*, 30–15.

Verón, E. (2014) 'Mediatization Theory', in Lundby, K. (ed.) *Mediatization of Communication*. Berlin: de Gruyter, pp. 163–172.

Vicari, S. (2015) 'Exploring the Cuban Blogosphere', *New Media & Society*, 17(9): 1492–1512.

Villi, M. (2012) 'Visual Chitchat: The Use of Camera Phones in Visual Interpersonal Communication', *Interactions: Studies in Communication & Culture*, 3(1): 39–54.

Virilio, P. (1997) *Open Sky*. London: Verso.

Voirol, O. (2005). 'Les Luttes pour la Visibilité', *Réseaux*, 1(129/130): 89–121.

von Uexküll, J. (2010) [1934/1940] *Foray into the Worlds of Animals and Humans*. Minneapolis, MN: University of Minnesota Press.

Wachelder, J. (2014) 'Toys, Christmas Gifts and Consumption Culture in London's Morning Chronicle', *Journal of the International Committee for the History of Technology*, 19(1): 13–32.

Waisbord, S. (2013a) 'A Metatheory of Mediatization and Globalization?', *Journal of Multicultural Discourses*, 8(3): 182–189.

Waisbord, S. (2013b) 'Media Policies and the Blindspots of Media Globalization', *Media, Culture & Society*, 35(1): 132–138.

Waisbord, Silvio (ed.) (2014) *Media Sociology*. Cambridge: Polity.

Wajcman, J. (2015) *Pressed for Time*. Chicago, IL: University of Chicago Press.

Wajcman, J., Bittman, M. and Brown, J. E. (2008) 'Families Without Borders', *Sociology*, 42(4): 635–652.

Walby, S. (2007) 'Complexity Theory, Systems Theory, and Multiple Intersecting Social Inequalities', *Philosophy of the Social Sciences*, 37(4): 449–470.

Wall, M., Otis Campbell, M. and Janbek, D. (2015) 'Syrian Refugees and Information Precarity', *New Media & Society*. Available at: http://nms.sagapub.com/content/early/2015/07/01/1461444815591967.full.pdf+html.

Wasserman, H. (2011) 'Mobile Phones, Popular Media, and Everyday African Democracy', *Popular Communication*, 9(2): 146–158.

Wasserman, S. and Faust, K. (1994) *Social Network Analysis*. Cambridge: Cambridge University Press.

Weber, M. (1911) 'Geschäftsbericht', in Deutsche Gesellschaft für Soziologie, *Verhandlungen des Ersten Deutschen Soziologentages*. Tübingen: Mohr Verlag, pp. 39–62.

Weber, M. (1947) *The Theory of Social and Economic Organization*. New York: Free Press.

Weber, M. (1972) [1921] *Wirtschaft und Gesellschaft.* Tübingen: Mohr Verlag.

Weber, M. (1978) *Economy and Society. Volume I.* Berkeley, CA: University of California Press.

Weber, M. (1988) [1904] *Gesammelte Aufsätze zur Wissenschaftslehre. Siebte Auflage.* Tübingen: Mohr Verlag.

Weick, K. E. (1979) *The Social Psychology of Organizing.* 2nd edn. New York: McGraw.

Weick, K. E., Sutcliffe, K. M. and Obstfeld, D. (2005) 'Organizing and the Process of Sensemaking', *Organization Science,* 16(4): 409–421.

Weimann, G. (2004) 'Cyberterrorism', *United States Institute of Peace.* Available at: http://www.usip.org/sites/default/files/sr119.pdf

Wellman, B. (1997) 'An Electronic Group is Virtually a Social Network', in Kieseler, S. (ed.) *Culture of the Internet.* Mahwah, NJ: Lawrence Erlbaum, pp. 179–205.

Wellman, B., Quan-Haase, A., Boase, J., Chen, W., Hampton, K., Diaz, I. and Miyata, K. (2003) 'The Social Affordances of the Internet for Networked Individualism', *Journal of Computer-Mediated Communication,* 8(3), doi: 10.1111/j.1083–6101.2003.tb00216.x.

Weltevrede, E., Helmond, A. and Gerlitz, C. (2014) 'The Politics of Real-time: A Device Perspective on Social Media Platforms and Search Engines', *Theory, Culture & Society,* 31(6): 125–150.

Wenger, E. (1999) *Communities of Practice.* Cambridge: Cambridge University Press.

Wessler, H., Peters, B., Brüggemann, M., Kleinen-von Königslöw, K. and Sifft, S. (2008) *Transnationalization of Public Spheres.* Basingstoke: Palgrave Macmillan.

Westlund, O. (2011) *Cross-media News Work.* Gothenburg: University of Gothenburg.

White, H. C. (2008) *Identity and Control.* 2nd edn. Princeton, NJ: Princeton University Press.

Whitson, J. R. (2013) 'Gaming the Quantified Self', *Surveillance & Society,* 11(1/2): 163–176.

Wieviorka, E. (2013) *L'Impératif Numérique.* Paris: CNRS.

Willems, H. (2010) 'Figurationssoziologie und Netzwerkansätze', in Stegbauer, C. and Häußling, R. (eds.) *Handbuch Netzwerkforschung.* Wiesbaden: VS, pp. 255–268.

Willems, W. (2014) 'Producing Local Citizens and Entertaining Volatile Subjects', in Butsch, R. and Livingstone, S. M. (eds.) *Meanings of Audiences.* London: Routledge, pp. 80–96.

Williams, B. (2006) 'Philosophy as a Humanistic Discipline' in Moore, A. W. (ed.) *Philosophy as a Humanistic Discipline.* Princeton, NJ: Princeton University Press, pp. 180–199.

Williams, D., Ducheneaut, N., Xiong, L., Zhang, Y., Yee, N. and Nickell, E.

(2006) 'From Tree House to Barracks: The Social Life of Guilds in World of Warcraft', *Games and Culture*, 1(4): 338–361.

Williams, R. (1965) *The Long Revolution*. Harmondsworth: Penguin.

Williams, R. (1976) *Keywords: A Vocabulary of Culture and Society*. London: Fontana / Croom Helm.

Williams, R. (1980) *Problems in Materialism and Culture*. London: Verso.

Williams, R. (1990) *Television: Technology and Cultural Form*. London and New York: Routledge.

Williamson, B. (2015) 'Algorithmic Skin: Health-tracking Technologies, Personal Analytics and the Biopedagogies of Digitized Health and Physical Education', *Sport, Education and Society*, 20(1): 133–151.

Wimmer, A. and Glick Schiller, N. (2002) 'Methodological Nationalism and Beyond', *Global Networks*, 2(4): 301–334.

Winocur, R. (2009) 'Digital Convergence as the Symbolic Medium of New Practices and Meanings in Young People's Lives', *Popular Communication*, 7(1): 179–187.

Winseck, D. R. and Pike, R. M. (2007) *Communication and Empire, 1860–1930*. Durham, NC: Duke University Press.

Winter, R. (2010) *Der produktive Zuschauer*. Zweite Auflage. Köln: von Halem.

Wittel, A. (2008) 'Towards a Network Sociality', in Hepp, A., Krotz, F., Moores, S. and Winter, C. (eds.) *Connectivity, Network and Flow*. New York: Hampton, pp. 157–182.

Wittgenstein, L. (1978) [1953] *Philosophical Investigations*. Cambridge: Wiley.

Wobring, M. (2005) *Die Globalisierung der Telekommunikation im 19. Jahrhundert*. Frankfurt am Main: Peter Lang.

Woelfer, J. P. and Hendry, D. G. (2012) 'Homeless Young People on Social Network Sites', *Proceedings of the SIGCHI Conference on Human Factors in Computing Systems*: 2825–2834.

Wolf, G. (2009) 'Know Thyself: Tracking Every Facet of Life, from Sleep to Mood to Pain, 24/7/365', *Wired*, 17(7), p. 92.

Wolf, G. (2010) 'The Data-driven Life', *The New York Times*, 28 April.

Wrong, D. (1994) *The Problem of Order: What Unites and Divides Society*. New York: Free Press.

Yannopoulou, N. (2013) 'User-Generated Brands and Social Media: Couch-surfing and Airbnb', *Contemporary Management Research*, 9(1): 85–90.

Yuan, E. J. (2013) 'A Culturalist Critique of "Online Community" in New Media Studies', *New Media & Society*, 15(5): 665–679.

Zaglia, M. E. (2013) 'Brand Communities Embedded in Social Networks', *Journal of Business Research*, 66(2/2): 216–223.

Zelin, A. Y. (2015) 'Picture Or It Didn't Happen: A Snapshot of the Islamic State's Official Media Output', *Perspectives on Terrorism*, 9(4). Available at: http://www.terrorismanalysts.com/pt/index.php/pot/article/view/445/html

Zerubavel, E. (1981) *Hidden Rhythms*. Berkeley, CA: University of California Press.

Zervas, G., Proserpio, D. and Byers, J. (2014) 'The Rise of the Sharing Economy', *Boston University School of Management*, 2013(16). Available at: http://people.bu.edu/zg/publications/airbnb.pdf

Zhao, S. (2006) 'The Internet and the Transformation of the Reality of Everyday Life', *Sociological Inquiry*, 76(4): 458–474.

Zhao, S. (2007) 'Internet and the Lifeworld', *Information Technology & People*, 20(2): 140–160.

Zhou, B. (2011) 'New Media Use and Subjective Social Status', *Asian Journal of Communication*, 21(2): 133–149.

Zolo, D. (1992) *Democracy and Complexity*. University Park, PA: Pennsylvania State University Press.

Zook, M. (2005) *The Geography of the Internet Industry*. Malden, MA: Blackwell Publishers.

Zukin, S., Lindeman, S. and Hurson, L. (2015) 'The Omnivore's Neighborhood? Online Restaurant Reviews, Race, and Gentrification', *Journal of Consumer Culture*. Available at: http://joc.sagepub.com/content/early/2015/10/13/1469540515611203.full.pdf+html.

Index